Powering the Unstoppable Green Shift

The Green Shift is unfolding. It is no longer a projection but a reality, unlocking a wealth of investment and business opportunities. In the face of environmental crisis, businesses, governments, and financial institutions must work together to drive the transition to sustainability.

This book takes the reader on a clear and illuminating journey through the dynamic landscape of our evolving decarbonising world. Rich with insightful analysis, the meticulously researched road map empowers business leaders, financial experts, and policymakers to navigate the various dimensions of climate action. Corporate and investment banking veteran Joseph Jacobelli analyses the treacherous transition facing small to large companies and contends that evolving public policy and new finance paradigms will successfully propel businesses to drive the unfolding of a carbon-neutral planet. He demystifies the intricate issues surrounding company strategies for achieving carbon neutrality and climate resilience, from the inevitable phasing out of fossil fuels to the difficulties of geopolitical interactions. This book enables readers to comprehend the complex kaleidoscope of decarbonisation topics and seize the emerging business and investment opportunities, with real-world examples serving as inspiration.

Powering the Unstoppable Green Shift is for those seeking to change their long-term strategies to account for the harsh realities of climate risk mitigation, invest sustainably, and create meaningful change – from corporate executives to financial professionals, policymakers to business consultants, nonprofit leaders to research analysts.

Joseph Jacobelli heads Single-Family Office Bourne Impact Capital and climate finance insights platform, actE. He is a recognised expert in climate business and finance, with over three decades in leading research and investment in clean energy. His upbringing in Europe and Asia developed a multicultural perspective that shapes his multidisciplinary approach to the energy transition. He regularly speaks at industry conferences and contributes to media platforms to advance climate awareness in business and finance. He holds a master's in international law from National Taiwan University and a bachelor of arts from the University of Queensland.

Powering the Unstoppable Green Shift

How Policy and Finance Transform Business to Lead Climate Action

Joseph Jacobelli

Routledge
Taylor & Francis Group
NEW YORK AND LONDON

Designed cover image: TRAVIEE.ART

First published 2026
by Routledge
605 Third Avenue, New York, NY 10158

and by Routledge
4 Park Square, Milton Park, Abingdon, Oxon, OX14 4RN

Routledge is an imprint of the Taylor & Francis Group, an informa business

ISBN: 978-1-041-12769-7 (hbk)
ISBN: 978-1-041-12768-0 (pbk)
ISBN: 978-1-003-66650-9 (ebk)

DOI: 10.4324/9781003666509

Typeset in Sabon
by Apex CoVantage, LLC

Dedicated to
Shirley, Jean-Luc, Luca, and Arin.
Grateful for your
unwavering encouragement
and
boundless love.

Contents

Foreword

The global energy system is undergoing the most profound transformation since the Industrial Revolution. For more than a century, hydrocarbons have powered economic growth, but today the urgency of climate change demands a decisive shift towards clean and sustainable energy. What was once the domain of a few early adopters – solar rooftops, corporate power purchase agreements, and battery storage – has become mainstream. This is not simply a matter of technology – it is a fundamental reordering of policy, finance, and business priorities on a scale that touches every citizen, every enterprise, and every government.

In *Powering the Unstoppable Green Shift*, Joseph Jacobelli captures this transformation with rare clarity. He shows that the path forward is neither linear nor comfortable – it is, as he rightly puts it, 'a bumpy flight'. Yet the book demonstrates that this turbulence masks an extraordinary truth: the green shift is no longer optional; it is unstoppable. This momentum is now undeniable because, in much of the world, renewable energy is not only cleaner but also cheaper. Solar and wind projects are increasingly outcompeting fossil fuels on cost, and the downward trajectory of clean energy prices makes the transition both an environmental imperative and an economic inevitability.

My own career has mirrored this journey. From founding a developer in India that was later acquired by Shell and Keppel to launching and then running a renewable business at TotalEnergies, I have seen first-hand the unique challenges and opportunities that the energy transition presents to governments, investors, companies, and individuals across Asia. At Peak Energy, backed by Stonepeak, one of the world's largest infrastructure funds, I have continued this work – developing projects that prove renewables are not only viable but also increasingly the most competitive choice.

What makes *Powering the Unstoppable Green Shift* so valuable is its multidimensional perspective. The author places climate science in conversation with policy frameworks, financial markets, and corporate strategy. Too often, these elements are examined in isolation; here, they are woven together into a single narrative that makes sense of the complexity. Whether describing the hurdles of financing bankable projects, the subtleties of carbon regulation, or the opportunities of corporate climate transition, the book provides both breadth and depth.

From these vantage points, I can confirm the truth of Joseph Jacobelli's central insight: government, finance, and business exist in a symbiotic relationship that will determine the speed and scale of the green shift. Policy signals, even imperfect ones, unlock capital. Finance, when paired with innovation, turns ambition into bankable projects. And business, through strategy and execution, delivers the tangible infrastructure of the transition.

The shift to renewable energy is not just about megawatts and molecules; it is about credibility, resilience, and long-term value creation.

This book provides an invaluable guide for leaders grappling with these realities. It equips policymakers with a clearer view of the trade-offs required, financiers with the tools to evaluate risks and opportunities, and corporations with a framework to integrate sustainability at the core of their business models. Above all, it reminds us that the success of the energy transition will depend on collaboration across sectors, government, finance, and business in a symbiotic relationship.

Powering the Unstoppable Green Shift is ultimately a hopeful book. It does not downplay the challenges, but it demonstrates that the solutions are within reach if we act with urgency and imagination. For those of us who have been in the boardrooms where these decisions are made, the arguments here ring true. For those just beginning their journey into the energy transition, the insights will be indispensable.

The task ahead is immense, but the direction is clear. The green shift is indeed unstoppable, and, with the guidance of works like this book, it is navigable.

Gavin Adda
Chief Executive Officer, Peak Energy Pte. Ltd.
(a Stonepeak Infrastructure company),[1] and
Former Chief Executive Officer of TotalEnergies Renewables
Asia Pte. Ltd. and Cleantech Solar Development Company Pte. Ltd.

Note

1 Author's note: Stonepeak is a leading alternative investment firm specialising in infrastructure and real assets with over $76 billion of assets under management globally according to the company, as of August 2025.

Foreword

The impacts of climate change are visible all around us – just as the World retreats from the multilateral political approaches that have driven so much investment and decarbonisation over the past decade. But is this an end to the green momentum? In this new book, Joseph Jacobelli argues just the opposite. *Powering the Unstoppable Green Shift* is a thoughtful, detail-rich compendium of information that shows why the economic decarbonisation imperative is here to stay – and what is required to make it even more effective.

During my years as UK Minister for Energy and Clean Growth and as the architect of the successful UN COP26 meeting in Glasgow, I experienced first-hand the delicate choreography required between government policy, financial markets, and corporate strategy to deliver effective and lasting decarbonisation. The energy system, as Jacobelli shows in detail, is especially complicated given the interplay of global and local forces, the persistence of fossil fuel in primary energy, and the need for new forms of government intervention to stimulate investments. The Offshore Wind Sector Deal I led in the United Kingdom demonstrated how targeted government intervention and a 'whole of ecosystem' mindset can successfully unlock private investment at an unprecedented scale in new renewable technology, and I agree with Jacobelli's central thesis that a strong relationship between government, finance, and business will ultimately determine our success in creating a carbon-neutral planet.

What strikes me most about this book is its practical grounding. Having written the United Kingdom's Clean Growth Strategy, I appreciated Jacobelli's unflinching examination of both opportunities and obstacles. His analysis of the 'bumpy flight' metaphor for the energy transition rings true; progress rarely follows smooth trajectories, yet the direction can always be clear with long-term thinking and policy, strategy, and financial alignment.

Two other aspects of the book also resonated with me. First, the author's experience in the financial sector provides crucial insights into how capital flows towards climate solutions. His point that projects must be 'bankable' may seem obvious, yet it represents a fundamental truth often overlooked in climate discussions – and his focus on how we need to move from vague words to specific contractual terms when it comes to green finance and taxonomies rings especially true. The second is his geographical knowledge and location. Too many books tackling the climate topic are written entirely from a European perspective, and although, as Joseph Jacobelli shows, Europe remains a leading force in the roll-out of policy and clean technology, his knowledge and inclusion of case studies from the ASEAN region, South Africa, China, and Australia underpin the global nature of this transition.

Finally, having made a transition myself, from government policy leader to private sector board member, advisor, and investor, I find Jacobelli's central thesis that "businesses are at the heart of this transformation" to be a compelling one. As he describes, the policy landscape is usually a jungle, governments often don't make logical long-term decisions, and few economies have the sort of road maps and symbiotic frameworks between the public and private sectors that we would wish for. When they do exist – they can be transformational, but even without them, the 'green shift' is indeed unstoppable.

Claire Perry O'Neill
Former UK Minister for Energy and Clean Growth; COP26 President – Designate; Director, Occidental Petroleum Corporation; Board Chair, Climate Impact X Ltd; Director, Singapore Exchange Limited; Co-Chair Global Imperatives Advisory Board, World Business Council for Sustainable Development; Strategic Advisor, Climate Investment; Advisor, Hysata Pty Ltd; Advisor, Unwritten.co; Senior Global Advisor, McKinsey & Company, Inc.

Disclaimer

The information contained in this work is provided strictly for general informational purposes and shall not, under any circumstances, be construed as, or relied upon in lieu of, professional, tailored financial or investment advice, nor shall it be deemed to constitute an offer, solicitation, invitation, or recommendation to buy, sell, subscribe for, or otherwise acquire or dispose of any securities, financial instruments, or investment products. The author may hold, may have previously held, or may in the future hold interests in one or more of the securities or financial instruments referenced herein. Recipients of this work are expressly advised that any decisions relating to investments, taxation, law, or other professional matters must be made only after obtaining independent advice from duly qualified professionals.

The author affirms that certain limited aspects of the preparation of this work were facilitated by artificial intelligence (AI) tools. Such assistance was confined strictly to ancillary functions, including research support, data organisation, and editorial refinement, with the purpose of enhancing efficiency and consistency in presentation. At no stage did AI tools originate or contribute to the formulation of ideas, the development of arguments, interpretive commentary, analysis, or policy recommendations contained herein. All substantive content, including insights, conclusions, and evaluative judgements, represents the independent and original work of the author.

All external sources and data referenced in this work have been manually reviewed, verified, and cited in accordance with the Oxford University Standard for the Citation of Legal Authorities (OSCOLA) and in line with recognised academic, professional, and legal standards.

Whilst the author has exercised reasonable care to ensure that the information contained in this work is, to the best of his or her knowledge, accurate as of September 2025 (unless expressly indicated otherwise), no representation, warranty, or guarantee, whether express or implied, is given regarding the accuracy, reliability, or completeness of any such information. Neither the author nor any associated party shall be liable in contract, tort (including negligence), or under any statutory duty for any loss, damage, costs, or expenses arising out of, or in connection with, any reliance placed upon the contents of this work.

Also by Joseph Jacobelli

Asia's Energy Revolution: China's Role and New Opportunities as Markets Transform and Digitalise (De Gruyter, 2021)

Acknowledgements

I decided to intentionally put the acknowledgements right at the beginning because my two-year journey with this book simply would not have happened without the encouragement, generosity, kindness, and support of some truly wonderful and extremely knowledgeable people. Saying 'thank you' too often may sound hollow, but in this case, every single 'thank you' is very much heartfelt and truly sincere. It is straight from the bottom of my heart.

Let me start with someone truly extraordinary: Shirley Chow. She was also the first person to read the final draft. It is a role she took on with much care and incredible insight, and I could not be more grateful. Shirley's unwavering support and constant encouragement were critical in the completion of the book.

I am also exceedingly indebted to Vincent Bourdarie in Taipei and Summer Huang in Shanghai, who were the second readers of the final draft. They devoted their time while being busy with their jobs. Their perspectives could not have been more different – and that's precisely what made their feedback so valuable. They offered thoughtful suggestions and raised questions that helped shape the book in ways I had not anticipated.

Special thanks to my exceptionally talented artist friend, Cyril, for the cover image featured in this book.

Back when the book was just a rough outline and a single poor draft chapter, a number of generous souls, all around the world, took time out of their busy lives to read through my early scribbles and share their thoughts. Their feedback helped me shape the direction of the book at a formative stage. I am sincerely grateful to Nancy Chen in Amsterdam; Keith Punzalan in Frankfurt; Grace Hui, Manshu Deng, Sam Hilton, and Steven Lu in Hong Kong; Douglas Wong in London; Larry Feign in Lisbon; Giorgio Fortunato in Singapore; Jonathon Ong in Sydney; and Thomas Jastrzab in Taipei. A special thanks also to Nick Smith in Adelaide for his insights on the green hydrogen section.

A big shout out to those six people who helped bring the concluding chapter to life. I am grateful once again to Vincent Bourdarie, Shirley Chow, Sam Hilton, Summer Huang, and Larry Feign, as well as Junior Isles in London. Your contributions made all the difference.

I would also like to express my gratitude to Meredith Norwich and Bethany Nelson at Routledge, Taylor & Francis, for their support and guidance throughout the publishing process. And a warm thank you to my co-agents, Chris Newson at NewsonWallwork and Marc Mikulich at Marc Mikulich Literary Agency LLC, whose help was always thoughtful and constructive.

Finally, I owe heartfelt gratitude to Professor Ling-Chen Chang, PhD, my master's thesis supervisor in Taipei in the 1980s. It was under her mentorship four decades ago that my passion for research truly took root. It is that foundation that has carried me through this entire project. I am also grateful to Apex CoVantage's Kousalya Vivekanandan for the great editing and production work.

Preface

I have been repeatedly amazed by the rapid pace of the energy transition.

Living in Hong Kong and frequently visiting the Chinese mainland, I witnessed tangible evidence that the shift was not only happening but accelerating. For example, Shenzhen, a city bordering Hong Kong with 18 million people, about the same as the Netherlands, is a leader in transport electrification. Its bus fleet of around 16,500 vehicles and taxi fleet of about 22,000 are entirely electric. The city had about 3,000 electric vehicles in 2014, including passenger vehicles, rising to over one million in 2024, accounting for about a quarter of the total number of vehicles on the city's roads. The city also boasts over 400,000 charging points, which go a long way towards addressing one of the biggest fears for drivers: range anxiety – the fear that an electric vehicle's battery would not last to reach its destination. Electric vehicle charging points are growing rapidly not just in China but in many other countries too. One can walk around the streets of cities like Paris and easily come across some charging points (see Figure 0.1).

The appearance of electric vehicles and charging points in our streets is only one of the many manifestations of the acceleration of the energy transition. This kind of pace was one of my motivations to start working in 2019 on my first book, *Asia's Energy Revolution: China's Role and New Opportunities as Markets Transform and Digitalise*, published in June 2021. It aimed to identify key drivers transforming the energy markets in Asia and provided some thoughts about their long-term outlook. While that work captured the broad strokes of change in Asia, the largest energy-consuming region in the world, it left me with a strong motivation to scrutinise and analyse the worldwide shift towards sustainability and the intricate forces propelling it forward. I wanted to delve deeper and contribute to the growing body of work on our global shift towards a sustainable future, and I devoted over two years to this endeavour.

In *Powering the Unstoppable Green Shift*, I aim to provide a clear, multidisciplinary portrait of the complex world of decarbonisation, spanning regions and sectors. The idea was not to write a guide or a textbook. It was to allow someone inquisitive about the energy transition to learn how to identify the crucial elements important to the sector, find direct or indirect investment opportunities in the field, or simply understand the business and finance elements of the transition better to satisfy one's curiosity.

I spent several decades working in investment banking and energy companies. I closely witnessed how public policy, the financial sector, and particularly corporations are central to driving efforts to minimise environmental damage. I believe that these three actors (government, finance, and business) exist in a symbiotic relationship that will ultimately determine our success in creating a carbon-neutral planet.

Figure 0.1 Vehicle charging point in Paris
Source: Paris Street by Joseph Jacobelli (April 2025).

From the phasing out of fossil fuels to the intricacies of investment instruments, I aim to dissect the multifaceted challenges and opportunities that define our transformative era.

I have organised the book into four sections. The first section offers a background on what our climate change crisis is all about. Apart from defining it and discussing the economic costs of inaction, I also analyse the energy landscape and briefly examine some of the business areas in the sector. Finally, I highlight the growth opportunity and some of the challenges faced. The second section discusses a necessary evil, policy. Policy is like the ignition key of a car. It is the initial spark but not the ultimate driver. Policy needs to provide a signal to businesses and investors. It needs to be a signal that policymakers are behind the transition. It does not really matter if the signal is a flickering, weak green light or a strong, bright one. As long as there is some kind of green light, business and the capital markets will take economic action. The next sections are about the closely interrelated actors: finance and corporations. I argue that there is an almost limitless number of business and investment opportunities and that there is ample capital available. But the projects must be 'good' or, in finance-speak, they must be bankable. So I evaluate in detail the different finance outlets and mechanisms and then dive into specific areas of application for this financing. In the fourth and final section, I selected some specific sectors and businesses that I believe typify the opportunities available and how corporates can participate.

Why focus on corporations and their climate transition plans? Simply put, businesses are at the heart of this transformation. They are largely involved in energy-transition-related investments, whether they be clean energy generation facilities or digital solutions. Their strategies, risks, and actions are pivotal in shaping our sustainable future. Of course, they do not operate in isolation. That is why I carefully evaluate the symbiotic relationship between these three key actors, especially business and finance. I firmly believe that there is no sustainable business without sustainable finance, and vice versa. And, of course, no business can be sustainable if it is not at the same time economically sustainable too.

Throughout these pages, I want to take the reader on a clear journey through the dynamic landscape of our evolving world. Ranging from small enterprises to multinational corporations, all face a treacherous transition as they navigate the shift from traditional energy systems to cleaner alternatives. I carefully analyse how evolving public policy and new finance paradigms are successfully propelling corporations to drive the unfolding of a carbon-neutral planet. I aim to uncover the immense business and investment opportunities that the energy transition offers us.

To make this complex subject accessible, I have filled these pages with real-world examples as well as a comprehensive set of fact-checked data. I also created a comprehensive glossary to help navigate the terminology. It is available on my website (asiacleantech-energy.com/terms) and will be regularly enhanced and updated. My goal is to empower the reader, whether that reader is a business leader, finance expert, policymaker, or simply someone curious about our sustainable future, to understand and engage with all the various complex and critical issues.

By the end of this book, I hope the reader will have a clear road map of how governments, corporations, and finance can converge to create a sustainable world.

The green shift is unstoppable, and understanding how the different elements work is crucial for anyone looking to thrive in our changing world. So, let us embark on this illuminating journey together as we explore how to power our way towards a cleaner, more sustainable future. The transition is not like taking a very comfortable and smooth flight. Rather, it is like a very bumpy flight. But it is a flight that is slowly but surely heading in the right direction.

Section I

Climate and decarbonisation

The landscape and the hurdles

Chapter 1

The high carbon crisis

Unveiling the urgency

> **Aims:**
>
> - Climate change and the escalating frequency and intensity of extreme weather events.
> - The scientific consensus on climate change and rising public awareness and action.
> - The significant economic costs and potential long-term impacts of climate change.

Are worries over climate change misplaced?

> Unless there was any lingering doubt, last year, 2023, made it clear that climate change is a clear and present danger for all of us. It was the hottest year in modern history. We saw extreme weather ravage every corner of the globe. Sea surface temperatures reached new highs and have not come down despite winter in the northern hemisphere, and the science is clear: the circumstances are about to get more dire in the years ahead.[1]

This is how a New York Times reporter, David Gelles, introduced a panel discussion on climate action at the 2024 World Economic Forum in Davos, Switzerland. At the same forum, the then US Special Presidential Envoy for Climate, John Kerry, called 2023 'the most climate disruptive, most climate consequential year in human history'.[2]

A great number of influential figures have made public statements to raise awareness of climate change and its effects. These voices span the globe and encompass a wide range of sectors. Political leaders, including Chinese President Xi Jinping, Indian Prime Minister Narendra Modi, and former US Presidents Barack Obama and Joe Biden, have all spoken on the issue. Religious leaders, such as Pope Francis, the Dalai Lama, and the Muslim Council of Elders, have also added their weight to the discussion. In the business world, figures like Microsoft founder Bill Gates, Virgin Group founder Sir Richard Branson, and NVIDIA co-founder Jensen Huang have highlighted the importance of addressing climate change. Moreover, global personalities, including British natural history broadcaster Sir David Attenborough, actor and former politician Arnold Schwarzenegger, and actor Matt Damon, have used their platforms to expand the message.

The frequency of extreme climate events is increasing as average temperatures steadily rise, warming the climate system. Several alarming studies indicate that global surface

DOI: 10.4324/9781003666509-2

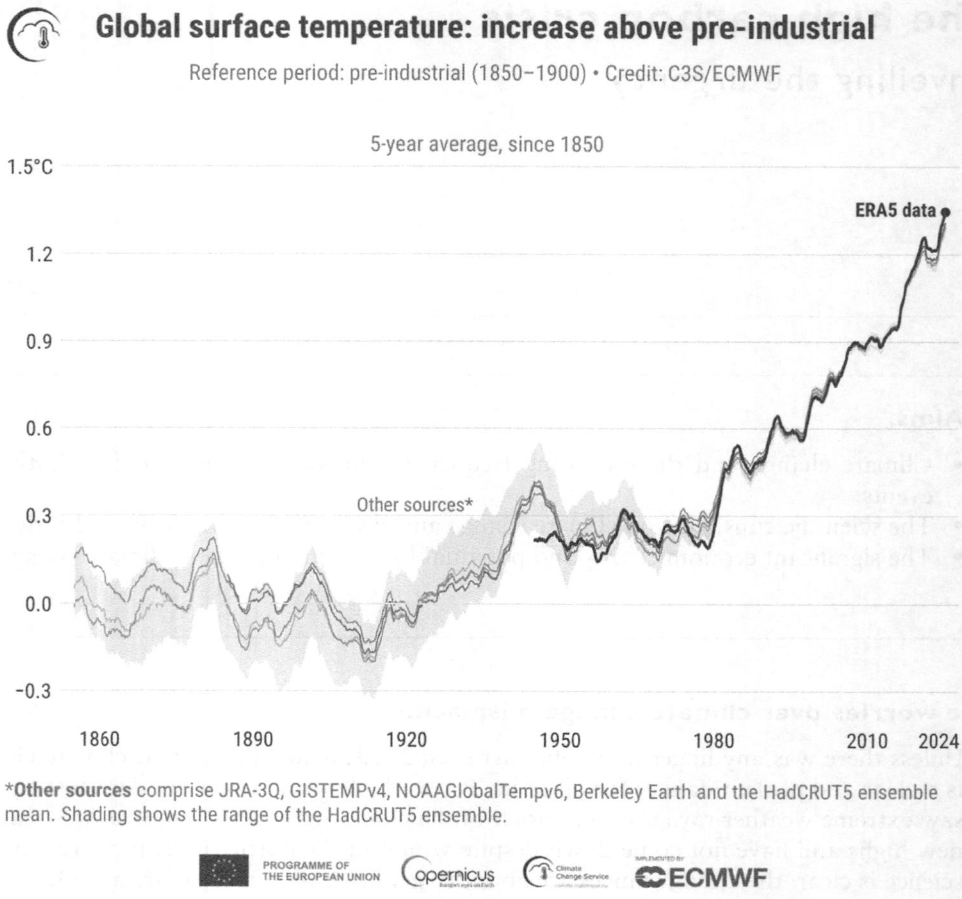

Figure 1.1 Global surface temperature: increase above pre-industrial levels

Notes: Increase above the average for the 1850–1900 designated pre-industrial reference period, based on several global temperature datasets, shown as five-year averages since 1850. Credit: C3S/ECMWF.

Source: Copernicus, 'Global Climate Highlights 2024 | Copernicus' (Copernicus.eu 10 January 2025). Available at: https://climate.copernicus.eu/global-climate-highlights-2024 accessed 4 July 2025.

temperatures have significantly exceeded pre-industrial levels, typically taken to mean between 1850 and 1900. The rising trend is consistently documented in reports from the Copernicus Climate Change Service, the Earth observation component of the EU's Space Programme (see Figure 1.1). For instance, a study published in *Nature*,[3] the British weekly scientific journal, concluded that the summer of 2023 in the Northern Hemisphere was likely the hottest in 2,000 years. This conclusion was reached through the analysis of tree rings from nine northern locations, combined with weather data from the mid-1800s onwards.

Recent meteorological data and the extrapolated estimate of the rise of temperatures over the next decades are worrying. Analysis by the Copernicus Climate Change Service found that the average temperature for 2024 was 0.72°C warmer than the 1991–2020 period and 1.6°C above the pre-industrial level (see Figure 1.2). Copernicus also said that

Region	Anomaly (vs 1991–2020)	Actual temperature	Rank (out of 85 years)
Globe	+0.72°C (+1.60°C vs pre-industrial)	15.10°C	1st highest (2nd - 2023)
Europe	+1.47°C	10.69°C	1st highest (2nd - 2020)
Arctic	1.34°C	-11.87°C	4th highest (1st - 2016)
Extra-polar ocean	0.51°C	20.87°C	1st highest (2nd - 2023)

Figure 1.2 Key temperature statistics for 2024

Notes: The estimates for the globe refer to the surface air temperature over land and ocean, and for Europe and the Arctic over land only. Sea surface temperature is computed for the 60°N–60°S domain.

Source: Copernicus, 'Global Climate Highlights 2024 | Copernicus' (Copernicus.eu 10 January 2025). Available at: https://climate.copernicus.eu/global-climate-highlights-2024 accessed 10 March 2025.

2024 was the warmest year on record since 1850; temperatures for 1850 are based on a multi-dataset record of global temperature going back to 1850.[4]

Millions of books, studies, and articles have been published on climate change by scientists, economists, and other experts. The colossal body of science tells us that the episodes of flooding, drought, heatwaves, and other combined extreme weather events of 2023 and 2024 will multiply and surely worsen over the next few years and decades.

At the state level, there is broad agreement globally that climate change is a problem that must be addressed. Over 190 countries signed the 2015 Paris Agreement, a legally binding international treaty on climate change. Many have submitted their individual national climate action plans, known as Nationally Determined Contributions (NDCs), under the agreement. As one would guess, harmonised action has been lacking and consistency in updating and enhancing these commitments has proven to be highly varied. Some very large economies have regularly updated their NDCs. These include Canada, China, the European Union (as a bloc), India, Japan, the United Kingdom, and South Korea. However, there have been some economically important jurisdictions that have not been consistent since 2015. They include Australia, Brazil, Russia, and the United States of America.

A large portion of the global population agrees with the scientific consensus that climate change is a serious worry and that it is an urgent and serious issue requiring prioritised climate action. About 80 per cent of people around the world want stronger climate action from their leaders, concludes a report by UNDP and the University of Oxford published in mid-2024.[5] The study covered over 73,000 people in 77 countries and showed a significant increase in climate concern, with 53 per cent of people reporting greater worry than the previous year. Notably, 72 per cent support a quick transition from fossil fuels, and 81 per cent seek more nature protection.

Opinions on climate change among the general population have shifted in recent years in key economies. In the United States, for example, the proportion of people alarmed or concerned about global warming increased by nine percentage points, according to a late 2024 study by the Yale Program on Climate Change Communication and George Mason University.[6] It was 54 per cent in December 2024 compared to 45 per cent in October 2014.

To tackle global warming, one of the urgent actions is addressing greenhouse gas emissions (GHGs). This is achieved chiefly through the decarbonisation of human activity.

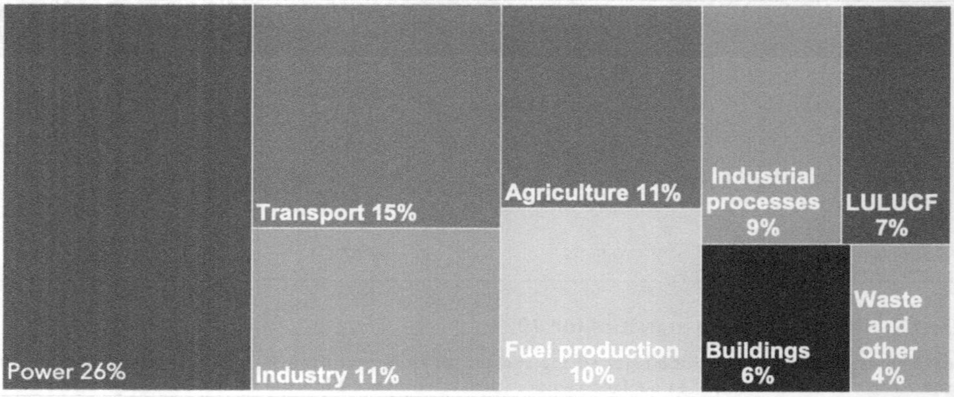

Figure 1.3 Climate change and global GHG emissions

Source: Author using information and data from United Nations Environment Programme, 'No More Hot Air . . . Please!' (United Nations Environment Programme 2024). Available at: https://wedocs.unep.org/bitstream/handle/20.500.11822/46443/EGR2024_ESEN.pdf?sequence=14&isAllowed=y accessed 13 March 2025.

Global warming and climate change are caused by GHG emissions, which blanket the Earth, trapping the sun's heat. The energy sector was the biggest contributor, about 68 per cent, to GHG emissions in 2023, according to the UN Environment Programme. The electric power sector was responsible for 26 per cent, transport for 15 per cent, industry for 11 per cent, fuel production for 10 per cent, and buildings for 6 per cent. The remaining 32 per cent was from agriculture; industrial processes; land use, land-use change, and forestry (LULUCF); waste; and others (see Figure 1.3).[7]

Rising global temperatures and GHG emissions disrupt weather patterns and ecosystems worldwide. The scientific conclusions were drawn by the Intergovernmental Panel on Climate Change (IPCC), the United Nations' body assessing the science related to climate change. This body, together with other organisations, has published valuable and influential studies on the impact of human-driven climate change. They range from the extremely accessible to the exceedingly technical. The study of changes in climate science is not new or recent.

The science of climate change has made huge advancements over the past two centuries. The foundation was laid in the 19th century by scientists like Joseph Fourier and John Tyndall, who proposed that the Earth's atmosphere traps heat and identified gases such as CO_2 and water vapour as key to this greenhouse effect. Svante Arrhenius quantified the relationship between CO_2 levels and global temperatures in 1896. He predicted that doubling atmospheric CO_2 would raise global temperatures by several degrees Celsius. The mid-20th century saw significant progress with the establishment of the Mauna Loa Observatory by Charles Keeling in 1958, providing the first continuous record of rising atmospheric CO_2 levels, known as the Keeling Curve. During the 1970s and 1980s, climate models became progressively sophisticated. Climate scientist James Hansen's 1988 testimony before the US Congress marked a pivotal moment, presenting compelling evidence that global warming was already detectable. The formation of the IPCC in 1988 consolidated the global research efforts.

Climate risks: the financial costs of climate inaction to economies

Rising global temperatures pose serious and far-reaching risks, affecting our planet and society in numerous ways. The United Nations[8] stressed that climate change generates several major issues. Hotter temperatures cause more frequent and intense heatwaves, which kill vulnerable people. Warmer temperatures intensify storms, hurricanes, and typhoons, which flood and significantly damage areas. Droughts and water shortages severely impact agriculture and communities. Notably, extreme flooding and drought may occur in the same locality, albeit at different times. These extreme changes force many species to adapt quickly or face extinction, disrupting ecosystems and food chains. Climate change also affects food production, leading to potential shortages and insecurity. Warmer temperatures facilitate the spread of diseases like malaria, and heat stress exacerbates respiratory and heart conditions, increasing health risks. Vulnerable communities face increased poverty and displacement from uninhabitable areas. Climate change disrupts natural cycles, like migration and reproduction, affecting ecosystem functions. Rapid habitat changes accelerate biodiversity loss, impacting ecosystem stability.

The escalating economic costs of climate change mean all these events have deep and long-lasting economic ramifications. The study of the financial burdens stemming from climate-related events is a rapidly growing field. The majority of long-term projections indicate that these costs are rapidly and significantly growing year by year. Our understanding of how different economies and sectors are being impacted is also growing. The reduction in global and national economic output is increasingly visible. One example in recent years is the increasing difficulty in obtaining homeowners' insurance in areas prone to natural disasters, like the Florida Keys in the United States, Townsville in Queensland in Australia, or coastal towns in East Anglia in the United Kingdom. Extreme climate events have significantly impacted real estate there. Property values have decreased as buyers face higher financial risk, may find it difficult to secure a mortgage, confront very high alternative insurance costs, or encounter reduced market liquidity.

There are countless studies examining the economic impacts of climate change, both on a large and small scale. Two illustrative examples from the countless studies examining economic impacts include a study by the European Central Bank (ECB) and a report in *Nature Communications*, a respected, peer-reviewed scientific journal. These studies provide valuable insights into the economic consequences of climate change.

The ECB article first offers some caution about modelling the economic impact of climate change in the long term. There are two fundamental necessary assumptions which are quite challenging. One is the changes in carbon emissions, especially as the world tries to progressively transition to net-zero carbon, one must make assumptions about the amount and the period of the reduction. This is especially important, if the transition-related public policies are 'well-conceived, well-communicated, and well-coordinated', the article correctly underlines. Another hurdle when making modelling assumptions is the changes in the climatic conditions. Every single year will be slightly different in terms of number of climate events and level of extreme weather.

The authors believe that unmitigated climate change is substantially worse for 'potential output' in the long term. Potential output is primarily an economic concept representing the maximum output an economy can support in the long term. It is composed of three parts: the capital stock (comprising all assets for the production process), the labour supply, and the Total Factor Productivity (how effectively capital and labour are used in the

	CAPITAL STOCK	LABOUR SUPPLY	TOTAL FACTOR PRODUCTIVITY
LONG RUN CLIMATE CHANGE	Shifts in tourism flows. Loss of agricultural land from higher temperatures, water stress and salinification of soil due to rising sea levels. Disruption of economic activity in coastal areas from higher sea levels. Loss of biodiversity and ecosystem services.	Higher rates of mortality and sickness. Higher regional structural unemployment from changes in tourism, for example. Climate induced migration.	Reduced labour efficiency from higher temperatures, including fewer hours worked. Capital invested in adaptation is less productive in aggregate and diverts resource is away from innovation.
EXTREME WEATHER AND CLIMATE EVENTS	Destruction of capital stock in disasters. Opportunity to replace old, destroyed capital with newer, more technologically advanced capital. Greater uncertainty and volatility reduce willingness to invest over long run.	Higher rates of mortality and sickness. Disaster induced migration. Loss of education and skills.	Disaster induced bankruptcies and localised reductions in access to finance cause reallocation between firms for better or worse. Rebuilding process distracts management, reducing overall productivity.
CLIMATE POLICY AND GREEN TRANSITION	Increase in stranded assets*. Higher energy costs from carbon taxes reduced funds for investment.	Skills mismatches increasing structural unemployment.	Reallocation of output between firms within sectors may prove more or less efficient. Environmental regulation reduces productivity, perhaps (more than) offset by innovation. Reduced impact of supply shocks arising from fossil fuels.

Figure 1.4 The impact of climate change on the components of potential output

Notes: (*) physical assets recorded on a corporate balance sheet whose investment value cannot be recouped and must be written off.

Source: European Central Bank, 'How climate change affects potential output' [2023] Economic Bulletin. Available at: https://www.ecb.europa.eu/pub/economic-bulletin/html/eb202306.en.html accessed 27 February 2024; Robeco, 'Sustainable Investing – Stranded Assets' (Robeco.com – The investment engineers). Available at: https://www.robeco.com/en-int/glossary/sustainable-investing/stranded-assets accessed 27 February 2024.

production process). The following table expresses some of the climate change effects on each of the three components of potential output at three levels: long-run climate change, extreme weather and climate events, and climate policy and the green transition. At this third level, for example, the impact on capital stock is an increase in stranded assets; assets that have become or are expected to become obsolete or uneconomical, such as a coal-fired power plant in a country that wants to phase out such plants (see Figure 1.4).

The other study is one conducted by two researchers at the Reserve Bank of New Zealand, Rebecca Newman and Ilan Roy. It was widely publicised by the World Economic Forum, an international non-governmental organisation focused on public–private cooperation. The article, titled 'The global costs of extreme weather that are attributable to climate change', found that the costs of extreme weather events caused by climate change were staggering. The researchers looked at events over a period of two decades, between 2000 and 2019. They concluded that in aggregate the total cost was $2.86 trillion. Newman and Roy highlighted that the economic costs can be evaluated in two ways. These include the direct economic damage occurring during or immediately after the event, and indirect economic losses involving the declines in economic value added resulting from the direct damage.[9] In the coming years, the number of events is likely to rise, so the $143 billion estimated cost may even turn out to be much higher. Swiss Re, an insurer, estimated that the cost could be as much as $23 trillion per year from global GDP while S&P, a research firm, estimated the cost of climate change at $13 trillion per year.[10]

The massive macroeconomic implications will also have many microeconomic ramifications. Corporations, large and small, will also be impacted. At a high level, climate-related risks include changes or disruptions in policy, legal regimes, technology, and reputation. There are many physical risks caused by a changing climate to a corporation's supply chain, labour health and productivity, operating costs, insurance costs, borrowing costs, or assets'

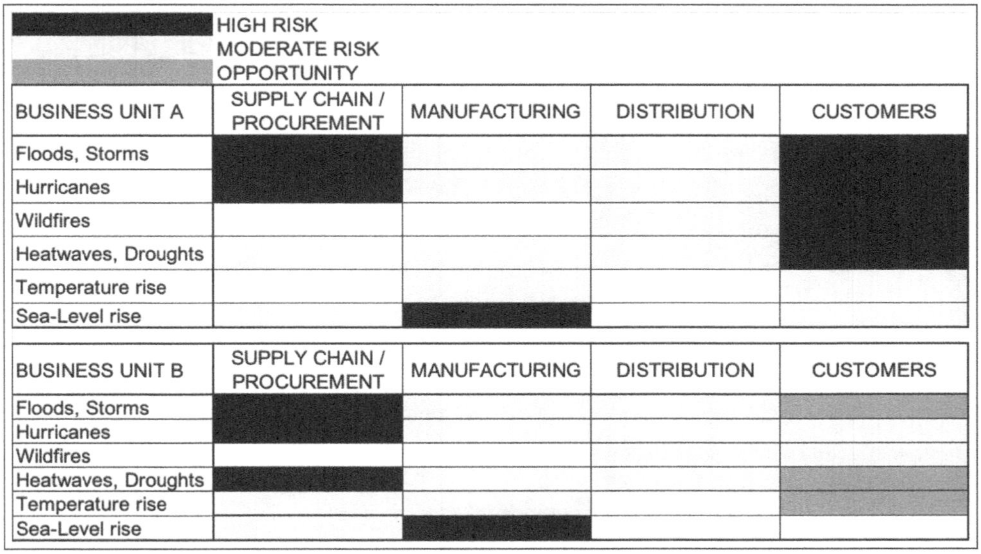

Figure 1.5 Climate effects on business units checklist

Source: Adapted by author. Data Source: PwC, 'Climate Change Risks on Business with 3 Real-Life Examples' (PwC16 May 2022). Available at: https://www.pwc.com/gx/en/services/sustainability/publications/risks-and-opportunities-of-climate-change-on-business.html accessed 18 February 2024.

depreciation, suggests PwC,[11] an accounting firm, and others. PwC also argues that corporations need to assess the effects of climate change on their supply chains, procurement, manufacturing, distribution, and customers. The firm created a checklist of effects which should be scrutinised (see Figure 1.5). It includes floods, storms, hurricanes, wildfires, heat waves, droughts, temperature rises, and sea level rises. Climate risks affect corporations in different ways. Figure 1.5 illustrates the hypothetical impact on two different companies. For one, climate change mostly translates into more risks. For another, while it presents some risks, it could also create some new business opportunities.

As mentioned, there is a great variety of studies today assessing the economic impacts. The Climate Policy Initiative is one of the several organisations which has tried to put a cost on climate inaction. The Climate Policy Initiative correctly underlines that if no energy transition action is undertaken – that is, current policies or business-as-usual scenarios – the world will be heading to warming of 3°C or higher, resulting in massive and disastrous human and economic losses. The organisation estimates that about $266 trillion in climate finance will be needed in the 25 years through 2050. It assumes that the annual climate finance requirement ranges from $5.4 to $11.7 trillion until 2030 and $9.3 to $12.2 trillion in the following two decades through 2050. These investments should reduce $1,266 trillion out of the estimated $2,328 trillion in losses caused by climate change between 2025 and 2100 based on a business-as-usual scenario.[12] Inaction comprises two main costs from negative climate-related impacts: the economic losses and the social costs, including those related to humans and the environment.

Other examples include reports and articles from Christian Aid, the US Congressional Budget Office, the International Chamber of Commerce, the US National Centers for Environmental Information, Responsible Business News, and the World Economic Forum (see Figure 1.6).

ORGANISATION / REPORT TITLE	SUMMARY	DATE
Christian Aid: Counting the Cost 2024: A year of climate breakdown	Ten most expensive climate disasters of 2024. $4 billion/each in damages, primarily insured losses.	Dec-24
Congressional Budget Office: The Risks of Climate Change to the United States in the 21st Century	Climate change could cut US real GDP by 4 per cent by 2100. Potential residential property losses: $930 billion due to sea-level rise. Rise of 0.61 - 1.22 meters: lost real estate property range $250 - $930 billion.	Dec-24
International Chamber of Commerce & Oxera: The economic cost of extreme weather events	Economic losses in 2014 - 2023 from 4,000 extreme weather events: $2 trillion. Economic damages $451 billion in 2022 - 2023, 19 per cent increase versus previous 8 years.	Nov-24
National Centres for Environmental Information: Billion-Dollar Weather and Climate Disasters	27 weather and climate disasters in US in 2024, at least $1 billion/each. Total about $182.7 billion, fourth highest on record.	Jan-25
Responsible Business News: Climate change's economic costs are six times greater than previously estimated	Economic costs could be six times higher than previously thought. Each additional degree Celsius of warming significantly impacts global GDP. Social cost of carbon far higher than previous estimates.	Jun-24
World Economic Forum: Climate change is costing the world $16 million per hour: study	Damage $1.7 - $3.1 trillion per year by 2050. Includes infrastructure, property, agriculture, and human health costs. Extreme weather events 2000 - 2019 cost estimate $2.8 trillion.	Oct-23

Figure 1.6 Economic costs of climate change sample of reports summaries

Sources: Christian Aid, 'What Climate Disasters Cost the Most in 2024?' (Christianaid.org.uk 30 December 2024). Available at: https://www.christianaid.org.uk/news/policy/costliest-climate-disasters-2024 accessed 15 March 2025. Congressional Budget Office, 'The Risks of Climate Change to the United States in the 21st Century' (Congressional Budget Office 19 December 2024). Available at: https://www.cbo.gov/publication/60845 accessed 15 March 2025. International Chamber of Commerce, 'New Report: Extreme Weather Events Cost Economy $2 Trillion over the Last Decade - ICC - International Chamber of Commerce' (ICC - International Chamber of Commerce11 November 2024). Available at: https://iccwbo.org/news-publications/policies-reports/new-report-extreme-weather-events-cost-economy-2-trillion-over-the-last-decade/ accessed 15 March 2025. NOAA, 'Billion-Dollar Weather and Climate Disasters | National Centers for Environmental Information (NCEI)' (www.ncei.noaa.gov2025). Available at: https://www.ncei.noaa.gov/access/billions/ accessed 15 March 2025. News RB, 'Climate Change's Economic Costs Are Six Times Greater than Previously Estimated - Responsible Business News' (Responsible Business News7 June 2024). Available at: https://responsiblebusinessnews.com/2024/06/07/climate-changes-economic-costs-are-six-times-greater-than-previously-estimated/ accessed 15 March 2025. Bennett P, 'Climate Change Is Costing the World $16 Million per Hour' (World Economic Forum 12 October 2023). Available at: https://www.weforum.org/stories/2023/10/climate-loss-and-damage-cost-16-million-per-hour/ accessed 15 March 2025.

The economic risks from climate change must be met with effective climate action, and governments must clearly state their stance on tackling climate change. Once this public policy is set, a variety of tools and mechanisms can be implemented. Especially important is the creation of administrative and supervisory structures able to focus on specific issues.

For example, creating a government department or agency dedicated to the supervision of decarbonisation efforts by industry participants is vital, as discussed in section two. First and foremost, the governments of individual nations must undertake effective climate action to address the economic risks of climate change (Section II of this book examines in depth the important role played by public policy and the reasons it is an absolute imperative to alleviate the negative impacts of climate change).

Notes

1 World Economic Forum (2024). *Climate and Nature: Seed Capital Needed | Davos 2024* (World Economic Forum) [online] <https://www.youtube.com/watch?v=WmsNALUSe0E&t=102s> accessed 19 January 2024.
2 World Economic Forum (2024). *Climate and Nature: Seed Capital Needed | Davos 2024* (World Economic Forum) [online] <https://www.youtube.com/watch?v=WmsNALUSe0E&t=102s> accessed 19 January 2024.
3 G Dickie, 'Summer 2023 Was the Hottest in 2,000 Years, Study Says' *Reuters* (14 May 2024) <https://www.reuters.com/business/environment/summer-2023-was-hottest-2000-years-study-says-2024-05-14/> accessed 17 May 2024.
4 Copernicus, 'Global Climate Highlights 2024 | Copernicus' (Copernicus.eu 10 January 2025) <https://climate.copernicus.eu/global-climate-highlights-2024> accessed 10 March 2025.
5 UNDP & Oxford University, *Peoples' Climate Vote 2024: Results* (The United Nations Development Programme (UNDP) and the University of Oxford 2024) <https://peoplesclimate.vote/document/Peoples_Climate_Vote_Report_2024.pdf> accessed 20 March 2025.
6 A Leiserowitz and others, *Climate Change in the American Mind: Beliefs & Attitudes, Fall 2024: Yale Program on Climate Change Communication* (Yale University and George Mason University, New Haven 2025) <https://climatecommunication.yale.edu/publications/climate-change-in-the-american-mind-beliefs-attitudes-fall-2024/> accessed 20 March 2025.
7 United Nations Environment Programme, *No More Hot Air . . . Please!* (United Nations Environment Programme 2024) <https://wedocs.unep.org/bitstream/handle/20.500.11822/46443/EGR2024_ESEN.pdf?sequence=14&isAllowed=y> accessed 13 March 2025.
8 United Nations, *Causes and Effects of Climate Change* (United Nations 2024) <https://www.un.org/en/climatechange/science/causes-effects-climate-change> accessed 17 February 2024.
9 R Newman and I Noy, 'The Global Costs of Extreme Weather that are Attributable to Climate Change' (2023) 14 Nature Communications 6103 <https://doi.org/10.1038/s41467-023-41888-1>.
10 M Gongloff, '$200 Trillion is Needed to Stop Global Warming. That's a Bargain.' *The Washington Post* (5 July 2023) <https://www.washingtonpost.com/business/energy/2023/07/05/-200-trillion-is-needed-to-stop-global-warming-that-s-a-bargain/929f606c-1b32-11ee-be41-a036f4b098ec_story.html> accessed 30 July 2023.
11 PwC, *Climate Change Risks on Business with 3 Real-Life Examples* (PwC 16 May 2022) <https://www.pwc.com/gx/en/services/sustainability/publications/risks-and-opportunities-of-climate-change-on-business.html> accessed 18 February 2024.
12 C Dreyer, *The Cost of Inaction* (CPI 4 January 2024) <https://www.climatepolicyinitiative.org/the-cost-of-inaction/#_ftnref1> accessed 4 March 2024.

Chapter 2

Four core market elements drive the energy landscape

Aims:

- The energy landscape's core elements: demand, supply, cost, and market system.
- Different electric power market mechanisms and their impact on the energy transition.
- Advancing the energy landscape: key hurdles and potential strategies.

For well over a century, the vision of a world powered by clean, renewable energy has persisted. This is evidenced by the words of Thomas Edison. The energy transition is not a recent concept; it has existed for many decades. Thomas Edison, whom the New York Times described as the 'godfather of electricity-intensive living' in a 2007 article, discussed the energy transition almost 120 years ago. He stated in 1910:

> When we learn how to store electricity, we will cease being apes ourselves; until then we are tailless orangutans. You see, we should utilise natural forces and thus get all of our power. Sunshine is a form of energy, and winds and tides are manifestations of energy. Do we use them? Oh, no; we burn wood and coal . . . There must surely come a time when heat and power will be stored in unlimited quantities in every community, all gathered by natural forces.[1]

Edison's 1910 vision, though decades old, resonates profoundly with today's urgent need to shift away from fossil fuels and embrace sustainable energy solutions. This chapter, and the remainder of this first section, will delve into how Edison's forward-thinking concepts have evolved, and the challenges and opportunities that lie ahead in realising his vision of a world not powered by fossil fuels.

Electricity and electrification are at the centre of today's energy transition and decarbonisation. Electric power from zero-carbon clean energy resources, such as hydroelectric power, solar, and wind, can replace fossil fuel-based energy supply. The electrification of some sectors, powered by clean energy, such as heating, manufacturing, and transport, can help in reducing GHG emissions. The electricity and energy landscape comprises many components. Three fundamental elements of the energy landscape are demand and supply, cost and the end-user price, and the market mechanism. A fourth element, and one which is growing and evolving the most rapidly, is technology. These four components exist in every

DOI: 10.4324/9781003666509-3

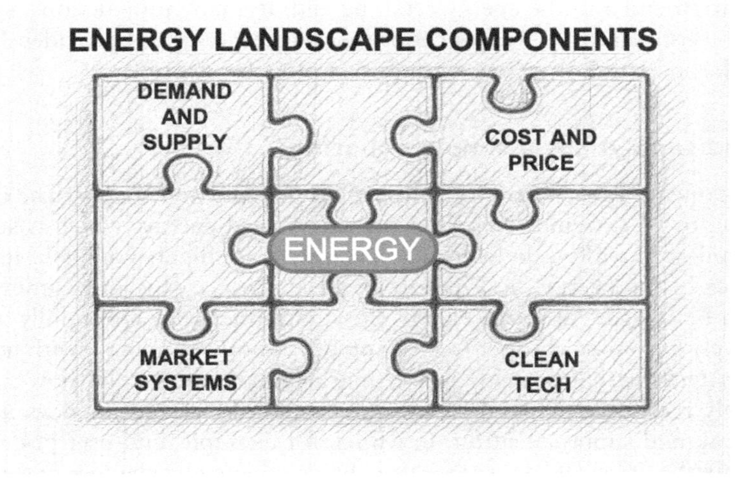

Figure 2.1 Fundamental components of energy landscape

Source: Author, original chart design (July 2025); background images sourced from OpenAI <https://chat.openai.com> accessed 4 July 2025.

region in the world, though their make-up will have significant regional differences. Not just country by country but also within regions of a country, particularly in nations with large land masses such as Australia, Canada, China, or Russia. In this chapter, the first three energy landscape elements, which drive the energy landscape, are examined. The fourth element, technologies, is dealt with separately in Chapter 3 (see Figure 2.1).

Demand and supply are core elements of the energy transition. Electricity demand must be accurately measured and forecasted, and if possible reduced. The sources of supply must meet normal demand as well as sudden surges. So there is a natural mismatch, as supply generally consists of predictable long-duration assets, whereas demand fluctuates. Constructing supply resource can take from a few days (such as for rooftop solar) to several years (such as for nuclear power plants), while their life cycles range from a few years (such as for energy storage) to several decades (such as for nuclear- or hydropower).

End users are a central element to the energy transition. Closely related to the end user are the cost of the delivered energy as well as the price paid by the end user. The consumer, as the chief revenue producer, is central to the energy markets. All consumers, be it residential, industrial, or commercial, want their energy to be priced as cheaply as possible and at the same time to be absolutely 100 per cent reliable. Something which is a tall order in a macroeconomic environment affected by such fluctuating and volatile factors as fossil fuel prices, inflation, interest rates, and supply chains. These are some of the factors which may raise the unit cost of the generation source. In the case of clean energy, such as solar or wind power, the upfront costs are high and inflation, interest rates, and bottlenecks will affect the cost of equipment and materials.

The third fundamental component of the energy landscape is the energy market mechanism. In its simplest form, an energy market is a place where energy is bought and sold. Globally, energy mechanisms differ drastically. At one end of the spectrum are closed market systems where there is a single producer and supplier. At the other end of the spectrum, there are fully open, competitive market structures where there are multiple actors at the energy generation end and the energy retailing end; in many jurisdictions, such as Europe or Japan, the consumer is allowed to choose the electricity or gas provider. In between the two ends of the spectrum, there are a number of other structures.

Demand and supply: not a simple equation

The first component of the electricity landscape is demand and supply. The concept seems, on the surface, to be extremely simple. Consumers need energy, which is supplied by the energy companies. In reality, the working parameters are highly complex. In part, because of the resource of the energy, and in part because, as of today, only limited amounts of electricity can be stored. Although energy storage technologies are rapidly advancing and are progressively becoming cheaper (see Chapter 3). Another anomaly with normal demand and supply patterns is that in many power markets the unit price of power does not necessarily sharply rise when demand is strong or supplies limited, nor does it plunge when demand is weak and supply plentiful. In China, for example, end-user prices are typically fixed, with only the prices of some generators being affected by changes in their input costs, because of government regulations.

When discussing demand, one must first differentiate between consumption and demand in the context of electricity. Consumption is the total amount of electricity used. Demand specifically refers to a specific moment, especially the peak. This is because if the demand is higher than the maximum amount of supply then there will be blackouts, which is why analysts and practitioners look at peak demand. Some, among the very many, key factors impacting electricity demand and consumption are the weather and temperatures, the time of day and day of the week, and population growth. These are easy and straightforward to understand and examine. Two other factors are economic activity and fiscal or financial incentives. Economic activity-driven unexpected electricity demand surges are not common in developed economies, especially because industrial production typically comprises a significantly smaller portion of GDP compared to emerging economies. In some jurisdictions, the long-term projections have in recent years been rising given the rapid expansion of data centres. Electricity demand driven by financial incentives can work in both negative and positive ways. When governments create subsidy systems for consumers, consumption may substantially rise as users take advantage of the lower tariffs, and this may also lead to energy wastage. Conversely, fiscal or financial incentives for energy efficiency can cut consumption. These incentives could be in the form of fines, grants, rebates, or taxes.

Global energy consumption rose at a compound annual growth rate (CAGR) of about 1.4 per cent between 2012 and 2022 (see Figure 2.2). This rate would have been much lower if it were not for users in the Asia Pacific region. About 79 per cent of the world's total energy consumption was in three regions. Asia Pacific was responsible for 46 per cent, Europe consumed a little over 13 per cent, and North America accounted for almost 20 per cent. The growth rates of each of these regions diverge greatly. Asia Pacific's was at 2.6 per cent, North America's at 0.6 per cent, while the whole of Europe was negative 0.9 per cent; for EU countries, it was negative 3.5 per cent.

The picture with electricity consumption is a little different from that of energy, with the latter also including coal, natural gas, and oil used by industry for uses other than power generation (see Figure 2.3). Its CAGR was about 2.5 per cent for the ten years through 2022, which was 80 per cent higher than that for energy. One of the key reasons for this differential is because of the electrification rate increase in some sectors, especially transport. In terms of growth rates, Asia Pacific's consumption rose at a CAGR of 4.6 per cent, North

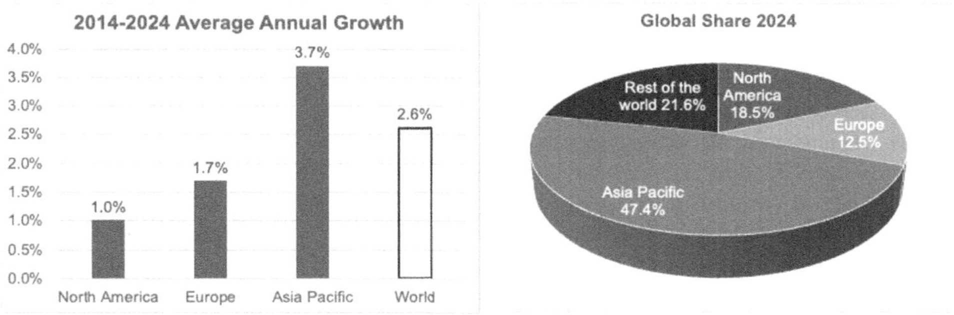

Figure 2.2 Energy consumption in key regions in 2024

Source: Author using data from Energy Institute, 'Energy Institute Statistical Review of World Energy' (Energy Institute Statistical Review of World Energy June 2025). Available at: https://www.energyinst.org/statistical-review accessed 4 July 2025.

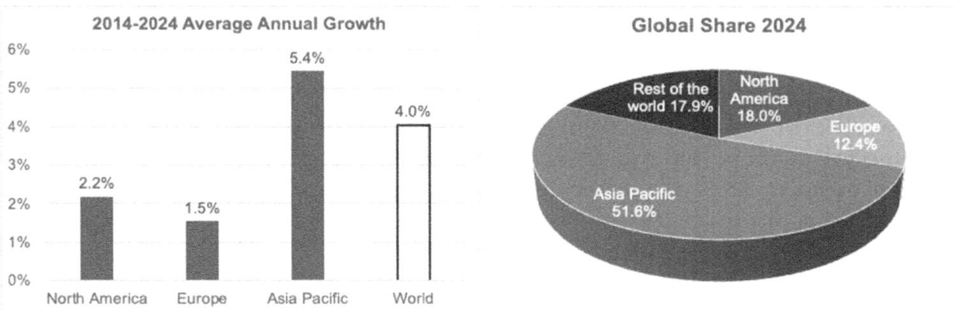

Figure 2.3 Electricity consumption in key regions in 2024

Source: Author using data from Energy Institute, 'Energy Institute Statistical Review of World Energy' (Energy Institute Statistical Review of World Energy June 2025). Available at: https://www.energyinst.org/statistical-review accessed 4 July 2025.

America's was 0.6 per cent, while for the whole of Europe it was negative 0.4 per cent, with that of EU states being a similar rate.

Electricity consumption is set to grow at a steady rate of 1 per cent to 3 per cent through 2050. One of the many long-term projections is a CAGR of electricity generation at 2 to 3 per cent, which is a highly realistic assumption.[2] There are at least two reasons driving the growth. As emerging economies continue to grow, industrial production and higher wealth per capita will mean more energy consumption relative to developed economies. If the world is roughly split into developed and emerging economies using the label OECD and non-OECD countries, about 61 per cent of global energy consumption in 2022 was from non-OECD countries. The emerging economies is the portion of the pie that will grow at a higher rate. As the world decarbonises, the rate of replacing technologies or processes that use fossil fuels (i.e., electrification) in such sectors as transportation (from the greater penetration of electric vehicles, for example) is also expected to steadily rise. Based on current planning scenarios, the share of electricity of all final energy consumption globally will rise to 28 per cent by 2050 from 23 per cent in 2030 (it was 22 per cent in 2020). Assuming global measures to achieve 1.5°C are successfully adopted to limit global warming, the share will grow to 51 per cent, instead of 28 per cent, by 2050 from 29 per cent in 2030.[3]

The upside to the 2 to 3 per cent electricity consumption CAGR would be higher global economic growth or a faster rate of electrification. The downside to this CAGR, apart from slower GDP growth, could be more intense and frequent extreme weather events as well as more stringent energy efficiency measures. It is important to note that some form of energy efficiency measures is already incorporated into most 1.5°C scenarios. Energy efficiency gains can be had in such areas as industrial, services, residential, and transport energy use. This would require highly aggressive public policy action, something which is typically politically difficult, no matter the political system of the jurisdiction in question. Reasons include acceptance from business and the public, concerns over the potential negative economic impact on growth, getting multiple and diverse parties to agree, and the amount of time that it takes to translate the measures into legislation. One of the earliest examples is the Kyoto Protocol, a global treaty aimed at cutting GHG emissions. It was the result of discussions at the June 1992 UNFCCC meeting in Rio de Janeiro. It was finally adopted in 1997 but did not fully come into force until February 2005. Another example is about the latest energy efficiency directive in the EU. The EU Energy Efficiency Directive took over two years to reach official agreement in September 2023. It is likely that it will take a further two years, if not longer, for all of the domestic parliaments to put these directives into national legislation. On the other hand, more frequent extreme climate events will create pressure to accelerate decision-making or the actual implementation of energy efficiency policies.

Supply is the other side of the coin. It must concurrently take two paths. It must be sufficient to meet demand peaks, and it must shift progressively away from fossil fuels by 2050. Meeting demand is, relatively speaking, easier than shifting fuels. It is just a mathematical calculation comprising the installed capacity (i.e., the maximum amount of electricity output generated at an installation) necessary (see Figure 2.4). The planners must assume a mid to long-term peak demand growth rate and plan to add capacity accordingly. Some countries, such as South Korea, have a rolling plan, the Basic Plan of Electricity Supply and Demand, for capacity addition. The plan is released periodically, adjusting the long-term

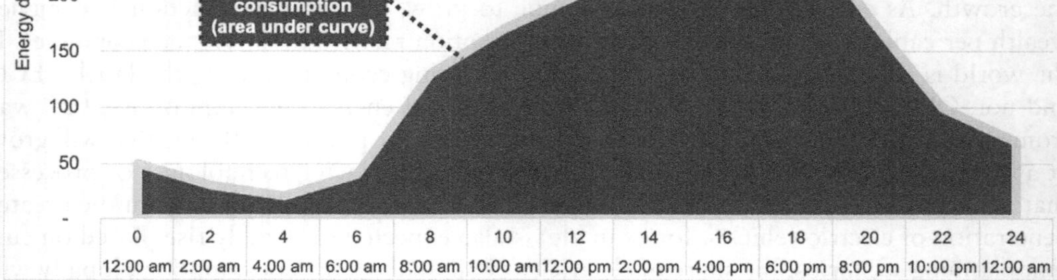

Figure 2.4 Growth in energy consumption versus peak demand (hypothetical)

Source: Author, original chart design (July 2025).

projections for factors such as changing economic conditions; the nation's tenth such plan was released by the Ministry of Trade, Industry and Energy in January 2023. More countries should adopt South Korea's approach but often there are too many players involved which makes it difficult for a government to construct such a plan.

Apart from having to accurately project peak demand, the other two challenges are securing plant construction permits on time as well as obtaining the necessary financing associated with the project. Historically, most countries have relied on fossil fuels-based electricity generation, especially on coal-fired power plants. Shifting future installed capacity away from fossil fuels in favour of clean generation is more challenging. Some of the difficulties include addressing infrastructural, economic, or technological dependence, as well as cost considerations, and domestic or international complexities. There also exists a difference between developed economies and emerging markets. In Europe and North America, the need for additional generation capacity in general is less urgent than in emerging economies given the lower growth rate in demand. The focus will be on building non-fossil fuel energy resources to replace existing fossil fuel assets.

For example, in Greece, there was a significant amount of clean energy additions in the past few years, especially solar PV and wind power, and a decline in fossil fuel capacity. It led output from clean energy sources representing 50 per cent of the total in 2024. At the same time, electricity consumption had been falling. It was about 56 TWh in 2024 compared to almost 64 TWh in 2008. The fall was principally due to such factors as the weak economy, a declining population, and energy efficiency improvements. The government expects demand to drop 6.2 per cent by 2030 from the level in 2020. This, however, is not negative for the growth of renewable energy capacity and related facilities in the country, such as energy storage, as much more clean energy capacity is being built and more is under planning.[4] In areas like the Asia Pacific region, which is dominated by emerging economies, the spending on the energy infrastructure would be much higher than in Europe or North America because in addition to replacing existing assets, a large amount of new capacity needs to be built given the higher growth rate in demand.

A final factor for the supply side of the equation is the transmission and distribution infrastructure. This is a serious constraint to supply at the best of times because of the high level of expenditure required, and, more often than not, because of such hurdles as delays in construction approvals, meeting ever-more restrictive environmental regulations, and public opposition, among other challenges. As the energy complex shifts away from fossil fuels, the grid infrastructure is an even bigger problem. This is because of the decentralised nature of energy from clean energy as this resource may not necessarily be close to demand centres and because of the intermittency; solar and wind power generation, unlike fossil fuel, cannot be on-demand and thus the technical management, mainly through digital solutions, is more complex. The EU is one of the many jurisdictions which has identified that the roll-out of electricity grids is urgent and crucial for the energy transition. It announced an action plan in late 2023 so that transmission distribution systems may operate more efficiently and be rolled out at a faster pace.[5] It set up a supportive legal framework for this purpose and estimated that almost €600 billion ($703.3 billion) will have to be invested. Some of the major areas in the action plan include long-term grid planning improvements, regulatory incentives' introduction, enhancing transparency and improved grid tariffs, raising grid financing access, and fast-tracking grids-permitting.

Most major international organisations involved in the energy sector highlight the importance and urgency to improve and expand electric power grid networks. The IEA's 'Electricity Grids and Secure Energy Transitions'[6] 2023 report, for example, stated that unless an adequate electricity transmission and distribution network is available, the energy transition will stall. The agency believes that the world will need to add or upgrade about 80,000 kilometres of network by 2040. This is roughly similar in size to today's total global grid network. At least $600 billion per year in investments will be required, double that of the past decade. Some of the challenges that need to be addressed include the timing mismatch between the construction of transmission and distribution lines and that of renewable energy projects. Grid projects take 5–15 years from conception to completion. Utility-scale renewable energy projects typically are constructed in just one to five years; although sometimes permitting – environmental approvals, building and construction permits, land use permits, and the like – will slow project construction. The IEA recommends that governments actively incentivise grid investments. This is especially important for Asia which accounts for 50 per cent of global consumption but also has several large grid companies in precarious financial health which may prevent them from adequately investing in expanding or improving grids. The IEA further highlights that securing supply chains and a skilled workforce are quite essential. This would be helped if governments were able to ensure that the grid companies have a secure and transparent project pipeline.

Costs and end-user prices: keeping them low

A second important element in the energy landscape is the total production cost of the electricity and the price paid by the end users. In the EU, electricity markets are fully liberalised. There is intense competition among the companies which sell electricity (known as retailers) to end users allowing them to shop around for the best price. Despite the open and free market, EU governments are sensitive to the price that consumers pay for energy consumption. In February 2022, Russia invaded Ukraine. It caused supply crisis in the energy fuels resulting in an immediate surge in the price of natural gas and oil, and thus electricity prices. This was one of the two reasons for the large 3 per cent fall in electricity demand in the EU in 2022 compared to a year earlier, the other being a mild winter. Several governments were concerned about the impact of the higher power prices on users and so enacted some temporary price relief measures. These included direct subsidies to electricity bills, reductions in energy-related taxes, or targeted assistance to lower income households. Apart from EU governments, globally governments, of whatever their political persuasion, are typically sensitive to the price consumers pay for their electricity, particularly during periods of high inflation and stagnant wages. In many cases, they directly or indirectly subsidise the price so that, for example, industry may remain competitive and households happy.

A significant challenge to decarbonisation is balancing economic viability and sustainability while maintaining affordable prices for consumers. The tools available to achieve this are simple. Governments can advance decarbonisation through direct investments, policy setting, financial incentives, and public–private partnerships. It will involve hundreds of billions of dollars in capital requirements. The investments must earn reasonable returns otherwise investors will not be incentivised. The combined end product, including the energy resource and its transmission and distribution, must be affordable to be economically sustainable.

Industry and households in different geographies will have different points of affordability depending on their economic level of development and their purchasing power. Typically, developed economies can afford higher energy prices whereas developing economies may not necessarily be able to afford them given the lower purchasing power. In Singapore and in Sierra Leone, the electricity cost as of March 2024 was $0.25 per kWh, though the purchasing power of households in the two countries is vastly different, for example.[7] The energy transition is global, so electricity prices during and post the energy transition must be affordable worldwide. The positive trend is that the output price of clean energy technologies, especially more established ones, such as solar and wind, has been declining in the past few years. The projections of most experts indicate that the cost of commercially available clean energy technologies will continue to decline. The key methodology to evaluate the trend is by examining the Levelised Cost of Energy (LCOE). It calculates the cost per unit of output from an energy generation project using a particular technology. Although the summation may appear complex, it can be simply explained. The elements include: (1) total initial investment cost of the project plus the combined total amount over the life of the project of (2) the operations and maintenance expenses, and of (3) the total fuel expenditure, if applicable. Other elements include: (4) the total useful life cycle of the project, (5) the sum of the electricity generated throughout the life of the project, and (6) the discount rate to determine the present value of future costs and benefits associated with an energy project. The chief variable assumption is the discount rate to be used.

The International Renewable Energy Agency, an intergovernmental organisation, is one of several entities providing LCOE calculations for mainstream clean energy technologies. These include solar PV, concentrating solar thermal power, onshore wind, and offshore wind. IRENA looked at the installation costs per kilowatt, the capacity factor (how much energy can be extracted from the capacity), and then the LCOE on a MWh basis (see Figure 2.5). The agency found that the installed costs of solar PV, concentrated solar, and onshore and offshore wind declined between 37 and 86 per cent between 2010 and 2023 depending on the technology. The capacity factor for these various technologies had improved by between 8 per cent and 83 per cent. Altogether, the LCOE declined between 63 per cent and 90 per cent during the period. Broadly, the fall drop was thanks to lower equipment costs, higher capacity factors (i.e., higher efficiency), and other factors. The other gains were driven by innovation, volume leverage, operational streamlining, technological advancement, economies of scale, and production optimisation. Hydro and geothermal experienced an increase in cost mostly due to issues specific to these resources. Hurdles include longer-than-expected

	Total installed costs (2023 USD/kW)			Capacity factor (%)			Levelised cost of electricity (2023 USD/kWh)		
	2010	2023	Percent change	2010	2023	Percent change	2010	2023	Percent change
Bioenergy	3 010	2 730	-9%	72	72	0%	0.084	0.072	-14%
Geothermal	3 011	4 589	52%	87	82	-6%	0.054	0.071	31%
Hydropower	1 459	2 806	92%	44	53	20%	0.043	0.057	33%
Solar PV	5 310	758	-86%	14	16	14%	0.460	0.044	-90%
CSP	10 453	6 589	-37%	30	55	83%	0.393	0.117	-70%
Onshore wind	2 272	1 160	-49%	27	36	33%	0.111	0.033	-70%
Offshore wind	5 409	2 800	-48%	38	41	8%	0.203	0.075	-63%

Figure 2.5 Renewable power generation costs in 2023

Notes: CSP = Concentrated Solar PV.

Source: Global weighted average total installed cost, capacity factor and LCOE trends by technology, 2010 and 2023, found at IRENA (2024), Renewable Power Generation Costs in 2023, International Renewable Energy Agency, Abu Dhabi.

development timelines, less 'easy' sites or more remote and difficult sites, and rising civil engineering related costs.

Few experts question today's price competitiveness of clean energy generation versus fossil fuel generation. In many countries around the world, wind or solar power is produced at a cost significantly lower than that of fossil fuel generated power. In the Asia Pacific region, for example, the production cost of electricity from renewable sources was 13 per cent lower than that from thermal coal in 2023, and is expected to be 32 per cent cheaper by 2030, according to an analysis published by Wood Mackenzie (or WoodMac), a leading global consultancy.[8] Thermal coal generation has been the fuel of choice for many countries in the region, especially for developing economies such as China and India, as historically it was the lowest priced fuel type.

Renewable energy's biggest challenge has been intermittency. It cannot be produced 24 hours a day, 365 days a year. This contrasts with energy generated from fossil fuels. In recent years, this problem has been addressed through energy storage with increasing success. The most common technologies currently are batteries and pumped storage; electricity is used to pump water up to a dam and, when required, the water is released to generate power. The major difference between the two energy storage technologies is that large-scale batteries can be deployed almost anywhere whereas locations for pump storage facilities are more limited. They require favourable geological and geographical elements. In the case of both technologies, the total cost per kilowatt-hour of output remains high as of 2024. This limits the volume of deployment of the two. In the case of batteries, the take-up rate will sharply rise in the coming years, thanks to expected rapid technological advances and sharp price reductions. An important element of the transition is examined in Chapter 3.

Electric power markets mechanisms: simple complexities

A third element of the energy landscape is the electric power market mechanism or market design operating in a particular jurisdiction.

Broadly speaking, there are two systems. The more traditional and established design is the regulated market (see Figure 2.6). It is a model established over many decades and that exists in some form in most countries around the world. In a regulated market, there is only one single company which is often majority or wholly owned by the state. It has a monopoly to produce, transmit, distribute, and retail all, or the great majority, of the electric power in a region or country. There exists little or no competition in any form. Frequently, some private generation facilities are allowed to alleviate the capital expenditure burden facing the monopoly utility. In some instances, the monopoly power utility even invests in upstream energy resources, including thermal coal and natural gas. This model is referred to as the vertically integrated monopoly utility electric power market model. Saudi Arabia's Saudi Electricity Company is an example of such kind of utility.

At the other end of the spectrum are fully deregulated or liberalised electric power markets (see Figure 2.7). This is also known as the complete retail competition electric power market model. Typically, there are several companies that own and operate the generation facilities. The electricity is managed by an independent system operator and traded in an exchange. The transmission and distribution of the power is handled by a separate company, typically one per region to avoid wasteful overlaps in infrastructure. The electricity is retailed by a distribution company or electricity supplier. Often, the companies owning generation facilities also have a power retailing arm. Such a market is fully open and competitive. The end user, be it a factory or a household, is free to choose their retailer. In

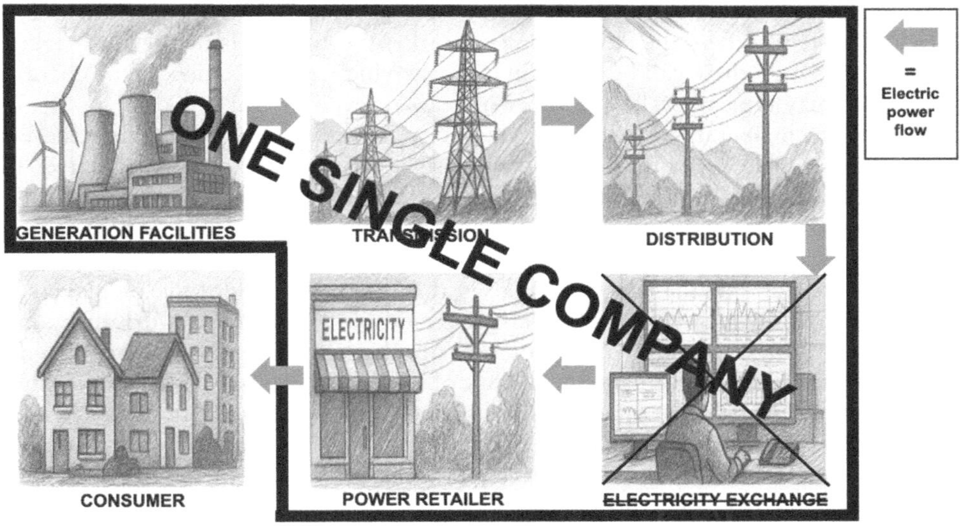

Figure 2.6 Regulated electric power market

Source: Author, original chart design (July 2025); background images sourced from OpenAI <https://chat.openai.com> accessed 4 July 2025.

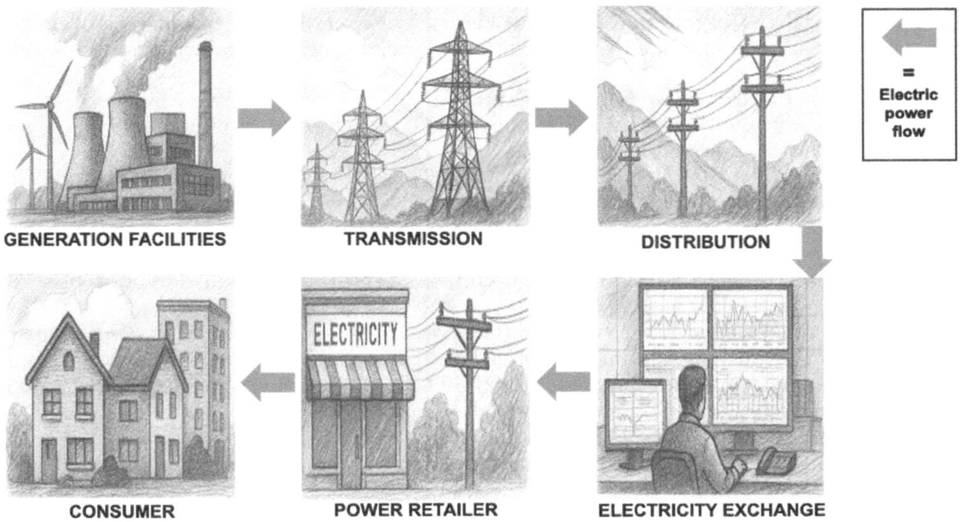

Figure 2.7 Deregulated electric power market

Source: Author, original chart design (July 2025); background images sourced from OpenAI <https://chat.openai.com> accessed 4 July 2025.

Australia, there are over 40 retailers supplying electricity to small energy customers. This is a large number of players given the relatively small size of the market with a population of less than 27 million people. These retailers often offer additional services to the customers ranging from other utility-like services such as gas and telecommunications to other customer products such as insurance and home security services. In some jurisdictions, there exist hybrid systems where the electric power market mechanism is neither fully regulated nor fully open. Often these can be found in markets which are in the process of liberalising, a route which may typically take a number of years or even several decades.

A nation which operates a regulated electricity market would find taking the energy transition path a little easier than a nation whose electricity market is deregulated. In the regulated market, typically, the state owns the electricity monopoly. If a country already has net-zero objectives coupled with a clear energy transition plan, it can direct the monopoly in whichever direction it wants and can execute the transition more swiftly. In an open and competitive market, the first challenge is that there is a multitude of players. Also in deregulated markets, the electric power price paid by the end user is driven by market forces, which at times can make prices volatile. Another challenge is that deregulated markets are relatively recent in terms of the history of the energy industry. They have only been around for about four decades or so, mostly starting from the early 1990s. As such, in many countries or regions, market designs are still undergoing some changes. This is something, for example, that the EU is currently working on. This makes the energy transition in such places as the EU or Australia a little bit trickier.

Notes

1 E Hubbard (ed), 'The Open Road – Afoot with the Fra: Thomas A. Edison' (1910) 5 The Fra: A Journal of Affirmation 6 <https://babel.hathitrust.org/cgi/pt?id=chi.65534236&seq=9> accessed 20 April 2024.

2 Enerdata, 'Global 2050 Projections for Total Electricity Generation | Enerdata' (eneroutlook.enerdata.net) <https://eneroutlook.enerdata.net/total-electricity-generation-projections.html> accessed 1 March 2024.

3 Statista, *Global Electrification Rate by Scenario 2030–2050* (Statista Research Department 19 January 2024) <https://www.statista.com/statistics/1417905/global-electrification-in-end-use-sectors-worldwide-forecast/> accessed 1 March 2024.

4 Low Carbon Power (ed), 'Understand Low-Carbon Energy in Greece through Data | Low-Carbon Power' (lowcarbonpower.org) <https://lowcarbonpower.org/region/Greece> accessed 24 April 2024.

5 European Commission, *Commission Sets out Actions to Accelerate the Roll-out of Electricity Grids* (European Commission 28 November 2023) <https://ec.europa.eu/commission/presscorner/detail/en/ip_23_6044> accessed 3 March 2024.

6 International Energy Agency, *Electricity Grids and Secure Energy Transitions Enhancing the Foundations of Resilient, Sustainable and Affordable Power Systems* (International Energy Agency 2023) <https://iea.blob.core.windows.net/assets/ea2ff609-8180-4312-8de9-494bcf21696d/ElectricityGridsandSecureEnergyTransitions.pdf> accessed 3 March 2024.

7 World Population Review, 'Cost of Electricity by Country 2022' (worldpopulationreview.com 2024) <https://worldpopulationreview.com/country-rankings/cost-of-electricity-by-country> accessed s20 March 2025.

8 M Lewis, 'Utility Solar Dethrones Coal as the Cheapest Power Source in Asia' *Electrek* (29 February 2024) <https://electrek.co/2024/02/29/utility-solar-dethrones-coal-as-the-cheapest-power-source-in-asia/> accessed 7 March 2024.

Chapter 3

The energy landscape

Technologies, the newer core element

Aims:

- The evolution of clean energy technologies and the transition from fossil fuels.
- Capabilities, challenges, and future potential of key technologies and solutions.
- Clean energy technologies' cost reductions, investment trends, and market differences.

In some energy circles, a phrase is often quoted: 'The Stone Age did not end for lack of stone, and the Oil Age will end long before the world runs out of oil'. It is attributed to Sheikh Ahmed Zaki Yamani who was a Saudi Arabian politician and Minister of Petroleum and Mineral Resources for several decades in the 1960s through the late 1980s. Sheikh Zaki Yamani used this analogy to emphasise that the transition to new energy sources is not because existing ones are exhausted but because better alternatives emerge. The fourth fundamental component of the energy landscape, technologies, is dealt with separately as it is one of the most important drivers of the transition.

Energy generation has historically been dominated by the use of natural gas, oil, or thermal coal. Today, mainstream resources are becoming more diversified. The fastest-growing segment is clean energy generation technologies. They include, but are by no means limited to, wind energy and solar power, increasingly coupled with battery-based energy storage. The shift is in large part due to the pollution emitted by burning fossil fuels. In some other jurisdictions, such as in China, the motivation is beyond climate change considerations. Other drivers include raising energy independence and security, economic benefits such as the creation of new industries and new jobs, and reducing energy price volatility driven by natural gas, oil, or thermal coal prices.

The first coal-fired power plant began operating in the 1880s, and fossil fuels have dominated electricity generation ever since, spanning nearly 150 years. Fossil fuel electricity production is a proven, reliable, and well-understood technology. Conversely, traditional energy companies often view renewable energy technologies, including mainstream options like solar and wind, as 'new'. These companies, resistant to change, prefer familiar methods. Despite the world installing hundreds of gigawatts of clean energy, large mainstream operators are only slowly acknowledging renewables as a viable additional energy source that could eventually replace fossil fuels.

DOI: 10.4324/9781003666509-4

The primary challenge cited is the intermittent nature of renewable energy, which may not meet sudden demand surges. However, two technologies secure renewables' continued growth: battery energy storage, with rapidly falling costs and significant technological advances, and digital technologies. Digital technologies and artificial intelligence (AI) optimise renewable energy systems by improving forecasting accuracy for variable sources like solar and wind, and enhancing grid management for better integration and stability. These digital solutions also automate maintenance and boost operational efficiency, reducing costs and maximising energy output.

Understanding decarbonisation requires grasping both the nature of clean energy technologies – from generation to distribution – and the broader landscape of solutions. Among the many evolving technologies, key emerging technologies in this space include energy storage systems (such as batteries), green hydrogen production, digital solutions (including AI applications), and small modular reactors.

Exploring clean technologies solutions

There are several ways to assess the development stage of a technology, from initial idea to full commercialisation. The IEA categorises this process into 11 development stages across six groups: concept, small prototype, large prototype, demonstration, market uptake, and mature (see Figure 3.1). This classification helps stakeholders understand the progress and potential of emerging technologies, making it a valuable tool for anyone involved in the energy transition.

The IEA is one of several international organisations and groups that track clean energy technologies. It established an open interactive database, the ETP Clean Energy Technology Guide, containing data on about 550 'individual technology designs and components across the whole energy system that contribute to achieving the goal of net-zero emissions'.[1] The IEA categorises technologies as 'fully mature' when they are extensively deployed and commercially viable, and 'emerging' when they are still in development or early stages of commercialisation. Some of the fully mature technologies include demand response, EVs, geothermal power,

STAGE OF DEVELOPMENT	PHASE	TYPE	REMARKS
CONCEPT	1	Initial idea	Basic principles have been defined
	2	Application formulated	Concept and application of solution have been formulated
	3	Concept needs validation	Solution needs to be prototyped and applied
SMALL PROTOTYPE	4	Early prototype	Prototype proven in test conditions
LARGE PROTOTYPE	5	Large prototype	Components proven in conditions to be deployed
	6	Full prototype at scale	Prototype proven at scale in conditions to be deployed
DEMOSTRATION	7	Pre-commercial demonstration	Prototype working in expected conditions
	8	First of a kind commercial	Commercial demonstration, full-scale deployment in final conditions
MARKET UPTAKE	9	Commercial operation in relevant environment	Solution is commercially available, needs evolutionary improvement to stay competitive
	10	Integration needed at scale	Solution is commercial and competitive but needs further integration efforts
MATURE	11	Proof of stability reached	Predictable growth

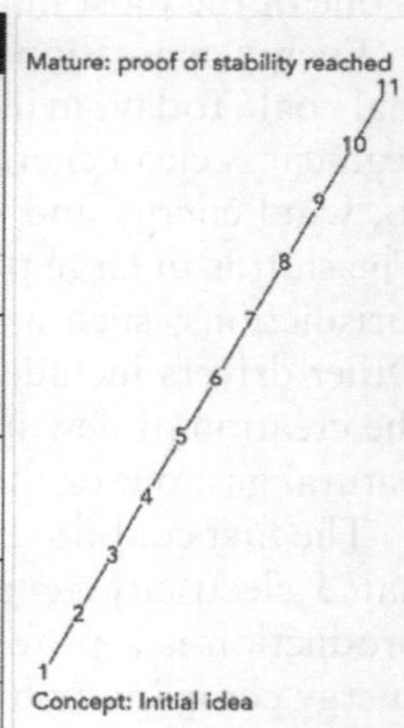

Figure 3.1 Clean technology stages of development

Notes: This is a work by the author derived from IEA material and the author is solely liable and responsible for this derived work. The derived work is not endorsed by the IEA in any manner.

Source: IEA, 'ETP Clean Energy Technology Guide – Data Tools' (IEA, 14 September 2023). Available at: https://www.iea.org/data-and-statistics/data-tools/etp-clean-energy-technology-guide accessed 8 March 2024.

grid-scale storage, hydro, nuclear, smart grids, solar PV, and wind. A small sample of technologies which are emerging or yet to reach full commercialisation include building-integrated PV, Carbon Capture and Storage (CCS), energy storage, flexible grids, green hydrogen, smart buildings, and sustainable building materials. It is important to note that the mature technologies are still evolving and improving. They are still undergoing further development. For example, solar cell manufacturers aim to raise the capacity factor of the cells (the percentage of time they generate electricity). Wind turbine manufacturers seek to improve the efficiency of wind turbines by such improvements as increasing the size of the blades.

Clean technologies' fast-evolving landscape

The general knowledge of clean energy technologies has sharply improved over the past few years as adoption of mainstream ones, such as solar and wind, has risen exponentially worldwide. For example, solar power generation capacity has grown over 1,000 per cent in the past ten years. It amounted to only 177 GW in 2014 compared to an estimated 2000 GW or so in 2024.[2] One of the great many resources to understand the clean energy space is from the American Public Power Association (see Figure 3.2). The various technologies are grouped into the three levels. First are the digital hardware and solutions which are common to all clean technologies. They include supervisory control and data acquisition (SCADA) systems, distributed energy resource management systems (DERMS), AI and data analysis tools, modern wireline or wireless communications, and cybersecurity protocols. Digital hardware and solutions have been at the centre of energy generation and the supply system for decades, but they are even more critical for clean technologies today.

A second group of technologies are those related to the generation, distribution, and consumption of energy. They include electrification, distributed energy resources (DERs) and load flexibility, community-scale generation, and utility-scale generation. When the world solely relied on large-scale power generation and distribution, distributed systems usually

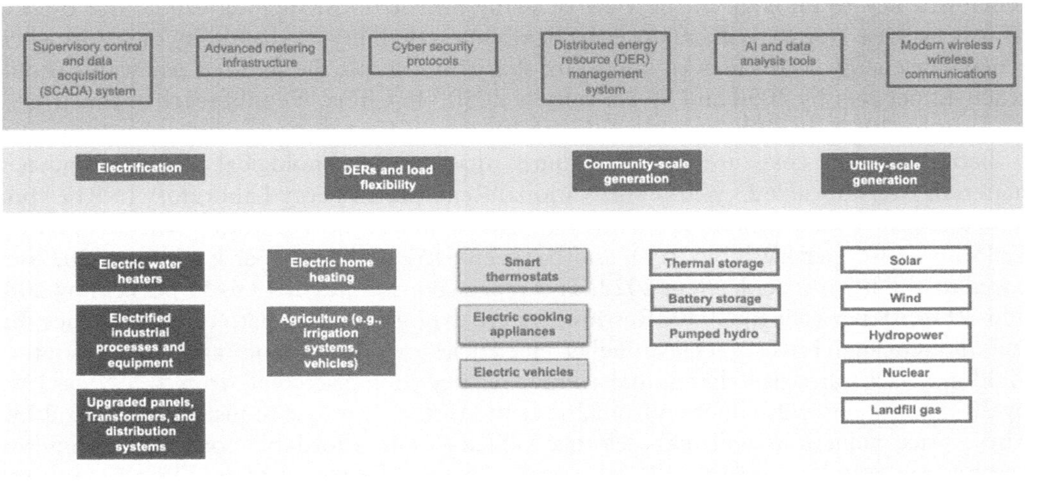

Figure 3.2 What technologies are necessary for a clean energy transition?

Source: American Public Power Association, 'What Technologies Are Necessary for a Clean Energy Transition?' (https://www.publicpower.org/8 November 2022). Available at: https://www.publicpower.org/periodical/article/what-technologies-are-necessary-clean-energy-transition accessed 31 March 2024.

made little economic sense. With the advent of distributed energy generation sources, such as rooftop solar PV or battery storage, new technologies need to be introduced.

A third group of technologies are consumer-related ones. They include electric water heaters, electrified industrial processes and equipment, upgraded panels, transformers, and distribution systems, together with electric home heating and solutions for agriculture, such as irrigation systems. There are also many behind-the-meter technologies (energy devices installed on the end-user side of their electricity metre). They include smart thermostats, electric cooking appliances and other smart home devices, as well as, arguably, electric vehicles.

Another critical group of technological solutions is related to community-scale generation specifically energy storage, including thermal storage, battery storage, and pumped hydro.

The last group is utility-scale generation technologies, with the most common ones being hydropower, nuclear energy, and landfill gas. The list is by far not fully complete. Especially, if one thinks of the hundreds of technologies and solutions on the watch list of the IEA, for example, found in a regular publication titled 'Clean Energy Market Monitor'.[3] In fact, the key technologies which the IEA monitors closely include solar PV, wind, nuclear, electric cars, heat pumps, and hydrogen electrolysers.

Batteries: transforming electricity into a commodity

Energy storage is critical to support clean energy generation, given that renewables can be interrupted by a lack of sun, a lack of wind, or an extraordinary weather event. This has been highlighted several times, albeit in different contexts. The US National Renewable Energy Laboratory (NREL), a national laboratory of the US Department of Energy, concluded that energy storage will be a major element of any electric power system in the future as energy storage can work in a variety of valuable roles.[4] For large-scale, or grid-scale, battery energy storage, the logistics and the cost are somewhat more challenging. Yet, it remains a key technology in the view of many jurisdictions, such as China and the EU. This is because storage will enhance the flexibility, reliability, and stability of a grid where renewable energy constitutes an important share. In Europe, the share of renewable should reach 42 per cent by 2030 and 89 per cent by 2050.[5] In China, it could reach as much as 75 per cent by 2050, according to BloombergNEF, a research firm.[6]

Battery storage costs are set to plummet, thanks to technological advances and new materials over the next 25 years. The National Renewable Energy Laboratory (NREL) projects that utility-scale lithium-ion battery systems with four-hour duration will cost between \$245 and \$403 per kWh by 2030, and between \$159 and \$348 per kWh by 2050, compared to about \$500 per kWh in 2022. This represents declines of 19 to 51 per cent by 2030 and 30 to 68 per cent by 2050. Researchers are exploring many battery technologies that use different materials to achieve higher efficiencies or rely on more accessible resources. Goldman Sachs forecasts that global average battery pack prices will drop to \$99 per kWh by 2025, a 40 per cent reduction from 2022, and further decrease to just over \$80 by 2030. These price reductions will make electric vehicles more affordable compared to internal combustion engines, boosting EV sales and increasing battery demand. This growth will create a virtuous cycle, further driving down battery costs as production scales up.

The IEA is another organisation closely monitoring the battery industry market trends and global competition. The agency believes that the global battery industry had reached a major turning point as of March 2025, with several notable developments reshaping the market landscape. In 2024, the industry achieved remarkable milestones as battery demand surpassed 1 TWh for the first time, coinciding with a 25 per cent increase in electric car sales to 17 million units. Crucially, average battery pack prices have fallen below $100 per kWh, widely considered the threshold at which electric vehicles become cost-competitive with conventional models. Global manufacturing capacity has expanded to 3 TWh, with projections suggesting this could triple within five years if all announced projects materialise.

China maintains its dominant position, producing over 75 per cent of global batteries with prices approximately 30 per cent lower than European counterparts and 20 per cent lower than North American manufacturers. Chinese battery prices decreased by nearly 30 per cent in 2024 alone, reflecting their competitive advantage. This superiority stems from extensive manufacturing expertise (having produced 70 per cent of all EV batteries ever made), integrated supply chains, and a strategic focus on cheaper lithium-iron phosphate (LFP) batteries, which cost about 30 per cent less than lithium nickel cobalt manganese oxide (NMC) alternatives. The intense competition amongst nearly 100 domestic producers further drives this price advantage.

The IEA stressed that the industry is entering a new phase characterised by increasing consolidation among manufacturers, standardisation of technologies, and government-led efforts to diversify supply chains geographically. Concerns about supply chain concentration have intensified, particularly following China's proposed export limitations on battery technologies. Addressing these challenges will require sustained investment, international collaboration, and strategic deployment of automation and innovation to compete effectively in this rapidly evolving market.

NREL categorises batteries into four types: electrochemical, mechanical, chemical, and thermal. These technologies exist at various stages of development and market readiness. Electrochemical options like lithium-ion and lead-acid batteries enjoy widespread commercial use, while flow and sodium-sulphur varieties remain in earlier commercialisation phases.[7] Many promising technologies await further development, such as calcium-oxygen batteries, which offer energy density comparable to lithium-ion alternatives but could prove significantly cheaper to produce when commercialised, owing to calcium's greater global abundance compared to lithium.[8]

Energy storage research encompasses numerous technologies suited to different applications. Systems suited for distributed services include flywheels, supercapacitors, and superconducting magnetic energy storage. Technologies better adapted for bulk storage comprise power-to-gas and pumped storage hydropower. Several options serve both distributed and bulk purposes effectively, including thermal energy storage, sodium-based batteries, flow batteries, lithium-ion batteries, and lead-acid batteries.[9]

The forecasting of the future cost and deployment volume of battery-based energy storage presents significant challenges due to several uncertainties. The dominant battery technology a decade from now might still exist only in research laboratories today. The materials required for leading battery types may be readily accessible or difficult to obtain. Additionally, the rate at which costs will decline remains uncertain. These factors make precise predictions about the evolution of energy storage markets particularly difficult.

Yet, examining the exponential growth in recent years and the consistently declining cost curve provides strong grounds for optimism regarding future growth and adoption rates of battery-based energy storage. The remarkable progress already achieved, together with intense research activity and increasing investment in China and the rest of the world, suggests that battery technology will continue its rapid advancement. This trend points towards a future where energy storage solutions become increasingly affordable and widely deployed across various sectors.

Tomorrow's new fuel: green hydrogen

Green hydrogen merits closer examination due to its immense promise, having attracted enormous interest and hundreds of millions of dollars in investment commitments in recent years.

Hydrogen production has a rich history dating back to the 17th century. Scientists identified the element in 1766, and by 1800, they discovered how to create pure hydrogen and oxygen through electrolysis using electricity and water. Today, several hydrogen production methods exist, with two being particularly widespread.[10]

Steam-methane reforming involves subjecting natural gas or another methane source to extremely high temperatures, between 700°C and 1,000°C, to generate hydrogen.[11] Electrolysis, the second major method, splits water using electricity.[12] This process produces no harmful by-products or emissions. When the electricity comes from clean energy sources such as renewables, the result is green hydrogen.

Various colour-based designations exist for hydrogen based on production methods (see Figure 3.3). Black Hydrogen comes from coal gasification. Grey Hydrogen results from steam reforming natural gas. Blue Hydrogen resembles Grey Hydrogen but incorporates CCS technology to reduce emissions. Pink Hydrogen emerges from electrolysis powered by nuclear energy. Yellow Hydrogen comes from electrolysis using solar energy. Turquoise Hydrogen results from pyrolysis using natural gas as the source material. The colour-coding system reflects the environmental impact of different production methods, with green hydrogen representing the cleanest option due to its reliance on renewable energy sources for the electrolysis process.

Hydrogen offers diverse applications in the energy transition, earning it the nickname 'Swiss army knife of decarbonisation'. Despite its versatility, infrastructure limitations, technical challenges, and economic constraints restrict its widespread adoption. Energy

Hydrogen Type	Process	Fuel Source
Black	Gasification	Coal
Blue	Steam reforming with Carbon Capture	Natural gas
Green	Electrolysis	Renewable energy
Grey	Steam reforming	Natural gas
Pink	Electrolysis	Nuclear energy
Turquoise	Pyrolysis	Natural gas
Yellow	Electrolysis	Solar power

Figure 3.3 What are the colours of hydrogen and what do they mean?

Source: Acciona Energy, 'What Are the Colours of Hydrogen and What Do They Mean?' (www.acciona.com.au 16 June 2022). Available at: https://www.acciona.com.au/updates/stories/what-are-the-colours-of-hydrogen-and-what-do-they-mean/?_adin=0745137403 accessed 28 March 2024.

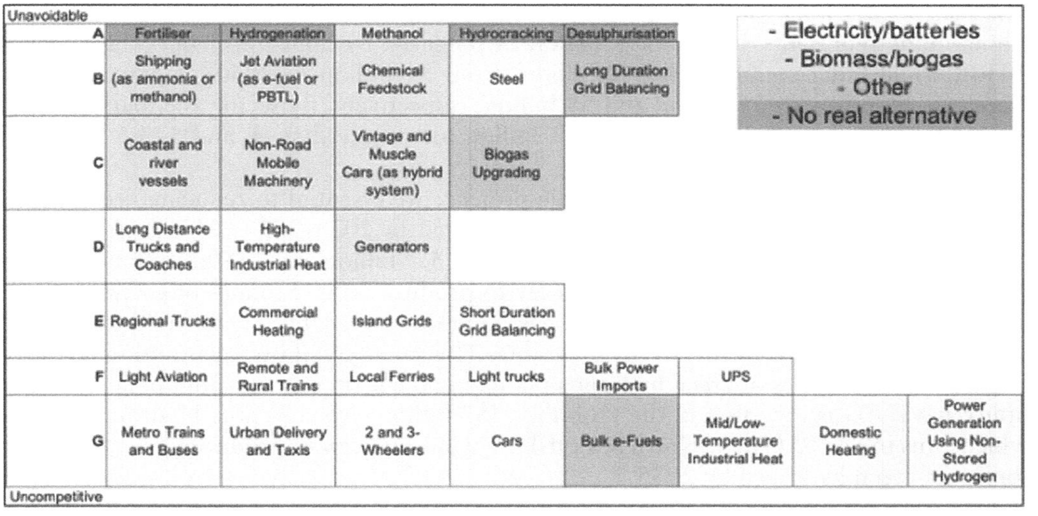

Figure 3.4 Hydrogen ladder 5.0

Source: Michael Liebreich/Liebreich Associates, Clean Hydrogen Ladder, Version 5.0, 2023. Concept credit: Adrian Hiel, Energy Cities. CC-BY 4.0

expert Michael Liebreich's 'Hydrogen Ladder' provides a clear framework for evaluating hydrogen's potential across various sectors.[13]

Liebreich argues that governments and businesses should focus their resources on the most viable hydrogen applications (see Figure 3.4). For instance, using renewable energy to produce hydrogen, storing it, and then converting it back to electricity proves inefficient due to substantial energy losses throughout this cycle. The 'Hydrogen Ladder' categorises hydrogen applications from 'A' to 'G', with 'A' representing uses with 'no alternative (though this does not mean the use case is growing)', 'B' indicating applications where 'decent market share is highly likely', and 'C' suggesting areas where 'some market share is likely'. Applications ranked 'D' through 'G' face significant challenges to commercial-scale adoption due to poor economic competitiveness.

This framework helps stakeholders prioritise investments and policy support for hydrogen technologies where they can deliver the greatest decarbonisation impact. By focusing on the most promising applications at the top of the ladder, stakeholders can maximise hydrogen's contribution to addressing climate change while acknowledging its limitations in less suitable contexts.

The production cost of green hydrogen remains prohibitively high. According to IRENA's 2021 study, green hydrogen costs between $4 and $6 per kilogram, roughly two to three times more expensive than grey hydrogen. However, electrolyser prices have fallen by about 60 per cent since 2010 and should continue dropping. Combined with growing economies of scale, these factors could reduce costs to $2 per kilogram by 2030 and potentially as low as $1 per kilogram by 2050[14]; one kilogram of hydrogen has an energy value equal to about 33 kWh.

Major Asian economies will help drive this cost reduction. China, India, Japan, and South Korea plan significant green hydrogen adoption for ammonia, iron, steel, and methanol production. China is currently the leader, as 80 per cent of the global capacity of electrolysers was based in the country, powered by 5.3 GW of energy from solar and wind sources.[15]

The Asia Society Policy Institute projects that this market will exceed $180 billion by 2050. China alone represents at least $85 billion of potential by 2050 (up from $22 billion in 2030), while India could reach $78 billion (from $4 billion in 2030). Japan and South Korea should grow to $9 billion and $8 billion, respectively. By sector, the market should exceed $49.1 billion for ammonia, $87.3 billion for iron and steel, and $43.5 billion for methanol.[16]

Industry experts believe that large-scale projects are essential to reducing green hydrogen costs. Several major initiatives were announced in 2023–2024. China Petroleum & Chemical Corp (known as Sinopec) is building a 5.7 billion yuan ($0.8 billion) plant in Inner Mongolia using solar and wind energy to produce 30,000 tonnes of green hydrogen annually.[17] A multinational consortium has committed $8.4 billion to build the world's largest green hydrogen facility in Saudi Arabia. This facility will use solar and wind power to produce 600 tonnes of green hydrogen per day in the form of green ammonia.[18] German utility RWE AG is investing in the €6 billion ($7 billion) Aqua Ventus Hydrogen project, which aims to use 10 GW of North Sea offshore wind capacity to produce up to one million tonnes of green hydrogen by 2035.[19]

However, significant challenges for green hydrogen remain. Australian businessman Andrew Forrest's Fortescue Metals Group has encountered setbacks in its green hydrogen initiatives in Australia and the rest of the world. High electricity costs and market pressures forced the company to scale back production targets and reduce its workforce. The viability of hydrogen production is questioned as it remains expensive compared to fossil fuels and battery technology. Additionally, Fortescue's renewable projects, funded by iron ore profits, face financial strain due to declining ore prices and China's economic slowdown.[20]

The growing trend of investment commitments is particularly evident in various regional mega initiatives throughout Asia, Europe, and North America.

According to Nick Smith, Managing Director of strategic and technical advisory firm Global Decarbonisation Advisory,[21] Australia has been a leader in the Asian green hydrogen effort alongside China, Japan, and Korea. The country launched its national hydrogen strategy in 2019, which was subsequently updated in May 2022. This revised strategy highlights green hydrogen's potential to attract A$300 billion ($197 billion) in investments for both domestic use and export. Smith highlights that the government wants to support building at least eight hydrogen hubs – clusters of large-scale demand – with A$464 million ($304 million) in funding. These hubs will likely be distributed across Australia with two each in Queensland, New South Wales, and Western Australia, plus one each in South Australia and Tasmania. Since early 2025, Australia's hydrogen sector has faced some challenges with the cancellation of the Queensland state government-backed, 2.24 GW Central Queensland Hydrogen Project. This follows the change in elected government and the decision for a Japanese off-taker to exit the project. Additionally, the South Australian government's 250 MW Hydrogen Jobs plan has been 'deferred' to allow for the allocated funding to be diverted to support the government's decision to force the Gupta Financial Group (GFG) and their Whyalla integrated steel works into administration. Smith adds that the Australian government's re-election in May 2025 provides policy certainty and consistency on a range of green hydrogen and green iron and steel supporting policies and investment opportunities in addition to ongoing renewable energy and infrastructure support.

The EU adopted its hydrogen strategy in 2020, outlining key actions including investment support, research funding, and production assistance involving both public and private sectors. The EU aims to produce 10 million tonnes of green hydrogen internally while importing another 10 million tonnes by 2030.[22] To achieve this goal, the European Hydrogen Backbone initiative was launched in 2020 with 33 energy infrastructure operators, including many European gas distribution utilities. This backbone will create infrastructure to produce and transport renewable and low-carbon hydrogen throughout Europe, comprising 53,000 km of pipelines (60 per cent repurposed and 40 per cent new) by 2040 at a cost of €80–€143 billion ($94–$168 billion).[23] Given the project's long timeline, total investment costs will likely increase.

North America had implemented various initiatives and incentives to promote green hydrogen production. In October 2023, the US Department of Energy announced that it would allocate $7 billion to create seven Regional Clean Hydrogen Hubs across the country to accelerate large-scale deployment of cost-effective clean hydrogen. The government offered a tax credit up to $3 per kilogram for clean hydrogen production, with amounts determined by the production process's carbon intensity. That same month, the Department selected specific projects for funding negotiations. These hydrogen hubs would play a vital role in reducing clean hydrogen costs and creating a sustainable market. Additionally, the Clean Hydrogen Manufacturing Initiative, supported by the bipartisan Infrastructure Law, had committed $750 million to improve clean hydrogen technologies, including electrolysers. All of these plans and allocations suffered cancellations, delays, and dislocations after Trump became president in January 2025, though in the long term, the country could still play catch-up with other countries. Canada has also announced support through its Canadian Hydrogen Strategy, directing substantial investments towards infrastructure development and research, particularly in Alberta, Ontario, and British Columbia provinces.[24]

Global Decarbonisation Advisory's Nick Smith argues that to enable projects that deliver and scale commercially competitive outputs and have strong community support,[25] it is important that harmonised regulations, codes, and standards are adopted to support efficient, effective, and safe hydrogen adoption. Efficient and effective regulations, codes, and standards are enhanced by research funding and collaboration to focus on known gaps in knowledge. These focus areas support appropriate management of technology, safety, and commercial risk and deliver an energy transition that is the lowest cost and maximises the benefits to communities and investors.

Smartening energy: AI and digital innovations in demand and supply

In 2021, the author of this book wrote extensively on the energy digitalisation revolution based on data available up to the end of 2020.[26] This predated the significant momentum AI gained in 2023 with the public release of Generative Artificial Intelligence.

The fundamental argument for digital solutions in the energy sector remains compelling. New digital technologies will deliver significant cost savings throughout the energy supply value chain, which will benefit both providers and consumers. They will enhance the economic and logistical viability of smaller projects such as mini-grids and distributed-energy systems. Additionally, these technologies will improve energy efficiency and conservation, creating a more sustainable and environmentally friendly energy supply. Furthermore, they will enable more flexible and cost-effective financing solutions, as well as reduce expenses in areas such as feasibility studies, legal fees, and other development costs. Digital solutions will also introduce new applications for financial transactions, including additional financing channels. All these developments will create numerous business and investment opportunities for both existing industry participants and new market entrants.[27]

Digital technologies and solutions can be categorised into three main groups, reflecting the diverse roles they play in the energy sector. The first group includes applications that balance the demand and supply of electricity, which ensures system equilibrium. The second group consists of applications aimed at process optimisation and that enhance the efficiency and effectiveness of internal operations. The third group is customer-service-oriented applications. These not only help the company secure more customers but also offer additional services to existing users, leading to increased revenues and other benefits. These groupings are discussed in Figure 3.5 in detail. Readers not familiar with some of the terminologies,

SYSTEM BALANCE	Smart Grid and Optimised Operations	**Smart Grid** Real-time condition monitoring and load, voltage, and frequency control via remotely controllable transformers, generators, and consumers **Optimised generation** Optimised operation of generation assets based on real-time monitoring, remote control, and direct communication with grid and market
	Smart Market and Flexibility Integration	**Integration of flexibilities** 'Flexibilisation' of existing generation units and consumers Creation of new flexibilities via storage units and sector coupling (e.g., batteries, e-mobility) Marketing of flexibilities of generators, consumers, and storage units (e.g., virtual power plants, operating reserve, demand-side management, demand response) **Smart market** Smart contracts High frequency microtransactions Peer-to-peer trades and peer-to-peer trading platforms Variable tariffs for (small) generators or consumers
PROCESS OPTIMISATION	Anomaly Identification and Predictions	Optimisation of forecasting for generation, demand, grid conditions, and prices. Minimisation of balancing energy Optimised anomaly detection, failure localisation, and remote fixing
		Predictive maintenance Digital twin for optimisation of operations and maintenance and lifetime extension Optimised strategic development of new business models, avoidance of risks, and optimised investment decisions Analysis of customer interactions (Net Promoter Score, reasons for leaving) and prediction of customer wishes and reactions
	Process Efficiency	Digital document management system Digitally supported work preparation and documentation (availability of documents and instructions, virtual reality training, augmented reality support) Robotic process automation (automation of reparative tasks), e.g., automated regulatory reporting Connected internal processes with digital processes of customers and suppliers
CUSTOMER ORIENTATION	Smart Home	**Smart home management and energy management services** Desegregation and visualisation of energy consumption in real time Energy-efficiency optimisation of appliances such as lighting, smart devices Optimisation of tariff and consumption by owner of solar PV system, energy storage, e-mobility charging, etc. Ambient assisted living and security systems
	Communication Channels	Digitalised customer communication channels and applications of bots (i.e., computing autonomous programs)
	Trust and Transparency	Automated billing based on real consumption Certification of origin of electricity Supplying the secure connection to the smart meter to third parties (e.g., for contracts submissions)

Figure 3.5 Digital applications

Source: Weigel P, 'Digital Applications in Energy Sector' (encyclopedia.pub 14 April 2021). Available at: https://encyclopedia.pub/entry/205 accessed 31 March 2024.

such as 'load monitoring' or 'the digital twins', may want to refer to the book 'Asia's Energy Revolution', also by this author.

AI represents another crucial area of digital technology development. It assists in various areas, with digital and physical analysis being the two most prominent. On the digital side, AI's remarkable capability to quickly analyse enormous, multi-layered and complex datasets enables radical improvements in demand response accuracy – determining how much electricity is needed where and when. On the physical side, AI assists in discovering and assessing new materials, such as those for energy storage. Google's Chief Sustainability Officer, Kate Brandt, believes that AI plays a major role in addressing climate change by supercharging climate solutions. She suggests that using AI to scale up proven applications and technology could help mitigate up to 10 per cent of GHG emissions by 2030. Brandt further highlights AI's significant opportunities in information optimisation and prediction.[28]

Grids are increasingly strained, and Virtual Power Plants (VPPs) and electric vehicle (EV)-related technologies exemplify the transformative AI applications in the energy transition and how they can support grids.

The EU faces significant challenges as it adds tens of gigawatts of solar and wind capacity annually through 2030, placing enormous strain on Transmission System Operators (TSOs). This expansion will increase total renewable energy capacity to approximately 1070 GW to 1200 GW by 2030, up from just under 400 GW in 2022. The EU aims for renewables to account for at least 42.5 per cent of final energy consumption by 2030, ideally reaching 45 per cent, compared to less than 23 per cent in 2022. The tripling of solar power capacity and doubling of wind energy capacity within such a short time frame will further stress the already stretched grid infrastructure in several EU member countries, as they must manage substantial energy supply from sources dependent on variable sun and wind patterns. According to the independent energy think tank Ember, 11 of 26 grids are not sufficiently accounting for renewables targets in their plans.[29] The EU estimates that over €580 billion ($680 billion) will be invested in grid improvements, with a substantial portion dedicated to digital solutions.

VPPs offer an effective digital solution for TSOs. These systems combine three key elements: distributed energy resources like solar panels and EV batteries, software-based technologies for effective energy management and dispatch, and information and communication technologies integrated with the Internet of Things. By leveraging VPPs, TSOs can achieve more efficient power grids, better balance intermittent-renewables integration, and improve overall grid stability and reliability. Additional advantages include providing continuous power supply, rapid or immediate availability, remote controllability, affordability, and cost savings for end users.

As Australian utility Origin Energy explains, VPPs can connect millions of energy assets across various locations, enabling the assets to work together effectively. Increased computing power leads to more efficient coordination, allowing assets ranging from home air conditioning systems to large industrial machines to operate in unison.[30] VPPs can process billions of data points in near-real time, including weather data, consumer information, electricity market data, and other sources. This information feeds into the VPP system, which continuously measures the overall power system, forecasts energy demand, and assesses available supply. AI significantly accelerates and enhances this entire process.

For VPPs to function effectively, smart meters must record consumer energy consumption data. While the EU is making progress in this area, it needs to accelerate smart meter adoption, as current levels remain below optimal. According to Berg Insights,[31] a consultancy, the EU27+3 (Norway, Switzerland, and the United Kingdom) should reach a penetration rate of almost 80 per cent by 2028, equivalent to 326 million smart meters, compared to just 56 per cent at the end of 2022. A study by the EU Directorate-General for Energy in March 2020 indicates that smart meter installation costs average €180–€200 ($211–$234) per metre while saving €270 ($316) per metering point in billing and achieving average energy savings of 2 to 10 per cent.[32] It is important to note that smart meter installation operates on a rolling basis, as their life cycle spans between 10 and 20 years.

The interaction between VPPs, EVs, and AI offers substantial long-term potential for operators and investors. EV battery quality continues to improve rapidly, providing users with longer ranges for the same energy consumption. Additionally, the cost of batteries for EVs and other storage forms has been steadily declining and is projected to continue falling. Currently, electricity for EVs flows unidirectionally from the grid to the vehicle via charging points. However, in recent years, companies worldwide have increasingly developed bidirectional or vehicle-to-grid (V2G) technologies (see Figure 3.6). These innovations allow EVs to function as small, on-site power plants, returning unused battery power to the electricity grid when needed, thereby becoming key components of VPPs. This helps balance the power grid and ensures steady energy supply, particularly in systems incorporating renewables. AI-driven technological breakthroughs optimise EV battery throughput while minimising impact on battery life cycles.

Some experts argue that China has already taken the leading role in V2G. The country is well on its way to transitioning from pilot projects to commercialisation. China has emphasised that one of its strategic focuses is to integrate EVs with the electric power grid through V2G. This will be chiefly driven by the National Development Reform Commission and the

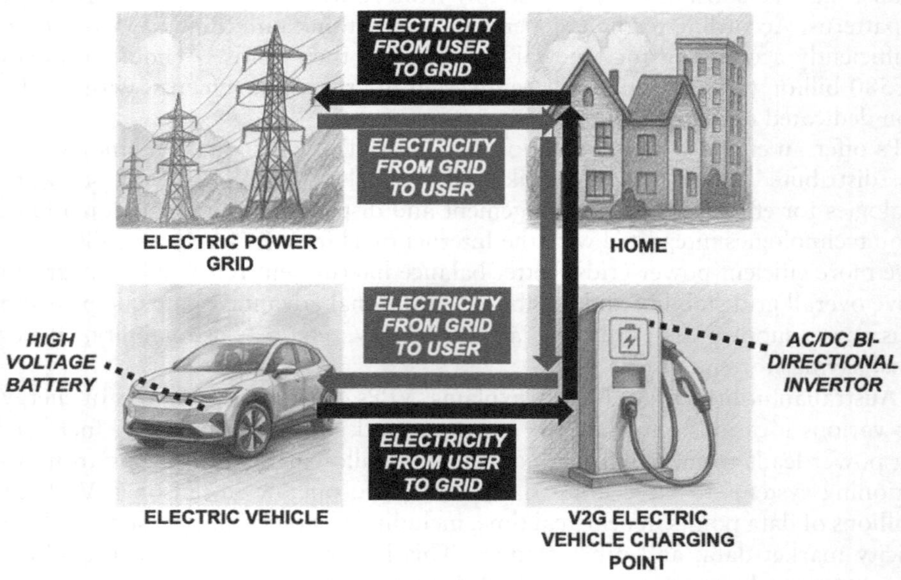

Figure 3.6 Vehicle-to-grid electric power flow

Source: Author, original chart design (July 2025); background images sourced from OpenAI <https://chat.openai.com> accessed 4 July 2025.

National Energy Administration. The objective is to establish by the end of 2025 comprehensive V2G infrastructure and policies in over nine 'demonstration' cities and over 30 pilot projects, also setting up large-scale technical and commercial viability. These initiatives come at a time when there were 22 to 31 million EVs at the end of 2024, depending on the source, with a projection, the number will exceed 100 million by 2030. Commercialisation is already quite advanced with several examples of testing activities. The largest Chinese electric power grid, the State Grid Corporation of China, released an app for cell phones which allows users to sell power from their EV back to the grid and includes real-time settlement. One user reported earning 114.86 yuan ($16.11) by discharging 42.54 kWh on 4 May 2025,[33] and another user – a company in Jiangsu's Changzhou – receiving a discharge income of 18.38 yuan ($2.58).[34] These are small amounts, but it is just the start.

There are also numerous V2G start-ups that have emerged around the world in recent years. StarUs Insights,[35] a database focused on start-ups and technologies, identified over 140 V2G solutions providers to watch in 2023. In Portugal, Pocityf,[36] established in 2019, concentrates on energy management and smart urban mobility, aiming to integrate V2G with solar power. In the United States, EnergyHub, a distributed energy management systems and software provider, partnered with Toyota to provide V2G services initially for Toyota and Lexus cars in Maryland,[37] in the United Kingdom, renewable energy supplier Octopus Energy launched a V2G tariff for customers in February 2024, offering EV owners free charging if they sell power stored in their vehicles back to Octopus Energy during peak hours. The company plans to expand this offering to other markets, including France, Japan, and New Zealand.[38] EV ownership has grown exponentially in the EU in recent years and is expected to continue its strong growth trajectory. This will translate into millions of batteries potentially available for VPP utilisation.

A growing number of companies are developing VPPs, with more likely to enter the sector. German electric utility company Next Kraftwerke GmbH operates in six EU countries and ranks among the major large-scale VPP operators. By the end of 2023, it had networked capacity of approximately 13.5 GW, involving almost 17,000 small producers, energy storage facilities, and commercial and industrial consumers. Another significant VPP market participant is German energy producer Sonnen GmbH, owned by Shell since 2019. The company provides home energy storage systems for private households and small businesses (with over 125,000 batteries installed) and operates in 11 countries across Asia, Europe, and North America. In Europe, Sonnen's VPP capacity stands at 250 MWh, with the aim to expand to 1000 MWh. A third example is Enel X, the energy supply and management services arm of Italian utility Enel, which serves 65 million customers and maintains 90 GW of installed capacity. Enel X has been highly active in the VPP space globally, exemplified by its October 2023 contract with the Australian Energy Market Operator to supply 120 MW of flexible demand capacity. Notably, several European energy technology manufacturers are also involved in the VPP sector, including ABB, Bosch, Schneider Electric, and Siemens.

The growth trajectory of VPPs in the EU and beyond is expected to accelerate sharply in the coming years. Multiple research firms project market expansion to between $10 and $24 billion from less than $2 billion, with compound annual growth rates exceeding 20 per cent. Spherical Insights & Consulting estimates that the global VPP market will grow from $1.8 billion to $13.7 billion by 2032.[39] Inkwood Research provides a more conservative estimate of $9.5 billion,[40] while Fortune Business Insights forecasts a substantial increase to $24 billion.[41]

Small but mighty: the rise of Small Modular Reactors

Small Modular Reactors (SMRs) are emerging as a promising solution for clean energy generation in the global push towards decarbonisation. This innovative nuclear technology is gaining significant momentum due to its flexibility, enhanced safety features, and streamlined installation process compared to traditional nuclear plants. According to the International Atomic Energy Agency (IAEA), nuclear reactors are classified by capacity: large conventional reactors at 700 MW or more, SMRs up to 300 MW, and micro-modular reactors (MMRs) up to 10 MW. SMRs offer considerable advantages over their larger counterparts, including the ability to be assembled in factories rather than on-site, simpler installation procedures, advanced safety mechanisms, reduced fuel requirements, and versatile deployment options that extend to remote and off-grid locations where traditional energy infrastructure might be impractical.

The global landscape of SMR development is remarkably diverse, with nearly 70 different designs at various stages of development and deployment. These technologies span several key categories that represent different approaches to nuclear power generation: 14 land-based water-cooled designs, 6 marine-based water-cooled systems, 14 gas-cooled reactors, 13 modular micro reactors, 11 molten salt reactor designs, and 10 liquid-metal fast-neutron systems. Each approach offers specific advantages for different deployment scenarios and energy needs, demonstrating the versatility of SMR technology. The development of these technologies is occurring across numerous countries, with Canada planning to begin construction of North America's first commercial SMR (the GE Hitachi BWRX-300) in 2025, with grid connection expected by late 2028. France is advancing multiple SMR designs through its France Relance 2030 funding programme, while Japan is exploring six different SMR designs and investigating hydrogen production applications using its operational High Temperature Engineering Test Reactor. South Korea has approved SMART technology and is developing the innovative i-SMR in partnership with Canada, while the United Kingdom features Rolls-Royce working on a 470 MW Pressurised Water Reactor. The United States has numerous projects underway from companies including NuScale, Westinghouse, and Holtec, alongside micro reactors and Generation IV technologies that prioritise sustainability, economic viability, safety, and reliability.

Two particular applications are driving the recent surge in SMR development: powering data centres for AI and providing clean energy for maritime shipping. The digital transformation and AI boom have created unprecedented demand for data centre capacity, which in turn requires substantial electricity generation. In the United States alone, data centre power demand grew from 58 TWh in 2014 to 77 TWh in 2023 and could potentially reach a staggering 580 TWh by 2028 – a 229.6 per cent increase according to the Lawrence Berkeley National Laboratory. SMRs provide an ideal power solution for these facilities, which typically require between 10 and 100 MW of continuous power. Notable projects in this space include Energy Northwest's collaboration with Amazon and X-energy, which aims to build four advanced SMRs generating approximately 320 MW with the potential to expand to 12 reactors. Additionally, Google announced a deal in late 2024 to procure up to 500 MW from SMRs developed by Kairos Power between 2030 and 2035. In the United Kingdom, Prime Minister Keir Starmer has announced the establishment of 'AI Growth Zones' to support data centres, beginning in Culham, Oxfordshire, which will explore renewable energy solutions including SMRs to sustainably power AI development.

The maritime shipping sector represents another promising application for SMR technology as this industry accounts for approximately 3 per cent of global CO_2 emissions and faces significant decarbonisation challenges. While nuclear propulsion is not new – being widely used by naval vessels of various countries – its application to commercial shipping could be transformative. A report by Lloyd's Register suggests that SMRs could revolutionise the maritime industry by providing safer, more reliable, and emissions-free shipping solutions. Norway's NuProShip project, led by shipbuilder VARD and supported by various maritime organisations, has evaluated 99 different reactor technologies and selected three promising designs for further development: Kairos Power's fluoride high-temperature molten salt reactor using tri-structural isotropic fuel particles; Ultra Safe Nuclear Corp's helium-cooled gas reactor also employing TRISO fuel particles; and Blykalla's lead-cooled reactor concept utilising uranium oxide as fuel. This initiative aims to create a commercially viable, zero-emission technology for deep-sea ships that meets the needs of all stakeholders and requires no subsidies once development is complete.

Despite the strong investment momentum and technological progress, SMRs face several significant challenges that must be addressed for widespread adoption. Achieving competitive cost per MWh is crucial for economic viability in energy markets, while regulatory barriers pose another major obstacle as existing nuclear frameworks often cater to larger, traditional reactors and require substantial adjustments for SMR deployment. Public resistance remains a concern, driven by safety worries, waste disposal issues, and fears of accidents, all of which can impede project progress. Environmental considerations extend beyond safe waste disposal to include potential impacts on local ecosystems during construction and operation. Additionally, technological hurdles such as ensuring reliability, efficiency, and cost-effective production must be overcome for SMRs to fulfil their potential. Nevertheless, industry experts remain optimistic that as the sector grows and matures, and as proven technologies are successfully deployed, the prospects for SMRs appear promising, particularly in their role supporting global decarbonisation efforts in energy-intensive sectors.

Notes

1 IEA, *ETP Clean Energy Technology Guide – Data Tools* (IEA 14 September 2023) <https://www.iea.org/data-and-statistics/data-tools/etp-clean-energy-technology-guide> accessed 8 March 2024.
2 AQ Al-Shetwi and M Zahim Sujod, 'Harmonic Distortion and Voltage Imbalance Study of Photovoltaic Power Plant Connected to the Malaysian Grid' (2018) 10 Journal of Telecommunication, Electronic and Computer Engineering (JTEC) 1 <https://www.researchgate.net/publication/323642562_Harmonic_Distortion_and_Voltage_Imbalance_Study_of_Photovoltaic_Power_Plant_Connected_to_the_Malaysian_Grid> accessed 17 March 2025; P Sánchez Molina, 'Global Installed PV Capacity Tops 2 TW' *PV Magazine International* (13 November 2024) <https://www.pv-magazine.com/2024/11/13/global-installed-pv-capacity-tops-2-tw/> accessed 17 March 2025.
3 IEA, *Clean Energy Market Monitor* (IEA 2024) <https://www.iea.org/reports/clean-energy-market-monitor-march-2024> accessed 31 March 2024.
4 I Chernyakhovskiy and others, 'USAID Energy Storage Decision Guide for Policymakers' (2021) <https://www.nrel.gov/docs/fy21osti/78815.pdf> accessed 2 April 2024.
5 E Krukowska and A Nardelli, 'EU Sees Electricity Production Doubling by 2050 to Reach Net Zero' (Bloomberg.com 24 January 2024) <https://www.bloomberg.com/news/articles/2024-01-24/eu-sees-electricity-production-doubling-by-2050-to-reach-net-zero> accessed 2 April 2024.

6 BloombergBNEF, 'Report Shows Way for China to Meet Climate Goals 10 Years Early' *BloombergNEF* (30 May 2023) <https://about.bnef.com/blog/report-shows-way-for-China-to-meet-climate-goals-10-years-early/> accessed 2 April 2024.
7 T Bowen and others, 'USAID Grid-Scale Energy Storage Technologies Primer' (2021) <https://www.nrel.gov/docs/fy21osti/76097.pdf> accessed 6 March 2024.
8 V Atkinson, 'Clever Cathode Design Opens Doors to First Rechargeable Calcium Battery' *Chemistry World* (7 February 2024) <https://www.chemistryworld.com/news/clever-cathode-design-opens-doors-to-first-rechargeable-calcium-battery/4018916.article> accessed 6 March 2024.
9 Bowen and others (n 7).
10 U.S. Energy Information Administration, 'Production of Hydrogen – U.S. Energy Information Administration (EIA)' (Eia.gov 23 June 2023) <https://www.eia.gov/energyexplained/hydrogen/production-of-hydrogen.php> accessed 28 March 2024.
11 Office of Energy Efficiency & Renewable Energy, 'Hydrogen Production: Natural Gas Reforming' (Energy.gov 2023) <https://www.energy.gov/eere/fuelcells/hydrogen-production-natural-gas-reforming> accessed 28 March 2024.
12 U.S. Energy Information Administration, 'Production of Hydrogen – U.S. Energy Information Administration (EIA)' (Eia.gov 23 June 2023) <https://www.eia.gov/energyexplained/hydrogen/production-of-hydrogen.php> accessed 28 March 2024.
13 M Liebreich, 'Hydrogen Ladder Version 5.0' (www.linkedin.com 20 October 2023) <https://www.linkedin.com/pulse/hydrogen-ladder-version-50-michael-liebreich/> accessed 30 March 2024.
14 IRENA, *Green Hydrogen Cost Reduction* (International Renewable Energy Agency 2020) <https://www.irena.org/-/media/Files/IRENA/Agency/Publication/2020/Nov/IRENA_Green_Hydrogen_breakthrough_2021.pdf?la=en&hash=40FA5B8AD7AB1666EECBDE30EF458C45EE5A0AA6> accessed 30 March 2024.
15 Global Energy Association, *Only Seven Countries Produce Green Hydrogen – the Global Energy Association* (The Global Energy Association – Global Energy 28 February 2025) <https://globalenergyprize.org/en/2025/02/28/green-hydrogen-produced-by-only-seven-countries/> accessed 5 July 2025.
16 A Hasanbeigi, C Springer, and A Sibal, *Green Hydrogen for Decarbonizing Asia's Industrial Giants: Analyzing H2 Electrolyzer Market Opportunity in Key Industrial Applications* (The Asia Society 2024) <https://asiasociety.org/sites/default/files/2024-04/ASPI_GreenHydrogen.pdf> accessed 13 April 2024.
17 China Petrochemical Corporation, 'Sinopec Launches the World's Largest Green Hydrogen-Coal Chemical Project in Inner Mongolia | China Sinopec' (www.sinopecgroup.com 22 February 2023) <http://www.sinopecgroup.com/group/en/Sinopecnews/20230331/news_20230331_502557647316.shtml> accessed 29 March 2024.
18 NEOM, 'NEOM Green Hydrogen Company Completes Financial Close at a Total Investment Value of USD 8.4 Billion in the World's Largest Carbon-Free Green Hydrogen Plant' (www.neom.com 22 May 2023) <https://www.neom.com/en-us/newsroom/neom-green-hydrogen-investment> accessed 29 March 2024.
19 Blackridge Research and Consulting, 'All You Need to Know about Aqua Ventus Wind-To-Hydrogen Plant Project' (www.blackridgeresearch.com 8 January 2024) <https://www.blackridgeresearch.com/project-profiles/wind-to-hydrogen-plant-aquaventus-green-hydrogen-project-germany> accessed 29 March 2024.
20 I Verrender, 'Has Andrew Forrest's Green Hydrogen Dream Evaporated?' *ABC News* (20 July 2024) <https://www.abc.net.au/news/2024-07-21/green-hydrogen-forrest-fortescue/104120492> accessed 9 March 2025.
21 Nick Smith, e-mail interview by Joseph Jacobelli (30 June 2025).
22 European Commission, 'Hydrogen' (energy.ec.europa.eu 2022) <https://energy.ec.europa.eu/topics/energy-systems-integration/hydrogen_en> accessed 29 March 2024.
23 European Hydrogen Backbone, 'The European Hydrogen Backbone (EHB) Initiative | EHB European Hydrogen Backbone' (ehb.eu) <https://ehb.eu/> accessed 29 March 2024.
24 P Fanailoo and A Goyal, 'The Hydrogen and Clean Fuels Industry in North America' (www.dnv.com 22 March 2024) <https://www.dnv.com/article/the-hydrogen-and-clean-fuels-industry-in-north-america/> accessed 30 March 2024.

25 Nick Smith, e-mail interview by Joseph Jacobelli (30 June 2025).
26 J Jacobelli, *Asia's Energy Revolution: China's Role and New Opportunities as Markets Transform and Digitalise* (De Gruyter 2021) 150.
27 J Jacobelli, *Asia's Energy Revolution: China's Role and New Opportunities as Markets Transform and Digitalise* (De Gruyter 2021) 150.
28 WSJ News, 'Why Google's CSO Thinks AI Can Combat Climate Change | WSJ Tech News Briefing' (www.youtube.com 18 December 2023) <https://www.youtube.com/watch?v=FcRjAblwyxw&t=36s> accessed 8 March 2024.
29 E Cremona and C Rosslowe (eds), *Putting the Mission in Transmission: Grids for Europe's Energy Transition* (Ember 7 November 2024) <https://ember-energy.org/latest-insights/putting-the-mission-in-transmission-grids-for-europes-energy-transition/> accessed 17 March 2025.
30 Origin Energy, *Artificial Intelligence and the Tech behind the VPP* (Origin Energy 12 May 2021) <https://www.originenergy.com.au/blog/virtual-power-plant/> accessed 21 May 2024.
31 Berg Insight, 'Smart Metering in Europe 18th Edition' (2024) <https://media.berginsight.com/2024/02/16191446/bi-sm18-ps.pdf> accessed 21 May 2024.
32 EU Directorate-General for Energy, 'Benchmarking Smart Metering Deployment in the EU-28 – European Commission' (energy.ec.europa.eu 18 March 2020) <https://energy.ec.europa.eu/publications/benchmarking-smart-metering-deployment-eu-28_en> accessed 21 May 2024.
33 中国经济网, '吴松泉：车网互动有望实现规模化商用' (Auto.cnr.cn 15 April 2025) <https://auto.cnr.cn/2015xc/20250415/t20250415_527135634.shtml> accessed 5 July 2025.
34 China Daily, 'State Grid Changzhou Completes Jiangsu's First V2G Settlement' (Chinadaily.com.cn 2025). <https://www.chinadaily.com.cn/a/202508/11/WS68995e3ca310724b60020efb.html> accessed 18 August 2025.
35 StarUs Insights, *10 Top Vehicle-To-Grid Startups to Watch in 2023* (StartUs Insights 22 April 2023) <https://www.startus-insights.com/innovators-guide/vehicle-to-grid-startups/> accessed 8 March 2024.
36 POCITYF, *Homepage* (POCITYF) <https://pocityf.eu/> accessed 8 March 2024.
37 Smart Energy International, *EnergyHub and Toyota North America Partner on Grid Balancing Programme* (Smart Energy International 11 March 2024) <https://www.smart-energy.com/industry-sectors/electric-vehicles/energyhub-and-toyota-north-america-partner-on-grid-balancing-programme/> accessed 2 April 2024.
38 N Carey, 'Octopus Energy Launches UK's First Vehicle-To-Grid Tariff for EVs' *Reuters* (15 February 2024) <https://www.reuters.com/business/energy/octopus-energy-launches-uks-first-vehicle-to-grid-tariff-evs-2024-02-15/> accessed 22 April 2024.
39 Spherical Insights, 'Global Virtual Power Plant Market Size | Report Forecast to 2032' *Spherical Insights* (November 2023) <https://www.sphericalinsights.com/press-release/virtual-power-plant-market> accessed 21 May 2024.
40 Inkwood Research, *Global Virtual Power Market Firecast 2024–2032* (Inkwood Research 2023) <https://inkwoodresearch.com/reports/virtual-power-plant-market/> accessed 21 May 2024.
41 Fortune Business Insights, 'Virtual Power Plant Market Size, Forecast | Global Report [2028]' (www.fortunebusinessinsights.com 16 May 2024) <https://www.fortunebusinessinsights.com/industry-reports/virtual-power-plant-market-101669> accessed 21 May 2024.

Chapter 4

Landscape outlook

Transitioning, growing, and facing challenges

Aims:

- The energy transition through the lens of the shift to clean energy and its impact.
- Different scenarios for the future clean energy landscape.
- Key energy transition barriers across policy, technology, environment, and finance.

Imagine the year 2100, where someone stands in awe, witnessing the mammoth shift that occurred in the energy supply mix all around the world in the previous 75 years or so. An energy revolution will have dethroned the once-dominant, polluting fossil fuels and replaced them with a reign of green and sustainable energy sources. It is a transformation that few expected a few years ago would succeed. The most dramatic of the changes will occur in the 25 years or so to 2050, though further decarbonisation transitions will continue thereafter. Especially that of the currently hard-to-abate industries, including cement, heavy-duty transport like aviation and shipping, and petrochemicals, for example. The radically changing energy landscape will have seen surprising growth in clean energy and related solutions despite the many hurdles and challenges that the energy transition faces.

The energy transition and its decarbonisation of our existing energy supply and consumption are changing the landscape in a great variety of ways, and not just through 2050 but well beyond. For example, two- or four-wheel internal combustion engine vehicles will not have been completely eradicated worldwide by 2050, only in some jurisdictions such as in EU countries, while the decline of their market share will progressively accelerate.

The public in general, and public policy in particular, will be regularly reminded over the coming years of the climate urgency as extreme climate events occur more frequently. A logical derivation is that such events will continue to modify public opinion, especially among those who today do not think that resolving climate issues is urgent or it needs to be addressed at all. Public awareness will continue to move, likely at a much faster speed, in favour of urgent and strong climate action. Public opinion fervour will drive policy and regulation to be even more aggressively aligned with climate action. The changing ecosystem will continue to create new business opportunities which will in turn influence, drive, and motivate finance and investments. Another consequence will be an acceleration in the electrification of key sectors, including transport and manufacturing. The shift to clean energy will be closely supported by technological and digital solutions innovation. In short, the changes to the energy landscape will be at a great many levels.

DOI: 10.4324/9781003666509-5

This leads to the examination of two key topics: the expected course and growth path of the energy shift in future years, and the most significant barriers that could hinder its progress.

The massively growing clean energy sector

Energy demand will post a healthy rate of global growth throughout the energy transition through 2050. Globally, it will partly be driven by economic growth, an expanding population, and higher rates of electrification. Also, as emerging economies progressively mature, their per capita energy consumption will grow exponentially. A dramatically important factor will be the location of the energy growth. This will be the Asia Pacific region. It already accounts for approximately half of the world's population, GDP, and energy consumption. Yet energy use is mostly in the region's emerging and developing economies. It is broadly expected that energy consumption in the Asia Pacific region will be several multiples higher than that of the two other key regions, Europe and North America, addressed in this book.

Experts at a great many organisations all agree that the world will see substantial growth in the two and a half decades to 2050. It cannot be emphasised enough how difficult it is to make long-term growth projections of clean energy sources and related technologies. There are extremely complex variables to take into consideration which highly distort forecasts. Some of the variables difficult to accurately forecast are the growth of energy storage, which will be driven by how soon they become economically attractive, advances in smart grids, and the rate of electrification for such industries as transport. The single most difficult factors to forecast in the medium to long term are public policy, governments' net-zero pledges, and their capability and capacity for them to be able to execute those pledges successfully.

The energy analysis work by the IEA is one of the most respected and widely cited. The IEA's World Energy Outlook[1] and Global Energy and Climate Model[2] reports are among the most publicised when it comes to publicly available forecasts on global energy trends. Its annual forecasts typically use three types of scenarios. The Net-Zero Emissions by 2050 scenario (NZE scenario), the Announced Pledges Scenario (APS), and the Stated Policies Scenario (STEPS).[3]

The NZE Scenario is the most bullish of the three, aiming to keep global warming below 1.5°C. It focuses on a quick roll-out of clean energy technologies, fostering international cooperation, and heavy investments in renewable energy. The NZE Scenario assumes that all climate promises are sped up with wealthy developed nations taking the lead. It aims for everyone to have access to electricity and clean cooking by 2030 and foresees a big move towards clean energy, supported by strong policies and tech advancements.

The APS assumes that all current climate promises, including national targets and long-term net-zero goals, are met on time. It shows how these pledges affect global energy use and emissions, pointing out the gap between current efforts and the Paris Agreement goals. This scenario assumes that countries stick to their promises; it does not expect extra policies beyond what has already been pledged. The APS shows a moderate push for decarbonisation, with carbon prices going up to encourage emission cuts, but not as fast as in the NZE scenario.

The STEPS is the most conservative of the three scenarios. It focuses on what current and upcoming policies can achieve by a certain date. It does not assume that all climate promises will be fully met. Instead, it looks at how existing and developing policies affect energy demand, supply, and emissions. STEPS reflects a world where energy changes are driven by actual policies, not just goals. It highlights the 'implementation gap' between what is

	(TWh)	2010	2022	2023	Stated Policies 2050	Stated Policies CAAGR (%) 2023 to 2050	Announced Pledges 2050	Announced Pledges CAAGR (%) 2023 to 2050	Net Zero Emissions by 2050 2050	Net Zero Emissions by 2050 CAAGR (%) 2023 to 2050
	TOTAL GENERATION	**21,511**	**29,145**	**29,863**	**58,352**	***2.5***	**70,564**	***3.2***	**80,194**	***3.7***
CLEAN ENERGY	**Renewables**	**4,209**	**8,567**	**9,029**	**42,770**	***5.9***	**58,611**	***7.2***	**70,963**	***7.9***
	Solar PV	32	1,294	1,612	21,557	*10.0*	28,996	*11.0*	34,069	*12.0*
	Wind	342	2,120	2,336	12,347	*6.4*	18,289	*7.9*	23,940	*9.0*
	Hydro	3,455	4,350	4,249	6,399	*1.5*	7,032	*1.9*	7,722	*2.2*
	Bioenergy	309	691	714	1,758	*3.4*	2,782	*5.2*	3,054	*5.5*
	of which BECCS	-	-	-	-	*n.a.*	481	*n.a.*	731	*n.a.*
	CSP	2	14	18	238	*10.0*	844	*15.0*	1,327	*17.0*
	Geothermal	68	97	100	384	*5.1*	567	*6.7*	739	*7.7*
	Marine	1	1	1	87	*21.0*	100	*21.0*	112	*22.0*
	Nuclear	**2,756**	**2,684**	**2,765**	**4,460**	***1.8***	**6,055**	***2.9***	**6,969**	***3.5***
	Hydrogen and ammonia	**-**	**-**	**-**	**89**	***n.a.***	**560**	***n.a.***	**987**	***n.a.***
FOSSIL FUELS	**Fossil fuels with CCUS**	**-**	**1**	**1**	**111**	***21.0***	**832**	***30.0***	**979**	***31.0***
	Coal with CCUS	-	1	1	29	*15.0*	634	*29.0*	605	*29.0*
	Natural gas with CCUS	-	-	-	82	*n.a.*	198	*n.a.*	374	*n.a.*
	Unabated fossil fuels	**14,458**	**17,765**	**17,941**	**10,806**	***(1.9)***	**4,400**	***(5.1)***	**206**	***(15.0)***
	Coal	8,671	10,451	10,648	4,256	*(3.3)*	1,193	*(7.8)*	-	*(35.0)*
	Natural gas	4,819	6,515	6,540	6,425	*(0.1)*	3,146	*(2.7)*	206	*(12.0)*
	Oil	968	800	753	126	*(6.4)*	61	*(8.9)*	-	*(25.0)*
	Clean Energy (TWh)	**6,965**	**11,251**	**11,794**	**47,319**		**65,226**		**78,919**	
	Clean Energy (%)	***32%***	***39%***	***39%***	***81%***		***92%***		***98%***	
	Fossil Fuels (TWh)	**14,458**	**17,766**	**17,942**	**10,917**		**5,232**		**1,185**	
	Fossil Fuels (%)	***67%***	***61%***	***60%***	***19%***		***7%***		***1%***	

Figure 4.1 World electricity sector growth scenarios (TWh)

Source: International Energy Agency, 'World Energy Outlook 2024' (International Energy Agency 2024). Available at: https://iea.blob.core.windows.net/assets/140a0470-5b90-4922-a0e9-838b3ac6918c/WorldEnergyOutlook2024.pdf accessed 19 March 2025.

promised and what is achieved, giving a baseline to judge current policies. This scenario expects slower improvements in energy access and more reliance on fossil fuels than the NZE and APS scenarios, with lower carbon prices due to limited policy efforts.

The IEA Global Energy and Climate model, as of October 2024 (see Figure 4.1), assumes a global population CAGR of 0.7 per cent between 2023 and 2050. The world's population would hit 9.68 billion by 2050, of which 49 per cent would be in Asia, and reach a global average urbanisation rate of 68 per cent, up from 57 per cent in 2023. It also assumes a GDP CAGR of 2.7 per cent, including 3.3 per cent for Asia, the fastest pace globally after Africa's 4 per cent.

The model provides a variety of other key assumptions including the evolution of prices between 2023 and 2050 of fossil fuels, that of CO_2, and of selected technologies such as utility-scale stationary batteries and EVs. Some forecasts are worth highlighting to gauge a sense of the long-term trajectory (note that more granular assumptions, details, and explanations are provided in the report). For crude oil, starting at $82 per barrel in 2023, the forecasted price by 2050 varies across scenarios: $75 per barrel under STEPS, $58 per barrel under APS, and $25 per barrel under NZE. For natural gas and thermal coal, the IEA focuses on China, Japan, the EU, and the United States, projecting declines in both fossil fuels across all three scenarios. The exception is natural gas in the United States, which the IEA expects to rise under the STEPS and APS scenarios. Carbon prices for electricity, industry, and energy production in selected regions are expected to significantly increase. It is important to also note that the model is forecasting the average price of hybrid and battery electric vehicles to decline by 2030, 2035, and 2050 under all three scenarios.

Power Market	Terawatt-Hours	Population	kWh per Capita
Taiwan	288.1	23,571,000	12,225
South Korea	620.3	51,269,000	12,099
Australia	273.6	25,804,000	10,601
Singapore	57.1	5,703,000	10,015
New Zealand	44.7	4,931,000	9,061
Japan	1,033.6	125,502,000	8,235
China	8,848.7	1,411,000,000	6,271
Malaysia	182.9	33,484,000	5,462
China Hong Kong SAR	36.2	7,496,000	4,834
Vietnam	260.0	97,338,000	2,671
Thailand	180.4	69,799,000	2,584
India	1,858.0	1,380,004,000	1,346
Indonesia	333.4	276,361,000	1,206
Philippines	114.4	113,122,000	1,012
Sri Lanka	16.9	21,670,000	781
Pakistan	145.8	231,405,000	630
Bangladesh	97.5	164,689,000	592
Total Asia Pacific	14,391.5	4,043,148,000	3,559

Figure 4.2 Per capita generation of key Asia Pacific economies

Notes: The generation amount for Hong Kong SAR, China, is somewhat distorted as a significant amount of electricity is imported from southern China.

Source: Author calculations (February 2024).

The World Energy Outlook projects that electric power generation should grow at a compound average annual growth rate of 2.5 per cent assuming STEPS, 3.2 per cent under APS, and 3.7 per cent under NZE. The rate for clean energy will be substantially higher. Solar, wind, hydro, bioenergy, CSP, geothermal, marine, nuclear, and hydrogen and ammonia on a combined basis will see a rate of 5.9 per cent, 7.2 per cent, and 7.9 per cent based on each of the three scenarios. This means that clean energy will grow between fourfold and sevenfold by 2050 compared to 2023. Its share of total generation will rise from 40 per cent in 2023 to between 81 and 98 per cent. Even under the more conservative scenario, the growth of clean energy over the next two and a half decades will be formidable.

Looking at the per capita electric power generation in each of the key electric power markets in the biggest region, Asia Pacific, one can get a sense of the potential growth in the region over the next 30 or 40 years (see Figure 4.2). The calculation factors in the total power generated in the economy divided by the total population in 2022. The output was 14,391.5 TWh and the population was 4.04 billion, resulting in a per capita generation of 3,559 kWh. The most developed power markets in the region were Taiwan, South Korea, Australia, Singapore, New Zealand, and Japan. Among these economies, the highest per capita number was 12,225 kWh and the lowest 8,235 kWh. Assuming that all countries reach the lowest per capita level, then over the next 30 or 40 years, electric power generation will grow about 131 per cent to 33,297 TWh. If all countries reach the highest level, electric power generation would grow 243 per cent to 49,429 TWh. This is not the result of sophisticated energy generation projection modelling. It is relatively simplistic, a back-of-the-envelope calculation. The purpose is just to give a general idea as to the potential upside.

Projections from a variety of experts all concur that while Asia's electric power demand is much larger than the rest of the world, it will be even bigger by 2050. One example is projections from Enerdata, an energy consultancy. It expects global power demand to grow at a CAGR of 3 per cent between 2020 and 2050, but that of the Asia Pacific region to rise almost threefold during the period.[4]

ENERGY SYSTEM MODEL	GLOBAL 100% RE	1.5°C SCENARIO	100% WIND- WATER-SOLAR (WWS)	1.5°C SCENARIO	NET-ZERO EMISSIONS (NZE)
Institution	LUT (2021)	UTS (2019)	Stanford (2022)	IRENA (2021)	IEA (2021)
Target(s)	100% renewable energy system by 2050	Achieving 1.5℃ by 2050 with primary energy supply based on 100% renewable energy	80% WWS by 2030; 100% WWS by 2050 for 145 countries	Energy transition pathway aligned with the 1.5°C target (net zero by 2050)	Net zero by 2050
Renewable energy share in total energy supply (TES) by 2050	100%	100% (<92%, including non-energy consumption, which will still include fossil fuels. Primary energy supply in 2050 will be based on 100% renewable energy)	100%	74% in total energy supply (90% in electricity generation)	67% in total energy supply (88% in electricity generation)
Energy sources included in 2050	Solar photovoltaic (PV), concentrated solar power (CSP), wind, hydropower, geothermal and bioenergy	TPED: solar, wind, hydro, geothermal, biomass, ocean energy (tidal and wave), natural gas, oil, coal (latter due to non- energy consumption)	Generation: wind, solar PV, CSP, geothermal, hydro and ocean energy. Heat: solar thermal, geothermal heat	TES: solar, wind, biogas, biomass, hydropower, geothermal, solar, ocean energy, natural gas, oil, coal and nuclear	TES: solar, bioenergy, wind, hydropower, geothermal, other renewables, nuclear, natural gas, oil and coal.
2050 share of electricity (electrification level)	89% (total primary energy demand)	92.3% (total final energy demand)	Efficiency measures result in total energy demand decreasing by 56.4%, so that remaining energy is nearly all (~99.1%) electricity: 85% higher than 2018 actual levels (total installed capacity)	51% of direct electricity in total final energy consumption and 14% from hydrogen	49% of electricity in total final energy consumption
Cumulative investment needed to 2050	$72 tn, noting net energetic yield per invested unit of capital in renewable electricity solutions far exceeds the one in upstream fossil fuels	$51 tn across the power sector (an average investment of $1,420 bn per year, 2015- 2050) $12.4 tn for the heating sector (an average investment of $344 bn per year, 2015-2050)	Around $61.5 tn Upfront costs are recovered through energy sales, covering WWS electricity; heat and green hydrogen generation; storage for electricity, heating, cooling and green hydrogen; district heating heat pumps; all- distance transmission; and distribution	$131 tn (annual funding requirement averaging $4.4 tn), adapted from planned government cumulative energy and energy related infrastructure investment strategies amounting to $98 tn by 2050	Annual average capital invested is indicated for 2030-2040-2050: - $40-50 tn, annual investments of 4-5 tn per year by 2030 - Almost $5 tn annually by 2040 - $4.5 tn annually by 2050
Job creation	134 mn by 2050 in the global energy sector*	47.8 mn energy-sector jobs by 2050 (up to 89% would be renewable energy jobs by 2030)	28.4 mn (net increase) by 2050	122 mn jobs in the global energy sector: - 43 mn directly in renewable energy - 25 mn in power grids and flexibility - 25 mn in energy efficiency - 2.24 mn in hydrogen	30 mn more people under NZE working in clean energy, efficiency and low-emissions technologies.

Figure 4.3 Overview of scenarios analysed

Notes: (*) = (Ram, et al., 2022). Edits to original: abbreviated million to 'mn', billion to 'bn', and trillion to 'tr'.

Source: IRENA Coalition for Action, '100% Renewable Energy Scenarios: Supporting Ambitious Policy Targets' (International Renewable Energy Agency 2024). Available at: https://mc-cd8320d4-36a1-40ac-83cc-3389-cdn-endpoint.azureedge.net/-/media/Files/IRENA/Agency/Publication/2024/Mar/IRENA_Coalition_100_RE_scenarios_2024.pdf?rev=5ef440b6087942e8a8eba687b65c25f9 accessed 13 May 2024.

IRENA has compiled an excellent summary of some of the most respected net-zero system scenarios published in recent years. It compares five energy scenarios for achieving global climate goals by 2050.[5] Three of these five scenarios aim for 100 per cent renewable energy (solar, wind, and the like) by 2050: the Lappeenranta University of Technology (LUT) Global 100 Per Cent RE Scenario, the University of Technology Sydney (UTS) 1.5°C Scenario, and the Stanford University's 100 Per Cent Wind-Water-Solar (WWS) Scenario. The other two scenarios aim for net-zero emissions by 2050, limiting warming to 1.5°C, and include nuclear, fossil fuels, and CCS technologies (Bioenergy with CCS, Direct Air Capture and Storage) to remove remaining emissions. These two scenarios, the IRENA 1.5°C Scenario and the IEA Net-Zero Emissions (NZE) Scenario, differ from the 100 per cent renewable scenarios as they do not exclude these technologies. All scenarios involve a rapid increase in renewable energy, especially solar and wind, by 2050, with milestones along the way.

The summary (see Figure 4.3) clearly compares six areas. The targets, the renewable energy share in total energy supply by 2050, the energy sources, the share of electricity in the energy mix or electrification level, the cumulative investment needed, and the estimated amount of job creation.

Navigating the energy transition challenges

There are several challenges facing the transition of our energy system (see Figure 4.4). It is critical to note that the challenges are not unknown. They are generally well recognised and understood. Principally thanks to the great work by many organisations including IRENA, the IEA, the UN, the World Economic Forum, the World Resources Institute (WRI), and dozens of others. The obstacles are many, but they are surmountable. A set of 11 types of hurdles have been identified, albeit this is by no means an exhaustive list. They have been broadly categorised into four baskets: public policy, technology, environment, and finance.

The power of public policy: the first critical lever

In public policy, the obvious first step is for a government to acknowledge climate change as a concern and to have undertaken, at the very least, minimal action. Beyond government

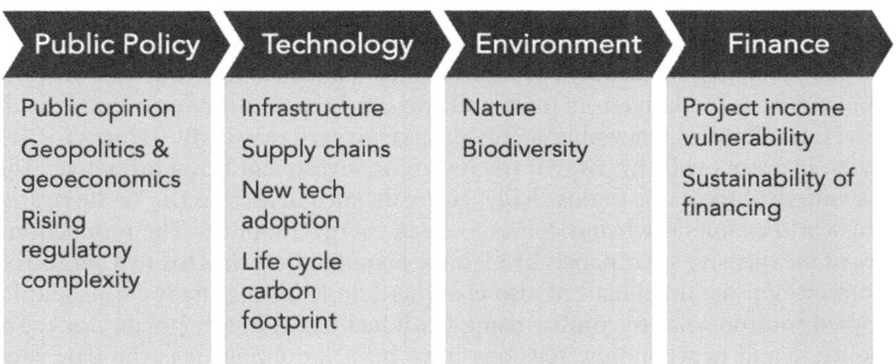

Figure 4.4 Hurdles to the energy transition

Source: Author, original chart design (April 2004).

policy, there are at least three state or public policy-related challenges. They include (Hurdle 1) public opinion, (Hurdle 2) geopolitics and geoeconomics, as well as (Hurdle 3) rising regulatory complexity.

Accurately predicting future global public opinion on the energy transition is next to impossible. Yet, two elements can be identified and evaluated. One is the visible impact of climate change. Another is the impact of the cost burden of the energy transition on consumers, whether households or industry.

As mentioned, in future years, the general public and policymakers will often be confronted with the pressing need to address climate change. This will be driven by an increase in extreme weather events, which are becoming increasingly common all around the world due to global warming. As a growing part of populations and businesses become affected, it is logical to deduce that these events will increasingly impact public sentiment, particularly among those who currently do not view climate change as an urgent issue. As extraordinary climate events continue to unfold, they will serve as stark reminders of the urgent need for action. This will lead to a rapid shift in public awareness towards the necessity of immediate and robust measures to combat climate change. The intensity of public opinion will exert pressure on policymakers and regulators, compelling them to align their actions more aggressively with climate mitigation efforts. In essence, the escalating frequency of extreme climate events will serve as a catalyst for change, transforming public opinion and driving policy and regulation towards more decisive climate action. This transformation is expected to occur at an accelerated pace, reflecting the urgency of the climate crisis. The intensity of public opinion will be a powerful force in pushing for more aggressive climate policies and regulations. Some of the climate change effects which may impact public opinion include higher home insurance costs, higher food prices, the unavailability of some foods, water scarcity impact on drinking water or water for crops irrigation, economic disruptions affecting sectors such as tourism or fishing, and a rise in migration and displacement creating masses of climate refugees.

The low cost of fossil fuels, especially thermal coal, in regions such as Southeast Asia, has made them a preferred energy source over non-fossil fuels. The public and corporations in these regions are not addicted to power generated from polluting fuels. They simply seek low-priced energy. Before the price of renewables started to sharply fall, there was limited interest in replacing polluting energy. As clean energy has become one of the most cost-effective ways to generate electricity in many regions today, the landscape is shifting. The public opinion challenge is with the investment requirements to transition our energy system which some people perceive as high. Even if the funding were to primarily come from governments, ultimately consumers would have to somehow foot the bill. Governments, financial institutions, and investors must find ways to keep end-user prices affordable while at the same time allowing renewable energy projects to earn reasonable returns to incentivise investments. Investors will shy away if the return on investment is not attractive. The problem and a variety of solutions to this challenge are detailed in Section III. Yet there are a great many real-world examples when it comes to clean energy adoption. The production of vast quantities of inexpensive solar panels by Chinese manufacturers has led to a surge in rooftop solar adoption not just in China but also elsewhere. In Pakistan, many farms and factories have adopted rooftop solar to combat rising fossil fuel-based energy prices,[6] for example.

Geopolitical and geoeconomic tensions have been mounting over the past few years. These have been made even worse by a rise in nationalism in some economically important countries such as China, Russia, and the United States. These conflicts affect the energy transition in at least two intertwined ways: cooperation and supply chains.

International cooperation is an important facet of the energy transition. Poor cooperation will affect supply chains by making it harder and more expensive to get materials or equipment. Cooperation has been attained through bilateral and multilateral agreements. Some decisions are best made at a global level rather than a state level for the world to reduce damage from a warming planet. The annual COP meetings organised by the UN have proven particularly useful in motivating climate change action in many nations. The last two international meetings on climate change, COP28 in late 2023 and COP29 in late 2024, proved yet again the critical importance of international collaboration and cooperation. The decision to transition away from fossil fuels and commitments to triple renewable energy capacity by 2030 are two of many examples of the importance of global cooperation. A report published by IRENA in 2023, *Geopolitics of the Energy Transition: Critical Materials*, explained that in a world where clean energy supply chains are global, the supply of critical raw materials is of utmost importance. Critical materials differ significantly from fossil fuels. The mining quantities are low.[7] Typically, their extraction generates smaller profits. Fossil fuels are burned immediately while critical materials become an integral part of energy transition assets, such as wind turbines. Finally, critical materials have the potential to be recycled compared to fossil fuels. At the same time, supply chain disruptions could delay the construction of a project or may increase the price of the renewable energy.

Climate-related regulation is witnessing escalating intricacy. The massive shift from fossil fuels to clean energy to decarbonise our economies is a relatively recent process. Much of the regulations and legislation at a domestic or international level did not take into consideration such a transition. The world has had to create new parameters to guide corporations and other entities. The transition is an evolutionary process as are the climate-related regulations guiding the transition. The process has expectedly not been a smooth one. Thousands of edicts have been issued around the world, and many will require a lot of tweaking. The Climate Change Laws of the World is a project jointly created by two think tanks, the Grantham Research Institute at London School of Economics, and the Sabin Centre at Columbia Law School. It has collected thousands of national-level climate change legislation and policies encompassing sectors such as energy, real estate, and transport from all around the world.

One of the many examples is the rules for corporations trading with the EU. The EU released a great number of regulations applying ESG standards between 2016 and 2023, and particularly since COP26 in December 2021. These standards raise pressure on companies in emerging markets to meet EU ESG requirements. Just in 2023, they included: the Carbon Border Adjustment Mechanism which applies a carbon tariff on carbon-intensive products; the Regulation (EU) 2023/1115 on deforestation-free products aimed at curbing the impact of EU economies on global deforestation and forest degradation; and the European Sustainability Reporting Standards requiring large corporations to publicly report on the social and environmental risks they face, including companies not based in the EU but with a presence in the EU.[8]

The construction of the massive body of climate-related legislation may impact corporations and others negatively, at least in the short term. They may create investment uncertainty as corporations are unsure as to how legislation will evolve and may thus decide to hold back funding new projects. It may also hold back innovation as capital funding is detracted. It raises administrative costs, including compliance, expenditure for corporations which may need to hire more people or rely on external advisors, something especially burdensome for the small- to medium-size corporations. It may slow down the energy transition because new rules and regulations can be confusing, conflicting, or inconsistent, in addition, the sheer volume of local, regional, national, and international rules may make it generally difficult or impossible for corporations to navigate.

An example is public policy issues in the United States in the last four presidential terms. Those under Presidents Obama, Trump, Biden, and Trump again. President Obama's policies, between 2009 and 2017, favoured promoting renewable energy sources. He announced the Clean Power Act, setting carbon emissions limits on power plants, in August 2015, for example. During the first Trump presidency, between 2017 and 2021, public policy was more in favour of fossil fuels and generally was full of scepticism towards climate risk and the need for an energy transition. Then, US policy changed again during the Biden presidency, between 2021 and 2025, as he held climate-related views similar to those of President Obama. Such massive shifts in policy nurture investment uncertainty and are highly unsettling for corporations that must execute long-term plans. In the second Trump presidency, starting in 2025, many, if not all, of Biden's pro-climate change policies were reversed as soon as the newly re-elected president entered the White House.

Sorting through the technology challenge

The energy transition faces at least four technology-related challenges. They include (Hurdle 4) infrastructure, (Hurdle 5) supply chains, (Hurdle 6) new tech adoption, and (Hurdle 7) life-cycle carbon footprint.

The infrastructure necessary to accommodate formidable additions of clean energy resources is lagging in many countries all around the world. At the centre are electric power grid systems. The lack of such infrastructure is a problem experienced in Asia, Europe, and North America. They pose a dual challenge to the energy transition. Transmission networks need to be built for new clean energy generation facilities. In addition, these networks need to be especially smart due to the intermittency (with renewables not necessarily available 24 hours a day) and non-dispatchability (production cannot be adjusted rapidly to meet changes in demand) of renewable energy. The IEA is one of the many voices emphasising that the lag in the building of the infrastructure has negative implications for global climate and energy goals. It is a massive task. Over 80 million kilometres of transmission and distribution lines must be built or overhauled around the world by 2040, the same amount of the length of the existing grids, stated the IEA.[9] Importantly, the issue is widely recognised, and governments are generally motivated to address the problem. Timing and technological advances are crucial. There are many promising technologies to improve existing grids being explored. One of the many is called the 'magic ball'. It is a bowling ball-sized device which fits around transmission wires to measure their temperature. It is supplied by a Norwegian technology company, Heimdall Power. The premise is that if the electricity transmission wires are cooler, they can transport more power. The 'magic ball', which can be installed on the wires using drones in under two minutes, allows operators to better utilise the transmission lines.[10]

Another technology-related challenge is the equipment supply chain. Especially because of China's great success. The nation has become today the largest and fastest-growing producer of clean energy equipment in the world. It has led for at least a decade. Its lead has expanded and should continue to widen at least over the next few years.[11] China achieved this dominant role for a variety of reasons. The principal one is simply the massive economies of scale. A scale so large that it has never been seen in history anywhere in the world.

The high dependence on China has been fuelling geopolitical tensions which, coupled with potential transport or other bottlenecks, highlight great supply chain risks to the energy transition. This is not the only potential supply chain risk. Raw materials dependence, such as those for batteries, is another.

The sixth hurdle is the slow adoption of new clean energy technologies. The reluctance is often due to a lack of confidence in the reliability of a new technology. Another reason is that typically when a new technology reaches full commercialisation, its price will remain high until mass production is reached. WoodMac, the consultancy, had identified and ranked 243 distinct technologies across ten transition themes.[12] The evaluation revealed which innovations are poised to reshape our energy systems and which may require additional policy support to overcome adoption barriers. There are many examples of existing technologies whose adoption has been slow.

Dynamic Line Rating (DLR) technology is a promising innovation for power transmission networks. By precisely measuring the thermal capacity of transmission lines in real time, DLR enables grid operators to safely increase capacity as renewable generation becomes the dominant source in power systems. The development of CCS technologies is progressing steadily, although significant economic hurdles remain. These technologies remain essential components of the decarbonisation strategy, particularly in industrial sectors where emissions are difficult to eliminate through electrification alone. Meanwhile, hydrogen technologies continue to develop, confronting substantial obstacles but maintaining their position as vital contributors to future deep-decarbonisation scenarios, especially for heavy industry and certain transport applications. Alternative battery chemistries, such as sodium-ion and solid-state batteries, show tremendous potential but require further development before they can effectively compete with established lithium-ion technology. In the transport sector, sustainable aviation fuels and low-carbon maritime fuels are gaining significant traction, though they face critical constraints regarding feedstock supply, which may limit their ultimate deployment scale.[13]

The final technology-related challenge is the emissions generated during the manufacturing process of clean energy equipment, also referred to as life-cycle emissions. While in operation, renewable energy technologies produce minimal or no emissions. However, there are emissions generated from the extraction of critical materials, the manufacture of the equipment, and the transportation of the product. Arguably, there is also exposure at the end of the life of the product. Wind turbines and solar cells will need to be dismantled, decommissioned, and disposed of.[14]

There are a great number of detailed scientific studies as to the full carbon footprint or total GHG emissions of each of the major electricity generation technologies, in particular, the carbon footprint related to the manufacturing of the equipment such as wind turbines (see Figure 4.5). The amount is calculated on the basis of grammes of CO_2 equivalent per kWh, and one such study, conducted by a UN agency, found that for thermal coal electric power generation the minimum amount of GHG emissions was 751 grammes of CO_2 equivalent per kWh and the maximum was 1,065. For thermal coal with CCS, the range was 147–469. It was 403–513 for combined-cycle natural gas and 49–220 for combined-cycle natural gas with CCS. The range for nuclear power was 5.1–6.4. For hydroelectric power, it was 6–147, a particularly wide range because of the sharp differences in construction and location of hydroelectric power projects. For concentrated solar PV, the range was 27–122 while for solar PV, it was 8–83. Finally, for onshore wind, it was 7.8–16.0 and for offshore wind, 12–23.[15]

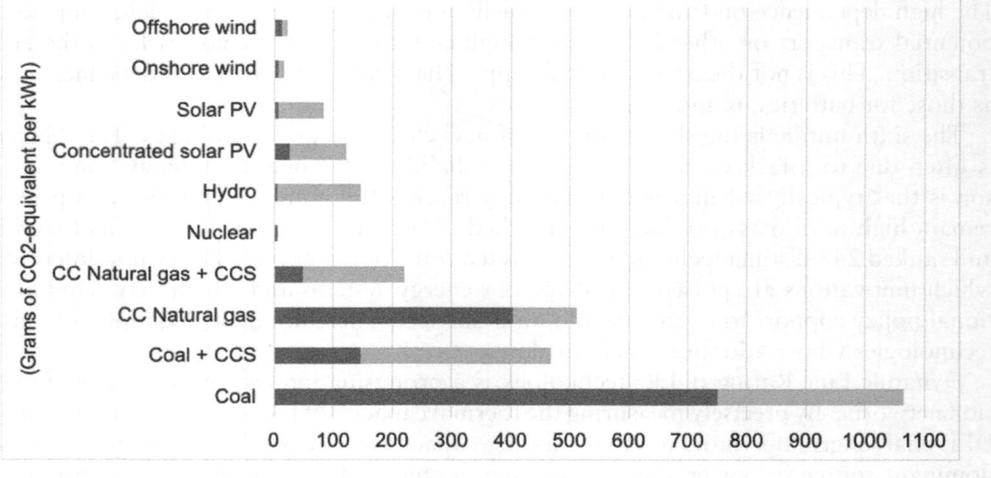

Figure 4.5 Life-cycle emissions by generation type

Source: Gibon T, Hahn Menacho Á and Guiton M, 'Life Cycle Assessment of Electricity Generation Options Life Cycle Assessment of Electricity' (United Nations Economic Commission for Europe 2021). Available at: https://unece.org/sites/default/files/2021-09/202109_UNECE_LCA_1.2_clean.pdf accessed 11 April 2024.

The often-overlooked challenge: the environment

There are many environmental challenges to the energy transition. Two of the key ones are (Hurdle 8) nature and (Hurdle 9) biodiversity.

The energy transition means an acceleration in the construction of renewable energy generation facilities. These projects will displace fossil fuel-based generation which causes enormous harm to the environment, including to the air, land, and water. While renewable energy projects cut air pollution and use less resources, they still require equipment and infrastructure. They will have an impact on ecosystems and biodiversity, the different kinds of life found in one area. At the equipment end, the main worry is over the GHG emissions during the life cycle of the product, such as a solar PV system or a wind turbine, as already explained. Also, there will be an environmental impact in the securing of the materials, such as the metals required, then in the production of the product and finally in its removal at the end of its life cycle. At the infrastructure end, the impact will depend on the technology. Utility-scale solar power generation facilities need substantial amounts of land which could modify and fragment some habitats. Such project would also need a supporting infrastructure beyond the solar panels. These could include the construction of access roads as well as electrical equipment. It could lead to the installation needing 2.5 times the area of the solar panels.[16] In the case of onshore wind farms, they could disrupt the migratory patterns of birds. Another dimension is that concerns by government authorities over ecosystems and biodiversity lead to stricter land use requirements, as is the case in some European countries. The additional step in the approval process could lead to project delays.

Overall, using renewable energy generation as one of the tools to transition our energy system away from fossil fuels has a net benefit. WWF, an environmental NGO, produced a study, *Building a Nature-Positive Energy Transformation*, analysing the risks posed by renewable energy to nature and people, together with the Boston Consulting Group, a consultancy. It found that '*an energy system powered by renewables will be far better across a range of metrics – 2–16 times better – for nature and people*'.[17] It found that renewable energy projects have a positive impact on key resources including air and water quality and biodiversity, especially, when considering what these projects replace, such as coal mining.

The importance of biodiversity is increasingly a factor in investment decisions, even for investments in the public markets. For example, the Head of Research and SRI, Nathalie Pistre, at Ostrum Asset Management, a fund management company with almost $400 billion under management, wrote that preserving biodiversity is now a central concern for investors. Pistre highlights that biodiversity significantly influences over half of the world's GDP. The vanishing of biodiversity poses a substantial risk to human livelihoods, food security, and public health. She comments that conscientious investors must crucially determine economic projects with the potential for sustainable growth. They should assess the effects of climate change and biodiversity loss on each sector and issuer. Furthermore, they should incorporate the potential risks that these 'externalities' could have on their growth path.[18] The fact that climate change is indivisibly linked to the biodiversity crisis is echoed by a great number of financial investors and is a concern for a great many governments, think tanks, and many other entities.

Financing: addressing income vulnerability and sustainability concerns

The fourth set of challenges to the energy transition relate to finance and financing. They include (Hurdle 10) project income vulnerability and (Hurdle 11) the sustainability of financing.

The world has been adding renewable energy at a fast pace in recent years. In 2023, for example, the deployment was led by the two mainstream technologies, solar PV and wind. Solar PV capacity jumped 85 per cent and that of wind rose 60 per cent, for a total of 540 GW, according to the IEA. This growth was concentrated in China and some advanced economies which accounted for 90 per cent of the newly added generation, says the IEA.[19] At COP28, there was a call for renewable energy capacity to triple by 2030.[20] Continued strong growth in the short- to mid-term can be expected, whether or not the tripling of capacity goal is fully met or not. A potential side effect from the massive growth in capacity is lower wholesale or market prices, which cut revenues and negatively affect the profitability of projects. Temporary oversupply of solar and wind power has led to lower prices, and even 'negative power prices', in the past in such markets as Australia and Germany. The occurrences were due to more electricity being available than demand due to abundant wind and solar irradiation. This creates much uncertainty for investors as to the long-term commercial viability of projects. The regulators in many electricity markets are conscious of this issue and will likely find solutions to address it. One of the many possibilities is the deployment of hybrid projects, such as PV and wind, coupled with large-capacity energy storage. In the long term, green hydrogen could also play a significant role, once the cost at production – and at delivery – is commercially competitive, something which will take many years. Another aspect of project income vulnerability is the level of interest rates, given that typically a clean energy project requires almost all or all of its capital expenditure upfront, rising or persistently high interest rates greatly reduce profitability for the project.

Another finance-related challenge is the insufficient funding for climate investments and the energy transition, particularly in less advanced economies. Public policy is the obvious starting point. An acceleration in investments was seen after two major economies launched their massive plans to promote investments in renewable energy projects. Specifically, the EU Green Deal and the US Inflation Reduction Act. The funding gap is exacerbated because the bulk of the world has faced for several years high interest rates and inflationary environment, as of early 2025 which makes raising capital more challenging. Complicating this picture is the high level of indebtedness among emerging market and developing economies. Project Syndicate, a media organisation, quoted a study by the Boston University Global Development Policy Centre which found that out of 108 such economies, 62 were at a high risk of debt distress while another 33 were 'severely constrained in their ability to access capital markets, owing largely to poor economic-growth prospects following the COVID-19 pandemic, advanced-economy interest-rate hikes, and below-investment-grade bond ratings'.[21] Funding hundreds of billions of dollars in the coming years is none the less looking brighter given the myriads of initiatives to allocate funding, with the EU Green Deal and the US inflation reduction act as two of several examples. A more detailed discussion of this area and other finance topics is in Section III.

Notes

1 International Energy Agency, *World Energy Outlook 2024* (International Energy Agency 2024) <https://iea.blob.core.windows.net/assets/140a0470-5b90-4922-a0e9-838b3ac6918c/WorldEnergyOutlook2024.pdf> accessed 19 March 2025.

2 International Energy Agency, *Global Energy and Climate Model Documentation-2024* (International Energy Agency 2024) <https://iea.blob.core.windows.net/assets/89a1aa9a-e1bd-4803-b37b-59d6e7fba1e9/GlobalEnergyandClimateModelDocumentation2024.pdf> accessed 19 March 2025.

3 International Energy Agency, *Global Energy and Climate Model Documentation -2024* (International Energy Agency 2024) <https://iea.blob.core.windows.net/assets/89a1aa9a-e1bd-4803-b37b-59d6e7fba1e9/GlobalEnergyandClimateModelDocumentation2024.pdf> accessed 19 March 2025.

4 Enerdata, 'Global 2050 Projections for Total Electricity Generation | Enerdata' (eneroutlook.enerdata.net) <https://eneroutlook.enerdata.net/total-electricity-generation-projections.html> accessed 12 April 2024.

5 IRENA Coalition for Action, *100% Renewable Energy Scenarios: Supporting Ambitious Policy Targets* (International Renewable Energy Agency 2024) <https://mc-cd8320d4-36a1-40ac-83cc-3389-cdn-endpoint.azureedge.net/-/media/Files/IRENA/Agency/Publication/2024/Mar/IRENA_Coalition_100_RE_scenarios_2024.pdf?rev=5ef440b6087942e8a8eba687b65c25f9> accessed 13 May 2024.

6 E360 Digest, 'Cheap Chinese Solar Panels Sparking a Renewable Boom in the Global South' *Yale e360* (25 February 2025) <https://e360.yale.edu/digest/China-solar-global-south> accessed 19 March 2025.

7 International Renewable Energy Agency, *Geopolitics of the Energy Transition: Critical Materials* (International Renewable Energy Agency 2023) <https://mc-cd8320d4-36a1-40ac-83cc-3389-cdn-endpoint.azureedge.net/-/media/Files/IRENA/Agency/Publication/2023/Jul/IRENA_Geopolitics_energy_transition_critical_materials_2023.pdf?rev=420aeb58d2e745d79f1b564ea89ef9f8>.

8 B Tansan, *Why Emerging Markets Need to Prepare for the EU's New Climate and ESG Regulations* (Tim Figures and others eds, BCG Global 6 November 2023) <https://www.bcg.com/publications/2023/how-emerging-markets-can-prepare-for-the-new-esg-regulations> accessed 2 April 2024. And information from various European Commission sites at https://commission.europa.eu/index_en.

9 P Hevia-Koch, A Rawlins Bilbao, and D Morris (eds), *The Clean Energy Economy Demands Massive Integration Investments Now – Analysis* (IEA 25 January 2024) <https://www.iea.org/commentaries/the-clean-energy-economy-demands-massive-integration-investments-now> accessed 8 April 2024.

10 R Kazmer, *'Magic Balls' Installed by Drones May Soon Be Revolutionizing the US Power Grid: 'Unrivaled Quality at Scale'* (The Cool Down 13 January 2024) <https://www.thecooldown.com/green-tech/magic-balls-power-lines-heimdall/> accessed 21 April 2024.

11 C Howe, 'Explainer: The Numbers behind China's Renewable Energy Boom' *Reuters* (15 November 2023) <https://www.reuters.com/sustainability/climate-energy/numbers-behind-Chinas-renewable-energy-boom-2023-11-15/> accessed 8 April 2024.

12 S Flowers, 'Wood Mackenzie' (Woodmac.com 30 May 2024) <https://www.woodmac.com/blogs/the-edge/the-coming-low-carbon-disruptors/> accessed 19 March 2025.

13 S Flowers, 'Wood Mackenzie' (Woodmac.com 30 May 2024) <https://www.woodmac.com/blogs/the-edge/the-coming-low-carbon-disruptors/> accessed 19 March 2025.

14 C Laurie, 'Renewable Energy Is Green, but We Can Make It Greener' (www.nrel.gov 24 February 2024) <https://www.nrel.gov/news/program/2024/renewable-energy-is-green-but-we-can-make-it-greener.html> accessed 10 March 2024.

15 T Gibon, Á Hahn Menacho, and M Guiton, *Life Cycle Assessment of Electricity Generation Options Life Cycle Assessment of Electricity* (United Nations Economic Commission for Europe 2021) <https://unece.org/sites/default/files/2021-09/202109_UNECE_LCA_1.2_clean.pdf> accessed 11 April 2024.

16 A Gasparatos and others, 'Renewable Energy and Biodiversity: Implications for Transitioning to a Green Economy' (2017) 70 Renewable and Sustainable Energy Reviews 161 <https://www.sciencedirect.com/science/article/pii/S1364032116304622?via per cent3Dihub> accessed 11 March 2024.

17 WWF, 'Building a Nature-Positive Energy Transformation' (wwf.panda.org 3 November 2023) <https://wwf.panda.org/wwf_news/?9967866/Building-a-Nature-Positive-Energy-Transformation> accessed 11 March 2024.

18 N Pistre, *Energy Transition and Biodiversity: A Difficult Union* (Ostrum Asset Management 19 June 2023) <https://www.ostrum.com/en/news-insights/insights/energy-transition-and-biodiversity-difficult-union> accessed 12 April 2024.

19 IEA, *Clean Energy Market Monitor – March 2024 – Analysis* (IEA March 2024) <https://www.iea.org/reports/clean-energy-market-monitor-march-2024> accessed 11 March 2024.

20 IEA, *Massive Expansion of Renewable Power Opens Door to Achieving Global Tripling Goal Set at COP28 – News* (IEA 24 January 2024) <https://www.iea.org/news/massive-expansion-of-renewable-power-opens-door-to-achieving-global-tripling-goal-set-at-cop28> accessed 11 March 2024.

21 R Ray and U Volz, *Making Climate Finance Affordable* (Project Syndicate 11 March 2024) <https://www.project-syndicate.org/commentary/lower-borrowing-costs-for-developing-economies-to-invest-in-climate-action-sdgs-by-rebecca-ray-and-ulrich-volz-1-2024-03> accessed 11 March 2024.

Section II

Singular driver in the multifaceted energy shift

Chapter 5

The many faces of the energy shift

Aims:

- The transition's complexity and the multiple disciplines and perspectives.
- The decarbonisation challenge's magnitude, financial scale, and knowledge gap.
- Approaches to navigating the transition, including the 'Energy Transition Pyramid'.

The energy transition is a complex and multifaceted challenge. It is like a cubist painting by Pablo Picasso, where objects are portrayed from a variety of viewpoints at once. In the same way, the energy transition must be viewed from a variety of perspectives. It is an intricate kaleidoscope of intertwined disciplines. These fields include accounting, economics, engineering, environmental science, finance, infrastructure, logistics, policy, politics, regulation, sociology, taxation, taxonomy, and technology. An additional layer of complexity is the overwhelming pressure to ensure the transition does not raise consumer prices. As Dr Faith Birol, head of the IEA, remarked in 2021, the energy transition is a 'herculean task'.

Understanding the multifaceted nature of decarbonisation, the energy transition, and the path to net zero is the first step for corporations, and other entities, to be able to successfully identify and navigate the opportunities and the risks to business and assets brought about by the energy transition. Its massive and complex nature must be put into context. There are several areas that must be grasped by all direct and indirect participants in the green shift. How large is the undertaking to transition to green? How difficult is it for decision-makers and other stakeholders to understand the transition? What are the disciplines involved? What is the role of capacity building and education? What are the possible approaches to evaluate and comprehend the energy transition?

Shifting away from fossil fuels: a huge task

The world has largely come together and agreed that climate action is as imperative as it is urgent. But looking at the task, the energy shift is beyond daunting. Transitioning to green is a mammoth global undertaking. The world's energy system needs to be transformed. The infrastructure to generate and deliver the energy must be partly revamped or retooled. Hundreds of billions of dollars must be invested in the next two and a half decades. Concurrently, apart from ensuring supply security, the energy must remain affordable, convenient for users, effective, environmentally sustainable, and as GHG emissions neutral as possible,

DOI: 10.4324/9781003666509-7

as Holger Hanselka, the president of a German university, commented.[1] Germany originally planned to shut down all of its nuclear and coal-fired generation facilities and replace the output with natural gas. Natural gas generation would have been a solid bridging solution given it does not have the decommissioning issues of nuclear and the high emissions of coal power. Russia's invasion of Ukraine forced the German government to rethink its over-reliance on sourcing gas from Russia. It then had to find ways to diversify its generation sources, including clean energy, to reduce gas consumption, and source the remaining gas from elsewhere. These complex parameters and shifts did cause some havoc, including temporary higher electricity prices for consumers.

Germany is, of course, not alone. Many other countries have to undertake the energy shift journey, which is a more arduous path for those nations without domestically available energy resources. For example, in the case of Japan, net energy imports amounted to almost 90 per cent of total energy supply in 2022, according to the IEA.[2] The global fossil fuel energy market is valued at several trillion dollars. One estimate puts it at over $7 trillion in 2022 and forecasts growth of almost 70 per cent to $11.8 trillion by 2032.[3] As such, at a minimum, the energy transition is aiming at reforming a $7-trillion market. Several organisations forecast a sharp drop in the use of fossil fuels through 2050 and further falls beyond that. One estimate forecasts the decline of between 55 per cent and 70 per cent in natural gas supply, a fall of 80 per cent to 85 per cent for coal, and a decrease of between 75 per cent and 95 per cent for oil, according to a report by the Energy Transitions Commission, a think tank.[4] While the IEA expects that global demand for natural gas and oil will peak by 2030, the 2050 net-zero emissions scenario implies consumption of the two fuels will drop by over 75 per cent.[5] Several studies have highlighted that long-term fossil fuel forecasts by various institutions and think tanks have tended in the past to slightly overestimate fossil fuel consumption and underestimate clean energy demand. This is unlikely to continue as clean energy growth continues to gain momentum.

Bridging the knowledge gap for key players

Understanding the transition undertaking is a major challenge for those whose job it is to drive change, including decision-makers in government or legislatures. After all, they are human and may neither have the background nor a comprehensive understanding of all of the complexities.

There are at least two solutions to address the knowledge gap problem. One is for government and related institutions to actively participate in capacity-building exercises organised by a myriad of entities. Another, and often concurrent, solution is to call in subject experts, including specialised consultancies such as Environmental Resources Management, McKinsey and Company, and Wood Mackenzie.

In terms of capacity building, there are a great number of entities which have the capability and the structure to help the various state institutions to build capacity for the energy transition. The capacity-building efforts might include training programmes and financing information exchanges. Many entities involved in the energy transition are helping. Some of these include international organisations such as some UN agencies, the IEA, and IRENA, regional and global multilateral financial institutions such as the Asia Development Bank and the International Finance Corporation, and regional entities such as the European Climate Infrastructure and Environment Agency. The latter, for example, delivers the necessary capacity building at national, regional, and even municipal levels. Capacity-building in public authorities involves technical support to clean energy transition plans and strategies. They need to learn how to switch from plans only focused on the energy sector to strategies also including climate and the transition. This, in addition to working to

> align existing plans to new, more ambitious targets of carbon neutrality . . . holistic planning and sectoral integration . . . secure stronger political commitment and resources to deliver the plans . . . develop governance structures to implement the change . . .[and] coherence with other strategies (National Energy and Climate Plans, Recovery Plans, Long Term Renovation Strategies, etc.).[6]

Capacity-building by non-institutional entities chiefly includes nonprofit organisations and think tanks as well as consultancies. The Climate Policy Initiative was founded by a university professor in 2009 with the aim to make climate a key part of economic planning. Through in-house experts and external partners, it gives government-related decision-makers and others, from finance professionals to academia, tools to execute sustainable economic development.[7] State recipients may also call in consultancies. Other participants active in capacity building are commercial financial institutions, especially the large global ones such as Bank of America, JPMorgan Chase, and UBS. The purpose is profit-oriented. They hope that the capacity building they undertake will reinforce their client relationships or lead to sourcing new clients. It would enable them to generate fees from such work as helping these clients to issue fixed-income instruments. For example, China issued a US-dollar-denominated green bond in the London Stock Exchange. The issuance's joint lead managers included the Bank of China, the Bank of Communications, HSBC, Barclays, and several other financial institutions.

Capacity-building is critically necessary for recipients to be able to grasp the complexities of the energy transition and learn how to make sustainable development, climate, energy transition, and the like as an integral part of policy setting and planning. Unfortunately, both the institutional capacity building and the calling-in-experts solutions add another layer and make policymaking less efficient and slower.

Navigating the interwoven complexities

What are the disciplines which practitioners must grasp when considering climate business, climate finance, and the energy transition in general, whether they are state planners, academics, business managers, or related roles? They probably need to have general knowledge in at least 14 separate disciplines.

Accounting

Financial regulators created new global rules to cater for the decarbonising landscape. Many are highly pertinent to the energy transitions. There is a massive volume of new rules and regulations, with each having its own complexities. The types of reporting include climate, sustainability, ESG, carbon disclosure, corporate social responsibility, and biodiversity reporting. Many of these rules will undergo tweaks and some will be overtaken by new ones. It is an evolutionary process.

Economics

The energy transition creates many new economic challenges for policymakers. It impacts a wide variety of economic areas. Some of these include investment and financing, labour markets, industrial policies, economic incentives such as carbon pricing, and many others.

Engineering

Technical issues refer to the operation and performance of existing clean energy technologies. They can include efficiency limitations, integrating existing electricity distribution and transmission networks, incorporating energy storage facilities, or sourcing production materials such as rare earths. Also, as the electrification rate in many sectors rises, there will be an enormity of technical considerations to address.

Environmental science

The transition commands global climate action commitments and this has forced a great number of governments to rethink their domestic environmental agendas and some of their conservation efforts. These include subjects as diverse as biodiversity-positive plans, preparing rural areas for the energy transition, balancing building new clean energy projects with land and water conservation, or natural resources management – for those nations that have such resources.

Finance

Finance is one of the fundamental disciplines in the energy transition given the investment scale required. Issues in the realm of finance include the financing mechanisms and sources for the high upfront costs of renewable energy projects, for the phasing down or phasing out of fossil fuels, or for the new or the revamping of the electricity distribution infrastructure required.

Infrastructure

The transition will require significant amounts of physical infrastructure changes. In energy, transmission-related investments will be crucial, and the planning is complicated. Areas include grid modernisation to expand networks and also to integrate clean energy sources; incorporating sizeable new amounts of energy storage, such as EV charging; making the infrastructure 'smart' through automation, digitisation, and AI incorporation; and accelerating cybersecurity measures to protect critical infrastructure.

Logistical

The transition creates new supply chains and the associated logistics, chiefly relating to the manufacturing process of clean energy-related equipment. At one end is the building, or reinforcing, of the supply chains of the input materials, such as the rare earths necessary for the permanent magnets of wind turbines. At the other end is ramping up the production capacity of the clean technologies. Also, new supply chains must be created for green input materials, such as bamboo, cork, and recycled steel.

Policy

The list of policymaking issues involved in the transition is extensive. It encompasses new or revised policies for virtually every single aspect of economic activity. They encompass many of the areas in this list of disciplines, such as economic incentives, resources allocation, and infrastructure planning. They must concurrently include consumer protection and empowerment as well as 'just transition' policies supporting workers and engaging with various communities.

Politics

Politics will drive transition-related policies and is intrinsically complicated and challenging to forecast. Domestically, one party or faction today may be in favour of climate-change-related policies, and the next day shift its views. Predicting this is next to impossible. Worldwide, at times, national interests will trump global interests and may affect a nation's intended climate actions.

Regulation

Regulations related to the energy transition are nascent, much like those in the accounting field. A significant portion of these climate- or energy transition-related regulations are still in the early stages of development and are subject to frequent modifications and fine-tuning. A beneficial aspect of this process is that necessary changes are typically extensively deliberated and debated, allowing practitioners to potentially anticipate upcoming alterations.

Sociology

Two of the many sociological issues related to the energy transition are a 'just transition' and public acceptance. The International Labour Organisation defines the 'just transition' as 'greening the economy in a way that is as fair and inclusive as possible to everyone concerned, creating decent work opportunities and leaving no one behind'.[8] Public acceptance means that public education programmes will be needed so the general public may accept new technologies and infrastructure and adopt new consumption behaviour.

Taxation

Transition-related fiscal considerations are closely linked but relatively separate from financial ones. They mostly involve governmental financial or economic entities. Governments can adapt carbon pricing mechanisms such as carbon taxes or emissions trading schemes. They may have to start subsidy reform, such as removing fossil fuel subsidies and creating green ones. Or they may need to address lower fiscal revenues from fossil fuels.

Taxonomy

In the transition, taxonomies play a central role. However, green taxonomies are still evolving. There are many developments at national levels as well as global ones. Issues include the need for a global harmonisation of definitions; creating hard approaches for the transparent verification of what is and is not 'green', to avoid greenwashing; or how to render taxonomies dynamic so they can be adjusted as technologies and environmental understandings evolve.

Technology

Technological issues revolve around the development of technologies which are still at the inception stage or that are yet to reach mass market. They encompass solar PV cells or wind turbines with higher efficiency, advanced nuclear power – such as small modular reactors, CCS and CCUS, marine and ocean energy technologies, battery energy storage, and geothermal systems as well as new materials or production methods for these technologies.

The role of education and the approaches

Public policy, which is chiefly written by governments, is the fundamental driver and starting point of the energy transition. Yet the mechanics of the transition are relatively new and typically there is limited understanding of the necessary educational tools or requirements. Public institutions, including universities, are generally behind the curve. It is urgent and imperative to have learning structures and systems readily and widely available so that bureaucrats, professionals, students, or workers alike can learn what the energy transition is all about. They must understand how one can play a role in executing one or more parts of the transition. They must be able to identify opportunities and risks related to climate and the transition. Government and all individuals and entities, from the state to civil society, directly or indirectly involved in the energy transition must be taught, and in some cases even retrained. Yet the task is not easy chiefly because transition-related education involves a paradigm shift. It is not just about energy. It is not a single subject, as it involves multiple ones. Energy transition education frameworks must be constructed from scratch, borrowing from a variety of disciplines, to equip everyone to execute policies and plans.

Evaluating the level of energy transition-related knowledge at public and private institutions would be a gargantuan task, if not simply impossible. Yet two deductions can be made: formal energy transition-related education is likely insufficient worldwide for today's needs, and it may particularly lack in emerging economies, arguably where it is most needed. A study by Norwegian researchers, Roman Vakulchuk and Indra Overland, released in 2024 sheds some light on this subject. Vakulchuk and Overland correctly emphasise that '*[The] energy transition involves the transformation of professions and labour markets, which in turn depend on the availability of a workforce with the right education and competence*'.[9] They also underlined that between 2010 and 2024 there had been a rising scarcity of skilled labour for renewable energy projects. They reviewed 18,400 universities around the world and created a dataset including 6,142 institutions where energy-specific education was offered. They found that fossil fuels-related education was growing while that for renewable energy lagged behind and that '*as many as 68 per cent of the world's energy-focused educational degrees were oriented towards fossil fuels, and only 32 per cent focused on renewable energy*'.[10] They also found that developing countries were lagging behind developed ones.

The positive trend is that since the Paris Agreement teaching capacity has been steadily growing. One informal survey, for example, found that the availability of sustainable finance courses had grown exponentially in the past three years at universities and other nonprofit organisations such as finance-related associations. The top universities in the world in 2024 ranked by Times Higher Education[11] were the University of Oxford, Stanford

University, the Massachusetts Institute of Technology, Harvard University, and the University of Cambridge. One offered a sustainable finance-related degree (Harvard), two offered courses on the subject (Oxford and Stanford), and another two offered sustainability as part of their finance degrees (Cambridge and MIT), as of 2023. In terms of non-tertiary institutional learning, one example is the CFA Institute, a global finance education nonprofit organisation. It principally provides a finance course for professionals – 200,000-strong worldwide – to obtain the widely respected Chartered Financial Analyst designation after a three-year, three-stage course. The institute started offering a specific climate finance-related course, the Climate Risk, Valuation, and Investing Certificate in 2024.

Evaluating the energy transition

It is no small feat to understand the various essential elements of the energy transition. It is a complex area with lots of dimensions and uncertainties,[12] as a recent blog stated. It is also the most complex undertaking humanity has ever embarked upon,[13] cleantech energy guru Michael Liebreich called it. Some want the complexity to sound even more complex, as a recent study underlined, 'expectations of a linear global transition have been shaken as climate goals coexist with priorities around energy security, energy access, and affordability'.[14] None of these statements is exaggerated.

The Energy Transition Pyramid (see Figure 5.1) offers a simplified way to better evaluate the individual elements of the energy transition. It can serve as the stepping stone for a variety of purposes to evaluate investments and for business transition planning. It contains four building blocks. These work with three specific drivers. The various disciplines mentioned earlier can also be placed in three broad baskets. The pyramid, the drivers, and the disciplines should enable a sound understanding and robust approach to the energy transition.

The four Energy Transition Pyramid building blocks are: government, finance, technology, and cost. The fundamental and primary building block for the world to achieve a net-zero, carbon-neutral economy is the ability for governments to establish a policy

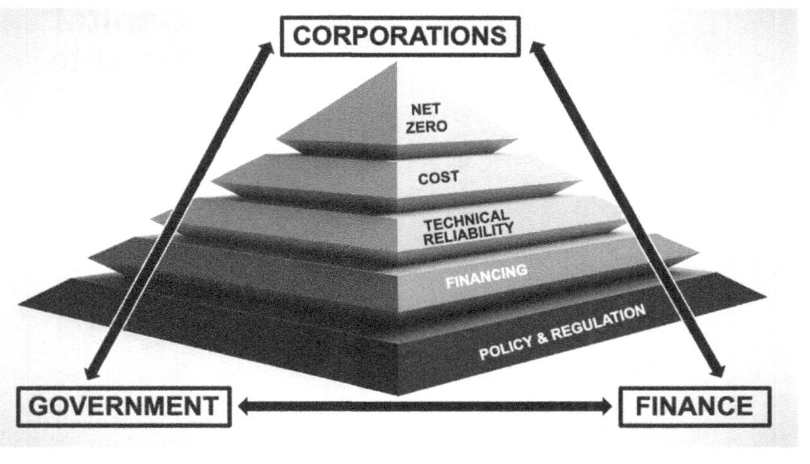

Figure 5.1 The Energy Transition Pyramid

Source: Author, original chart idea and design (June 2025); background image generated Image generated by Google Gemini, from the prompt 'Three-dimensional pyramid', accessed 11 June 2025.

framework, no matter if it is policy heavy or policy light. A government's climate action declaration must come together with or be soon followed by the establishment of a series of regulations and institutions. Once these foundations are firmly anchored, they will set in motion a circular causality, a dynamic interplay between government, business, and finance. The next building block is that the financing needs must be sourced, coupled with the related regulatory, financial or accounting compliance. These two building blocks are primordial. The first is considered in the next chapter while the second block is examined in Section III. The third block is to make sure that the business models and the technologies and solutions deployed are technically and technologically reliable and sustainable. The final block is cost. Once the first three blocks are achieved, it must be determined that the clean energy source is produced at an economically attractive, competitive, and sustainable cost, so that the prices paid by consumers may stay low and affordable.

A second perspective on the Energy Transition Pyramid is that there is a clear intersection and overlap of three elements, all part of the Pyramid. They are government, corporations, and finance. The three elements are interlocked and must work together for climate-aligned strategies to be successful, regardless of whether these are strategies stemming from government, corporations, or the financial sector.

The various disciplines can be placed into three broad baskets. The first basket comprises macro-related disciplines. Another basket includes energy transition assets and related disciplines. A third basket encompasses capital-markets-related disciplines.

Macro-related factors include economic, policy, political, regulatory, and sociological disciplines, and possibly taxonomic factors as well (see Figure 5.2). Those related to assets, or businesses, include environmental, infrastructure, logistical, technical, and technological disciplines. Finally, related to capital markets are accounting, financial, fiscal, and taxonomy disciplines.

The Energy Transition Pyramid and the approaches of examining the issue from three different perspectives may seem rather theoretical. To understand the practical implications

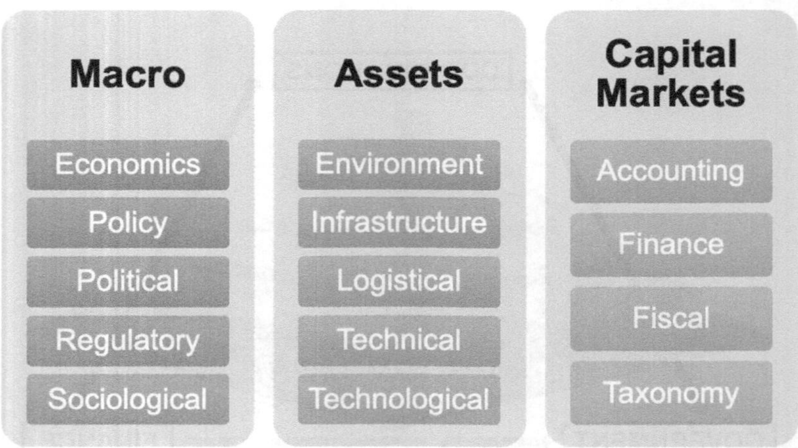

Figure 5.2 The baskets of disciplines

Notes: Taxonomy could also be included as a 'macro' factor.

Source: Author, original chart design, June 2025.

of the triadic relationship between government, business, and finance, it is helpful to provide a real-world case study. One such example could be the development of the wind energy industry in the United Kingdom.

Wind power accounts for about a quarter of the United Kingdom's total electricity output. It may sound small, but the growth in wind power's share has been remarkable. The contribution has grown exponentially in recent years. Wind power generation doubled between 2007 and 2010. This trend continued in 2012, 2015, and 2022, reaching an impressive output of 80.2 TWh and a total installed capacity of over 28 GW in 2022 (see Figure 5.3).

The starting point to this remarkable development was the government's policies promoting renewable energy. The interest was first highlighted in the mid-1970s as a reaction to the global oil crisis of 1974. It did not gain significant momentum until the 1990s and saw a step change with more concrete and effective policies in the 2000s. A policy milestone was the launch of the Renewables Obligation in 2002, where renewable energy generators were paid a premium above the market price for their output. From 2014, the Contracts for Difference scheme paid these producers a fixed price set through a competitive bidding process. Also, in 2010, a Feed-in Tariff scheme was set up to pay residential and commercial users a tariff for power generated from their own solar panels or wind turbines. Interestingly, during the first two decades (2000s and 2010s), policy and regulation were not consistent and, some would argue, overly weak when compared to regional neighbours such as Germany. They drew much criticism domestically and from abroad.

Yet, the policies did boost investors' confidence. The nation added over 25.2 GW between 2002 and 2022, a 58-fold rise, higher than the 12-fold average increase for the whole of Europe.[15] The government stated that it had been able to attract almost £200 billion ($270 billion) in investments in low-carbon energy since 2010. The wind industry drew some of the world's largest companies involved in renewable energy, including Denmark's Ørsted, the Spanish/German Siemens Gamesa Renewable Energy, Denmark's Vestas Wind

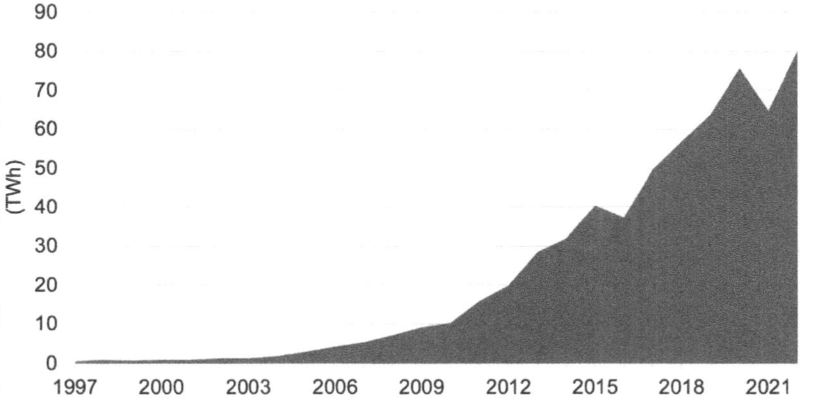

Figure 5.3 UK wind energy generation (1997–2022)

Notes: Unit TWh. The 2021 wind turbine output was lower than that of a year earlier due to low wind conditions.

Source: Energy Institute, 'Energy Institute Statistical Review of World Energy' (Energy Institute Statistical Review of World Energy 26 June 2023). Available at: https://www.energyinst.org/statistical-review accessed 25 December 2023.

Systems, the United States' General Electric (specifically GE Renewable Energy), and Sweden's Vattenfall. Many private equity firms and infrastructure funds have also been keen to invest in the United Kingdom's wind sector, including Canada's Brookfield, Australia's Macquarie, as well as the United Kingdom's Global Energy Group, GLIL Infrastructure, and Greencoat Capital. Often these entities do not invest alone. These projects are often co-investments. Typically, to maximise capital sourcing and diversify project risk in one's portfolio, as few investors like to put all of their eggs in one single basket. The investment approaches and models, together with the financing structures and tools, are key components of the whole picture.

The financing of wind energy projects has been a mixture of government funding and private investment. National financial institutions have played an important role at the public end. Institutions such as the UK Infrastructure Bank, the British Business Bank, and UK Research and Innovation, a national funding agency investing in science and research. They had also involved multilateral public financial institutions such as the European Investment Bank, prior to the United Kingdom's departure from the EU. These institutions have provided a steady stream of long-term commercial bank loans together with commercial banks from the United Kingdom and abroad, including Barclays, HSBC, Lloyds Banking Group, Royal Bank of Scotland, Santander, and Société Générale.

The United Kingdom's track record and the climate action announced by the current UK government, elected in 2024, mean that in the British Isles the triadic relationship – government, investors, and finance – is solid and should continue to thrive in the future as recent events testify. The government of former UK Prime Minister Boris Johnson publicised The Ten Point Plan for a Green Industrial Revolution in late 2020.[16] The points in the plan included the promotion of established clean technologies such as EVs, offshore wind, and nuclear power as well as newer solutions such as CCUS and green hydrogen. It also addressed low-carbon buildings and transport, restoring nature, making London as a green global finance centre, as well as supporting the development of zero-carbon aviation and shipping. Achieving each of the ten aims is exceedingly complex, and each faces a great number of specific hurdles. It will certainly take many years before some of the benefits from at least some of the individual points are felt. Yet, the ones involving offshore wind and other more established clean technologies should be relatively less tricky to execute.

The United Kingdom had been led by the Conservative Party since 2010. The new Labour government has many radically different policies but when it comes to the national energy transition, there has been continuity or fine-tuning in the policies. Labour has repeatedly stated that one of its missions is to 'make Britain a clean energy superpower'.[17] An aim not radically different from that of previous administrations. This kind of policy stability and consistency will continue to incentivise corporations and other investors in the nation's wind industry as well as reassure lenders to existing and future projects.

One of the attractions and motivations is the lower unit costs of renewables than gas-fired power plants. The UK government has estimated that for projects commissioned in 2030, the unit cost of electricity would be about £139 ($188) per MWh for gas generation, versus £39 ($53) per MWh for offshore wind farms, £37 ($50) per MWh for onshore wind, and £37 ($50) per MWh for large-scale solar power generation.[18] Importantly, the lower costs would only be attractive to investors if they still allow for sustainable margins. Obviously, apart from the attractive cost gap, the projects must be economically viable and financially sustainable in the long term to attract investors.

Notes

1 Helmholtz Association, *The Herculean Task of Transforming the Energy System* (Helmholtz-Gemeinschaft Deutscher Forschungszentren 27 January 2023) <https://www.helmholtz.de/en/newsroom/article/the-herculean-task-of-transforming-the-energy-system/> accessed 25 April 2024.
2 IEA, *Japan – Countries & Regions* (IEA) <https://www.iea.org/countries/japan/energy-mix> accessed 28 April 2024.
3 Precedence Research, 'Fossil Fuels Market Size to Hit USD 11.78 Trillion by 2032' (www.precedenceresearch.com2023) <https://www.precedenceresearch.com/fossil-fuels-market> accessed 25 April 2024.
4 The Energy Transitions Commission, *Fossil Fuels in Transition: Committing to the Phase-down of All Fossil Fuels* (Energy Transitions Commission November 2023) <https://www.energy-transitions.org/publications/fossil-fuels-in-transition> accessed 28 April 2024.
5 IEA, *Oil and Gas Industry Faces Moment of Truth – and Opportunity to Adapt – as Clean Energy Transitions Advance – News* (IEA 23 November 2023) <https://www.iea.org/news/oil-and-gas-industry-faces-moment-of-truth-and-opportunity-to-adapt-as-clean-energy-transitions-advance> accessed 28 April 2024.
6 M Sansoni, 'Capacity Building in Public Authorities Technical Support to Clean Energy Transition Plans and Strategies in Municipalities and Regions' (2021) <https://cinea.ec.europa.eu/system/files/2021-07/%281%29%20Technical%20support%20to%20clean%20energy%20transition%20plans%20and%20strategies%20in%20mu.pdf> accessed 28 April 2024.
7 Climate Policy Institute, *2022 Impact Report* (Climate Policy Institute 2023) <https://www.climatepolicyinitiative.org/wp-content/uploads/2023/10/CPI-2022-IMPACT-REPORT.pdf> accessed 28 April 2024.
8 United Nations Development Programme, *What is Just Transition? And Why Is It Important?* (UNDP Climate Promise 2022) <https://climatepromise.undp.org/news-and-stories/what-just-transition-and-why-it-important> accessed 28 April 2024.
9 R Vakulchuk and I Overland, 'The Failure to Decarbonize the Global Energy Education System: Carbon Lock-in and Stranded Skill Sets' (2024) 110 Energy Research & Social Science 103446 <https://www.sciencedirect.com/science/article/pii/S2214629624000379> accessed 28 April 2024.
10 R Vakulchuk and I Overland, 'The Failure to Decarbonize the Global Energy Education System: Carbon Lock-in and Stranded Skill Sets' (2024) 110 Energy Research & Social Science 103446 <https://www.sciencedirect.com/science/article/pii/S2214629624000379> accessed 28 April 2024.
11 Times Higher Education, *World University Rankings* (Times Higher Education (THE) 25 September 2023) <https://www.timeshighereducation.com/world-university-rankings/2024/world-ranking> accessed 28 April 2024.
12 University College London, *Decarbonising Energy and the Energy Transition* (The Bartlett 19 April 2021) <https://www.ucl.ac.uk/bartlett/news/2021/apr/decarbonising-energy-and-energy-transition> accessed 20 December 2023.
13 Michael Liebreich, *The Energy Transition Is the Most Complex Undertaking Humanity Has Ever Embarked Upon* (World Economic Forum 28 November 2018) <https://www.weforum.org/communities/gfc-on-energy-transition/>.
14 International Energy Forum with S&P Global Commodity Insights, *Shaping a Living Roadmap for Energy Transition* (International Energy Forum 2023) <https://www.ief.org/news/energy-transition-requires-deeper-northsouth-collaboration-report> accessed 27 December 2023.
15 Calculation by Author from Data Sourced from Energy Institute, *Energy Institute Statistical Review of World Energy* (Energy Institute Statistical Review of World Energy 26 June 2023) <https://www.energyinst.org/statistical-review> accessed 25 December 2023.
16 HM Government, 'The Ten Point Plan for a Green Industrial Revolution' (2020) <https://assets.publishing.service.gov.uk/media/5fb5513de90e0720978b1a6f/10_POINT_PLAN_BOOKLET.pdf> accessed 22 December 2023.
17 The Labour Party, *Switch on Great British Energy* (The Labour Party 2023) <https://labour.org.uk/missions/clean-energy/> accessed 27 December 2023.
18 Department for Energy Security & Net Zero, *Electricity Generation Costs 2023* (Government of the United Kingdom 2023) <https://assets.publishing.service.gov.uk/media/6556027d046ed400148b99fe/electricity-generation-costs-2023.pdf> accessed 4 January 2024.

Chapter 6

The policy landscape is usually a jungle

Aims:

- How countries are setting and implementing net-zero targets: variations and best practices.
- The crucial role of governments in driving climate action.
- National climate actions adequacy and gaps between current efforts and net-zero goals.

An unsung hero of global climate agreement, Christiana Figueres, pointed out the complexities with climate-action policy setting. In a TED talk, Figueres discussed the 2015 Paris Agreement, when nations united to combat climate change globally, agreeing to limit warming to 1.5 to 2.0°C above pre-industrial levels. Figueres said: '*2009, Copenhagen . . . after years of working toward a climate agreement,. . . governments convened in Copenhagen and failed miserably*'. 2015, Paris: '195 governments got together and unanimously – if you've worked with governments, you know how difficult that is – unanimously decided to intentionally change the course of the global economy'.[1] The Agreement has been criticised by many for its lack of strong enforcement and voluntary national pledges (NDCs) that may fall short of limiting warming to 1.5°C, yet it remains a vital milestone in global climate action.

Governmental climate policies are the bedrock of the energy transition. It is only through government influence that the shift to clean energy technologies can be effectively promoted, and the required infrastructure can be put into place. Governments hold the power to safeguard consumers and workers who will face the brunt of these changes. Concurrently, they have the responsibility to shape public policy to prevent any adverse environmental effects during this transition. This can be achieved by crafting and implementing policies aimed at achieving net-zero emissions. The policymaking broadly involves a two-stage process. A government must first reasonably clearly stipulate its net-zero mission statement which can be referred to as 'Level One Actions'. Then, it must build rules, regulations, and other parameters, which can be called 'Level Two Actions', with or without key stakeholders. Countries in Asia, Europe, and North America have generally taken different pathways and at different paces. Yet for the majority of these nations, the ultimate direction is the same: a carbon-neutral economy and society.

DOI: 10.4324/9781003666509-8

Net-zero policymaking is neither a chicken-or-egg situation

The importance of government action when it comes to climate change cannot be understated. It is mentioned throughout the book because of its primordial importance. Governments must step up and take the lead. Market forces and technological developments alone are not sufficient drivers. It is not a chicken-or-egg situation; policy must come first.

The first step for any government, or 'Level One Actions', is the declaration of its long-term vision. They typically do so by announcing and subsequently regularly updating their NDCs. Each country that ratified the 2015 Paris Agreement – a legally binding international treaty on climate change adopted by 196 parties – must formulate and implement a comprehensive plan to cut emissions and prepare for the impacts of climate change.[2] The plan must be reviewed and updated every five years to reflect the nation's own progress as well as the changing climate landscape. Apart from the NDC, governments must design a net-zero path.

The Climate Action Tracker, an independent scientific project tracking government climate action and measures, summarises well the ideal scope, architecture, and transparency needed by governments (see Figure 6.1). Scope-wise, first, a government has to set a net-zero target year. Typically, this is 2050. Some developing countries, such as China, have opted for 2060 carbon neutrality. Others have even set 2070, such as Indonesia, for example. It will also have to state emissions coverage, the impact on aviation and shipping, and reductions or removals outside of its own borders. It will have to structure the relevant legal works, split out reduction and removal targets, and set a review process. Finally, it will have to transparently report carbon dioxide removal, specify related comprehensive planning, as well as report on the clarity or fairness of the target. It is tireless and voluminous work, and a major challenge for any government no matter its size or stage of economic development.

Once the top-line policies are in place, 'Level Two Actions' must typically be unleashed. Actions such as mandating climate risk disclosure requirements for corporations are driven by financial regulators. The actions come in a variety of shapes and sizes. There are distinct and large variations from country to country. Sometimes, there are even sharp differences in rules and goals within one single country, such as in the United States. The detailed regulations usually tend to be highly complex and are designed and often executed with the help of many domain experts. It is worth noting that the burden of implementing the often-onerous rules and regulations often falls mostly on corporations.

SCOPE	**Target year**		
	Emissions coverage	**International aviation and shipping**	**Reductions or removals outside of own borders**
	All sectors and gases	Net zero target covers all emissions from international aviation, shipping	Reaching net zero within own borders
ARCHITECTURE	**Legal status**	**Separate reduction & removal targets**	**Review process**
	Legally binding target	Separate targets for emission reductions and removals	Legally binding review of target and progress against it at regular intervals
TRANSPARENCY	**Carbon dioxide removal**	**Comprehensive planning**	**Clarity on fairness of target**
	Transparent & scientifically robust assumptions on LULUCF, and carbon removals & storage	Transparent, scientifically robust pathway / intermediate targets with clear measures to achieve net zero	Clear statement on why target is fair

Figure 6.1 Good practice for ten key elements of national net-zero target setting

Source: Climate Action Tracker, 'Evaluation Methodology for National Net Zero Targets' (climateactiontracker.org 23 June 2021). Available at: https://climateactiontracker.org/publications/evaluation-methodology-for-national-net-zero-targets/ accessed 30 December 2023. Text partly edited by author.

The multi-agency approach: Hong Kong

Hong Kong ranks as one of the top financial centres in the world. The territory is part of the People's Republic of China, which ratified the Paris Agreement in September 2016. This automatically committed the Hong Kong Special Administrative Region's government to follow China's NDC, although it can set up more ambitious targets than the rest of the nation. The government started declaring concrete climate action plans in January 2017, launching a climate action plan in 2021. It had set such targets as an absolute carbon emission reduction of between 26 and 36 per cent and a carbon intensity reduction target of between 65 and 70 per cent by 2030, versus the 2005 base year, as well as cutting carbon emissions by 50 per cent, and reaching net zero by 2050.

The city is very keen to become a green finance hub for the region. For this, it is using a multi-agency, multi-pronged approach. An example of this approach is with the issuance of two plans. The government's Climate Action 2030+ plan and the Climate Action Plan 2050 included the involvement of a total of 16 agencies.

In the climate action-related regulation for corporations, there are many actors involved in executing a variety of climate-linked regulations (see Figure 6.2). The key ones are the Hong Kong Monetary Authority (the quasi-central bank); the Securities and Futures Commission (the capital markets regulator); the Environment and Ecology Bureau; the Financial Services and the Treasury Bureau (the environment and the finance ministry-equivalent); Hong Kong Exchanges and Clearing (the stock exchange); as well as the Insurance Authority (the insurance regulator) and the Mandatory Provident Fund Schemes Authority (the pension funds regulator). These bodies coordinate – or at least try to coordinate given the complexity of the issues and the conflicts of interest – through the Green and Sustainable Finance Cross-Agency Steering Group which focuses on managing climate-related risks in the financial industry, promoting green and sustainable investments, and aligning with the government's climate goals.

One of the many tasks the Steering Group has to set by 2025 is climate-related disclosures for corporations. These are to be in line with the suggestions by the Task Force on Climate-Related Financial Disclosures across some sectors, including the asset management, banking, insurance, and pension fund sectors.[3] It is also trying to establish 'a local

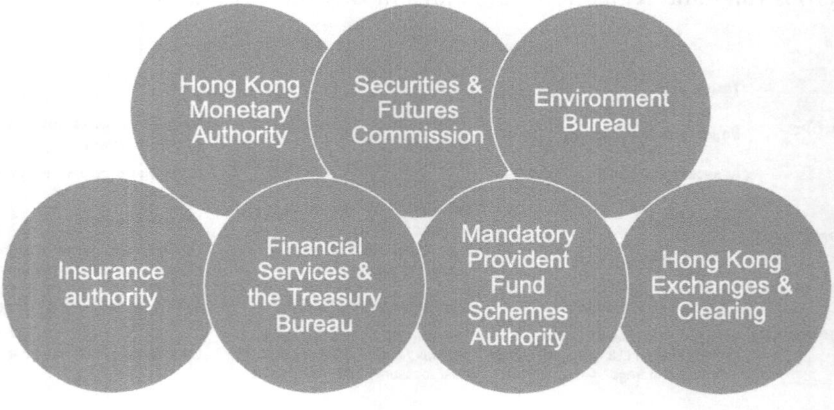

Figure 6.2 Hong Kong Green and Sustainable Finance Cross-Agency Steering Group
Source: Author, original chart design, June 2025.

green classification framework, capacity building, market opportunities, data and technology, etc., seeking to comprehensively develop green and sustainable finance'.[4] Concurrently, many of these bodies are issuing related guidelines. For example, the Securities and Futures Commission amended the Fund Manager Code of Conduct to take 'climate-related risks into consideration in their investment and risk management processes and make appropriate disclosures' and also provided clarifications on the expectations on the rules for unit trusts and mutual funds to enhance their Environmental, Social, and Governance disclosures' comparability, transparency, and visibility.[5]

The SFC itself is actively taking several sustainable finance-related actions, many related to corporate sustainability disclosures. They include aligning with such international standards as those from the ISSB which include GHG emissions disclosures by listed companies. Also, it has been working on establishing a voluntary code of conduct for ESG ratings and has asked product providers to raise governance, transparency, and the management of conflict of interest within the ecosystem. The SFC has worked hard to collaborate not only with local agencies but also with international bodies, for example, it is a very active member of such organisations as the International Organisation of Securities Commissions.[6]

A resource-rich, policy-poor nation: Australia

Another example of a national approach in climate action – policy first then rules-and-guidelines construction later – is Australia. It is an example of what not to do. Events in recent years in the country are evidence of the intersection of climate policy, climate business, and climate finance.

Australia should have long been a clean energy, green, sustainable, and decarbonisation leader, not just in Asia but globally.[7] Less fossil fuels and more renewables should have long been a national priority. Instead, it became a lagger due to a dearth of supportive federal government policies. However, the nine straight years of conservative, climate-denying government thankfully ended in May 2022.

Energy-wise, the nation is one of the richest in the world. Domestic advocates for the acceleration of decarbonisation in the country have faced formidable barriers over the past decade or so. These barriers have particularly included the fact that the country has massive reserves of fossil fuels, and that they have been vital resources for domestic energy production, and they have an outsized impact on the economy, particularly in terms of exports. Past governments had exploited this as an economic advantage. However, in today's world, where we are transitioning to a low-carbon economy, this blessing may have turned into a curse.[8]

With the sixth largest land mass on earth and a relatively small population, the country's renewable energy resources significantly surpass the national energy consumption requirements. Around the nation, it is easy to identify renewable energy resources, such as the many areas with strong wind speeds and high solar irradiation. At the same time, its 1 per cent global share of global emissions is tiny. Some numbers are helpful to put Australia in the global context.

Australia, also known as the Land of Plenty or the Lucky Country, had a population of about 26.5 million people in 2023. It accounted for just 0.3 per cent of the world's population (see Figure 6.3). Its GDP represented 1.6 per cent of global GDP, energy consumption was 1 per cent of the total, while its per capita energy consumption was almost 300 per cent higher than the world average, partly reflecting the fact that it is a developed economy.

	AUSTRALIA	WORLD
Population (millions)	26.5	8,090.0
GDP ($ billion)	1,728	106,170
Energy consumption (Exajoules)	6.0	619.6
Energy consumption/capita (Gigajoules)	227.6	76.6
Oil (%)	36.0	31.7
Coal (%)	25.1	26.5
Gas (%)	23.9	23.3
Renewables (%)	15.0	14.6
Nuclear (%)	-	4.0

Figure 6.3 Basic Australia and global energy statistics

Source: Calculation by author from data sourced from Energy Institute, 'Energy Institute Statistical Review of World Energy 2024' (Energy Institute Statistical Review of World Energy June 2024), as well as from worldmeters.info and tradingeconomics.com

Previous governments reduced the amount of fossil fuels in the pie but not as much as they could have – or should have. In its energy mix, the contribution of oil was 14 per cent higher than the global average, coal was 5 per cent lower, and natural gas was 3 per cent higher. Consumption from renewables was 3 per cent higher. Yet, the share of renewables should be much higher given its vast clean energy resources. How vast? Let's take its solar power potential. The nation's annual average solar energy is 58 million petajoules (over 16 million TWh) per year, roughly 10,000 times more than the nation's energy consumption, according to Geoscience Australia, an Australian government agency.[9]

The Australian renewables market sent negative market signals to investors for almost a decade. It suffered from a massive climate policy vacuum. The pre-2022 administration, a coalition led by the Liberal Party, was at the helm of the nation from 2013 and did not embrace climate change. The party's philosophy was to deny climate change. This has not changed now that the party is in opposition. Recently, for example, its climate change and energy spokesperson, Ted O'Brien, stated that it opposed the government's target to triple renewable energy by 2030.[10] When in government, it previously rescinded a carbon price mechanism, starting in 2013 – basically almost as soon as they came to power.[11] In 2015, the government carried out what some called greenwashing as it declared an emissions reduction goal of 26 to 28 per cent below 2005 levels by 2030. However, the goal included a carbon accounting loophole which led to widespread accusations that it was 'cheating' on the Paris Agreement, according to various media and independent analysis (the nation's climate action policies are further discussed in the next section).[12]

There was a significant shift post-2022 in terms of domestic investment in energy transition-related projects as well as the level of interest from foreign investors. The momentum was weak pre-2022 due to regulatory uncertainty. Post-2022, better regulatory visibility led to an increase in global capital as well as in project volume.

Tracking transparency in policy implementation

Government climate action policies must be clearly communicated to the market. A lack of transparency will raise the perceived investment risk. Investors expect the government to provide clear signals that it supports climate action and clear policies. It does not matter to the markets if the policies are at an early stage of development as long as the development process remains transparent through such mechanisms as regular private-public consultation. Failure to provide transparency has a variety of negative side effects. It can deter investment outright. It could mean that if the investment goes ahead, it will require a higher risk premium given the higher risk.

The global scorecard of government climate policies and real-world action has been poor. Despite most nations in the world agreeing in Paris in 2015 to limit climate warming to 1.5°C, the current trajectory is for a catastrophic 2.5°C.[13]

Putting this into context, the world is headed for a climate disaster. This is consistently being confirmed by a great many scientific reports. One of the many is the Emissions Gap Report 2023 by the UN Environment Programme issued just ahead of COP28.[14] The report offered several gloomy conclusions, including that 2022 emissions were record high, that NDCs hardly progressed in the previous year, and that if current policies are continued and no acceleration is undertaken, then the world will hit a 3°C increase.

The Climate Action Tracker was formed in the late 2000s by two nonprofit research organisations,[15] Climate Analytics and NewClimate Institute. The Climate Action Tracker's independent scientific analysis measures climate action by governments. It tracks the pledges of 39 countries which on a combined basis account for 85 per cent of global emissions, including the world's largest polluters and some smaller emitters as a representative sample.

The Climate Action Tracker assessed that none of the world's largest polluters had taken sufficient action in line with the Paris Agreement's goal of limiting warming to 1.5°C. As of March 2025, the organisation was pessimistic that the world will meet this goal. The Climate Action Tracker wrote that based on the current government-published pledges, the world is headed for a temperature rise of 2.5°C by 2100.

The actions of nine countries were assessed as being critically insufficient (see Figure 6.4). The actions of another six were highly insufficient, and those of 15, including the EU, were

CRITICALLY INSUFFICIENT	HIGHLY INSUFFICIENT	INSUFFICIENT	ALMOST SUFFICIENT	1.5°C PARIS AGREEMENT COMPATIBLE
Argentina	China	Australia	Bhutan	
Indonesia	Egypt	Brazil	Chile	
Iran	India	Canada	Costa Rica	
Mexico	New Zealand	Colombia	Ethiopia	
Russian Federation	Singapore	EU	Kenya	
Saudi Arabia	South Korea	Germany	Morocco	
Thailand		Japan	Nepal	
Türkiye		Kazakhstan	Nigeria	
Viet Nam		Peru	Norway	
		Philippines	The Gambia	
		South Africa		
		Switzerland		
		UAE		
		USA		
		United Kingdom		

Figure 6.4 Climate action tracker countries' thermometer

Notes: Highlighted countries are in the three regions of focus in this book, namely Asia, Europe, and North America.

Source: Climate Action Tracker, 'Climate Action Tracker: Countries' (Climateactiontracker.org December 2023). Available at: https://climateactiontracker.org/countries/ accessed 12 January 2024.

insufficient. Only ten had undertaken sufficient action; they include Bhutan, Chile, Costa Rica, Ethiopia, Kenya, Morocco, Nepal, Nigeria, Norway, and The Gambia.

Notes

1 C Figueres, 'The Inside Story of the Paris Climate Agreement' <https://www.ted.com/talks/christiana_figueres_the_inside_story_of_the_paris_climate_agreement/transcript> accessed 21 March 2025.

2 United Nations Framework Convention on Climate Change, *The Paris Agreement* (United Nations Climate Change 2015) <https://unfccc.int/process-and-meetings/the-paris-agreement> accessed 29 December 2023.

3 Hong Kong Monetary Authority, *Hong Kong Monetary Authority – Cross-Agency Steering Group Launches Its Strategic Plan to Strengthen Hong Kong's Financial Ecosystem to Support a Greener and More Sustainable Future* (Hong Kong Monetary Authority 17 December 2020) <https://www.hkma.gov.hk/eng/news-and-media/press-releases/2020/12/20201217-4/> accessed 8 February 2024.

4 The Government of the Hong Kong Special Administrative Region, 'LCQ22: Formulating Environmental, Social and Governance Standards' (www.info.gov.hk 12 July 2023) <https://www.info.gov.hk/gia/general/202307/12/P2023071200223.htm> accessed 8 February 2024.

5 Green and Sustainable Finance Cross-Agency Steering Group, 'Markets & Regulation | Hong Kong World's Sustainable Finance Hub' (sustainablefinance.org.hk 2021) <https://sustainablefinance.org.hk/en/markets-regulation> accessed 8 February 2024.

6 MPFA Channel, 'MPF Symposium (24 February 2025) (English Only)' (YouTube 16 April 2025) <https://www.youtube.com/watch?v=qUxhFRjyWzE> accessed 18 June 2025.

7 J Jacobelli, 'Australia Must Be a Decarbonisation Leader Not a Laggard' *The Energy Industry Times* (1 August 2021) 14.

8 J Jacobelli, 'Australia Must Be a Decarbonisation Leader Not a Laggard' *The Energy Industry Times* (1 August 2021) 14.

9 Geoscience Australia, 'Solar Energy' (Ga.gov.au 2019) <https://www.ga.gov.au/scientific-topics/energy/resources/other-renewable-energy-resources/solar-energy> accessed 10 January 2024.

10 A Morton, 'Coalition Opposes Australia Tripling Renewable Energy, Backs Nuclear Power Pledge at Cop28' *The Guardian* (9 December 2023) [online] <https://www.theguardian.com/australia-news/2023/dec/10/coalition-tells-cop28-it-will-tback-tripling-of-nuclear-energy-if-peter-dutton-becomes-prime-minister> accessed 21 January 2024.

11 Parliament of Australia, 'Carbon Price Repeal Bills: Quick Guide' (www.aph.gov.au 20 November 2013) <https://www.aph.gov.au/About_Parliament/Parliamentary_Departments/Parliamentary_Library/pubs/rp/rp1314/QG/CarbonPriceRepealBills> accessed 12 January 2024.

12 H Nott, 'Is Australia Really Meeting Its Kyoto and Paris Targets for Carbon Emission Reductions?' *Australian Associated Press* (31 January 2019) <https://www.aap.com.au/factcheck/is-australia-really-meeting-its-kyoto-and-paris-targets-for-carbon-emission-reductions/> accessed 12 January 2024; Climate Analytics, *No Legal Basis for Australia's Use of Kyoto Credits* (Climate Analytics 11 December 2019) <https://climateanalytics.org/press-releases/no-legal-basis-for-australias-use-of-kyoto-credits> accessed 12 January 2024.

13 The higher the number, the more severe the effects on people, wildlife, and ecosystems will be. An enormous amount of literature is available on the subject. One of the best-known sources is the Synthesis Report of the Sixth Assessment Report released by the Intergovernmental Panel on Climate Change on 22 March 2023 (see https://www.ipcc.ch/report/ar6/syr/).

14 United Nations Environment Programme, *Emissions Gap Report 2023: Broken Record – Temperatures Hit New Highs, yet World Fails to Cut Emissions (Again)* (United Nations Environment Programme 2023) Emissions Gap Report 2023: Broken Record© 2023 United <https://doi.org/10.59117/20.500.11822/43922> accessed 8 February 2024.

15 Climate Action Tracker, 'Climate Action Tracker: About' (Climateactiontracker.org 2016) [online] <https://climateactiontracker.org/about/> accessed 17 January 2024.

Chapter 7

Public policy

The many shades of green

Aims:

- Climate action initiatives across key areas in Asia, Europe, and North America.
- Overall trajectory and effectiveness of climate action efforts in the three key regions.
- Government approaches to addressing climate change in three key regions.

Lima, the capital of Peru, is famous for having some of the worst traffic congestion and heavy pollution. Back in 2010, the government brought in a law to try to make life easier for cyclists and get more people on their bikes. However, it did not work well. By 2019, less than 1 per cent of journeys in the city were being made by bicycle. Then COVID-19 hit, and suddenly nearly 100 kilometres of proper, separated cycle lanes were built, resulting in cycling popularity rising, with 6.2 per cent of trips being made by bike by 2021. The city planned to build over 1,300 kilometres of cycle paths by 2040.[1] The initial policy had the best of intentions but failed to deal with the practical problems. Once the practical problems were understood and addressed, the policy became a success.

There are many shades of green in terms of transition-related climate actions in the three largest continents. Understanding these different shades of green will support evaluating the general trajectory of climate action over the next few years together with some of the most likely steps. We specifically focus on three continents: Asia, Europe, and North America, because it is these three regions that most urgently need effective climate action by governments, as they are the key global emitters of GHGs around the world.

To put this into context, globally 23 economies accounted for about 80 per cent of emissions in 2023, based on calculations from data from the European Union (see Figure 7.1). A total of 17 economies of the 23 belong to one of these three continents. These 17 are responsible for almost half of global emissions and for over 84 per cent of the total GHGs from these 23 economies. The worst culprits are China, which was responsible for 30.8 per cent of the total, the United States accounting for over 11.5 per cent, and India making up 8 per cent.

The direction, structure, and pace of government climate action witnessed in Europe versus North America are markedly different. Europe is by far the most advanced of the regions. It has been the gold standard, the pioneer, and the pathfinder when it comes to climate action. The divergence between Europe and North America, on the one hand, and Asia on the other, is even more astounding. On average, governments in the Asia region have been laggards. To comprehend the big picture in each of the regions, specific economies,

DOI: 10.4324/9781003666509-9

COUNTRY IN 2023	PERCENTAGE OF GLOBAL GHGS	ASIA	EUROPE	NORTH AMERICA
China	30.83%	■		
United States	11.53%			■
India	7.99%	■		
Russia	5.17%			
Brazil	2.51%			
Indonesia	2.32%	■		
Japan	2.01%	■		
Iran	1.93%			
Saudi Arabia	1.56%			
Canada	1.45%			■
Mexico	1.38%			■
Germany	1.32%		■	
South Korea	1.26%	■		
Türkiye	1.17%		■	
Australia	1.11%	■		
Pakistan	1.03%	■		
Viet Nam	1.01%	■		
South Africa	1.01%			
Thailand	0.85%	■		
France and Monaco	0.75%		■	
Nigeria	0.74%			
United Kingdom	0.73%		■	
Italy, San Marino / Holy See	0.72%		■	
COUNTRIES TOTAL	**23**	**9**	**5**	**3**
GHGS TOTAL	**80.38%**	**48.42%**	**4.69%**	**14.35%**

Figure 7.1 Greenhouse gases (GHGs) emissions of top 80 per cent global emitters

Notes: This is a work derived by the author from European Union material and the author is solely liable, and responsible for this derived work. The derived work is not endorsed by the European Union in any manner.

Source: European Commission, 'EDGAR - the Emissions Database for Global Atmospheric Research' (Europa.eu 2024. Available at: https://edgar.jrc.ec.europa.eu/report_2024 accessed 30 July 2025.

or group of economies, have been selected. Five areas are used to grasp the general trends in Asia: ASEAN,[2] Australia, China, Japan, and India. For Europe, the European Union 27 (EU27) in addition to one ex-EU member, the United Kingdom, was singled out. For North America, the most representative economy is the United States as it is by far the largest and most important economy in that region.

To provide a concise overview of the current state of global climate action across various jurisdictions, the analysis presents a selection of illustrative examples rather than an exhaustive list. The objective is to offer a snapshot of current initiatives to enable one to estimate the overall trajectory of climate action efforts. In essence, only a curated selection is examined, akin to a tasting menu, instead of the full breadth of the climate action buffet.

Asian climate policies range far and wide

Asia is the biggest region in the world demographically, economically, and in terms of energy. It is the most populous continent in the world by a very large margin. The region, including South Asia and the Pacific, accounts for between 50 per cent and 60 per cent of the world's population, depending on how the region is defined. It is especially diverse in terms of population, culturally, geographically, and in terms of political systems. The region contains the world's two most populated nations, China and India. It also includes some of the world's smallest populations, including Nauru, Tuvalu, and Palau, which have a combined population of 42,000, as of 2022. The landmass of each of the three nations – Australia, China, and India – ranks among the seven biggest in the world. They have some of the oldest cultures

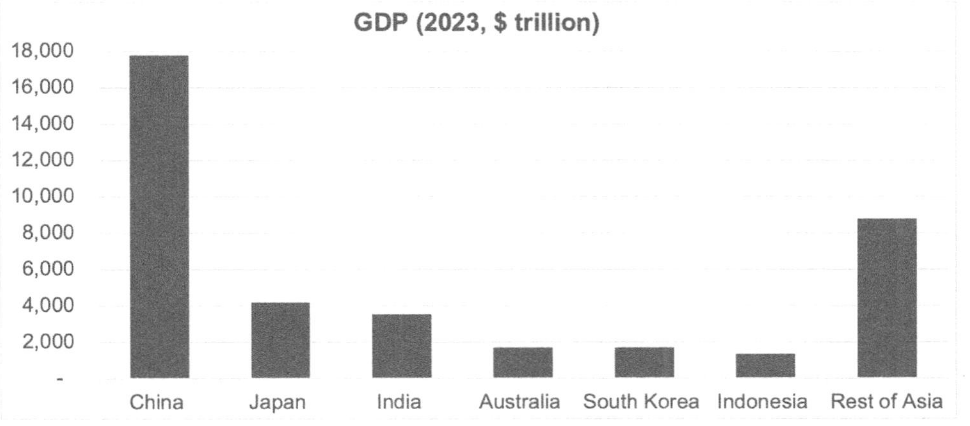

Figure 7.2 Asia Pacific's largest nations by GDP

Source: Trading Economics. https://tradingeconomics.com/matrix?g=asia; https://tradingeconomics.com/matrix?g=australia

on earth, a multitude of religions, and a countless number of languages and dialects. Politically, they range from absolute monarchies to military dictatorships to liberal democracies.

Economically, the majority of the population in the region lives in developing economies. The only developed ones are Australia, Japan, New Zealand, Singapore, and, some argue, South Korea. It is in most of these jurisdictions that we find more progressive governmental climate action. The largest six nations accounted for over 77 per cent of the region's combined 2023 GDP. They include China, Japan, India, Australia, South Korea, and Indonesia (see Figure 7.2).

A variety of examples of climate action by the governments of ASEAN, Australia, China, Japan, and India provide a helpful and practical window as to the developments in the region in general.

ASEAN: surprisingly coordinated on some fronts

The climate action scorecard of ASEAN member nations is quite eclectic. One of the ways, albeit a simplistic one, to compare and contrast climate action of governments is the number of submissions to the NDCs registry of the United Nations Framework Convention on Climate Change (see Figure 7.3). Through submissions and updates, individual countries communicate to the UNFCCC the nation's climate action ambitions aimed at cutting their GHG emissions to meet the Paris Agreement's targets. Singapore, Thailand, and Vietnam have been the most active nations within ASEAN. The three members have had three submissions each. This is quite a high number given that only Australia, Brazil, and Japan have had more – four each. Cambodia, Laos, Malaysia, and Myanmar had two. Brunei and the Philippines only had one. Still, the net-zero emissions target year for most is 2050. Indonesia set 2060 and Thailand set 2065. Myanmar and the Philippines are lagging behind. They had not submitted a target as of January 2024. The NGO Climate Action Tracker only assesses five out of the ten member states. It found the announced climate action plans of Indonesia, Singapore, Thailand, and Vietnam to be critically insufficient, while those of the Philippines were insufficient. The scorecard of Indonesia and Vietnam is surprising and that of Myanmar and the Philippines is even more surprising given that these four nations are amongst the most susceptible in the world to climate change-induced natural hazards.[3]

	Version	Date	Latest	Target	Climate Action Tracker
Brunei Darussalam	1	30.12.20	First NDC	2050	N/A
Cambodia	2	31.12.20	Updated submission	2050	N/A
Indonesia	3	23.9.22	Enhanced NDC	2060	Critically Insufficient
Laos	2	11.5.21	Updated submission	2050	N/A
Malaysia	2	30.7.21	Updated submission	2050	N/A
Myanmar	2	3.8.21	Updated submission	No Target	N/A
Philippines	1	12.4.21	First NDC	No Target	Insuffient
Singapore	3	4.11.22	Second Update of First NDC	2050	Critically Insufficient
Thailand	3	2.11.22	Second Updated NDC	2065	Critically Insufficient
Vietnam	3	8.11.22	2022 update	2050	Critically Insufficient

Figure 7.3 ASEAN members' climate action summary profile

Notes: This is a work derived by the author from the UNFCCC and from the Climate Action Tracker material and the author is solely liable and responsible for this derived work. The derived work is not endorsed by the UNFCCC and the Climate Action Tracker in any manner.

Sources: Columns 1-3: United Nations Framework Convention on Climate Change (2024). Nationally Determined Contributions Registry. [online] Unfccc.int). Available at: https://unfccc.int/NDCREG accessed 24 January 2024.; Columns 4-5: Climate Action Tracker (n.d.). Net Zero Targets. [online] climateactiontracker.org). Available at: https://climateactiontracker.org/countries/ accessed 21 January 2022]; various public media.

While the climate action scorecard of ASEAN governments is not bright, the same cannot be said about the strong collaboration and cooperation when it comes to key regulatory financial institutions. They have made significant advances in a short period of time by aligning transition-related rules and regulations. The result is the equivalent of inviting three dozen people for a meal and expecting them all to consume exactly the same type and volume of food. Quite an unlikely feat. Getting ten central banks, monetary authorities, and other national financial institutions to all agree not just about one but on several parameters is a great achievement. Specifically, ASEAN created a taxonomy board through four sectoral bodies related to each nation's banking, capital markets, and insurance sectors. The taxonomy is an essential guide and is imperative for the identification and classification of green and sustainable plans, projects, and the like. A green taxonomy itself only provides the criteria for what should be considered green. It does not imply the legal enforcement of green project compliance. However, it is the basis of such compliance. The legal enforcement will occur through various measures such as legislation, regulation, and reporting requirements, for example. The tough part was for all of the various representatives to agree on common points which could be applied throughout ASEAN.

The taxonomy was driven by the member states' public institutions responsible for national monetary affairs, including monetary policy and money supply, such as the central banks and finance ministries. The ASEAN Taxonomy Board published the second version of its taxonomy for sustainable finance in 2023.[4] It produced a presentation,[5] which summarised the taxonomy and underlined some key takeaways. It highlighted the reasons for its need, its importance, and its utility. Some of the most salient points are worthy of mention. The common taxonomy prevents the regional approach from being fragmented and it raises investor confidence by providing clarity to them. It is important because it consolidates the efforts of a great number of different institutions, and it gives all states a common and united ASEAN voice. Other points the Board correctly publicised are that in addition to raising investor confidence, it is of utmost importance for domestic and other financial institutions active in the ASEAN region as it allows them to better navigate the rules and regulations. It also provides them with the ability to gauge climate and sustainability risks related to lending and investment activities. Finally, it drives a more coherent policymaking at the national level.

The Board mentioned that the taxonomy is a living document. In fact, the first version was released in August 2022, the second version in March 2023, and an update to that version was published in June 2023.[6] The taxonomy, just like the energy transition, is far from static. It is consistently and constantly evolving.

One final area worthy of mention for our understanding of what is happening in the ASEAN region is some of the themes that the Board is pursuing. The region is keen to ensure that the ASEAN Taxonomy is aligned with national ones and that it is strongly correlated, or at least, is interoperable with taxonomies elsewhere in the world, such as with that of the EU. It also stressed that the data must be available, transparent, and of high quality.

The taxonomy also tries to be more accessible as green taxonomies can sometimes be daunting. It adopted a traffic light approach: Green as Tier One, Amber as Tier Two, and Red as Tier Three, as a classification system for the evaluation of the sustainability level of a particular economic activity (see Figure 7.4). The activity must contribute to one of four

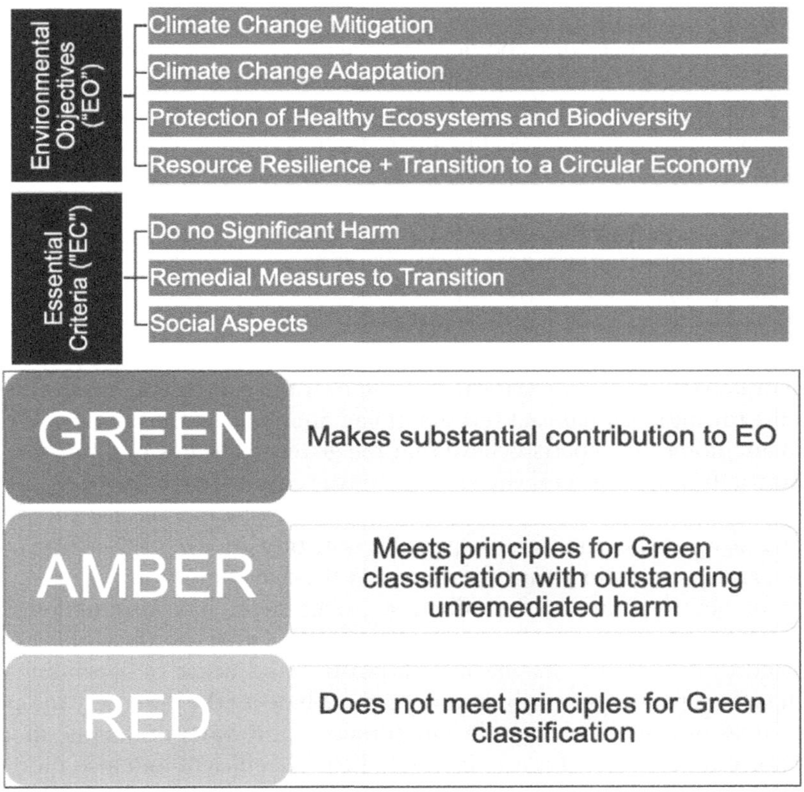

Figure 7.4 ASEAN Taxonomy Version 2: classification framework

Notes: This is a work derived by the author from Rajah & Tann Asia material and the author is solely liable and responsible for this derived work. The derived work is not endorsed by Rajah & Tann Asia in any manner.

Source: Rajah & Tann Asia (2023). Regional Sustainability Update: ASEAN Taxonomy V2 – Enabling a Just Transition Towards Sustainable Finance Adoption by ASEAN. [online] Rajah & Tann Asia, pp.2–3). Available at: https://www.ahp.id/clientalert/2023_04_ASEAN-Taxonomy-V2-Enabling-Just-Transition.pdf accessed28 January 2024. Rajah & Tann Asia is a network of legal practices in Asia.

environmental objectives as well as meet several critical criteria. To be labelled Green, the activity must produce a substantial contribution to an environmental objective. At the other extreme, to be labelled Red, the economic activity does not meet any of the principles for green classification.

Australia: getting its act together . . . finally

In the case of ASEAN, the climate action regulatory snapshot was the NDCs of member states and the coordinated establishment of a harmonised ASEAN taxonomy for sustainable finance. In the case of Australia, the nation's NDC and evaluation of primary climate action, including institutional formation, are profiled.

Australia suffered a major national policy vacuum due to the previous climate change-denying government. Since the election of the new pro-climate leadership in May 2022, the Albanese government, strong climate action policies are being executed. The government promulgated the Climate Change Act 2022 and the Climate Change (Consequential Amendments) Act 2022 in September 2022. It also established a 'super' ministry in July 2022, the Department of Climate Change, Energy, the Environment and Water (DCCEEW).

The Climate Change Act 2022 codified Australia's NDC commitments. It set itself to cut emissions to 43 per cent from 2005 levels by 2030 and reach net zero by 2050. The government highlighted some of the impacts of the emissions cut target. Federal or State projects and contracts would see an increase in climate-related clauses. There could be an increase in ESG-linked pricing for debt-financing as the financing can be linked to emissions reductions; whereby, if they are not achieved, the interest rate may rise. Government departments' focus on approving projects will be increased which will help with the reduction target and expand emissions reduction reporting obligations.[7]

The Climate Action Tracker's overall rating of Australia's climate action efforts is poor. Its policies and actions against the model domestic pathways point to a 3°C world and are thus insufficient.[8] Those of its NDC target are rated almost sufficient, pointing to a 2°C world. The organisation is quite critical because it evaluates that the government failed to deliver despite the initial climate actions that it had announced. The Climate Action Tracker as well as many domestic experts believe that the government has been far too kind to the fossil fuel sector. It offered several suggestions for the country to improve its climate action. These include less reliance on carbon offsets, stopping fossil fuels sector support, speeding up fossil fuel power generation plants phasing out, transitioning the nation's industry to new exports, and encouraging transportation sector decarbonisation.

Apart from new legislation, the Albanese government has also undertaken institutional changes. One was the creation of the DCCEEW. The response to the creation of the DCCEEW and to its activities has been both positive and negative depending on whether the reaction is from pro- or anti-Albanese corners. Whatever the difference in opinions, putting the key areas of climate, energy, the environment, and water under one single umbrella makes an enormous amount of sense. It should be more efficient and also more effective in executing policies. The DCCEEW unsurprisingly faces many challenges. Some are legacy ones due to the inaction from the many previous conservative governments for nearly a decade. Others are due to a multitude of factors, including the strong lobbying muscle of the fossil-fuel industry.

The DCCEEW has publicised several clear mandates and just over 16 months from its establishment, it was subject to a detailed audit. The Department had clearly publicised its purposes. Among these, some of the more significant ones were to push climate action, enable the energy system to transition, and encourage net-zero emissions while preserving its 'affordability, security, and reliability', as well as protecting and sustainably managing environmental resources.[9] Despite its short life, the DCCEEW has revealed several initiatives. Two examples are 'Rewiring the Nation' and the 'Capacity Investment Scheme'. The former aims at raising the accessibility and affordability of clean energy nationwide and invests A$20 billion ($13 billion) to upgrade the nation's power grid.[10] The latter aims at attracting new capital into renewable and clean dispatchable capacity. It will use competitive tender bids for projects amounting to 32 GW by 2030, fill any gap created by the shutting of coal-fired power plants, and support the national, ambitious yet achievable, 82 per cent of electricity from renewables target by 2030.[11]

Australia's independent audit authority, the Australian National Audit Office, published a report titled 'Governance of Climate Change Commitments' with the results of an independent performance audit of the DCCEEW in October 2023. The office found three issues. The measures to support the execution of the government's climate change action were only partly effective. Key strategies, plans, and others had not been delivered for use. Lastly, the Department was unable to show its level of contribution to the total emissions reduction. The office also publicised five recommendations, all of which were accepted by the DCCEEW, including developing a framework to measure the DCCEEW's contribution to the national emissions cut objectives, for example.[12]

The Albanese government also strengthened existing climate change related institutions such as the Climate Change Authority, the Australian Climate Service, and the Clean Energy Finance Corporation. It also set up Environment Information Australia, part of DCCEEW, to be the source of nationwide environmental data and information. It is also in the process of creating a national environmental agency, the Environment Protection Australia.[13]

Japan: from laggard to leader?

The third largest economy in the world, Japan, holds a significant position in the global energy transition discourse. It is a key energy market in the Asian and global contexts as well. The country's approach to addressing climate change raises various important considerations. These include queries about the declared national priorities, additional priorities that might exist, the policies that have been promoted, any priority areas that may have been overlooked, the effectiveness of policy implementation, the specific objectives set, the progress made so far, and the projected outcomes leading up to 2050.

The Japanese government's primary concern and national priority has been energy supply security for many decades. Transitioning away from fossil fuels would address this concern as clean energy can be produced domestically without the need to import any type of energy commodity. The various energy crises of 1973, 1979, 2008, and 2021 put a strain on the global supply of energy commodities. Oil prices increased sharply in the first three crises. The price of all three fossil fuel commodities shot up during the 2021 crisis. The fact that all of its fossil fuel energy resources are transported by ship, together with strained geopolitical relations with China and a volatile North Korea are factors that arouse domestic energy-supply concerns. Following the first energy crisis, the nation diligently tried to diversify its energy resources. Oil as a percentage of total energy consumption dropped to a share of 37 per cent in 2022 from about 77 per cent in 1973. That of coal rose to almost 28 per cent from about 16 per cent. That of natural gas jumped to over 20 per cent from just over 1 per cent. Oil replacement was also helped by nuclear energy which accounted for less than 1 per cent in 1973 and reached a high of over 13 per cent in 2010, the year before the disastrous Fukushima Daiichi Nuclear Power Plant accident on 11 March 2011.

Another priority that is not highlighted as often as energy security is the country's economic exposure to volatile oil, gas, and coal prices and the very high price residential, commercial, and industrial users have to pay. The nation spends over a hundred billion dollars in energy commodities imports every year. The more renewable energy replaces fossil fuels, the lower the import bill and the exposure to price fluctuations. Yet the approach by various Japanese administrations has been weak, despite the fact that currently the bulk of the nation's power comes from imported fossil fuels which have seen sharp volatility in recent years, especially after Russia's invasion of Ukraine. Their feeble attempts are surprising given that renewable energy can help the nation to attain energy independence. It would not only raise energy security but also lead to lower and less volatile electric power prices for consumers. A study by the Renewable Energy Institute showed that Japan has the potential for solar PV capacity to rise 3.5 times by 2035 from the 2023 levels to 280 GW, and for wind power to increase 13 times to 60 GW. The increase could lead to 80 per cent of electricity supply from clean energy. Also, it could drive down prices. Estimating the average electricity bill for end users is complex as Japan is an open and competitive market. For reference, and to give a flavour of the levels, retail prices for households – which are typically higher than those for commercial and industrial users – in the greater Tokyo area stood at about 28,879 ($195.15) per MWh as of January 2024.[14]

Examining wholesale market prices reported by the Japan Electric Power Exchange provides an idea (see Figure 7.5). The highest level (taking out an anomaly of 63,070 yen ($426.21) per MWh in January 2021) was 26,190 yen ($176.98) in March 2022, and the lowest 4,310 yen ($29.13) was achieved in July 2020. As of June 2024, it stood at 10,200

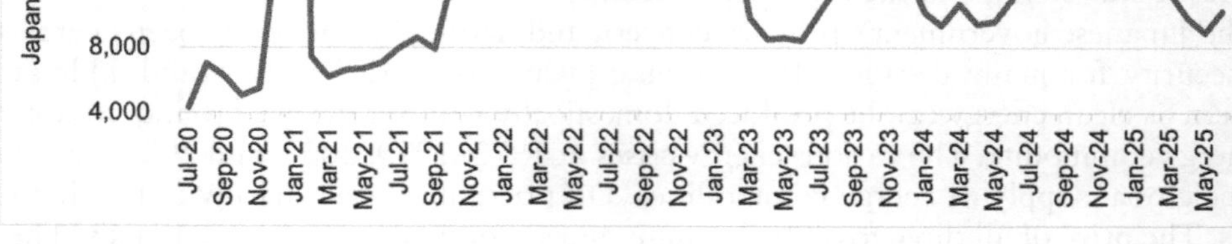

Figure 7.5 Japan Electric Power Exchange average monthly system prices

Notes: Total system price day ahead market.

Source: Japan Electric Power Exchange, 'Day Ahead Market | Trading Market Data | Trading Information | JEPX' (www.jepx.jp 2 May 2024). Available at: https://www.jepx.jp/en/electricpower/market-data/spot/ave_month.html accessed 2 May 2024.

yen ($68.93).[15] A massive volatility. The Institute estimated that the cost of solar PV by 2030 would be about 5,000 yen ($33.79), onshore wind power should be around 6,600 yen ($44.60), and offshore wind could be less than 10,000 yen ($67.58).

The government has not been as aggressive as it should be in its promotion of climate action. It submitted its first intended NDC in July 2015. Its last update was submitted to the UNFCCC secretariat in October 2021. Between the first submission and the latest one, the NDC target was raised to 46 per cent below 2013 levels by 2030, from 26 per cent. In early 2023, government issued the Green Transformation Basic Policy. Two measures of this policy were bond issuance and carbon pricing. It wanted to issue sovereign green bonds, the Japan Climate Transition Bonds, worth some 20 trillion yen ($135 billion) over a period of ten years which would be a market catalyst to achieve 150 trillion yen ($1.01 trillion) in private-public energy-transition investments. A second measure was the implementation of growth-oriented carbon pricing. This involves charging some formal carbon tax on imported fossil fuels from fiscal 2028 and also the start of emissions trading scheme called the green transition (or GX) Emissions Trading Scheme which began operations in fiscal 2023.

Together with many others, the Climate Action Tracker finds that government policy and other climate action overly prioritise economic growth and energy security, with insufficient emphasis on more aggressive decarbonisation efforts. In fact, overall climate action has been weak and a disappointment to most experts, and to many who follow the Japanese energy sector. Japan continues to heavily rely on fossil fuels for its energy, and the development of renewable energy has been slow. Mika Ohbayashi, a Director at Japanese think tank Renewable Energy Institute, is one of many experts who staunchly believes Japan can do much better and potentially become an energy transition leader.[16] The Institute is an organisation focused on renewable energy policy research because it believes that Japan has the financial capital, the human capital, and the technology to advance renewable energy. Unfortunately, a big problem is there is a lack of policies to implement renewables, Obayashi said in a podcast in early 2023. She believes that even when Japan decided to pursue offshore wind more aggressively, the amount installed has proven to be small, especially when compared to what neighbour China has managed to achieve. It is worth noting that when it was declared at COP28 that the world would triple its renewable energy capacity and double the rate of energy efficiency by 2030, the Japanese government did not as of May 2024 declare a sharp uptake of clean energy in the country.

In terms of energy transition solutions, Japan has overestimated the role that nuclear power, CCUS, and green hydrogen will play. All three of these solutions are more geared towards the long term. Of the three technologies, only nuclear energy is currently economically viable whereas the two other solutions would be at a high cost per unit of energy supplied, when compared to renewable energy solutions even when coupled with energy storage.

Japan also wants to export its green transformation policy, an international strategy it calls the Asia Zero Emission Community (AZEC) announced in January 2022. AZEC seems difficult to implement according to many experts including Teruyuki Ohno, an Executive Director at the Renewable Energy Institute.[17] AZEC revolves around the Japanese government's aim to support Asian countries in their decarbonisation. Ohno is sceptical on the government's game plan of realising carbon reductions and also on its economic viability. He highlights that on paper AZEC is dedicated to supporting Asian countries, particularly Southeast Asia, with their renewable energy deployment. However, the government's administration and the Ministry of Economy, Trade and Industry erroneously believe that

Southeast Asia's renewable energy resources potential is too small. For example, the minutes of one of the Ministry's subcommittees emphasised that 'the fast-growing economies in Asia are forced to use fossil fuels, a major source of greenhouse emissions, but also a region with large CO_2 sequestration potential'. It is an erroneous starting point because government has used this thesis for promoting CCS. In other words, converting existing thermal power plants into zero emissions plants by capturing the carbon emitted and storing it, as well as using coal-ammonia co-firing; this involves using ammonia to replace some of the coal and then burning the ammonia together with the coal. Actually, environmentally, this process does not substantially reduce emissions and would still produce emissions higher than gas power plants.

The world should be phasing out fossil fuel generation in the 2030s, but this is not Japan's vision. There is a cost issue. Thermal coal generation in Southeast Asia is already more expensive than solar PV, for example. Using CCS or Ammonia, which are technically complicated and expensive technologies, would render the cost per unit of output extremely expensive, at least 20,000 yen ($135) per MWh in Japan. Ohno also questions whether this can be done at scale. On CCS, he thinks that while it could make sense for some hard-to-abate sectors, government targeting coal-fired power plants generation with CCS accounting for 30 per cent of the electricity mix makes little sense. In addition, Japan would have to find storage sites. Something not realistic in a country with limited suitable sites. Of course, it could be exported to Southeast Asia or Australia, but this would create another set of technical and financial challenges. Mathematically, it would mean that Japan would have to export a massive amount of its stored emissions, potentially around one-quarter or so.

China: a global green leader

The global shift to green is rich in massive and complex topics. China's climate action, though, may certainly be among the most sizeable and complicated of the topics, especially given its global role as the world's clean energy leader. One perspective is to scrutinise the topic through the lens of track record rather than just publicised policies and objectives. As well as from the nation's own lens. This includes examining domestic priorities, the policy landscape and likely developments, involvement in international dialogues, and major domestic challenges.

The domestic priorities are not too different from those of other large energy-consuming nations such as the United States or block of nations such as the EU: economic growth, jobs, and energy security. Today, China has established a gigantic renewable energy manufacturing capacity. It is the world's largest producer of solar PV systems, wind turbines, and lithium-ion batteries, for example. This capability did not exist just a few decades ago. It appeared in the 2000s and began to rapidly grow in the 2010s. Initially, it was less a manifestation of environmental considerations or national climate action. It was just another export-oriented industrial sector that the country could advance to spur economic growth and create new jobs. Also, the first development of domestic renewable energy manufacturing capacity revolved around solar PV and was driven by 'returning entrepreneurs' who borrowed funds from local banks with the support of local administrations. At the time, the sector was not dominated by State Owned Enterprises and was not 'the realisation of strategic central government industrial policy'.[18] That came later with the wind sector and then the energy storage industry. By the 2010s, the importance of renewables as a long-term solution for energy security was becoming increasingly obvious. Until the 1980s, nearly all of domestic electric power was produced from domestic thermal coal. China is convinced that a heavy reliance on coal-fired generation is no longer a viable long-term solution. Planners now want to rely on clean energies including nuclear power, solar, and wind. Its clean energy equipment leadership together with its publicised climate action should mean China will continue to build non-fossil fuel generation capacity rapidly in the coming years.

China's policy landscape has perhaps not been well-advertised by government entities. Its climate action is well aligned with those of other energy transition leading nations. However, it is currently rated highly insufficient though by Climate Action Tracker Initiative.[19] Since September 2020, it has undertaken to reach carbon emissions peak before 2030 and then reach carbon neutrality before 2060. It submitted these goals in its updated NDC to the UNFCCC in 2021. Consultancy DNV[20] projected that peak carbon could be reached as early as 2026 in a 2024 report. Something which is highly possible but in part dependent on the growth trajectory of the Chinese economy. In its March 2024 Report on the Work of Government (Work Report), Premier Li Qiang maintained or reinforced the nation's existing climate action. The 13,700-word English translation of the Work Report directly mentions 'green' 15 times, the 'environment' 23 times, and 'carbon' 25 times. It also directly referred to climate-related action multiple times. The Work Report dedicated a whole section to '[Enhancing] ecological conservation and promoting green and low-carbon development'. This underlined the government's absolute focus and commitment in growing the green low-carbon economy. It said that

> [China] will advance the energy revolution, tighten control over fossil fuels consumption, and work faster to develop a new energy system. We will step up the building of large-scale wind and photovoltaic power bases and transmission routes and promote the development and use of distributed energy sources. We will enhance power grids' capacity for absorbing, distributing, and regulating clean energy and create new ways of storing energy and encourage the use and international mutual recognition of green electricity. We will see that coal and coal-fired power play their crucial role in ensuring energy supply and our energy supply meets the needs of economic and social development.[21]

This long quote is important because it clarifies what China is working on. The Work Report is always quite carefully crafted and typically includes objectives and policies which are actually already being successfully implemented.

DNV also expects that the share of renewable energy in the total electric power generation capacity of 8.7 TW by 2050 would increase to 88 per cent.[22] The combined share of solar and wind power will rise to 77 per cent by 2050 from 50 per cent in 2030 and 30 per cent in 2022. The most high-profile point of contention, which has drawn much criticism by international observers, is coal plants which will be built at an annual rate of 20 GW or so between 2020 and 2029. The total will begin to phase down in the 2030s and start phasing out in the 2040s. Coal capacity, DNV estimates, should account for 13 per cent of the total but just 3 per cent of output. The current idea is twofold: the plants will be modern and efficient, and their rate of utilisation will be low as they will mostly be used to stabilise the grid. DNV's other important projections are that oil consumption will peak in 2027, that natural gas usage will peak in the 2030s, and that the nation will proactively use its carbon markets.

China's climate action faces major domestic challenges. It needs to build more energy supply given new demand as its economy progressively matures. It must build massive amounts of clean energy capacity. It must raise the level of electrification of the transportation, buildings, and industrial sectors. All this expansion will also require the country to at least double the size of its transmission and distribution grid networks. It plans to seek additional solutions, more advances in the mainstream clean energy technologies, such as higher efficiency solar panels or offshore wind turbines, as well as introducing other new clean energy technologies, such as green hydrogen, new energy storage solutions, new digital tools, including AI-driven ones, and many other areas.

The country is extremely well-positioned for its climate action to leap forward, thanks to the consistent, and relatively transparent, government policy. This is also aided by its dominance of clean technologies value chains including energy storage, EVs, solar, and wind. It dominates this space because today it manufactures products of high quality, and can produce these technologies at scale, and at attractive prices, notes consultancy Wood Mackenzie.[23]

India: the waking energy consumption giant

India is another key actor in Asia's energy consumption. While the nation is similar in population size to China, the economies of the two are sizeably different. For example, when looking at electric power generation, China's output is massively larger than India's. India generated 1,958 TWh in 2023, about one-fifth that of China's 9,456 TWh, which represents 31.6 per cent of the world's total versus just 6.5 per cent for India.

The nation's domestic priority in energy is similar to that of other sectors: economic growth. The current national government administration has been re-elected for a third term. The focus of the Indian government which was re-elected for a third term in June 2024 should continue to be to turn India into one of the world's economic powerhouses. In fact, several organisations project that it will become the world's third largest economy by the early 2030s. To achieve this, much effort has been spent by the Modi government on stimulating economic growth – including attracting foreign direct investment, financial inclusion initiatives, and infrastructure development – reducing bureaucratic hurdles for business, and tax reforms. Growing electric power generation capacity to fuel this growth is quintessential. Historically, the priority has been on building coal-fired power plants, though recently it has wanted to accelerate the pace of renewables additions. Internationally, India has been wanting to be portrayed as a green agenda champion, especially since the fall of 2023 when it hosted the G20 summit, though it failed to clarify its position on coal generation, which not only dominates its electricity mix but also is likely to continue to do so in the short term, based on current national electricity plans.

The nation's NDC calls for reaching net zero by 2070, 20 years beyond most large economies and 10 years after China. The Climate Action Tracker assessed that the policies necessary to drive its target were lacking as of the end of 2023. It found that there was 'no information or underlying analysis available on the anticipated pathway or measures to achieve net-zero emissions'.[24] An example of the lack of transparency is with regard to the percentage of clean energy output. In its 2022 NDC update, the government announced that it targeted a cumulated installed capacity from non-fossil fuel sources of 50 per cent by 2030. The generation output from one MW of wind or solar power is significantly lower than that from coal or gas power, so the installed capacity numbers are not as relevant and meaningful as the share in the percentage of generation. On the plus side, this target has progressively increased since its initial commitments made in 2015. An article by the Centre on Global Energy Policy at Columbia University cited an estimate from the Central

Electricity Authority of the Ministry of Power that the share would be at least 64 per cent, and noted that 60 per cent was highly achievable.[25]

The consultancy Wood Mackenzie offered an evaluation on how India can effectively action its climate policies through four steps. It suggests that, firstly, the nation must leverage one of its greatest assets, its vast human resources. It should be more aggressive in its use of renewable energy and other low-carbon technologies and cut its dependence on coal and oil. It should also redesign its economy, energy system, and bureaucracy to attract the private sector so that a public–private partnership can drive the green agenda faster. Finally, it could aggressively pursue international cooperation and partnerships to build out its domestic energy transition.[26]

Rapidly building new capacity to meet peak demand could be the biggest challenge for India over the next 25 years or so. Driving strong economic growth and aggressive decarbonisation at the same time is a challenge faced by most developing countries. Given the nation's size and relatively low generating capacity for the size of its economy, the challenge will be even more massive for India. Global investment bank Goldman Sachs does not believe the nation's decarbonisation goals will easily be met in the short- to medium term.[27] It argues that it will be difficult to meet peak demand. It estimates about 47 GW in peak power demand shortfall by the fiscal year 2032 (March 2033). It underlined that the peak shortage gap of 9 GW seen in the previous ten years may progressively worsen; during the period, the country added about 71 GW while peak demand rose by 80 GW. Not all experts necessarily share this opinion, but it is a potential challenge nonetheless if clean energy generation coupled with energy storage is not rapidly built.

India faces a unique challenge in balancing economic growth with its climate action goals. Ensuring a prosperous economy without a significant increase in energy consumption or carbon footprint is a critical hurdle. No other nation must navigate this delicate balance on so massive a scale.

Europe: the uniting union

Climate action by the member states of the EU has been far from perfect. Yet, despite its numerous imperfections, it has nonetheless proven excellent, even becoming best-in-class based on its track record. As an article by C Dupont et al. rightly states, 'the [EU] portfolio of domestic climate mitigation policy measures is one of the most advanced in the world . . . [and]. . . the EU has long aimed to be an exemplary climate policy and governance leader'. The group has made enormous progress in a wide variety of areas, even considering the challenge of catering to the diverse needs of its 27 member states. Four key areas can be evaluated to understand the current state of climate policy and the energy transition in the region. The history of climate action in the EU is rich and complex, offering valuable lessons for other countries and regions. The policies implemented have led to a significant number of successes in the past two and a half decades. At the same time, some of these policies have drawn criticism both within and outside the EU, and some of the targeted future climate actions face significant challenges.

Long timeline

The year 2025 marks the 35th anniversary of the EU's climate policy formulation. This journey began in 1990 when the issue of climate change was first brought to the attention of the European Council. The path towards implementing measures to combat climate change has not been straightforward. It has been filled with challenges and obstacles. Despite this, the EU has managed to launch a significant number of initiatives that positively impact the climate, setting a pace that outstrips many other regions.

A brief overview of these progressive steps best illustrates the positive actions taken[28]:

- **1990.** The 1990 IPCC report triggered climate policy dialogues, including cutting GHG emissions, raising energy efficiency, and building renewable energy capacity.
- **1991.** 'Specific Actions for Vigorous Energy Efficiency' programme launched.
- **1992.** Common standards for key electric appliances adopted.
- **1993.** Member states required to limit GHG emissions and promote renewable energy.
- **1997.** Adoption of Kyoto Protocol commitment to reduce emissions in a basket of six GHGs by 8 per cent.
- **2003.** Creation of a scheme for GHG emission allowance trading within the community, the EU Emissions Trading System.
- **2007.** '20-20-20 by 2020' goal for GHG emissions (cut of 20 per cent vs. 1990 levels), renewable energy (20 per cent of total energy consumption), and energy efficiency (increase of 20 per cent).
- **2014.** New targets set for cutting GHG emissions, raising energy efficiency, and additional renewable energy capacity by 2030.

Subsequently, two programmes involving a series of legislative proposals were introduced. The 'Clean Energy for all Europeans' package was released in 2016 and adopted in 2019. In 2021, the 'Fit for 55' plan was proposed. This package was part of the European Green Deal, a set of policies aimed at putting the EU 'on the path to a green transition, with the ultimate goal of reaching climate neutrality by 2050'.[29] The 'Clean Energy for all Europeans' included directives related to emissions trading, energy efficiency, renewable energy, and energy performance of buildings. New regulations were introduced on effort sharing, 'Land Use, Land Use Change and Forestry' (LULUCF), governance, and, in 2019, the electricity markets. The other was the 'Fit for 55' and covered a new emissions trading system for transport and buildings, a carbon border adjustment mechanism. It set directives on energy efficiency, energy performance of buildings, renewable energy, and energy taxation. There were also new regulations on CO_2 emission standards for cars and vans, LULUCF, social climate fund, and sustainable maritime fuels. It also addressed methane emissions in the energy sector, and sustainable aviation fuels.[30]

The climate action 'wins'

The EU's efforts since 1990 have yielded a series of major 'wins'. They can be roughly categorised into two overlapping baskets: policy-and-regulations 'wins' and on-the-ground 'wins'.

Policy and regulations-wise, the breadth and depth of the climate mitigation policy measures that have been implemented by the EU are breathtaking, by global standards. The policy framework seemed ambitious when announced but has nonetheless been achievable. Its global leadership on this front is beyond question. Many observers believe that the climate action work undertaken inspired many countries to set or raise environmental standards and clean energy sources standards. It also influenced the establishment of climate-related policies and regulations in other countries. By evaluating the EU experiences, these countries could assess which policies proved more successful or impactful than others. Another major area of influence has been on climate regulation catering specifically to industry and corporations. The group has been a global pioneer in the implementation of disclosure, accounting, and reporting rules related to carbon, climate, the energy transition, and decarbonisation. These were issued by various agencies, including the European Parliament, the European Council, and the European Commission. They range widely from building standards to reporting standards to mandatory targets.

One example is energy efficiency. The EU worked aggressively in this area since the early 2010s, with the first directive promulgated in November 2012 (see Figure 7.6). It was then amended six years later, in December 2018 and subsequently changed in October 2023. Each time, the obligations were made stricter. Energy efficiency has been a top priority given it is 'closely linked to its three main pillars: security (security of supply, import independence, safe production), sustainability (reducing greenhouse gas (GHG) emissions) and competitiveness (affordable energy for end-users)', noted global consultancy Deloitte in 2016.[31] The 2023 directive calls for the lowering of energy consumption EU-wide by at least 11.7 per cent by 2030. The objective is an average of 1.5 per cent in 2024 and 2025, gradually getting to 1.9 per cent by the end of 2030. The directive tackles some not-easy-to-abate areas, such as buildings. They are responsible for 40 per cent of energy consumption and 36 per cent of GHG emissions in the EU. Energy efficiency improvements in old buildings, some centuries old, are complex and expensive. The targets call for an annual energy consumption of 1.9 per cent for the public sectors, for 3 per cent of buildings to be renovated annually into nearly net zero and also published new obligations for efficient district heating systems.[32]

Some of the 'physical wins' include GHG emissions, carbon trading, renewable energy, and energy efficiency.

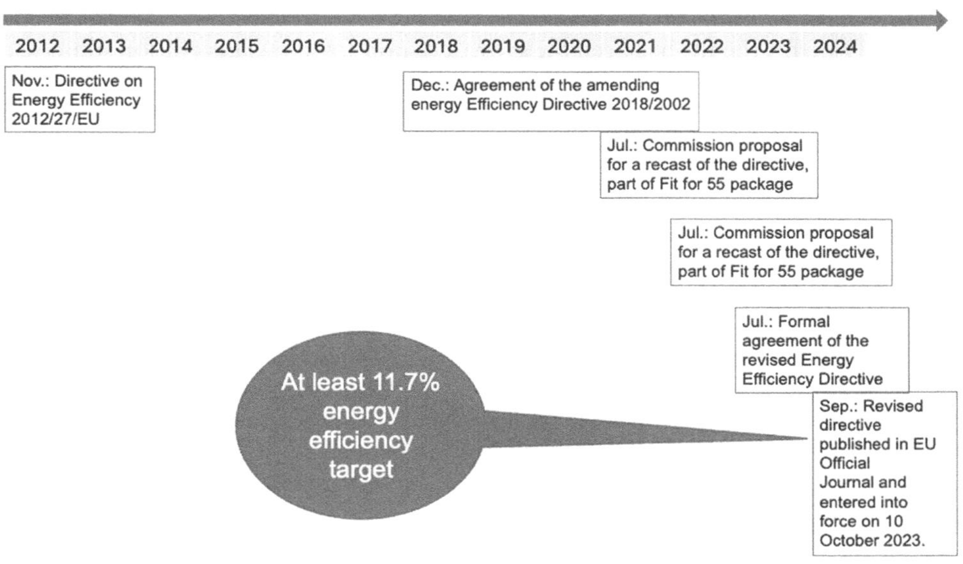

Figure 7.6 EU energy efficiency policy evolution

Source: Author, original chart design (February 2025) based on media and EU sources.

First and foremost, the member states managed to meet many of their GHG emissions goals. Compared to the 1990 levels, it stabilised CO2 emissions by 2000, cut them by 8 per cent between 2008 and 2012, and reduced them to 20 per cent by 2020. In fact, they had fallen by 32.5 per cent compared to 1990 levels in 2022, said the EU's Directorate-General for Environment in March 2024. Oberthür and Dupont highlight that the EU can achieve the 40 per cent reduction by 2030 with new measures, and perhaps the 55 per cent updated target involving carbon removal options, though additional measures would be required. The 2040 goal is yet to be agreed on while the 2050 carbon neutrality objective still remains.

The EU Emissions Trading System was the first carbon trading market in the world and remains the biggest as of 2024; though, over the next few years, China's will become far larger. It uses the 'cap-and-trade' mechanism which limits total GHG emissions for a specific sector, creating an emission allowance trading market to reduce emissions annually. The system evolved in four separate phases over the past 20 years. The first, between 2005 and 2007, was a pilot phase. During this period, nearly all permits were handed out for free. Subsequent phases required concrete emissions reduction targets. In Phase 2, from 2008 to 2012, the market was rebooted, and Phase 1 allowances could no longer be used. The 2008 economic slowdown resulted in a credit surplus forcing average prices down. In Phase 3, from 2012 to 2020, national caps were removed, while EU-wide ones were set, and more industries and gas types were added. Phase 4 began in 2021 and will end in 2030, with yet lower caps, which ultimately should fall to almost zero by 2039. Today's Emissions Trading System covers all member states as well as Iceland, Liechtenstein, and Norway. It effectively reduces GHG emissions as polluters pay for their emissions, generating income to finance some of the EU's energy transition efforts. In 2023, the value of EU Emissions Trading System permits trade on the European Energy Exchange amounted to €770 ($903) billion, equivalent to about 87 per cent of the world's carbon market, according to London Stock Exchange Group data. The global carbon markets created by the EU are increasingly important to the financing of the energy transition globally.

Another 'win' for the EU has been the growth of non-fossil fuel generation sources, especially renewable energy. The overall share of gross final energy consumption from renewable energy sources for the EU member states increased to 23 per cent in 2022, from 9.6 per cent in 2004, based on data provided by Eurostat, the statistical office of the EU. EU-wide, it ranged from a high of 66 per cent in Sweden to a low of 13 per cent in Ireland. In 2020, it had reached 22.04 per cent, 204 basis points higher than the 20 per cent target it had set in 2009, when it was 13.9 per cent (see Figure 7.7).

It had also set itself a target for renewable energy for transport of 10 per cent by 2020, from 1.8 per cent in 2005.[33] It beat this target too, attaining 10.3 per cent. It subsequently fell to 8.7 per cent in 2022 likely due to COVID-19 pandemic related reasons.

A fourth achievement is the EU-wide energy efficiency gains. In the 20-year period through 2020, the group realised a decrease in the total energy consumption of 11.5 per cent in primary energy and 7.4 per cent in final energy. This decrease was accompanied with a drop in energy intensity and energy consumption per capita.

Immediate challenges and criticisms

The EU's energy transition faces several immediate challenges in the mid-2020s. Some of these largely originate from public resistance to certain measures in specific demographics. One perspective is from Dr Benny Peiser,[34] a climate change denier. Peiser argued that growing protests across Europe in 2024 against ambitious net-zero plans and targets were caused

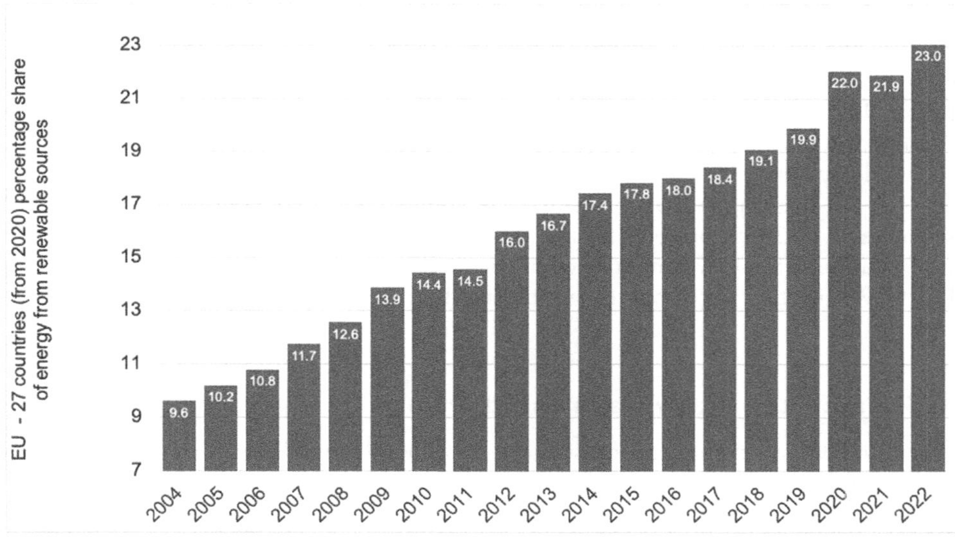

Figure 7.7 Overall share of energy from renewable sources

Notes: 2004–2022 (gross final energy consumption percentage).

Source: Eurostat, 'Share of Energy from Renewable Sources' (Europa.eu 5 April 2024). Available at: https://ec.europa.eu/eurostat/databrowser/view/nrg_ind_ren__custom_11321453/default/table?lang=en accessed 12 May 2024.

by rising costs associated with achieving net zero, and that these economic concerns are making these policies increasingly unpopular, particularly with far-right populist parties. He further suggests that concerns about the cost of living, including high energy prices and economic stagnation, have eclipsed climate change worries for many Europeans. However, it is important to note that such concerns have been a recurring theme throughout the EU's two decades of climate targets setting. The EU's successes, despite their fluctuations and non-linear nature, are undeniable. These include demonstrable progress in reducing GHG emissions, the ongoing effectiveness of the carbon trading system, a rise in the share of energy generated from renewable sources, and improvements in energy efficiency. A prime example is the 2018 Yellow Vest Protests (*mouvement des gilets jaunes*) in France. These protests erupted in response to the French government's sharp increase in diesel fuel taxes, sparking violent demonstrations. On the surface, it may have appeared as an anti-green rally, but observers emphasise that this was not an anti-environmental movement. It was a reaction to broader living cost concerns, encompassing the economy, government services, and affordability. Notably, the 2018 events and similar protests across Europe in recent years have not derailed the overall trend towards stricter emission reduction measures.

In addition to the actual short-term bumps, as for many aspects of the energy transition worldwide, the EU's plans have faced many criticisms at various times. In the 2020s, one criticism focused on the target to cut GHG emissions by 90 per cent compared to the 1990 levels. A commendable aim but one which will require over-relying on relatively unproven and often highly expensive technologies such as carbon removal. Another often voiced reproach is that there is a lag effect in the implementation of climate policies at the individual member state level, states the Climate Action Tracker. A third area is the commitments on the part of member states. For example, the European Parliament had approved a renewable energy binding target of 42.5 per cent, plus a 2.5 per cent top-up, by 2030. However, when individual states submitted their National Energy and Climate Plans, which included their contributions for reaching the goal, it proved that the sum fell short and resulted in a misalignment with EU targets, according to the Climate Action Tracker.[35] A fourth criticism is that wind capacity is being added at a pace slower than necessary, something largely due to red tape for the approval of projects. The zone should be installing about 200 GW in the seven years to 2030, projects industry association WindEurope. This capacity addition is equal to about 28.6 GW annually whereas 33 GW per year is needed for the EU to meet its 425 GW objective necessary to get to the 42.5 per cent binding target, WindEurope believes.[36]

United States: the highly fragmented union

The drive for environmental progress faces roadblocks anywhere in the world, with economic downturns, political gridlock, and social resistance often stalling even the most ambitious plans, at least temporarily. But no major nation has seen swings in environmental policy as dramatic as the United States. Since environmental issues became one of the top global concerns in the 1990s, the United States has been characterised for its frequent policy shifts and reversals, a trend that shows no signs of abating. This inconsistency and volatility make it difficult for the United States to chart a transparent and consistent course on climate action.

Presidential swings and the energy transition

The first step in evaluating climate action in the United States is to look at its track record since the 1990s. The United States has a complex policy implementation system given the powers of the federal government and those of individual states. To understand the history and the current state of climate action in the nation, the primary focus is on the record of the federal government. Broadly speaking, since at least the 1990s, climate action policies, and their execution, have mostly been driven by democratic presidents.

In the past 20 years or so, through 2025, the United States has had five presidents altogether serving eight four-year terms. Three were from the Democratic Party and two from the Republican Party.

Democrat Bill Clinton (January 1993–January 2001) was pro climate action and is best remembered for his administration issuing the Climate Change Action Plan in October 1993. The plan aimed to reduce GHG emissions to 1990 levels by the year 2000 through a mixture of voluntary measures, market-based incentives, and regulatory standards. Democrat Barack Obama (January 2009–January 2017) was also in favour of action to mitigate climate change. Among his administration's many actions, a key one was the Clean Power Plan proposed by the Environmental Protection Agency in June 2014, with the final version released in August 2015. Democrat Joe Biden (January 2021–January 2025) held the same beliefs as Clinton and Obama on the climate. An observer noted that the United States has made more progress in addressing climate change during the Biden administration than under any other previous presidency. An important action was that the United States submitted its NDC to the UNFCCC in April 2021, just three months after Biden's inauguration. The United States then pledged for GHG emissions cuts of at least 50 per cent below 2005 levels in 2030 – and, importantly, the Inflation Reduction Act, which included a climate-smart package.[37]

On the other hand, the record of the two presidents from the republican party has not been supportive of climate action. George W Bush (January 2001–January 2009) did not implement any major climate-action policy during his tenure. In fact, two months after his inauguration, he announced the United States would not apply the 1997 Kyoto Protocol even though it had been brokered by former Vice President Al Gore and signed by Bill Clinton. Donald Trump (January 2017–January 2021, and January 2025 to date) too did not support climate action. Many would argue that he is a climate change denier and staunchly 'anti-environment'. Five months after his first-term inauguration, he formally withdrew the United States from the Paris Agreement and undertook a great number of regulatory rollbacks to weaken environmental protection and back the fossil fuel industry,[38] highlighted the Brookings Institution, a US think tank. Trump took similar actions after being inaugurated for his second term.

Climate action-wise, the United States made enormous progress under the Biden administration. Some observers even argued that it had regained its international climate leadership. The administration overturned about two dozen fossil fuel-related actions by Trump. At the same time, it undertook several consequential climate initiatives that have been implemented. There were at least 30 such initiatives, according to Legal Planet,[39] a collaborative source of climate policy and environmental law by the UC Berkeley School of Law and UCLA School of Law. It counted four major international actions: rejoining the Paris Treaty, appointing a Special Presidential Envoy for Climate, its NDC submission, and ratifying the Kigali Amendment to the Montreal Protocol, which is aimed at limiting the use of hydrofluorocarbons (HFCs, which are super-warming chemicals). Another ten were cross-sector actions, including the Inflation Reduction Act. Another five focused on emissions from the transportation sector and included the bipartisan Infrastructure Act. A further 11 action points were specifically directed at emissions from the energy sector (see Figure 7.8).

Terms	Name	Party	GHG Emissions Reduction Goals
20 January 1993	Bill Clinton	Democratic	Yes
20 January 1997	Bill Clinton	Democratic	Yes
20 January 2001	George W Bush	Republican	No
20 January 2005	George W Bush	Republican	No
20 January 2009	Barack Obama	Democratic	Yes
20 January 2013	Barack Obama	Democratic	Yes
20 January 2017	Donald Trump	Republican	No
20 January 2021	Joe Biden	Democratic	Yes
20 January 2025	Donald Trump	Republican	No

Figure 7.8 US presidents and climate action

Source: Author, original chart design, June 2025.

Among all of these Biden administration initiatives, perhaps the two most significant ones were the already mentioned US Inflation Reduction Act of 2022 (IRA) and the US Infrastructure Investment and Jobs Act of 2021 (IIJA), also referred to as the Bipartisan Infrastructure Law.

Most provisions of the 2022 US IRA become effective in January 2023. The US Environmental Protection Agency highlighted that it was the major climate action in the nation's history. It offers 'funding, programs, and incentives to accelerate the transition to a clean energy economy and will likely drive significant deployment of new clean electricity resources' and encourages the reduction of 'renewable energy costs for organisations . . .[including]. . . businesses, nonprofits, educational institutions, and state, local, and tribal organisations'.[40] The hope is that more than 20 tax incentives would boost investments in clean energy and manufacturing. The IRA motivated plans for the expansion or creation of new clean energy manufacturing facilities for clean energy related equipment worth some $80 billion in private investments in the 12 months of existence.[41] Investment Bank Goldman Sachs estimated that the act could have stimulated as much as $11 trillion in infrastructure investments by 2050. It also noted that $290 billion could had been invested annually for the reinvention of the US energy system by 2032.[42]

The 2021 US IIJA was passed earlier than the IRA. Its impact on US climate action was significant but not as massive as that of the IRA. It too offered some incentives for clean energy investments, as well as for energy efficiency and energy infrastructure. The Department of Energy at the time stated that the act would allow the manufacture of clean energy technologies in the United States and that it would boost its competitive position in the global clean energy market by as much as $23 trillion by 2030. It added that it would instigate investments of over $7 billion in the supply chain for batteries, provide an additional $1.5 billion for clean hydrogen sector, produce $750 million worth of grants for advanced energy technology manufacturing projects in coal communities, invest over $4.5 billion in energy efficiency, and allocate tens of billions of dollars in investments and grants for modernising and expanding the electric power grid so that it could especially cope with the deployment of clean energy sources.[43]

Bipartisan upheavals

The discussion and analysis in this book revolve around the energy transition and not political or geopolitical discussions. However, one area which needs to be factually highlighted is that when it comes to the United States, it is difficult to avoid the elephant in the room: the bipartisan approach to climate action, with two seemingly equally powerful parties adopting distinctly opposite views. The two major acts promulgated by the Biden administration were game changers in favour of climate change. However, neither was universally endorsed. For example, while the US IRA won the votes of all Democrats in Congress, every single Republican member of Congress voted against it. Subsequently, House Republicans voted over 30 times in favour of repealing the climate provisions of the law, though they were unsuccessful each time as of May 2024.[44]

Confusingly for those not intimately familiar with US politics, the IRA has been especially beneficial to the economies of individual states controlled by the Republican Party. Georgia is emerging as a key hub for clean energy in the United States, one of several Republican-led states benefiting from a surge in renewable investments, boosted by Biden's climate policies. At the same time, House Republicans continue to attack the IRA.[45] Iowa,

South Dakota, Kansas, Oklahoma, and North Dakota are all states controlled by the Republican Party, and the share of electric power output from wind energy accounted for between 37 per cent and 62 per cent of the total, the largest share of any state in 2022, based on data analysed by Dr Hannah Ritchie, a data scientist.[46] The motivation has been the cost attractiveness as well as abundant wind resources. Also, approximately 70 per cent of wind generation in the nation is in Republican states. The largest producers, in terms of output being Texas (113.9 TWh in 2022), Iowa (44.7 TWh), Oklahoma (37.4 TWh), and Kansas (29.5 TWh), which are all states held by the Republican Party. In the case of solar, which has a smaller share of electricity output in the United States, the picture is more mixed. The top four states in terms of electricity from solar power are all controlled by the Democratic Party. While in terms of total output from solar PV, two of the top five (California with 62.5 TWh and Minnesota with 14.3 TWh) are Democrat and three (Texas with 25.4 TWh, Florida with 14.1 TWh, and North Carolina with 12.1 TWh) are Republican.[47] Some believe that Democrats-controlled California will lose its solar generation crown to Republicans-controlled Texas in the next years, thanks to some massive investments in solar projects in the state. One example is the $600 million 452 MW solar farm installed by Solar Nova or the 1,200 MW project by SB Energy which has a PPA with Google for 942 MW of the project.

The Republican Party won the US November 2024 presidential election and won a majority in both the House of Representatives and the Senate. As of June 2025, many of the Biden-era initiatives had been decimated mostly via presidential executive order. The brutal politics has created regulatory uncertainty and should make future administration's climate action relatively arduous. From the perspective of domestic and overseas investors alike, this level of uncertainty will drive many to postpone investment decisions or even force them to invest elsewhere. Global energy consultancy Wood Mackenzie projected that the US energy sector would receive around $7.7 trillion in investments between 2023 and 2050 based on policies in place prior to Trump's second term, including the IRA and the IIJA. However, it estimates that this amount would decline by at least 13 per cent of $1 trillion, should Republicans manage to change the key policies that are currently driving low-carbon energy and infrastructure advances.[48]

Energy transition booming landscape hindered by major hurdles

Even during the Biden presidency, projects faced major delays. As of mid-2024, clean energy projects in the United States were experiencing delays averaging 15 months beyond scheduled start dates, despite incentives from the IRA. In the previous four years or so, 62 GW of capacity had been delayed, with solar projects representing two-thirds of this postponed capacity, followed by wind (22 per cent) and battery storage (12 per cent). Only 29.8 GW was expected to become operational by the end of 2024, with a mere 22 per cent of projects delayed in 2023 having been commissioned by mid-2024.[49]

The Trump administration is likely to also hinder new projects. In early 2025, French utility EDF suffered a substantial $940 million write-down on its Atlantic Shores offshore wind project near New Jersey, mirroring Shell's similar financial hit earlier in the year when it withdrew from the partnership. This setback exemplified the broader struggles facing the US offshore wind industry under President Trump's freezing of new leasing arrangements, particularly affecting New Jersey's renewable energy ambitions. The state's energy regulator recently cancelled its fourth offshore wind solicitation after multiple bidders withdrew, leaving Atlantic Shores isolated, a pattern emerging across the sector with Ørsted, the developer, abandoning its Ocean Wind project in 2023 and Eversource Energy recording $1.6 billion in wind project write-offs last year. Public sentiment remains divided, with concerns persisting about transparency, environmental impacts, and economic consequences for coastal communities.[50]

President Trump clearly stated his disdain for clean energy projects, wind energy in particular, in a message on his social media platform, Truth Social, three days after his inauguration on 20 January 2025. The president stated,

> [A] special thank you to great New Jersey congressman Jeff Van Drew for his fight against a large-scale windmill disaster off the coast of southern New Jersey. It needed massive government subsidy that was impossible to justify. Hopefully the project is dead and gone, as almost all unsightly and environmentally unsound windmill project should be. Congratulations to the great people of New Jersey. You have finally won your war on stupidity.[51]

Notes

1 The World Bank, *Reality Check: Lessons from 25 Policies Advancing a Low-Carbon Future* (World Bank 19 September 2023) <https://www.worldbank.org/en/news/feature/2023/09/19/climate-policies-with-real-world-results> accessed 21 March 2025.

2 The Association of Southeast Asian Nations is a political and economic union of ten countries in Southeast Asia, albeit the group is not as harmonised as the EU as ASEAN is an intergovernmental organisation, while the EU is a supranational organisation. The nations include Brunei Darussalam, Burma, Cambodia, Indonesia, Laos, Malaysia, the Philippines, Singapore, Thailand, and Vietnam.

3 G Butler, 'The Nine Countries Most Threatened by Climate Change are All in Asia, Report Finds' *Vice* (2019) [online] <https://www.vice.com/en/article/7xgdgq/nine-countries-most-threatened-by-climate-change-crisis-disaster-hazard-all-asia-report-finds> accessed 24 January 2024.

4 ASEAN Taxonomy Board, *ASEAN Taxonomy for Sustainable Finance Version 1* (ASEAN Taxonomy Board 2021) [online] <https://www.sfinstitute.asia/wp-content/uploads/2022/11/ASEAN_Taxonomy_V1_F.pdf> accessed 25 January 2024.

5 ASEAN Taxonomy Board, *PowerPoint Presentation: ASEAN Taxonomy for Sustainable Finance Version 2* (ASEAN Taxonomy Board 2023) [online] <https://www.sfinstitute.asia/wp-content/uploads/2023/06/ASEAN-Taxonomy-for-Sustainable-Finance-Version-2-Webinar-on-9-June-2023.pdf> accessed 25 January 2024.

6 ASEAN Taxonomy Board, *ASEAN Taxonomy for Sustainable Finance Version 2* (2023) [online] <https://www.sfinstitute.asia/wp-content/uploads/2023/06/ASEAN-Taxonomy-Version-2_.pdf> accessed 25 January 2024.

7 T Fotheringham and C Robertson, *Australia's Climate Change Act: Potential Implications on the Private Sector* (DLA Piper 2023) <https://www.dlapiper.com/en-cn/insights/publications/2023/03/australias-climate-change-act-potential-implications-on-the-private-sector> accessed 30 January 2024.

8 Climate Action Tracker, 'Climate Action Tracker' (Climateactiontracker.org 2023) [online] <https://climateactiontracker.org/countries/australia/policies-action/> accessed 30 January 2024.

9 Department of Climate Change, Energy, the Environment and Water, *Corporate Plan 2022–23* (Commonwealth of Australia 2023) <https://www.dcceew.gov.au/sites/default/files/documents/corporate-plan-2022-23.pdf> accessed 29 January 2024.

10 Department of Climate Change, Energy, the Environment and Water, 'Rewiring the Nation – DCCEEW' (Dcceew.gov.au 30 August 2023) <https://www.dcceew.gov.au/energy/renewable/rewiring-the-nation> accessed 29 January 2024.

11 Department of Climate Change, Energy, the Environment and Water, 'About the Capacity Investment Scheme – DCCEEW' (Dcceew.gov.au 15 December 2023) <https://www.dcceew.gov.au/energy/renewable/capacity-investment-scheme> accessed 29 January 2024.

12 Australian National Audit Office, 'Governance of Climate Change Commitments: Department of Climate Change, Energy, the Environment and Water Australian National Audit Office' (2023) <https://www.anao.gov.au/sites/default/files/2024-01/Auditor-General_Report_2023-24_10.pdf> accessed 29 January 2024.

13 Department of Climate Change, Energy, the Environment and Water, 'EPBC Act Reform – DCCEEW' (Dcceew.gov.au 2022) <https://www.dcceew.gov.au/environment/epbc/epbc-act-reform> accessed 9 February 2024.

14 TEPCO Energy Partner, 'Fuel Cost Adjustments, Etc. Included in Electricity Rates for January 2024 | TEPCO' (www.tepco.co.jp 29 November 2023) <https://www.tepco.co.jp/en/ep/about/newsroom/press/archives/2023/20231129_01.html> accessed 2 May 2024.

15 Japan Electric Power Exchange, 'Day Ahead Market | Trading Market Data | Trading Information | JEPX' (www.jepx.jp 2 May 2024) <https://www.jepx.jp/en/electricpower/market-data/spot/ave_month.html> accessed 2 May 2024.

16 The Asia Climate Finance Podcast, 'Japan Domestic and Global Green Growth Ambitions' (31 January 2023) <https://theasiaclimatefinancepodcast.buzzsprout.com/1951932/12141804-ep26-japan-domestic-and-global-green-growth-ambitions-ft-mika-ohbayashi> accessed 30 April 2024.

17 J Nahm, 'How Solar Developed from the Bottom-Up in China' (*UC Institute on Global Conflict and Cooperation Blog*, 15 March 2023) <https://ucigcc.org/blog/how-solar-developed-from-the-bottom-up-in-China/> accessed 4 May 2024.

18 J Nahm, 'How Solar Developed from the Bottom-Up in China' (*UC Institute on Global Conflict and Cooperation Blog*, 15 March 2023) <https://ucigcc.org/blog/how-solar-developed-from-the-bottom-up-in-China/> accessed 4 May 2024.

19 Climate Action Tracker, 'China: Policies & Action' (climateactiontracker.org 22 November 2023) <https://climateactiontracker.org/countries/China/policies-action/> accessed 5 May 2024.

20 DNV, *China's Energy Transition Outlook* (DNV AS 2024) <https://www.dnv.com/publications/China-energy-transition-outlook/> accessed 5 May 2024.

21 State Council, 'Full Text: Report on the Work of the Government' (english.www.gov.cn 12 March 2024) <https://english.www.gov.cn/news/202403/13/content_WS65f0dfccc6d0868f4e8e5079.html> accessed 5 May 2024.

22 DNV, 'China's Energy Transition Outlook 2024' (www.dnv.com 2024) <https://www.dnv.com/publications/China-energy-transition-outlook/> accessed 19 June 2025.

23 Wood Mackenzie, *Not Made in China: The US$ 6 Trillion Cost of Shifting the World's Clean-Tech Manufacturing Hub* (Wood Mackenzie 2024) <https://www.woodmac.com/news/opinion/not-made-in-China-the-us$6-trillion-cost-of-shifting-the-worlds-clean-tech-manufacturing-hub/> accessed 5 May 2024.

24 Climate Action Tracker, 'Net Zero Targets' (climateactiontracker.org 4 December 2023) <https://climateactiontracker.org/countries/india/net-zero-targets/> accessed 6 May 2024.

25 K Deb and N Roy, *COP28: Assessing India's Progress against Climate Goals* (Insights from the Center on Global Energy Policy 1 December 2023) <https://www.energypolicy.columbia.edu/cop28-assessing-indias-progress-against-climate-goals/> accessed 6 May 2024.

26 P Sharma and others, *Chance of a Lifetime – Can India Show the Developing World a Unique Path to Net Zero?* (Wood Mackenzie 2024) <https://www.woodmac.com/horizons/india-net-zero-path/> accessed 6 May 2024.

27 A Bahadur and N Bhandari, *Balancing Growth with Decarbonisation* (The Goldman Sachs Group, Inc 2023) <https://www.goldmansachs.com/intelligence/pages/gs-research/balancing-growth-with-decarbonisation/report.pdf> accessed 8 May 2024.

28 A Prahl and E Hofmann (eds), 'European Climate Policy – History and State of Play' (climatepolicyinfohub.eu 14 November 2014) <http://climatepolicyinfohub.eu/european-climate-policy-history-and-state-play.html#footnote12_f9frg53> accessed 10 May 2024.

29 European Council, 'European Green Deal' (www.consilium.europa.eu 2023) <https://www.consilium.europa.eu/en/policies/green-deal/> accessed 10 May 2024.

30 C Dupont and others, 'Three Decades of EU Climate Policy: Racing toward Climate Neutrality?' (2023) WIREs Climate Change <https://wires.onlinelibrary.wiley.com/doi/epdf/10.1002/wcc.863> accessed 9 May 2024.
31 Deloitte Conseil, *Energy Efficiency in Europe: The Levers to Deliver the Potential* (Deloitte Conseil 2016) <https://www2.deloitte.com/content/dam/Deloitte/global/Documents/Energy-and-Resources/energy-efficiency-in-europe.pdf> accessed 11 May 2024.
32 European Parliament, *Energy Saving: EU Action to Reduce Energy Consumption* (European Parliament President's Office 18 March 2024) <https://www.europarl.europa.eu/topics/en/article/20221128STO58002/energy-saving-eu-action-to-reduce-energy-consumption> accessed 11 May 2024.
33 European Environment Agency, 'Use of Renewable Energy for Transport in Europe' (www.eea.europa.eu 24 October 2023) <https://www.eea.europa.eu/en/analysis/indicators/use-of-renewable-energy-for> accessed 12 May 2024.
34 Friends of Science, 'Dr Benny Peiser: Europe's Net Zero Rebellion and the Implications for Canada' (www.youtube.com 17 April 2024) <https://www.youtube.com/watch?v=sllhp8X_eFg> accessed 10 May 2024.
35 Climate Action Tracker, 'EU: Policies & Action' (climateactiontracker.org 6 February 2024) <https://climateactiontracker.org/countries/eu/policies-action/> accessed 12 May 2024.
36 WindEurope, *Wind Energy in Europe: 2023 Statistics and the Outlook for 2024–2030* (WindEurope 28 February 2024) <https://windeurope.org/intelligence-platform/product/wind-energy-in-europe-2023-statistics-and-the-outlook-for-2024-2030/> accessed 12 May 2024.
37 T Higgins, R Chang, and D Lespier, *The Biden Administration Has Taken More Climate Action than Any Other in History* (The Center for American Progress 6 March 2024) <https://www.americanprogress.org/article/the-biden-administration-has-taken-more-climate-action-than-any-other-in-history/> accessed 19 May 2024.
38 S Gross, *What is the Trump Administration's Track Record on the Environment?* (The Brookings Institution 4 August 2020) <https://www.brookings.edu/articles/what-is-the-trump-administrations-track-record-on-the-environment/> accessed 19 May 2024.
39 E George, *30 Major Climate Initiatives under Biden* (Legal Planet 13 May 2024) <https://legal-planet.org/2024/05/13/fifteen-major-climate-actions-under-biden/> accessed 19 May 2024.
40 US EPA, 'Summary of Inflation Reduction Act Provisions Related to Renewable Energy' (www.epa.gov 21 November 2022) <https://www.epa.gov/green-power-markets/summary-inflation-reduction-act-provisions-related-renewable-energy> accessed 21 May 2024.
41 D McCarthy and MV Olano, 'The US Climate Law is Fueling a Factory Frenzy. Here's the Latest . . .' *Canary Media* (16 August 2023) <https://www.canarymedia.com/articles/clean-energy-manufacturing/the-us-climate-law-is-fueling-a-factory-frenzy-heres-the-latest-tally> accessed 22 May 2024.
42 Goldman Sachs, *The US is Poised for an Energy Revolution* (Goldman Sachs 17 April 2023) <https://www.goldmansachs.com/intelligence/pages/the-us-is-poised-for-an-energy-revolution.html#:~:text=Goldman%20Sachs%20Research%20estimates%20that> accessed 22 May 2024.
43 US Department of Energy, 'DOE Fact Sheet: The Bipartisan Infrastructure Deal Will Deliver for American Workers, Families and Usher in the Clean Energy Future' (Energy.gov 9 November 2021) <https://www.energy.gov/articles/doe-fact-sheet-bipartisan-infrastructure-deal-will-deliver-american-workers-families-and-0> accessed 22 May 2024.
44 Higgins, Chang, and Lespier (n 37).
45 O Milman, 'Republicans in the US "Battery Belt" Embrace Biden's Climate Spending' *The Guardian* (22 February 2023) <https://www.theguardian.com/environment/2023/feb/22/climate-spending-republican-states-clean-energy-funding> accessed 21 May 2024.
46 H Ritchie, *Republican States Are Going Strong on Solar and Wind, but Not for the Climate* (Sustainability by Numbers 1 January 2024) <https://www.sustainabilitybynumbers.com/p/red-states-renewables> accessed 22 May 2024.
47 H Ritchie, *Republican States Are Going Strong on Solar and Wind, but Not for the Climate* (Sustainability by Numbers 1 January 2024) <https://www.sustainabilitybynumbers.com/p/red-states-renewables> accessed 22 May 2024..

48 V Volcovici, 'A Trump Presidency Would Risk $1 Trillion in Clean Energy Investment, WoodMac Says' *Reuters* (17 March 2024) <https://www.reuters.com/sustainability/climate-energy/trump-presidency-would-risk-1-trillion-clean-energy-investment-woodmac-says-2024-05-16/> accessed 22 May 2024.

49 V Srivastava, 'Project Delays Are Holding Back Clean Power Installation, Report Says' *Reuters* (8 May 2024) <https://www.reuters.com/sustainability/climate-energy/project-delays-are-holding-back-clean-power-installation-report-says-2024-05-07/> accessed 20 March 2025.

50 B Lepic, 'EDF Takes $940m Hit as It Abandons Wind Project off New Jersey' *Splash247* (24 February 2025) <https://splash247.com/edf-takes-940m-hit-as-it-abandons-wind-project-off-new-jersey/> accessed 20 March 2025.

51 B Lepic, 'EDF Takes $940m Hit as It Abandons Wind Project off New Jersey' *Splash247* (24 February 2025) <https://splash247.com/edf-takes-940m-hit-as-it-abandons-wind-project-off-new-jersey/> accessed 20 March 2025.

48. V. Volcovici, [illegible] Trump Rescinds Wind Rules [illegible], Reuters, 12 March 2025, https://www.reuters.com/[illegible], accessed 22 March 2025.
49. V. Srivastava, 'Project Delays Are Holding Back Clean Power Installation, Report Says', Reuters, 13 May 2024, https://www.reuters.com/sustainability/[illegible]-back-clean-power-installation-report-says-2024-05-13/, accessed 20 March 2025.
50. [illegible] 'Trump [illegible] Halts [illegible] Wind Farm [illegible]', 24 February 2025, https://[illegible], accessed 20 March 2025.
51. [illegible], 'EDF Takes $940m Hit as It Abandons Wind Project off New Jersey', [illegible] February 2025, https://[illegible], accessed [illegible] March 2025.

Section III

Financing transition finance

Chapter 8

The realm of climate finance

Aims:

- Approaches to navigating the complexities of climate finance.
- Identifying financing options available for energy transition projects.
- Evaluating optimal financing tool or tools for climate projects and solutions.

In the late 1970s, Apple founders Steve Jobs and Steve Wozniak were working on the first computer prototype. It was not until this prototype was ready that they sought financing. In finance, this is known as the 'project-led approach'. It is the preferred approach found in corporate finance textbooks and literature. For energy transition projects and solutions, arguably, it should be a 'financing-first approach'. Much of the capital needs to be in place, or at least needs to be committed, first. The number of potential transition-related projects is enormous. The lion's share of these projects is in well-understood, proven technologies and solutions. What is crucial for governments, financial institutions, and corporations is clear definitions and standards of the technologies and solutions, such as technical specifications, when allocating the financing.

For companies keen on adopting the energy transition, the availability of funding is vital. Like most big infrastructure or real estate projects, clean energy assets usually need a hefty investment upfront. Take, for instance, solar rooftops above residential homes or utility-scale solar farms. One needs cash for the equipment, buying or leasing the land, construction, and all sorts of other initial costs. Once the project is complete, the variable costs, such as labour and maintenance, are minimal. What exactly is climate finance? Is it something everyone understands? Is it easy to secure? Who are the main players involved? And, crucially, why should businesses care about green finance? How relevant is it to them?

The scope of climate finance

Defining the definitions

Defining financial terms tailored to address environmental and climate-change-related issues is no simple task. One might argue about the importance of defining these terms, especially given the rapid evolution of climate finance-related terminology. Indeed, some

DOI: 10.4324/9781003666509-11

may legitimately question whether any effort should be devoted to this at all. However, the answer is unequivocal: it is an imperative endeavour.

This book does not function as a textbook. It focuses on equipping the reader with the practical tools and mechanisms needed to understand and operate in the field of climate finance. Navigating this complex and rapidly evolving field requires grasping a specific set of terminology. Definitions are crucial at this stage, as terms like 'climate', 'conservation', 'environmental', 'green', 'sustainable', and 'transition' finance are still often used interchangeably, yet are distinct concepts. Interchangeably, because there currently still are many overlaps in the terminology.

To add to the confusion, some jurisdictions, such as China and the EU, have adopted slightly different definitions, as shown in the chart on sustainable finance from an OECD briefing (see Figure 8.1). All in all, it is still a nascent and evolving field, so the terminologies are not quite fixed. Yet, clear classifications are quite critical for many entities, especially crucial when it comes to regulation and greenwashing, for example. It is essential for practitioners to adopt more precise and more uniform language as emphasised by the UK-based think tank Green Finance Institute in a report published in 2023. This is important because failing to do so may put a corporation in jeopardy. The Institute believes that a driver of greenwashing in the field of ESG has been the lack of accurate language combined with asymmetric expectations and understanding for many years.[1] There are efforts in place to find common ground for green taxonomies. In late 2024, the International Platform on Sustainable Finance presented a comparison of the green finance taxonomies between China, the EU, and Singapore. In future, this will allow for a green financial product to meet the green taxonomies of these three regions.[2]

	Taxonomies		Definitions		
	China	EU	France	Netherlands	Japan
SOURCES					
Sovereign Green Bond			●	●	
Green loans definitions in legislation	●	●	●	●	
Green bonds definitions in legislation	●	●	●	●	●
INCENTIVES					
Interest rate incentives	●		●	●	
Tax incentives or subsidies	●		●	●	●
Monetary policy/collateral incentives	●				
OBJECTIVES					
Social objectives included	●	●	●		
Climate change adaptation		●	●	●	●
Climate change mitigation	●	●	●	●	●
Water and marine protection	●	●	●	●	●
Pollution prevention and control	●	●	●	●	●
Waste and recycling	●	●	●	●	●
Ecosystems/Biodiversity	●	●	●	●	●

Figure 8.1 Sustainable finance definitions and taxonomies

Note from a briefing based on the OECD report: Developing Sustainable Finance Definitions and Taxonomies, OECD Publishing, Paris, https://doi.org/10.1787/134a2dbe-en.

Source: OECD Environment Directorate, 'Developing Sustainable Finance Definitions and Taxonomies a BRIEF for POLICY MAKERS' (2020). Available at: https://www.oecd.org/en/publications/developing-sustainable-finance-definitions-and-taxonomies_134a2dbe-en.html accessed 4 June 2024.

Overlapping terms

When it comes to capital going towards projects or solutions dedicated to mitigating climate change, energy transition, decarbonisation, and related areas, as of today, the most commonly used terms can appear highly confusing. Three of the most common terms are 'green finance', 'sustainable finance', and 'climate finance'. A simple yet tangible approach is to use Google Trends to identify the most popular terms (see Figure 8.2). Examining the median of the weekly average score for the five years to June 2025, the most commonly used search term was 'green finance', with a score of 42 (100 most popular, 0 least popular). 'Sustainable finance' and 'climate finance' scored 21 and 14, respectively. When examining the median of the weekly average score for one year, the values are higher. 'Green finance' was 60, 'sustainable finance' 26, and 'climate finance' 21. There are of course other terms including conservation finance, environmental finance, and transition finance. To address the differences, the definitions from two or more sources are examined for each of the individual terms.

Climate finance

The UNFCCC, the Climate Policy Initiative, and others argue that it is the financing for climate change mitigation and adaptation projects. The European Environment Agency[3] says that mitigation refers to the prevention or reduction of GHG emissions into the atmosphere to lessen the impact on climate change. It argues that adaptation generally refers to implementing actions that prevent or minimise the causes of climate change, or the leveraging

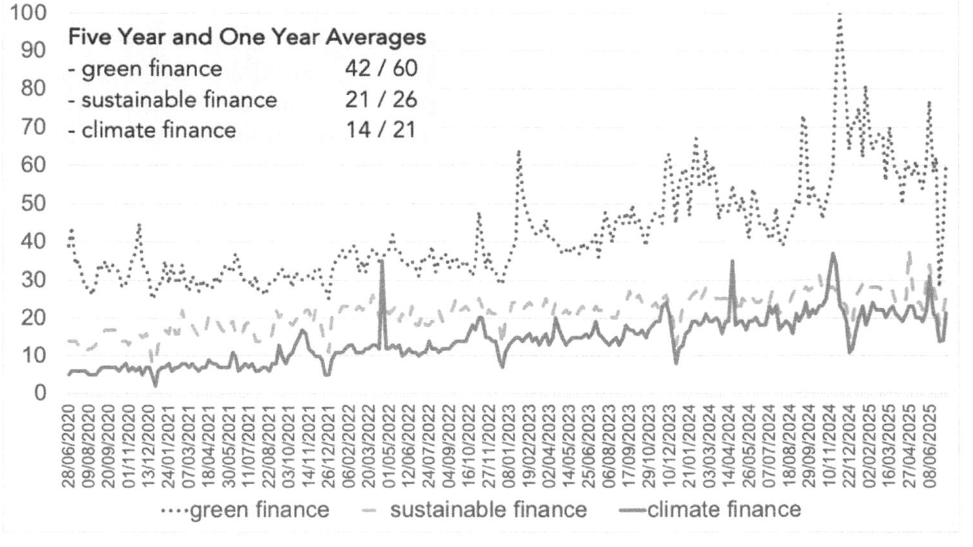

Figure 8.2 Google Trends for green, sustainable, and climate finance

Note from Google Trends: Numbers represent search interest relative to the highest point on the chart for the given region and time. A value of 100 is the peak popularity for the term. A value of 50 means that the term is half as popular. A score of 0 means that there was not enough data for this term.

Source: Compiled by author, 29 June 2025, using data from Google Trends (https://www.google.com/trends).

of opportunities which will be created.[4] Mitigation projects can include such measures as renewable energy and electrified transport. Adaptation projects can comprise activities aimed at building climate resilience such as habitat conservation or sustainable land management. The financing can be local, national, or cross-border. It can come from any source, including public, private, or alternative sources.[5] The Climate Policy Initiative adds that the capital has to be directed towards the transition to a low-carbon economy.[6] Financial website Investopedia adopts a narrower, and perhaps less common, definition emphasising that climate finance is the use of financial institutions or technologies to develop environmental sustainability, including developing new renewable energy projects. It adds that a narrower definition revolves around specifically transferring capital from developed economies to emerging ones.[7]

Conservation finance

Conservation finance is a term that tends to occasionally appear and so deserves to be profiled. One definition is from the Global Environment Facility which provides and mobilises funds to aid developing countries in meeting their economic goals. Its definition is that conservation finance involves investment strategies that leverage cash flows generated through sustainable ecosystem management. The funds have a dual purpose: supporting ecosystem conservation and providing returns to investors.[8] A global professional alliance of conservation finance experts, practitioners, and organisations, The Conservation Finance Alliance, further adds that the investment strategies and funding must support incentives to realise nature conservation outcomes.[9]

Green finance

The term green finance is often commonly used in publications, particularly those from commercial banks and other financial institutions. Put simply, it is any capital directed to projects, enterprises, or other activities aiming to have a positive environmental outcome. The World Economic Forum defines it as a structured financial activity, product, or service – including loans, debt mechanisms, and investments – focused on a better environmental outcome.[10] The definition by British banking group Lloyds is even simpler, it underlines the importance that the loans or investments must support environmentally friendly activities, such as the construction of environmentally friendly infrastructure.[11] In several of its briefings, the European Parliament wrote that it is about collecting funds that address the areas of climate and the environment as well as improving the financial risk management in these two areas.[12] The UN's definition specifically mentions that it is about raising the volume of financial flows from all types of sectors which is dedicated to sustainable development. In addition to flows from banks, micro credit, insurance, and other investments are also included. The UN believes that it is key to balance three factors: environmental and social risks management, securing opportunities which offer a decent rate of return, and that can provide greater accountability.[13]

Environmental finance

Unlike some of the other terminology, environmental finance is not frequently found in publications by financial institutions. Perhaps because the term 'environment' has connotations of nonprofit activities. It is however easily found in the education field. One source, education-focused website EnvironmentalScience.org, states that the first time 'environmental finance' was used in the academic education context was by Richard L Sandor, famous for being the father of the financial futures markets and products, among other things. In 1992, during his tenure as an adjunct professor at Columbia University, he taught a course that emphasised the intersection of environmental finance, economics, and market analysis. The course aimed to look at the funding of conservation initiatives, enhance businesses' environmental impact without compromising profitability, and improve the quality of life of communities.[14]

Sustainable finance

Sustainable finance is often accompanied by 'green' to highlight the environmental aspects of the financing, in addition to the multiple dimensions of sustainability. The European Investment Bank notes that it is about including ESG considerations in the investments processes, which will lead to more investments in sustainable projects and activities in the long term.[15] The OECD is one of several organisations which dug deep into the definition of sustainable finance. In its book Developing Sustainable Finance Definitions and Taxonomies, Green Finance and Investment,[16] it evaluated this issue in great detail, including looking at definitions in such diverse jurisdictions as the EU, Japan, and China. The OECD contended that clear definitions and taxonomies can yield numerous potential benefits, such as enhancing market clarity. Defining more precisely and consistently what constitutes green and sustainable investments will promote investment by raising investor confidence and providing assurance to investors. Among the other potential benefits are the facilitation of tracking sustainable finance flows, enabling more accurate measurements, and enforcing policy actions, such as the setting of incentives. UK and Hong Kong commercial banking group HSBC is one of the many institutions benefitting from clear definitions and taxonomies. It believes that sustainable finance and investment encompass financial services that incorporate ESG criteria into business and investment choices. These services include financing, investing, and related activities aligned with the UN SDGs, including the goals of the Paris Agreement. The bank designates facilities as sustainable finance or investment based on validation by relevant business governance forums.[17]

Transition finance

Green, environmental, sustainable, or transition finance started to be commonly used perhaps in the early 2010s. Transition finance, on the other hand, became more commonplace in the 2020s. Broadly speaking, transition finance is financial support aimed at reducing CO_2 emissions from high-polluting industries and facilitating the shift towards a low-carbon economy, argue Winnie Mak and Andres Vinelli in a paper[18] for the CFA Research and Policy Centre. They add that despite the critical role played by transition finance in achieving net-zero targets, it still lacks clear-cut definitions and standards. They also note that there is currently no global consensus on which activities or companies qualify for this type of financing, and that international organisations have yet to endorse specific transition finance instruments. The Glasgow Financial Alliance for Net Zero has stated that a definition of transition finance should be constructed on four high-level financing strategies: climate solutions, aligned, aligning, and managed phase out. The Institute for Energy Economics and Financial Analysis, a think tank, provided an analysis[19] of these four strategies and concluded that they need to be significantly more nuanced (see Figure 8.3).

GFANZ FOUR TRANSITION FINANCING STRATEGIES	CATEGORIES FOR ACTIVITIES AND ENTITIES	KEY CONSIDERATIONS WHEN SCREENING OPPORTUNITIES				SUGGESTED RELATIONSHIPS AMONG GENERAL, GREEN TRANSITION FINANCE	
		Science based taxonomy tool	Feasibility assessment	Use-of-proceeds criteria	Transition plan assessment		
CLIMATE SOLUTIONS	SUSTAINABLE AND ENABLING ACTIVITIES	✓	-	✓	-	GREEN FINANCE	
	SUSTAINABLE AND ENABLING ENTITIES	✓	-	✓	-	GREEN FINANCE (pure-play or use-of-proceeds ringfencing)	
ALIGNED	ALIGNED ENTITIES	-	✓	-	✓	TRANSITION FINANCE (high emitting 'hard-to-abate' sectors)	GENERAL FINANCE (other sectors)
ALIGNING	ALIGNING ENTITIES	-	✓	-	✓	TRANSITION FINANCE (high emitting 'hard-to-abate' sectors)	GENERAL FINANCE (other sectors)
	TRANSITIONAL ACTIVITIES	✓	✓	✓	-	TRANSITION FINANCE	
MANAGED PHASEOUT	MANAGED PHASEOUT ACTIVITIES	✓	✓	✓	-	TRANSITION FINANCE	

Figure 8.3 Think-tank view on GFANZ transition financing strategies

Notes: Original chart title: IEEFA's View: GFANZ's four strategies provide a high-level view, but FIs will need more nuanced considerations when screening opportunities.

Source: Leung K, 'Beyond COP28: Financial Institutions Should Adopt Nuanced Transition Finance Frameworks to Support Net Zero' (Institute for Energy Economics & Financial Analysis 2024). Available at: https://ieefa.org/resources/beyond-cop28-financial-institutions-should-adopt-nuanced-transition-finance-frameworks accessed 18 August 2024.

The preferred term used in this book is 'climate finance' as the principal actors discussed throughout chiefly relate to corporations and financial institutions. 'Climate finance' addresses the funding for climate change mitigation and adaptation, and it aligns with the carbon emissions reduction focus of the energy transition. Also, the term 'climate finance' does not negate the purposes of 'green' or 'sustainable' finance, for example. In the choice, there was a preference for 'climate' over 'transition'. Based on current definitions, 'climate' is a little broader in scope than 'transition'. It addresses a broader range of climate-focused investments and activities, ranging from renewable energy projects to reforestation efforts. These are all areas corporations or financial institutions could participate in. 'Transition finance', at least for now, seems to refer a little more specifically to those sectors which must target lowering their emissions, such as fossil fuel-based energy supply, transport (aviation, rail, shipping, and the like), or other heavy polluting industries such as cement, chemicals, and steel. Also, 'climate' can include mitigation and adaptation, two initiatives that corporations can adopt in their transition strategies.

One cannot overemphasise that in the short- to medium term, probably over the next five to ten years, definitions will become significantly more granular. In the long term, all types of finance and financing tools will fully integrate the 'green' or 'climate' or 'transition' elements of finance. It will be an element to be considered for all forms of financing and financial products. For example, today equity analysts value a company based on common measures to gauge the value of a listed company such as Price to Earnings, Enterprise Value to Earnings Before Interest, Tax, Depreciation, and Amortisation, as well as Discounted Cash Flow. Over the next few years, analysts will have to include a climate element to the valuations. This is because a company which is not 'green' may be valued at a discount to one which is. Many investment banks already use ESG scorecards, and such an approach will have to be fully integrated into the valuation methodology in the near future.

Everything from loans to insurance will inherently have a climate impact component. It will be mandatory for climate risks to be carefully assessed. Approving a loan or an insurance product for a corporation will have to involve making sure it is climate-neutral or climate-positive. While a variety of terms exist today, with overlapping definitions, the ultimate goal is a future where all financing inherently considers all forms of environmental impacts.

Notes

1 The Green Finance Institute, *Transition Finance: New Asset Class or Emperor's New Clothes?* (The Green Finance Institute 2023) <https://www.greenfinanceinstitute.com/wp-content/uploads/2023/12/Transition-finance.pdf> accessed 30 May 2024.
2 Monetary Authority of Singapore, 'The International Platform on Sustainable Finance Presents the Multi-Jurisdiction Common Ground Taxonomy to Enhance Interoperability of Taxonomies across EU, China and Singapore' (Mas.gov.sg 14 November 2024) <https://www.mas.gov.sg/news/media-releases/2024/multi-jurisdiction-common-ground-taxonomy> accessed 6 July 2025.
3 European Environment Agency, 'What is the Difference between Adaptation and Mitigation?' (www.eea.europa.eu 30 October 2023) <https://www.eea.europa.eu/en/about/contact-us/faqs/what-is-the-difference-between-adaptation-and-mitigation> accessed 9 June 2024.
4 United Nations Climate Change, 'Introduction to Climate Finance' (Unfccc.int 2022) <https://unfccc.int/topics/introduction-to-climate-finance> accessed 9 June 2024.
5 United Nations Climate Change, 'Introduction to Climate Finance' (Unfccc.int 2022) <https://unfccc.int/topics/introduction-to-climate-finance> accessed 9 June 2024.
6 A Falconer and M Stadelmann, 'What is Climate Finance? Definitions to Improve Tracking and Scale up Climate Finance. A CPI Brief Acknowledgements' (2014) <https://climatepolicyinitiative.org/wp-content/uploads/2014/09/Climate-Finance-Brief-Definitions-to-Improve-Tracking-and-Scale-Up.pdf> accessed 9 June 2024.
7 J Fernando, C Rhinehart, and J Ma, 'Climate Finance: Meaning, Contributors, Example' *Investopedia* (31 July 2023) <https://www.investopedia.com/terms/c/climate-finance.asp> accessed 9 June 2024.
8 The Global Environment Facility, 'Conservation Finance' (2018) <https://www.thegef.org/sites/default/files/publications/GEF%20Assembly_ConservationFinance%20Factsheet_9.4.18.pdf> accessed 9 June 2024.
9 D Meyers and others, *Conservation Finance: A Framework* (Conservation Finance Alliance 2020) <https://static1.squarespace.com/static/57e1f17b37c58156a98f1ee4/t/5e8c97ecf33f8960fc2cbda3/1586272239963/Conservation+Finance+Framework.pdf> accessed 9 June 2024.
10 S Fleming, *What is Green Finance and Why is It Important?* (World Economic Forum 9 November 2020) <https://www.weforum.org/agenda/2020/11/what-is-green-finance/> accessed 9 June 2024.
11 S Wire, 'What is Green Finance?' (www.lloydsbankinggroup.com 31 May 2024) <https://www.lloydsbankinggroup.com/insights/green-finance.html> accessed 10 June 2024.
12 S Spinaci, 'BRIEFING EPRS | European Parliamentary Research Service' (2021) <https://www.europarl.europa.eu/RegData/etudes/BRIE/2021/679081/EPRS_BRI(2021)679081_EN.pdf> accessed 9 June 2024.
13 UNEP, *Green Financing* (UNEP – UN Environment Programme 23 January 2018) <https://www.unep.org/regions/asia-and-pacific/regional-initiatives/supporting-resource-efficiency/green-financing> accessed 9 June 2024.
14 S Jaworski (ed), 'Environmental Finance: Who, What, Where, Why, and When' (www.environmentalscience.org) <https://www.environmentalscience.org/environmental-finance#:~:text=Environmental%20finance%20is%20a%20field%20that%20on%20the> accessed 9 June 2024.
15 E Kreivi, *What is Sustainable Finance* (European Investment Bank 3 April 2023) <https://www.eib.org/en/stories/what-is-sustainable-finance> accessed 9 June 2024.
16 OECD Environment Directorate, 'Developing Sustainable Finance Definitions and Taxonomies: A Brief for Policy Makers' (2020) <https://www.oecd.org/environment/cc/developing-sustainable-finance-definitions-and-taxonomies-brief-for-policy-makers.pdf> accessed 4 June 2024.

17 HSBC, *HSBC Sustainable Finance and Investment December 2023: Data Dictionary* (HSBC 2023) <https://www.google.com.hk/url?sa=t&source=web&rct=j&opi=89978449&url=https://www.hsbc.com/-/files/hsbc/investors/hsbc-results/2023/annual/pdfs/hsbc-holdings-plc/240221-hsbcs-usd750-bn-usd-1-trn-sustainable-financing-and-investment-ambition-data-dictionary–2023.pdf%3Fdownload%3D1&ved=2ahUKEwiN9ICMqc-GAxXz-gIHHZIVAeEQFnoECBMQAQ&usg=AOvVaw16Wrv26-Ll1qWpnBo0-vO> accessed 9 June 2024.

18 W Mak and A Vinelli, *Navigating Transition Finance: An Action List* (CFA Institute Research and Policy Center 2024) <https://rpc.cfainstitute.org/research/reports/2024/navigating-transition-finance> accessed 10 July 2024.

19 K Leung, *Beyond COP28: Financial Institutions Should Adopt Nuanced Transition Finance Frameworks to Support Net Zero* (Institute for Energy Economics and Financial Analysis 2024) <https://ieefa.org/resources/beyond-cop28-financial-institutions-should-adopt-nuanced-transition-finance-frameworks> accessed 18 August 2024.

Chapter 9

The ecosystem

Financing, actors, and tools

Aims:

- Understanding the profile of climate capital providers.
- Recognising the differences between the major actors.
- Discovering the numerous and different types of capital provision.

The Redstone Concentrated Solar Thermal Power Project in Northern Cape province, South Africa shows how today's clean energy projects can secure funding from multiple sources. It is an innovative $724 million, 100 MW solar plant with energy storage facilities able to store energy for up to 12 hours, using a technology called molten salt tower and will generate 480 GWh per year (Figure 9.1 is a simplified schematic representation of a solar thermal

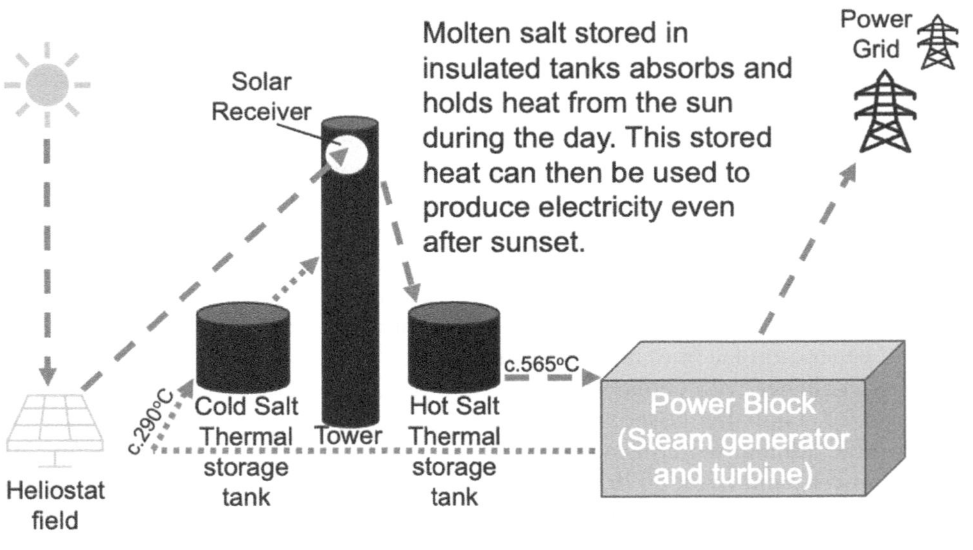

Figure 9.1 Simplified solar thermal plant with heliostats and molten salt storage

Source: Author, original chart design (September 2025). Generic background images from OpenAI, https://chat.openai.com accessed 29 June 2025.

DOI: 10.4324/9781003666509-12

power project with heliostats and molten salt energy storage). What made this project work financially is the combination of different sources of capital so that the investment risk can be spread out among investors. Saudi Arabia-listed ACWA Power Company, which controls 35 per cent, was the major equity investor. The South African government created a supportive programme with guaranteed power purchase agreements. State institutions like the Industrial Development Corporation of South Africa also put in significant funding. The African Development Bank acted as the lead arranger and Coordinating Bank with financing also secured from leading international and South African financial institutions including ABSA Bank, CDC Group, Development Bank of Southern Africa (DBSA), Deutsche Investitions- und Entwicklungsgesellschaft (DEG), Nederlandse Financierings-Maatschappij voor Ontwikkelingslanden (FMO), Investec Bank, Nedbank Limited, and Sanlam Limited.[1]

The flows of climate-dedicated capital

Capital dedicated to energy transition-related projects has many features that are different from capital dedicated to traditional mainstream infrastructure projects such as the financing project. The most important reason for such differences is the nature of the financing target. A green target requires relatively newer approaches and considerations.

The construction of a new regular office building compared with that of a new green office building is quite different. Regular office buildings are mainstream, and in major urban metropoles, such as Hong Kong, London, or New York, there is deep and broad experience in constructing such buildings. This typically makes the planning and design of a standard office building relatively quicker and smoother. While environmental and energy efficiency factors are to be considered, they may not necessarily be prioritised. Green office buildings may have some added complexities. There is a need for more planning and design considerations while sustainability factors will be the priority. Regular ones would use standard construction materials and methods. Green ones would use some materials which are not widely common, such as recycled ones; the sourcing of the materials would have to be carefully planned as they could have a high carbon footprint at source, and the construction methods would also have to be adjusted compared to traditional ones, such as the minimising of waste or the energy consumption during construction. A green office would have to include such features as the maximisation of natural light and ventilation, energy-efficient heating and cooling systems, or systems which minimise the use and wastage of water. Another feature is that green buildings will have to be designed so that they can be certified as green. Certifications such as BREEAM (Building Research Establishment Environmental Assessment Method) in the United Kingdom or LEED (Leadership in Energy and Environmental Design) in the United States. The importance of the nature of the financing targets is the same for energy supply sources. There are many differences between fossil fuel-based generation facilities and clean energy ones.

Another challenge with climate-dedicated capital is the familiarity of the subject by the entity involved. Globally, governments, financial institutions, and others are likely to be generally more familiar with the factors that they need to consider when lending money to a coal-fired power plant or an oil drilling project. These industries have a longer history than onshore or offshore wind farms, for example. There is a wide gap between those countries where clean energy is common because a large number of projects have been completed, and those nations where clean energy has lagged behind. For example, Chinese financial institutions are quite fluent in assessing clean energy project risks and have become highly efficient in green credit.[2]

Admittedly, the education trajectory is encouragingly positive. There is anecdotal evidence that in the financial sector, for example, internal and public training programmes have grown exponentially. This trend should result in staff members gaining a greater understanding of topics such as climate risk management, including analysis, measurement, and disclosure, as well as integrating climate considerations into their work processes. They are also helped by organisations' publishing standards and regulations as to what is a green activity such as the International Financial Reporting Standards foundation on accounting and sustainability disclosure standards or the Principles for Responsible Investment, a UN supported initiative advocating the integration of ESG factors into investment decisions, so that investors may better understand their responsibilities and gain clarity on sustainable investments, including the associated rules and regulations. This educative process should progressively allow financial actors to make better decisions when raising capital for business or lending to climate mitigation investment projects such as for the construction of a renewable energy generation facility or for a corporation to switch its internal combustion engine vehicle fleet to EVs.

While it is important to understand the targets of climate-dedicated capital flows, it is also imperative to understand the sources of the capital and the principal actors involved. States are involved in climate financing in a variety of ways. It may include national governments, sub-national ones, such as states or provinces, or even a local authority in a city or a county. Financial lending institutions can take the form of multilateral development banks or commercial banks. Then there are institutional investors which can be directly or indirectly involved in the capital flow. Also important are other private sector sources which can include family offices, NGOs, philanthropies, venture capital, individual investors, and even communities. Another major set of actors are corporations. Importantly, these actors can work alone or together with other actors. A corporation may directly invest in a climate-related or energy transition project alone or together with an institutional investor, such as a private equity firm. There has been an increasingly significant amount of interplay between actors. As energy transition investments grow exponentially, this trend will not only continue but also gain more momentum.

The main actors and financing

Financing from the state and state-linked entities

National governments are one of the actors directly investing capital into energy transition projects. Some of the high-profile ones are China in Asia, the United States in North America, and France and Germany in Europe – as well as the EU itself.

There are several ways by which States support capital investments into net-zero-related projects. They can invest in projects directly. They can co-invest directly. They can create structures under a Public–Private Partnership umbrella which can boost capital flows in energy transition-related projects by offering grants, loans, loan-guarantees, subsidies, or tax incentives.

Direct investments by government

An example of a direct investment in the energy transition by a national government is the United Kingdom's EV infrastructure strategy. The government committed to invest at least £1.6 billion ($2.2 billion) in EV charging infrastructure to accelerate the adoption of EV in 2022. It aimed to raise the number of public charging points to 300,000 by 2030. Part of the investment, about £500 million ($675 million), is to be devoted to public charging points at local communities, ranging from cities to rural villages throughout the country.[3] In the United States, as part of the Bipartisan Infrastructure Law, the Biden administration announced a similar strategy to that of the United Kingdom in 2022. The US Transportation and Energy departments announced that $5 billion would be made available to expand the EV charging infrastructure throughout the country. The aim was to build out the number of charging points along major highways as well as in rural and underserved communities.[4] But investments are not limited to EV charging infrastructure. Also in the United States, the Department of Energy announced a $104 million investment package in 2024 dedicated to energy conservation projects and clean energy generation facilities, amounting to about 27 MW, at 31 federal locations. The department underlined that the investment would result in $29 million worth of savings in energy and water costs in the first year of operation. The investment was the first of three disbursements amounting to a $250 million funding approved under the Bipartisan Infrastructure Law.[5]

Government direct investments also go towards climate adaptation projects such as reforestation. The Canadian government is working towards planting two billion trees (the '2 billion Trees Programme') over ten years between 2021 and 2031. Justin Trudeau, the former Prime Minister, had announced the programme in 2019 pledging C$3.2 billion ($2.3 billion) towards the planting.[6] The programme provides federal funds to provinces, territories, cities, and others. Many other countries, including Australia and the United States, have also pledged tree planting programmes in recent years. These programmes may also come under the form of direct funding, subsidies, or grants.

Co-financing

Co-investments are quite common in both developed and developing countries. It can be partnerships with corporations, financial investors, or even with NGOs or philanthropies. It can also be in projects which use mainstream technologies – carrying low to medium investment risk – such as solar plants or offshore wind farms, or in those using less widely adopted technologies – carrying medium to high investment risk – such as CCS or green hydrogen. Generally speaking, there are more examples of governments investing in projects involving newer technologies. This is because projects using mainstream technologies are more likely to be able to source capital from investors or loans from banks. In recent years, government co-investment involvement has been in a wide range of projects involving newer technologies. Examples include the Norwegian or UK government's involvement in CCS projects in their respective countries. In Norway, the government invested 27 billion Norwegian kroner ($2.7 billion) into the Longship CCS project. The project is to capture CO_2 from cement production and waste incineration and then transport and store it under the North Sea. The project should be completed in phases by 2026.[7] Other examples range from the Canadian government involvement in a tidal power project in Nova Scotia to the Kenyan government involvement in geothermal energy developments.

Grants and subsidies

Governments deploy grants, loans, loan-guarantees, subsidies, or tax incentives to accelerate net-zero-related projects or to make the financing of hard-to-finance projects easier and more bankable. There are hundreds of thousands of examples worldwide with amounts ranging from a few thousands of dollars to billions – given the wide range of project sizes or the maturity of the technology or solution. The concept can be further illustrated with some specific examples: India's smart cities financing, and Hong Kong and Singapore's green financial platforms creation and financial support towards clean energy generation projects.

In 2015, India launched the Smart Cities Mission. It has aimed at transforming 100 cities by integrating technology, enhancing infrastructure, promoting sustainable development, and creating a clean and sustainable environment. The areas of special focus have been efficient public services, sustainable mobility, smart energy, and water management. It involves collaboration between central and state governments, the private sector, and local communities. The government initially committed 480 billion Indian rupees ($5.5 billion) in financial support over five years. Today, the project is still ongoing. The government had completed 7,142 of 8,009 individual projects and deployed about 1,433 billion Indian rupees ($16.3 billion) out of a projected 1,641 billion Indian rupees ($18.6 billion) as of June 2024, based on Ministry of Housing and Urban Affairs data. The projects are wide-ranging in nature and scale. They included energy generation, water treatment facilities, sewage treatment, digital solutions, and public space development. The financing for the projects did not solely come from the central government of India. It included matching funds from individual states, municipal bonds issuance, tax increment financing (the incremental taxes created by the project), loans from financial institutions, and private sector funding.[8] Overall, the Smart City Mission has been relatively successful. It offers a good example of the positive mobilisation of external resources through alternative financial structures as well as instruments, such as Public–Private Partnerships and municipal bonds, as noted by the World Economic Forum.[9]

Governments' participation in net-zero projects is not limited to physical assets. Two of the many examples are the green financing platform in Singapore and the green fintech start-up programme in Hong Kong.

Singapore is a global leader in the promotion of green finance. In late 2022, the Monetary Authority of Singapore launched a S$5 million ($3.9 million) Asia Climate Solutions Design Grant and Convergence Blended Finance. It provides early-stage grant funding for the 'proof of concept and feasibility studies on innovative and scalable blended finance solutions to fund sustainability projects'. The programme also aims to 'mobilise capital into high impact target sectors that are significantly under-capitalised in Asia, such as early-stage climate adaptation and mitigation technology, clean energy access, sustainable transport, sustainable cities and infrastructure, sustainable agriculture, and nature-based solutions'.[10] While the absolute amount may seem small, this is only one of many initiatives undertaken by the Singapore government.

In early 2024, the Hong Kong government announced a new subsidy scheme focused on green fintech start-ups to boost sustainability data. The start-ups it seeks should have some expertise in collecting, analysing, and reporting sustainability-related data. A senior official highlighted that Hong Kong has about a thousand fintech companies which supply technological solutions on ESG analytics, reporting, and related subjects.[11] Sustainability disclosures for corporations are of central importance to the future development of climate finance in Hong Kong or anywhere else in the world. The government will further support start-ups in five climate finance-related areas: 1) green and digital finance and investment (such as green tokenised bonds or green insurance products); 2) ESG disclosure, compliance, and regulatory reporting (such as listed companies' disclosure and compliance or regulatory and supplier reporting); 3) carbon trading, analytics, and technology (such as carbon credit trading or carbon registry and trading infrastructure); 4) ESG data, intelligence, and analytics (such as ESG data collection and aggregation or ESG rating of companies and funds); and finally 5) ESG and climate risk modelling and assessment (such as bank climate modelling or insurance underwriting climate analysis).[12]

A relatively widespread form of government support globally is that of financial backing for clean energy generation projects. The most common format has been Feed-In Tariff (FIT) policies. A form of FIT was introduced under the Carter administration in the United States in the late 1970s, as part of the Public Utility Regulatory Policies Act signed in 1978. However, often Germany is recognised as implementing the FIT earliest policy in 1990. Within just ten years, dozens of countries had adopted their own versions. Depending on the jurisdiction, FIT policies can be applicable to a narrow type of producers, such as large-scale renewable energy generation projects, or a wide range of producers, including factories, farmers, households, and private investors. In its simplest form, FIT policies offer the renewable energy producers a guaranteed, long-term unit price which can be at or above average market electricity prices, as well as guaranteed access to the power grid. The three-decade-old system has seen many tweaks depending on the country and in some it actually disappeared altogether in favour of some other types of renewables. Utility solar PV in China is an example.

Apart from FIT policies, there are many other forms of government financial support for renewable energy projects, such as tax incentives, subsidies, and contracts-for-differences. The United States has federal tax incentives, known as the Renewable Electricity Production Tax Credit. It is a tax credit, providing up to 1.5 US cents/kWh or 2.75 US cents/kWh, depending on the energy type, produced by eligible renewable energy sources. The 2022 IRA mandates new wage and apprenticeship requirements for systems over 1 MW commissioned after 2021. Tax credits begin at 0.30 or 0.55 US cents/kWh based on the energy type and increase to the full amount when these standards are met.[13]

One example of a subsidy is India's support for small solar PV rooftop systems for households. In March 2024, the nation announced that its cabinet had approved about $9 billion to install rooftop solar and provide electricity for 10 million households. The programme includes central financial assistance for residential rooftop solar. Specifically, 60 per cent for the costs of 2 kW systems and 40 per cent for one between 2 kW and 3 kW. At the then benchmark prices, it will mean a 30,000 Indian rupees ($340) subsidy for 1 kW systems, 60,000 Indian rupees ($681) for 2 kW systems, and 78,000 ($885) for systems above 3 kW.[14]

The provision of grants is another common form of government support towards clean energy projects aimed at cutting the national carbon footprint. The United Kingdom has been highly focused on ways to decarbonise as well as reduce the overall energy bill for households and enterprises. One of the many targets is heating and cooling systems. Using such equipment as air source heat pumps, the carbon footprint can be reduced and the energy bill cut. An area which is not solely aggressively targeted in the United Kingdom, but throughout the whole of Europe.

Heat pumps extract the required energy from ambient air so that they may supply cooling and heating. The purchase price of these systems has been falling sharply in recent years, though they still remain more pricey than conventional systems. Government grants make it more attractive for end users to retrofit or for new users to opt for air-source heat pumps or similar systems. The benefits are many. They include better air quality, lower CO_2 emissions, lower energy use and bills, and in some cases – depending on the type of equipment – less maintenance compared to traditional systems, which also results in lower running costs. Overall, heat pumps are at least three times more efficient than natural gas boilers, for example. The United Kingdom created a programme to expand the penetration. The boiler upgrade scheme began in 2020 and provides grants to homeowners. The average installation cost is £10,000 ($13,504) to £14,000 ($18,906) for an air source heat pump and £14,000 ($18,906) to £35,000 ($47,265) for ground source heat pumps. The scheme provides £7,500 ($10,128) per household to help offset these costs. In late 2023, the government announced that it would allocate an extra £1.5 billion ($2 billion) for the period from 2025 through 2028. This, together with a £400 million ($540 million) energy efficiency grant, is to be launched in 2025.[15] The idea behind such grants is that a more attractive price for the end user will raise the volume of products sold, which in turn will help the progressive reduction of the price. A similar approach has been adopted in a great number of countries in other areas, such as EVs and e-bikes.

Financing from banks

Development banks

Multilateral Development Banks play a crucial role in climate finance for many important reasons. These financial institutions fall into three broad categories: those with a global presence and mandate, those with regional mandates, and national institutions with international operations. Major multilateral development banks include the World Bank, the European Bank for Reconstruction and Development, and the Asian Infrastructure Investment Bank. At the regional level, key institutions comprise the Asian Development Bank, the African Development Bank, and the New Development Bank. Finally, examples of significant national development banks with international reach include the Brazilian Development Bank, the China Development Bank, the Development Bank of Southern Africa, and Germany's KfW Bankengruppe.

The ways development banks play a critical role in climate finance are not simply limited to their financing muscle. They offer policy support, technical expertise, collaboration facilitation, and risk management, including the de-risking of investments. Providing funding is the very essence of these banks. Today, most have recognised that the energy transition is a major priority, and they must be a central participant in the financing of transition-related projects and solutions, including renewable energy generation, energy efficiency, and grid modernisation projects. Their participation is especially important in developing countries which have more limited access to financing. Also, these banks typically have a great amount of influence on governments. With their broad experience and extensive expertise, they can support governments in setting or improving policies and regulations that drive the energy transition. They can also provide significant technical assistance which can be tailored to the specific needs of a specific country. Their regional or global position allows them to structure ways for different countries to collaborate and coordinate, have more aligned efforts, and use resources more efficiently. Their work also allows them to broaden this collaboration and coordination to the private sector and other stakeholders. Finally, they can help in managing risk. Low- or zero-carbon projects and solutions can be complex and present many risks. These banks can help with risk mitigation by providing instruments like guarantees and insurance to attract the private sector. Guarantees, insurance, blended finance, currency hedging support, and other mechanisms can also help with partially or fully de-risking an energy transition project. For example, let's take a country which wants to invest in green hydrogen but has no prior experience in this area. Such a project could be viewed as high risk and may not be able to attract investors. The support of one or more development banks would allow the projects to go ahead as the development banks could finance the feasibility study as well as part or all of the construction costs.

Ten major development banks[16] have grouped together to jointly announce several climate finance-related commitments.[17] They want to strengthen collaboration with clients, development partners, civil society, the private sector, and others to reduce poverty and inequality and address the crises. For this purpose, they announced in 2022 a climate finance commitment of $61 billion for low- and middle-income economies, and almost $100 billion in all economies where they operate. One year later, at COP28, they reaffirmed their commitment to socially inclusive, gender-responsive, and nature-positive climate and development action. They plan to achieve this through an increased focus on measuring results and outcomes, analytics for impact, long-term strategies, country-level collaboration, attracting private capital at scale, and supporting efforts on adaptation and disaster risk management. They are also committed to strengthening collaboration on nature, water, health, and gender. They will boost their joint action on climate and development, strengthen collaboration to scale up finance and enhance results measurement, bolster country-level collaboration, and increase co-financing and private sector engagement. In an ideal world, these ten banks as well as others could adopt common principles, taxonomies, and even action plans. It is not impossible that this will happen in future as the climate urgency becomes increasingly evident to them. For now, it is a positive development that these entities are at least banding together to announce joint commitments. It is a big step forward.

Another example of a joint approach on the part of MDBs is related to nature. A group of MDBs set up the 'Task Force on Sustainability-Linked Sovereign Financing for Nature and Climate'. The task force will exclusively focus on 'debt-for-nature' swaps. This tool is used to reduce the sovereign debt of a nation which needs to protect its ecosystem. One way of achieving such cuts is the MDBs purchasing a sovereign bond issued by the nation and then replacing this bond with an eco-labelled one carrying a lower coupon. 'Debt-for-nature'-related bonds are attractive to some institutional investors given the MDBs' backing. This format is by no means new. It has been reported that it first began in the 1980s. Over 140 deals have been completed as of November 2023. The Nature Conservancy, a global environmental organisation, identified that at least $800 billion worth of sovereign debt could be swapped into 'debt-for-nature'.[18] In 2021, the small Caribbean nation of Belize used such a mechanism. A subsidiary of The Nature Conservancy lent Belize funds to buy back its entire external commercial debt, a $553 million 'superbond', at a discounted price of 55 cents in the dollar. This was financed by issuing $364 million in 'blue bonds', arranged by Credit Suisse, with insurance from the US government's International Development Finance Corporation. This resulted in a low-interest loan with a 10-year grace period and a 19-year maturity. In exchange, Belize committed to spend approximately $4 million annually on marine conservation until 2041, aiming to double its marine-protection parks from 15.9 per cent to 30 per cent of its oceans by 2026. An endowment fund of $23.5 million will support conservation efforts post-2040.[19] Another example is the Ecuador deal in May 2023. It executed the largest 'debt-for-nature' swap on record, according to Reuters, by issuing a new 'blue bond'. This bond would allocate at least $12 million annually towards the conservation of the Galapagos Islands, a globally significant ecosystem. Ecuador secured around $1.6 billion of the country's debt at a nearly 60 per cent discount with Credit Suisse's assistance. The $656 million 'Galapagos Bond', which matures in 2041, offers investors a 5.645 per cent interest rate. The bond features an $85 million 'credit guarantee' from the Inter-American Development Bank and $656 million in political risk insurance from the US International Development Finance Corp, reducing its risk profile.[20]

Another example of MDBs' climate financing is the backing of energy-transition-focused private equity funds. The SUSI Asia Energy Transition Fund was formally launched in May 2023 with $120 million in assets. Key shareholders of the fund include some private investors as well as seven development finance institutions: the Asian Infrastructure Investment Bank, Austria's OeEB, the Belgian Investment Company for Developing Countries, the Netherlands' FMO, Norway's Norfund, Sweden's Swedfund, and the United Kingdom's British International Investment. The fund concluded seven investments including energy efficiency, a development platform for utility-scale renewables, and distributed solar PV solutions for commercial and industrial customers, with companies in Malaysia, the Philippines, Singapore, Thailand, and Vietnam.[21] For example, the fund is cooperating with renewable energy projects developer BayWa r.e. for investments in solar rooftop PV of up to 20 MW in Indonesia, Malaysia, the Philippines, Thailand, and Vietnam.[22]

Given the important role that multilateral development banks play in financing and advancing the energy transition, it is worth briefly highlighting some case studies involving some specific MDBs including the Asian Infrastructure Investment Bank, the KfW Bankengruppe from Germany, and the Inter-American Development Bank.

An interesting collaborative work by MDBs is The Asian Infrastructure Investment Bank (AIIB) and the Global Energy Alliance for People and Planet (GEAPP) forming a significant strategic partnership at COP27, committing to mobilise up to $1 billion for green energy transition and renewable energy projects throughout Asia and beyond. This collaboration targets three key areas: grid-based renewables, distributed renewables, and fossil fuel transitioning initiatives. This marks AIIB's first partnership with a global philanthropic foundation-led initiative, enhancing its capacity for co-financing operations and private capital mobilisation. The partnership will direct capital to eligible countries that satisfy both AIIB's strategies and policies while aligning with GEAPP's charitable objectives.[23]

In a related development, AIIB updated its Energy Sector Strategy (ESS) in November 2022. This revised strategy excludes most coal investments, introduces new restrictions on gas and oil financing, and increases focus on renewable energy and climate adaptation finance. Despite these positive steps, the updated ESS contains significant shortcomings. Critics note loopholes remain that permit fossil fuel financing, and the strategy lacks clear commitments to address important areas such as energy access and gender equality. As a result, while representing progress, the ESS falls short of meeting the ambition required by both the UN SDGs and the Paris Agreement.[24]

Another key global MDB making significant impact is the Inter-American Development Bank (IDB). Through its private sector arm, IDB Invest has committed a $50 million loan to Allkem for the Sal de Vida lithium project in Argentina. This investment actively promotes low-carbon and climate-resilient private sector development in the region. The ambitious project aims to produce 15,000 metric tons of lithium annually, create approximately 1,000 jobs, and strengthen domestic supply chains. What makes this financing particularly noteworthy is its structure as both a green and sustainability-linked loan, with specific targets for women's workforce participation, renewable energy utilisation, and emissions reduction. The project incorporates a comprehensive action plan addressing social and environmental criteria while aligning with multiple UN SDGs.[25]

A final instructive example comes from KfW Bankengruppe, a regionally headquartered MDB from Germany. This German state-owned investment and development bank, acting on behalf of the German Federal Ministry for Economic Cooperation and Development, recently formalised two substantial loan agreements with the State Bank of India and the Indian Ministry of Finance. These agreements, totalling €200 million ($234 million), bring KfW's cumulative support for the German–Indian solar partnership to approximately €1 billion ($1.17 billion) since 2017. The financing specifically targets the expansion of India's solar energy infrastructure to meet growing energy demands through renewable sources. Projects implemented under these new contracts will reduce India's GHG emissions by 650,000 tons annually. The partnership has already achieved remarkable results, installing 4 GW of output capacity, providing 5 million people with electricity from renewable sources, and preventing roughly 6 million tons of CO_2 emissions each year across India.[26]

Commercial and investment financial institutions

Commercial and investment banks differ from MDBs in many ways. When it comes to climate finance, a key difference is that MDBs are principally moved by domestic or global policies whereas commercial financial institutions are typically driven by regulation and income generation. These financial institutions have an unexpectedly dynamic relationship with the energy transition. As they have different activities outside lending, they are also impacted in a multitude of different ways. They are corporations working with corporations as clients, so they struggle, in particular, institutions with a global business scope – to balance regulations against their clients' interests and needs. At the same time, the climate dimension seriously increases the complexity of risk management for the commercial banks.

Lending by commercial banks

These financial institutions have an unexpectedly dynamic relationship with energy transition. Their business is directly and indirectly impacted by climate change. Internally, financial institutions need to make at least three adjustments: for their emissions, their reporting, and their internal training. Emissions-wise, by the very nature of their business, their direct carbon footprint is relatively low. Out of the 11 sectors, as defined by financial services firm MSCI, the finance sector on average has one of the lowest CO_2 direct emissions footprints together with the communication services, healthcare, and real estate sectors. To cut these, they can focus on their operational emissions from such sources as heating and cooling at their offices, their company-owned vehicles, or directly owned data centres, for example. Reporting-wise, financial institutions must set up internal systems for the monitoring of their direct emissions. Training-wise, internal staff must receive extensive and regular training to better understand how to use ESG principles, sustainability standards, and the like in their day-to-day business. This is absolutely imperative as rules and regulations related to climate are evolving rapidly. These three adjustments to cut their CO_2 can be easily attained.

At the same time, the business that financial institutions conduct with their clients is generally climate-negative. The CDP, an NGO, produced a study concluding that 556 financial institutions disclosed environmental information for 2022 through its climate change questionnaire. The reported financed emissions – the emissions associated with the investments made by the clients of the institutions – on average were 750 times larger than the reported operational emissions. Specifically, they were 11,000 times higher for North

American institutions, 270 times higher for those in the Asia Pacific region, and 250 times higher for European ones.[27] So, while the activities of commercial or investment banks have traditionally revolved around lending, they must provide many more services than just lending money. Many institutions strive to be a one-stop shop for financial solutions to their clients. These include client services such as asset management, financial advisory, foreign exchange, insurance, investments, payment, or wealth management. Some even have arms which do direct investments. So while their own carbon footprint could be low and falling, that of their portfolio may remain stubbornly high. They could be providing foreign exchange services to an oil company, or insurance services to a company which owns coal-fired power plants, or bond issuance advisory services to a steel company.

Many prominent financial institutions, especially the large international banks, have committed to a net-zero portfolio by 2050 given regulatory and stakeholders pressures. They need to find a balance between meeting climate regulations and their clients' requirements and needs. A significant number of the world's leading financial institutions have pledged to achieve net-zero emissions in their investment portfolios as of July 2023, according to a study by the NewClimate Institute,[28] an NGO. This group includes 37 of the top 50 asset managers, 24 of the top 50 asset owners, and 33 of the top 50 banks. Achieving a net-zero portfolio means that the clients that the bank deals with must have, on an aggregate basis, zero emissions. It can raise the amount of exposure to corporations with near-net-zero or net-zero activities, and with those that have a pathway to net zero by 2050. At the same time, that can terminate the relationships with those who do not have such strategies or offer their expertise, services, resources, and finance to accelerate their clients' transition.

Given the complexity of the relationships that banks may have in terms of the types of services provided, it is no easy task to build a net-zero portfolio. While the global commitment by banks has a positive track record in recent years and the momentum is strong, it has created a variety of intense debates as of 2024. For example, some of the largest global investment banks are arguing that a significant portion of their underwriting activities should be exempt from net-zero targets. Some of the world's largest investment banks have been lobbying to exclude chunks of their underwriting activity from net-zero targets, in a debate that threatens to slow their progress on decarbonisation, reported the Financial Times. The same article quotes NGOs such as Urgewald and the Rainforest Action Network stating that more than a third of the $669 billion in financing provided to fossil fuel companies in 2022 by the world's 60 largest banks was through underwriting bonds and equities. This means that a significant portion of the banks' support for the oil, gas, and coal sectors was not in the form of direct loans. Rather, it was through facilitating the issuance of financial instruments.[29]

Commercial banks can be global, regional, and national (see Figure 9.2). They all have different lending policies and pressures. For now, global banks lead the way when it comes to climate finance. It is important to distinguish the current differences between global and domestic commercial banks. Some factors are not necessarily related to climate finance but are still crucial. Global banks have a greater reach given that they have operations in multiple jurisdictions whereas domestic banks typically are limited to their home markets. They are subject to the green lending regulatory framework in each of the markets they operate while being subject to higher scrutiny as well as having to follow international reporting standards. For domestic banks, green lending reporting is typically less developed. They enjoy more diverse funding and can easily diversify their portfolios compared to the domestic banks. On their environmental performance, they are typically more high profile and so more of them are forced to target higher internal environmental sustainability standards

	GLOBAL COMMERCIAL BANKS	DOMESTIC COMMERCIAL BANKS
OPERATIONS	Operate in multiple jurisdictions	Primarily home market focus
SCALE	Larger asset base, diverse funding, easily enter large-scale climate financing	Limited global assets and funding sources
REGULATION	Higher scrutiny, varied reporting standards, may follow international standards	Green lending reporting not yet mature
CAPITAL	Access to diverse funding, can diversify portfolios more easily	Limited balance sheet, harder to attain diversified green portfolio
ENVIRONMENTAL PERFORMANCE	Higher profile requires more transparency on sustainability	Environmental performance and green lending vary widely
RISK MANAGEMENT	Greater experience in green lending, better risk management tools, higher risk tolerance	Less experience, lower risk tolerance in green lending
CLIMATE POLICIES RESPONSE	Higher response	Responses vary, often less influenced by environmental considerations
GREEN ASSETS	Keen on aligning emission reduction goals with investments	Attraction to green lending varies, generally less than global banks
STAKEHOLDER ENGAGEMENT	Experience with diverse stakeholders, including environmental groups	
CORPORATE FOCUS	Focus on mid to large corporations	Serve small to medium enterprises
GLOBAL COLLABORATION	Increasing collaboration with domestic banks	Increasing collaboration with global banks

Figure 9.2 Climate finance capability of global and domestic banks

Source: Author, original chart design (June 2025).

while facing more scrutiny on their green lending, especially financed emissions. They typically respond more proactively to changing climate policies. The behaviour of domestic banks is typically less influenced by environmental considerations, at least for now. They are usually keen to increase green assets in their portfolio which allows them to align emission reduction goals with investment opportunities. A final difference is with risk management. Typically, they have greater experience and expertise in green lending risk management leading to better risk management tools enabling them to have higher risk tolerance relative to domestic banks. For example, a global bank can significantly lower its risk exposure by entering into a green loan together with one or more other banks. Such syndicated loan approach is also quite typical with MDBs as well. The global players also have greater capacity to evaluate client risk.

This in no way means that global banks are better than domestic banks when it comes to green lending. Climate finance is a relatively new field, and it is still evolving and developing. As it matures, it will be easier for domestic banks to adopt global best practice when it comes to internal environmental sustainability considerations and climate considerations with their lending and the other financial services they offer.

Banks' approaches and strategies

Global banks play a significant role in financing the global transition to a low-carbon economy, but their approaches and strategies vary greatly. As of April 2025, the 15 largest commercial banks in the world had an aggregate total assets base of almost $52 trillion (see Figure 9.3). Six of these banks are headquartered in China and have about $27.4 trillion in total assets. Four are US-based and have a total of $11.3 trillion. Three are European with assets of $8.5 trillion. Finally, two are headquartered in Japan and hold $4.6 trillion in assets. Understanding the actions of these banks in green or climate finance is important in assessing the progress towards a sustainable economy.

Rank	Name	Headquarters	Total assets ($B)	Accounting principles
1	Industrial and Commercial Bank of China Ltd. (1398-SEHK)	China	6,688.7	IFRS
2	Agricultural Bank of China Ltd. (1288-SEHK)	China	5,923.8	IFRS
3	China Construction Bank Corp. (939-SEHK)	China	5,558.4	IFRS
4	Bank of China Ltd. (3988-SEHK)	China	4,803.5	IFRS
5	JPMorgan Chase & Co. (JPM-NYSE)	US	4,002.8	US GAAP
6	Bank of America Corp. (BAC-NYSE)	US	3,261.5	US GAAP
7	HSBC Holdings PLC (HSBA-LSE)	UK	2,989.8	IFRS
8	BNP Paribas SA (BNP-ENXTPA)	France	2,809.8	IFRS
9	Crédit Agricole Group	France	2,693.6	IFRS
10	Mitsubishi UFJ Financial Group Inc. (8306-TSE)	Japan	2,628.1	Japanese GAAP
11	Postal Savings Bank of China Co. Ltd. (1658-SEHK)	China	2,340.7	IFRS
12	Citigroup Inc. (C-NYSE)	US	2,152.0	US GAAP
13	Bank of Communications Co. Ltd. (3328-SEHK)	China	2,041.5	IFRS
14	Sumitomo Mitsui Financial Group Inc. (8316-TSE)	Japan	1,977.2	Japanese GAAP
15	Wells Fargo & Co (WFC-NYSE)	US	1,929.9	US GAAP
	China headquartered banks	**6**	**27,356.5**	
	Europe headquartered banks	**3**	**8,493.2**	
	US headquartered banks	**4**	**11,346.1**	
	Japan headquartered banks	**2**	**4,605.3**	

Figure 9.3 The world's 15 largest banks by assets, 2025

Notes: Cumulated assets by geography of headquarters calculated by the author; all data as of 8 April 2025; please refer to the source for full set of footnotes and remarks.

Source: Jimenea A, Wu J, Terris H, Singh Y, and Lozano C 'The World's Largest Banks by Assets, 2025' (S&P Global 2025). Available at: https://www.spglobal.com/market-intelligence/en/news-insights/articles/2025/4/the-worlds-largest-banks-by-assets-2025-88424232 accessed 29 June 2025.

CHINESE AND EUROPEAN BANKS: BEST GLOBAL PRACTICE AND CRUCIAL TO THE DEVELOPMENT OF CLIMATE FINANCE

Chinese banks are the major ones that cannot be ignored. Their role is crucial to the development of climate finance due to the size of the Chinese economy, the nation's leading role in the energy transition, their state ownership provides them with a sovereign or near sovereign credit rating, and the massive size of the balance sheet of the top six banks: the Agricultural Bank of China, the Bank of China, the Bank of Communications, the China Construction Bank, the Industrial and Commercial Bank of China, and the Postal Savings Bank of China. Given the State is their majority shareholder, when discussing these six banks, the emphasis is on what the government policies are. Financing the energy transition and path to net zero is a key national priority for the Chinese government. Chinese President Xi Jinping himself pointed out in October 2023 at the Central Financial Work Conference, a key twice-a-decade financial policy meeting, that the financial sector should provide high-quality services for economic and social development in five major areas. One of the five areas he mentioned is green finance, reported the People's Daily.[30]

While President Xi, together with the State Council and the Central Party Committee, drives green finance policies, the implementation has been left to several other bodies. They include the People's Bank of China, the Ministry of Finance, the Central Financial Commission, the National Development and Reform Commission, the Ministry of Ecology and Environment, the National Financial Regulation Administration (formerly the China Banking and Insurance Regulatory Commission), the China Securities Regulatory Commission, and the State-owned Asset and Administration Commission. In other words, the bureaucratic oversight is a heavy and complex one for the banks.

China has been making efforts to develop common finance-related policies and regulations, but authorities recognise that there is still work to be done. In particular, there are opportunities to harmonise some areas with international standards. For example, a recent paper suggested several 'low-hanging fruit' initiatives, such as establishing unified ESG disclosure standards and making them mandatory. The paper also recommended expanding the grading criteria of financial institutions to include more instruments, improving ESG risk management for Chinese companies in the 'new three' industries (EVs, lithium batteries, and solar panels) and promoting the growth of third-party accreditation agencies. These measures could help to further align China's financial sector with global best practices and support the country's transition to a more sustainable economy.[31] Figure 9.4 presents potential acts of support towards green finance in China.

The Industrial and Commercial Bank of China and other banks have quite a lot to say about their climate finance activities. The priorities of the Industrial and Commercial Bank of China,[32] the largest bank in the world by total assets, unsurprisingly match the five priorities set by the central government, which include green finance. Its climate finance spreads to all of its main activities, including lending, bonds issuance and investing, equities, wealth management, and direct investments. These activities expanded significantly in the past few years, making the bank a large and active actor in the Chinese green space. Its green loans portfolio increased about 1 trillion yuan ($140 billion), up about 20 per cent year over year, to 6 trillion yuan ($841 billion) as of December 2024. It issued green bonds domestically amounting to 110 billion yuan ($15 billion) and ten overseas ones worth a total of $21.7 billion during the year. In its investment activities, it participated in the underwriting of 153 ESG bonds, including green bonds and sustainability-linked bonds, raising 475.7 billion yuan ($67 billion), including lead underwriting 166.9 billion yuan ($23 billion) worth. It also invested in domestic green bonds adding 40.6 billion yuan ($5.7 billion), up 363.5 per cent in the year, for a cumulative 290.9 billion yuan

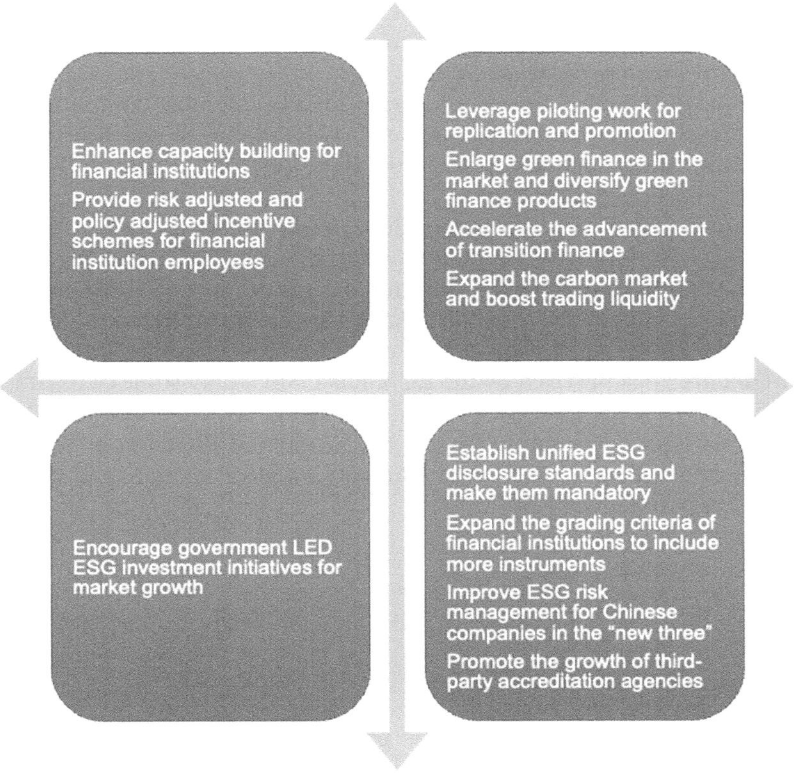

Figure 9.4 Heat map of potential actions on green finance development

Source: Zhang J, Ziying S and Nedopil Wang C, 'New Report: China Green Finance Status and Trends 2023-2024' (https://greenfdc.org/3 April 2024). Available at: https://greenfdc.org/China-green-finance-status-and-trends-2023-2024/ accessed 25 June 2024.

($41 billion). Its fund management arm, ICBC Credit Suisse Asset Management, held over 40.3 billion yuan ($5.7 billion) in 'green'-related equities involved in environmental protection and new energy. It had issued and managed 77 green public fund products with a value of 177.7 billion yuan ($25 billion); this subsidiary is a joint venture with defunct Swiss bank Credit Suisse taken over by another Swiss bank, UBS, in 2023. Its banking services for high-net-worth individuals, ICBC Wealth Management were keenly involved in climate finance products, it reports. Finally, its direct investment arm, ICBC Investment, increased its climate finance investments by 30.6 per cent or 13.8–60.0 billion yuan ($1.9–$8.4 billion) cumulatively during the year.

The bank was also highly proactive in internal or operational green activities. It accelerated its work on domestic climate risk management involving all of its business, its risk management, and its internal audit departments, referring to these as the first, second, and third lines of defence. It is also further developing the climate risk profile of its clients. Finally, it is progressively strengthening the management of its own carbon footprint, including consumption of water, electricity, and office paper. Its efforts translated in getting a rating of 'A' by financial services firm MSCI's ESG Ratings in 2023, the highest rating then assigned to the Chinese banking industry.

All in all, large Chinese domestic banks are doing well on the climate finance front internally and externally, though they will need to continue to improve and also raise the level of transparency in climate-related areas.

Western European financial institutions are probably the most committed in the world when it comes to climate finance-related areas. This applies to the four European commercial banks ranking among the top 15 in the world by total assets: BNP Paribas, Crédit Agricole, HSBC, and Banco Santander.

Commercial banks operating in Western Europe face different climate-related pressures. They have to follow the climate-related policies in the countries they operate in. They are supervised by the nation's supervisory body and, in some of the jurisdictions, they are supervised by the ECB as well (refer to Figure 9.5). This creates differences in the regulation and policies that dictate their business and strategies. BNP Paribas, Crédit Agricole, and Banco Santander are all supervised by the ECB. For HSBC, only some of its branches where it operates are supervised by the ECB, including France, Luxembourg, and Malta. As a UK-headquartered bank, it is supervised by the Prudential Regulation Authority, a body under the Bank of England – the United Kingdom's central bank – and by the Financial Conduct Authority (see Figure 9.5).

Figure 9.5 Countries whose banks are European Central Bank supervised entities

Source: Author (June 2025). Map created using MapChart (https://www.mapchart.net/).

Climate change and environmental degradation pose significant risks to the economy and financial sector. The ECB has set three objectives to address these risks. Firstly, it aims to better understand, monitor, and manage climate-related risks in monetary policy, investment operations, and the financial system. This involves assessing the economic impact of climate policies and exploring the relationship between climate, nature, and the economy. Secondly, it supports the transition to a carbon-neutral economy by promoting sustainable finance and creating incentives for a greener financial system. Finally, it aims to foster wider action by improving general understanding of climate and nature-related risks, collaborating with European and international partners on climate and sustainable finance topics, improving transparency, and reducing its own environmental impact. Achieving these objectives will help the ECB to maintain price stability and ensure the safety of banks.[33]

Rating agency Moody's highlighted that the ECB plans to expand its focus on climate change in 2024 and 2025, as part of its climate and nature work plan. It wants to address nature-related risks, promote greener monetary policy, and assess the impact and risks of transitioning to a green economy. The ECB wants institutions to adopt a strategic and comprehensive approach to climate-related and environmental risks. It set deadlines for banks to meet supervisory expectations on climate and environmental risks by the end of 2024, including full integration into the Internal Capital Adequacy Assessment Process (ICAAP) and stress testing. Other initiatives for 2024 and 2025 include assessing banks' alignment with supervisory expectations, incorporating climate risks into prudential frameworks, contributing to stress testing and scenario analysis, exploring the economic implications of climate adaptation policies, and integrating green transition policies into macroeconomic models. Furthermore, the ECB will consider environmental aspects in the preparatory phase of designing a digital euro and overseeing financial market infrastructures, and even in the eco-design of the next euro banknote series.[34]

The ECB has taken numerous steps to ensure that the banks it supervises fully take into consideration climate-related and environmental risks in all of their workflows. In a speech, a senior member of the ECB emphasised that it first started discussing such risks with the banks in 2019. He believes that there has been clear progress in the integration by banks of climate-related environmental risks in their strategy, governance, and risk management. He added that materiality assessments and business environment scans by banks in general were more robust in 2024 versus 2019. However, a number of them were not adequately performing these tasks and now face periodic penalty payments until they address this issue. The objective is for all banks under its supervision to fully meet all of the ECB's expectations by the end of 2024.[35] Notably, the periodic penalty payments can be steep. As much as 5 per cent of a bank's average daily turnover for up to six months, after which other actions can be taken by the ECB, according to the ECB website.

As is frequently the case with many climate actions, there are many voices critical of the ECB. Chiefly, arguing that the ECB has not done enough. Perhaps the most contentious area is that banks have no limitations in providing credit to highly polluting sectors such as steel manufacturing, fossil fuel-based power production, or aviation. The ECB believes that the banks need to maintain their relationships with companies involved in these sectors so that it can help these companies to gradually transition away from their highly polluting activities. For example, environmental NGO Greenpeace published a report in March 2024 highlighting that some banks supervised by the ECB, such as BNP Paribas, Santander, Deutsche Bank, ING Group, and Rabobank, had lent around €256 billion ($300 billion) between 2016 and early 2023 to companies whose operations destroy critical nature and threatened the climate.[36] While this issue has become a highly visible hot topic of debate in the European context, it is actually an issue found in many different jurisdictions around the world.

In the United Kingdom, while the Prudential Regulation Authority is very much separate from the ECB, especially after the United Kingdom left the EU, it is just as concerned about banks' approaches to managing their financial risks from climate change. The Authority's Rulebook includes a chapter on climate risk. It stresses that climate change poses financial risks through physical and transition risk factors. It explains that physical risks can include extreme weather events as well as long-term shifts in climate, while transition risks come from the adjustment towards a low-carbon economy. Liability risks may also arise from parties seeking to recover losses from those held responsible. It states that these risks are far-reaching, uncertain, and dependent on short-term actions. The magnitude of financial risks will depend on future scenarios, with a 'too little, too late' scenario potentially resulting in severe financial risks.[37] In its 2024 Business Plan, published in April 2024, the Prudential Regulation Authority said that it would examine the progress by banks in assessing their climate risk. It added that it would offer tools and other guidance to help them.[38] So while perhaps slightly behind the ECB, the trajectory is clearly for further regulation and tighter measures.

French multinational bank BNP Paribas and UK-based banking giant HSBC are two prominent financial institutions which can be examined as examples of climate strategies and risk management practices of European banks. Like any other major banks, there are two climate aspects: the internal aspect and the other external one. Both have been active in formulating clear internal and external climate change related strategies.

BNP Paribas has declared that it is committed to create a sustainable low-carbon future for clients and the world in 2021. Its 2025 strategic plan placed sustainability at the heart of its strategy, with five priority themes aligned with clients' objectives and the UN SDGs. It said that climate is central to the priority theme of transitioning towards carbon neutrality and that it is also deeply connected to other themes such as the circular economy, natural capital and biodiversity, as well as sustainable savings, investments, and financing.[39] Internally, the bank is aggressively addressing its own climate-related metrics and climate risk management. Its actions include internal carbon-lowering measures in all of its different business, including asset management, wealth management, and real estate, as well as training its employees, almost 190,000 worldwide, on climate-related issues.

From the external business perspective, BNP Paribas is already providing significantly more loans to low-carbon energies, including renewables, biofuels, and nuclear, than to fossil fuels, including coal, gas, and oil; €32 billion ($38 billion) to renewables, biofuels, and nuclear compared to €17.3 billion ($20.3 billion) to coal, gas, and oil. It aims for the amount to rise to €40 billion by 2030, which will mean it will have completed the transition of more than 90 per cent of its financing activities towards low-carbon energy production. It has specific credit reduction targets by 2025 in at least nine sectors. For the oil and gas, power generation, and automotive sectors, they were set in 2022. For the steel, aluminium, and cement sectors in 2023. And for the aviation, shipping, and commercial real estate sectors in 2024. It will also fully exit financial activities related to coal in the EU and OECD by 2030 while dedicating €200 billion ($234 billion) to the transition of its corporate clients to a low-carbon economy, through green loans, green bonds, and financing to low-carbon technologies.[40]

HSBC believes that its net-zero transition plan is one of the bank's four strategic pillars. Internally, it aims at entrenching net zero across in the organisation by deploying risk-based, proportionate, and iterative approach to support the transition to net zero in the markets it serves. Practically, it wants to have a net-zero-carbon footprint in its operations, including its supply chain, by 2030. It will reduce carbon emissions from its consumption and subsequently replace the remaining emissions with low-carbon alternatives. This would include buying high-quality carbon offsets as well as entering into clean energy procurement agreements. Other measures, including asking suppliers to disclose their emissions to the NGO CDP, accelerate the use of EVs, reduce business travel, and cut water consumption in its offices. Externally, it targets to provide and facilitate $750 to $1,000 billion for sustainable financing and investment to its customers by 2030.

HSBC partners with its stakeholders to support systemic change through new and existing partnerships and industry alliances. The bank says it has assessed its balance sheet, including using scenario analysis to understand the impact of climate risk on the business, and found no material impact on the financial statements for the year ended 31 December 2023. It is focused on raising the percentage of climate finance and investments in terms of balance sheet-related transactions, in its capital markets and advisory business, and in net new ESG and sustainable investing flows. When it comes to credit, it wants a net-zero portfolio by 2050, or what it calls 'net zero in its financed emissions'. In the short term, it will combine on-balance sheet financed emissions and facilitated emissions – the emissions derived from the facilitation of a financial transaction – targets for two emissions-intensive areas: the oil and gas, and the power and utilities sectors, and plans to disclose the combined progress for both sectors.[41]

UNITED STATES AND JAPANESE BANKS: PRACTICES IN CLIMATE FINANCE ARE LAGGING

Among the largest 15 banks globally, those headquartered in the United States have not been as proactive on the climate front. This is likely due to the high politicisation of the issue from the polarised views on the subject by the two main political parties. Domestic policies influence the big three banks – Bank of America, Citigroup, and JPMorgan Chase – as between half and two-thirds of their revenue originates from North America. It was not until late 2023 that Federal agencies supervising US banks addressed climate-related financial risk management, when the Fed finalised a set of principles for financial institutions with assets greater than $100 billion. The principles provide a high-level framework for addressing physical and transition risks associated with climate change. They cover various aspects of risk management, including governance, policies, procedures, strategic planning, data measurement, and scenario analysis. The principles do not prohibit or discourage banks from providing services to any specific class or type of customer, as long as they comply with applicable laws and regulations.[42] This means that they are free to offer their financial services to the fossil fuel industry, for example. The big three banks have issued climate-related actions, but these have typically neither been consistent nor provided clear and detailed targets. This lack of disclosure has worsened since the election of President Trump in January 2025.

Among the three US banking giants, JPMorgan Chase and Citigroup seem to have clearer climate actions than Bank of America. The two banks have individual climate reporting unlike Bank of America, which on its website only releases its responses to climate-related surveys from such bodies as CDP.

All three banks aim at net zero for their internal operations by 2030 and for their financing portfolios by 2050. The commitments are set to match international best practices rather than being mandated by government policy or regulatory bodies. Also, the internal climate action oversight by both JPMorgan Chase and Citigroup is more robust. JPMorgan Chase has appointed several senior sustainability roles firm-wide who are responsible for climate-related strategy and execution matters. Roles such as climate risk executive, global head of sustainability, head of green economy banking, as well as asset management and private banking heads of sustainable investing. Citigroup has had a similar approach. In addition to this comprehensive climate action supervision, they both strive to reduce the carbon footprint of their operations in ways similar to those of Chinese or European banks. They are executing on initiatives such as reducing the amount of energy consumption in general, raising the direct amount of clean energy as a percentage of total energy consumed, or transitioning their vehicle fleets away from internal combustion engine vehicles to EVs.[43]

In its latest annual report, for the year 2023, the Bank of America does not clearly provide great detail on internal and external climate action. Similar to other financial institutions, it classifies climate risk into physical risk and transition risk. Its approach to managing climate risk involves regular discussions by senior management, the Board, and its committees, and a Climate Risk Council. The corporation has committed to achieving net zero before 2050 and has set interim targets for 2030 for financing activities, operations, and supply chain. It says it has a $1.5 trillion sustainable finance goal, with $1 trillion dedicated to supporting the transition to a low-carbon economy. It underlines that achieving these goals may require technological advances, clearly defined road maps, better emissions data reporting, new standards and public policies, and strong engagement with stakeholders.[44]

One example of criticism towards Bank of America comes from As You Sow, a US-based shareholder advocacy NGO. While the bank committed to achieving net-zero emissions for its financing activities in the auto, energy, and power sectors by 2030 and also has signed the Net Zero Banking Alliance Commitment Statement, As You Sow notes that there is a lack of clear disclosure regarding the bank's transition planning. As of November 2023, shareholders still do not have sufficient information to determine whether the bank was on track to meet its targets. Additionally, As You Sow points out that the bank's annual disclosures do not provide clear information on how non- or slow-transitioning companies in high-emitting sectors will impact the bank's ability to meet its 2030 targets. These omissions make it difficult for investors to assess potential misalignments between the bank's 2030 targets and its clients' transition progress, as well as any proactive actions the bank is taking to address such misalignments.[45]

Another of the many criticisms has been towards its financing of fossil fuel industries. Bank of America had received praise from climate activists in 2022 for pledging not to finance new coal mines, coal-burning power plants, or Arctic drilling project. In the ESG policy update released in December 2023, it backtracked on these commitments, stating that such projects will be subject to 'enhanced due diligence' instead. This is most likely due to the increasing backlash from Republican lawmakers against corporations that consider ESG factors in their operations, as some media reports have indicated.[46]

The big three US banks and other large financial institutions are likely to progressively improve their climate action efforts over the coming years. However, at present, they are falling behind and have not taken sufficient measures to match the global best practices set by Chinese or European banks in addressing climate change. A former high-ranking official at the US Department of the Treasury[47] has pointed out that the guidance provided by various US financial agencies is largely discretionary, and the United States is currently lagging behind its G20 counterparts in addressing the financial implications of climate change. This view is widely shared by industry experts and is clearly reflected in the limited climate action taken by the big three US banks compared to their global peers. The US financial regulators' slow response to climate change risks puts them out of step with the international consensus on the financial risks posed by climate change.

Similar to US climate action, climate action by Japanese financial institutions has lagged that of Chinese or European banks. This includes that of the Japanese banks' regulator, the Financial Services Agency, and the nation's central bank, the Bank of Japan. The two bodies, for example, are still in the process of setting up climate scenario analysis for the country's largest financial institutions. They announced that they are working on climate-related scenario analysis in the banking sector in May 2024. The exercise will build on an initial analysis carried out in fiscal 2021, through March 2022. The new analysis will focus on risks associated with bank lending within a shorter time frame and will use common scenarios for climate-related risks in the 2024 financial year, through March 2025. The two also plan to conduct a similar scenario analysis for the insurance sector.

Environmental campaigners have long pushed for more systematic collection of data on global banks' financed emissions, as the world's 60 biggest banks are estimated to have provided $6.9 trillion in financing to the fossil fuel industry over the past eight years.[48] Mitsubishi UFJ is the fourth largest lender in the world to the fossil fuel industry with about $308 billion in financed emissions cumulatively between 2016 and 2023. Sumitomo Mitsui is the ninth largest with around $213 billion. In the top ten banks financing the fossil fuel sector, there is another Japanese bank, Mizuho, with about $273 billion cumulatively (see Figure 9.6).

While the two banks have made some efforts in their climate strategies, oversight is still an issue. In April 2024, for example, a coalition of climate groups filed shareholder

BANK (STOCK CODE AND EXCHANGE)	TOTAL FOSSIL FUEL FINANCING ($, billion)
JPMorgan Chase & Co. (JPM-NYSE)	430.4
Citigroup Inc. (C-NYSE)	396.3
Bank of America Corp. (BAC-NYSE)	333.2
Wells Fargo (WFC-NYSE)	307.7
Mitsubishi UFJ Financial Group Inc. (8306-TSE)	296.3
Mizuho (8411-TSE)	272.5
Royal Bank of Canada (CAD-TSX)	256.5
Barclays (BARC-LSE)	235.2
Sumitomo Mitsui Financial Group Inc. (8316-TSE)	212.2
UBS (UBSG-SWX)	210.7

Figure 9.6 Total fossil fuel financing by major global banks

Note: This report was a joint effort among Rainforest Action Network (RAN), BankTrack, Center for Energy, Ecology, and Development, Indigenous Environmental Network (IEN), Oil Change International (OCI), Reclaim Finance, the Sierra Club, and Urgewald. The finance data was co-researched with significant contributions from Profundo.

Source: Various Non-Profit Organisations, 'Banking on Climate Chaos: Fossil Fuel Finance Report 2024' (Banking on Climate Chaos 2024). Available at: https://www.bankingonclimatechaos.org accessed 29 June 2024.

proposals with Japan's top three banks, including Mitsubishi UFJ and Sumitomo Mitsui Financial Group, calling for stricter board oversight of climate-related risks. It marked the first time such groups targeted the boards of these banks as a way to pressure them on climate change. The proposals focus on board oversight of climate-related business risks and seek to make the banks disclose how they evaluate competency for such oversight. This represents a strategy shift from proposals in 2023, which require banks to disclose credible transition plans to meet 2050 carbon-neutral targets. The latest proposals reflect governance standards set by the International Sustainability Standards Board requiring disclosure around how governance bodies oversee sustainability-related risks. The proposals were voted by the banks' annual general meetings in June 2024 but faced high hurdles and were not approved. In 2023, proposals received only around 20 per cent backing from shareholders. Climate resolutions commonly take the form of proposals to amend a company's articles of incorporation, which in Japan requires a two-thirds majority. While no climate resolutions were passed, the pressure will continue to prompt further policy changes at banks. Climate groups are also calling on the banks to disclose how they assess fossil fuel sector clients' climate change transition plans and what they plan to do if clients fail to produce credible plans.

Mitsubishi UFJ released its 'carbon neutrality declaration' in May 2021. It broadly followed the script of action points of other major global banks, such as BNP Paribas and HSBC. It announced that it wanted to achieve net-zero emissions in its finance portfolio by 2050 and in its own operations by 2030. But, at the time, the Japanese banking giant provided fewer tangible targets. It began to develop a transition plan in line with the transition plan guidance of the November 2022 Glasgow Financial Alliance for Net Zero. Targets came through in April 2024 with its Climate Report. It says that this report showcases the progress and achievements of the bank's efforts towards decarbonisation, including its transition plan and decarbonisation approach. It highlighted the importance of client engagement and support, including transition finance, in realising steady progress in decarbonising carbon-intensive industries and regions. It also acknowledges the need to balance decarbonisation efforts with economic development, particularly in Asia, where energy demand will continue to increase.

Mitsubishi UFJ's four main strategies are to cut emissions from its own operations, engage and support clients, reduce emissions from its financed portfolio, and implement effective risk management and governance. These strategies are closely aligned to global best practice. The first of the specific measures was to provide an interim target for internal emissions. It will reduce emissions from its own operations by 50 per cent by the end of fiscal 2026, through March 2027, and net zero by March 2031. It also set interim targets for reducing emissions from its finance portfolio for its key sectors: power generation, oil and gas, commercial and residential real estate, steel, shipping, as well as new targets for the automotive, aviation, and coal sectors. The bank's cumulative sustainable financing stood at 27.7 trillion yen ($187 billion) at the end of September 2023. It raised its March 2031 target to 100 trillion yen ($676 billion) from 35 trillion yen ($237 billion).[49] Similar to peers, the bank also spelled out detailed climate risk management mechanisms as well as raising internal engagement and internal training programmes.

Sumitomo Mitsui, like Mitsubishi UFJ, has been slow in setting detailed plans compared to global best practices. In a May 2024 presentation, the bank acknowledged three challenges. While its credit portfolio aims to achieve net-zero emissions by 2050, the bank anticipates an increase in GHG emissions in its portfolio in the short to mid term. The bank needs to address clients who face difficulties in transitioning to a low-carbon economy, including those in jurisdictions where government policies are not yet aligned with a 1.5°C scenario and those in industries requiring structural transformation. Lastly, the bank highlighted the cost burden. Companies need to pass on transition costs, while at the same time, governments must balance economic efficiency with stable supply and decarbonisation. This while limiting price increases for consumers. Similar to its global peers, Sumitomo Mitsui plans to increase its climate finance. It aims at 50 trillion yen ($338 billion) by March 2030 from 24 trillion yen ($162 billion) for the fiscal year ending March 2024. The bank has set mid-term targets for the power, oil and gas, coal, automobile, steel, and real estate sectors but has not yet set targets for agriculture, aluminium, and cement.[50]

The big two Japanese financial institutions have made some progress in recent years, and the trajectory towards change and reaching global best standards is positive. Another example of the big two catching up is that both are early adopters of making disclosures aligned with the Taskforce on Nature-related Financial Disclosure, which offers a framework for risk management and disclosure to enable companies and financial institutions to recognise, evaluate, handle, and, when necessary, disclose issues related to nature.[51]

The Net Zero Banking Alliance (NZBA), established under the Glasgow Financial Alliance for Net Zero during COP26, aims to mobilise the financial sector in support of the global net-zero transition. Member banks of the NZBA have pledged to achieve net-zero emissions by 2050, focusing not just on their direct emissions but also on the emissions they finance across the economy, known as Scope 3 emissions. Additionally, these banks have set interim targets for 2030 to significantly reduce emissions in the most critical and high-emitting sectors.

The NZBA tripled its membership since April 2021 to 128 banks from 44 countries, managing a combined total of $47 trillion in assets, as of June 2025. The alliance prioritises sectors that contribute significantly to global GHG emissions, both from energy use and non-energy processes. These sectors include heavy industries such as aluminium, cement, and steel, which are pivotal in the decarbonisation effort.[52] By focusing on these areas, the NZBA aims to drive meaningful reductions in emissions and support the transition to a more sustainable economy.

However, as of June 2025, the number of banks participating had declined. Mitsubishi UFJ Financial Group, Japan's largest lender, left the NZBA, following similar exits by Nomura Holdings and Sumitomo Mitsui Financial Group. This trend mirrors withdrawals by major US and Canadian banks, influenced by shifting environmental policies. The NZBA, once representing over 40 per cent of global banking assets, is now reviewing its strategies, potentially removing the requirement for members to align with a 1.5°C global warming limit. Mitsubishi UFJ Financial, previously a steering group member, maintained its commitment to addressing climate change despite this departure.[53]

Financing from private capital – direct and indirect investors

Financial investors are a critical source of climate finance. They are important, if not even more important, than multilateral and commercial banks. These can be categorised into two baskets: direct and indirect investors. These two types can be further split into 15 types of financial institutions, as shown in Figure 9.7.

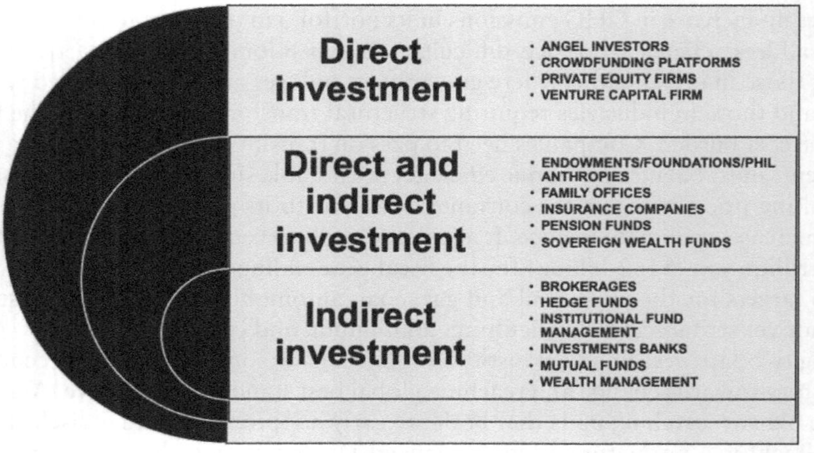

Figure 9.7 Financial institutions involved in climate finance

Source: Author, original chart design (June 2025).

Five Types of investors have capital that they can invest directly or indirectly, such as buying the shares of a company involved in the energy transition or investing in a fund which in turn buys such shares, for example. These include family offices, insurance companies, pension funds, and sovereign wealth funds, as well as a fifth type which comprises endowments, foundations, and philanthropies.

Another four types of entities are typically solely direct investors comprising angel investors, crowdfunding platforms, venture capital firms, and private equity firms.

There are another six kinds of institutions that are indirect investors in the energy transition. They include brokerages, hedge funds, institutional fund management, investment banks, mutual funds, and wealth managers. The type of institution, its investment activity, and the type of climate action must not be narrowly defined since there are many areas of overlap and also many exceptions to the rule. Yet it is important to understand the nature of these various sources of capital, as well as the opportunities and challenges they face, in order to effectively navigate how private capital for climate action can be mobilised.

Firstly, one must consider the institutions that are genuinely committed to supporting a net-zero 2050 world. For example, some institutions have joined global alliances to show their commitment, but many have not. One example is the Glasgow Financial Alliance for Net Zero (GFANZ). This group represents a united front of prominent financial institutions worldwide, dedicated to expediting the reduction of carbon emissions in the global economy. It shares the common aim of adhering to the Paris Agreement. There are no less than eight sector-specific alliances. They encompass banking, asset managers, financial service providers, investment consultants, venture capital, export credit agencies, asset owners, and Paris-aligned asset owners. Both of the last two initiatives aim to address climate change by mobilising the financial sector but are slightly different. The Paris-Aligned Asset Owners focus on aligning investment portfolios with the Paris Agreement, while the Net-Zero Asset Owner Alliance focuses on transitioning investment portfolios to net-zero GHG emissions by 2050 or sooner.

Direct and indirect capital driving the energy transition

Family offices, insurance companies, pension funds, sovereign wealth funds, endowments, foundations, and philanthropies have roles, structures, and purposes that vary widely. The chief commonality is that they can invest directly or indirectly in energy transition-related companies, projects, solutions, assets, and the like.

Family offices and insurance companies invest internal capital. They typically have external investors, though, much like the other types of financial institutions, they do co-invest to diversify and lower the risk profile of their portfolios. Family offices usually have low public transparency about their investments. That of insurers is medium to high. Pension funds typically have external capital, and the transparency is similar to that of insurers. The fourth type is amongst the most diverse ones. Endowments, foundations, and philanthropies – and we could put some NGOs in this bucket as well – may hold financial assets or receive donations, with their transparency can be anywhere from inexistent to very high (see Figure 9.8).

The total amount of capital invested in energy transition-related assets by these four types of institutions is difficult to narrow down due to limited data availability. While some insurers, pension funds, and many endowments, foundations, and philanthropies disclose their investments, reporting is seldom mandatory and is neither widespread nor standardised. Estimates, derived by piecing together information from numerous sources, suggest that the total capital available for investment by these institutions must be in excess of $50 trillion as of 2023. Family offices, which typically manage the private wealth of one or a few families, are the most private of investors. In contrast, other institutions are generally more public, and many are more likely to reveal their climate action involvement. For example, a survey found that 68 per cent of pension funds in the United States had committed to net-zero alignment, 11 percentage points more than the same survey had found in 2022. It highlighted that among these pension funds, 90 per cent were targeting net-zero compliance by 2050 at the latest.[54]

Insurers and reinsurers are deeply concerned about climate change as it presents significant challenges to their industry through various risks, according to a report by international

	Source of investment capital	Investments disclosure
Family offices	Internal	Low
Insurance companies	Internal	Medium to High
Pension funds	External	Medium to High
Endowments, foundations, philanthropies	Internal and External	Low to High

Figure 9.8 Capital source and transparency of investors investing directly and indirectly

Source: Author, original chart design (June 2025).

law firm Norton Rose Fulbright. The main risk categories are physical risks from extreme weather events, transition risks from shift to a low-carbon economy, and liability risks from legal claims related to climate impacts. These risks have caused a rise in insurance claims and a widening of the protection gap, or uninsured losses, in recent years. The report's authors believe that collaboration is necessary for the industry to adapt. One form of collaboration is through Public–Private Partnerships, as initiatives like flood insurance programmes and risk-reduction incentives can help manage risk and ensure affordability. Another is through data sharing and innovation, as collaboration can improve risk assessment, encourage investment in climate solutions, and lead to innovative insurance products. Three successful collaboration examples include the United Kingdom's Flood Re programme, which reduces premiums for flood-prone households, the United States' National Flood Insurance Program, which provides federal flood insurance, and incentives for risk mitigation such as discounts for homeowners who invest in hurricane or flood protection measures.[55]

However, there are challenges to collaboration. Regulation may restrict the ability of the insurers to set premiums reflecting risk, and implementing risk-reduction measures can be expensive. Additionally, there are uncertainties regarding the effectiveness of adaptation investments in reducing risk. The Norton Rose Fulbright report suggests that the insurance industry cannot address climate change alone and comes to the important conclusion that collaboration between insurers, governments, regulators, and policymakers is crucial to develop innovative solutions, promote risk reduction, and ensure a resilient future. These suggestions are already being implemented in more than one jurisdiction globally.

One example of recent efforts is that by several re/insurance firms, including Alliant, AXA, Gallagher Re, Howden, Mosaic Insurance, Munich Re, and WTW. They have recently backed the Joint Declaration launched at COP28. The declaration aims to promote sustainability-linked sovereign financing for nature and climate in countries from the Global South, nations with a low level of economic and industrial development. Signatories include major multilateral development banks and other international organisations. A global task force has been formed to achieve this objective, and the re/insurance providers have committed to collaborating with the task force and working with governments to lower borrowing costs for developing nations. The firms have pledged to support the issuance of sustainability performance-linked sovereign debt instruments to tackle the interconnected crises of debt, climate, and nature.[56]

Insurers can positively impact the energy transition in at least three ways. They can direct their investments towards energy transition-related companies, projects, and assets. They can collaborate with their clients, government, and other institutions to foster awareness and encourage climate-positive actions and behaviours. They can de-risk clean energy investments through leveraging their risk management expertise, as well as possibly offer financial coverage and longer policy terms.

Like insurers, many pension funds have actively taken climate action. They have had strong incentive to address climate change, as it can impact their business in several ways. Firstly, the bonds, equities, and real estate and other assets they invest in face physical risks, transition risks, and liability risks, similar to insurers. They have a fiduciary duty to act in the best interest of their beneficiaries, necessitating effective risk management to avoid financial losses resulting from climate change. Lastly, investments may become stranded assets due to climate change or the shift towards a low-carbon economy. For instance, a coal-fired power plant could lose much of its net present value due to regulatory changes, such as emissions abatement, carbon pricing, or technological advancements.

Capital allocation into climate solutions by pension funds has been growing rapidly over the past few years. There are many examples of pension funds setting a target allocation, as a percentage of assets under management, or designating a specific amount of capital towards climate-themed and sustainable opportunities. The US-based California State Teachers Retirement System, or CalSTRS, in September 2021 pledged to achieve net-zero GHG emissions across the CalSTRS Investment Portfolio by 2050. It has a 1 per cent target allocation to climate and low-carbon-themed private investments within the portfolio. The total portfolio mounted to $358 billion as of May 2025, including $3,673 million in 'sustainable investment and stewardship strategies public and private investments'.[57] Canadian-based Caisse de Dépôt et Placement du Québec has targeted to decarbonise its investment portfolio since 2017. It had C$58 billion ($42 billion) in low-carbon assets, a $40 billion increase since 2017, as of the end of 2024. The pension fund also said that it had been able to lower the carbon intensity of its portfolio by 69 per cent from 2017, exceeding its 60 per cent by 2030 target. It had about 80 per cent of its total portfolio, or about C$358 billion ($259 billion), in assets with a low-carbon footprint. It added that C$6.2 billion ($4.5 billion) was allocated to transition assets to decarbonise the highest emitting sectors.[58] UK-based Border to Coast Pensions Partnership earmarked £1.35 billion ($1.8 billion) for private markets climate investments over a three-year period starting 2022. Netherlands-based PGGM, a firm investing on behalf of pension fund clients, allocated 18 per cent of the total assets under management for sustainable development investments.[59]

Researcher Clara McDonnell examined the development of climate strategies among the largest US and EU pension funds. McDonnell discovered that these funds have incorporated climate factors into their investment strategies for over two decades. However, she highlights several limitations to the effectiveness of pension fund strategies for climate mitigation, despite the rapid expansion of their climate initiatives. Although pension funds frequently use language that aligns with the objectives of phasing out fossil fuels, their reactions to fossil fuel company actions reveal a degree of complacency and acceptance of the minimal, often insincere, measures taken by these companies. To become active participants in the fossil fuel phase out, pension funds will likely need to fundamentally reconsider and redefine their role in addressing the climate crisis.[60]

The direct investors: from angel investors to established PE players – their pivotal role

There are at least four types of investing institutions which are typically solely direct investors. The four can be broadly sorted by the amount of capital they manage. Angel investors and crowdfunding platforms are generally regarded as being small with investments as little as a few hundred dollars. Venture capital firms are usually viewed as small to medium in size. Private equity (PE) firms are typically considered medium- to large-size investors, some with the capacity to invest several billion dollars in one year.

PE firms are the second most important protagonist in the financing of the energy transition after the banking sector. Its role can be profiled by understanding the wants and needs of PE players and by some examples illustrating the approach.

First, it is useful to distinguish PE investments from infrastructure funds. The investment focus of PE firms is to seek to acquire stakes in companies with a view to improve the companies' profitability. Infrastructure funds' investments typically will target physical infrastructure assets. The two commonly have different investment horizons. PE firms would look at investing over a period of five to ten years whereas infrastructure funds would look at longer-term returns. In terms of the return spectrum, PE would tend to invest in high-risk, high-return assets but infrastructure funds usually prefer lower risk, stable returns. Finally, PE firms typically focus on the value appreciation of their investment from an eventual exit while infrastructure funds are more likely to look at steady recurring cash flows generated from the asset.

PE firms primarily invest in relatively mature companies, unlike venture capital, with the aim of increasing their value or realising returns before exiting the investment. PE firms raise capital to launch funds, operating as general partners and managing investments in exchange for fees and a share of profits. Some firms specialise in specific categories of PE deals, including distressed investing, growth equity, sector specialisation, secondary buyouts, and carve-outs. The buyout remains a common PE deal, involving the acquisition of an entire company, while carve-outs involve buying a division of a larger company. In a secondary buyout, a PE firm buys a company from another PE group. Other exit strategies include selling the portfolio company to a third-party, known as a 'trade sell', or an initial public offering (IPO). PE firms often implement plans to increase the investment's worth, such as cost cuts, restructuring, or utilising special expertise. Industry surveys suggest that operational improvements have become the main focus for PE managers. However, debt remains a significant contributor to PE returns though this is easier in a low or falling interest rate environment.[61] The volume of capital transacted by private equity firms annually over the five-year period ending in 2023 fluctuated significantly, ranging from $474 billion in 2023 to $1,184 billion in 2021, according to one estimate.[62] This variability can be attributed to several factors, including inflationary pressures, increasing interest rates, and unstable geopolitical conditions, all of which have a broader impact on capital markets, including stock markets.

In recent years, the activity of PE firms in the energy transition space has sharply accelerated. Part of the reason is that the energy transition being a fast-growing market requiring vast amounts of capital. Also, many PE firms need to decarbonise their portfolios. This can be due to some pressure by regulators, consumers, B2B customers, or investors, including pension funds and insurance companies. Some PE firms have already committed to helping companies in their respective portfolios to reach net zero by 2050. They include Blackstone, Carlyle Group, KKR, and TPG Capital.

The consensus view in mid-2025 is that PE firms are playing an increasingly important role in funding the energy transition. Firms such as Apollo, KKR, and Brookfield are raising energy transition funds, and a new generation of venture capital groups is emerging with a focus on sustainable investment and decarbonisation. It is impossible for the transition to succeed without private capital due to the scale of the financing challenge, the tens of trillions of dollars needed through at least 2050. PE teams are often well-suited to backing complex energy projects, thanks to their expertise in spotting and executing investments in complex environments and their higher risk appetite. At the same time, these investments carry novel risks, including first-of-a-kind technology risks, heavy dependence on government policy and regulation, and reputation risks linked to allegations of 'greenwashing'. To cope with these challenges, private equity funds have adopted longer time horizons for some funds and launched multi-fund strategies that enable businesses to stay out of public markets for longer.[63] For example, Blackstone has seen strong demand for energy transition infrastructure opportunities. It had raised a cumulative $3.24 billion as of April 2024 for its Energy Transition Partners IV fund, with a focus on clean energy infrastructure investments. The fund was launched in 2022 with a $6 billion target, but the firm expected a final close of $4 billion or more as of April 2024. Investors include Teacher Retirement System of Texas and Minnesota State Board of Investment. The fund is the successor to Blackstone Energy Partners III, which generated a 33 per cent net internal rate of return in the first calendar quarter of 2024.[64]

The profile of the types of investments led by PE firms in the energy transition can be illustrated by three examples based on data from announcements. A US-based PE firm acquisition of an energy company in Germany, a US-based PE firm stake in a US power utility, and a Canadian-based PE firm investment plans in India.

One of the largest deals by a private equity firm in the 12 months to July 2024 was the acquisition by a KKR-led consortium of Encavis AG, a German-based renewable energy company. Encavis AG is listed on the German stock exchange (on the MDAX of Deutsche Börse) and is one of the leading independent clean power producers in Europe. The company operates onshore wind farms and solar parks in 12 countries, with a total generation capacity of over 3.5 GW. Of this capacity, 2.2 GW is attributable to Encavis AG, and an additional 1.2 GW of capacity is under construction, with 830 MW attributable to the company. Other group companies include Encavis Asset Management, which offers fund services to institutional investors, and Stern Energy S.p.A., based in Italy, which provides technical services for photovoltaic systems across Europe. Encavis announced that the strategic partnership with KKR would enable the power producer to accelerate growth in all segments. The company had previously targeted an attributable capacity of 5.8 GW by 2027, but it has since raised that target by over 20 per cent to 7 GW. KKR has committed to supporting Encavis for continued growth beyond this target. The €2.8 billion ($3.3 billion) takeover of Encavis was announced in March 2024 and was completed in November. KKR is leading a consortium that includes Viessmann GmbH & Co., a German family business, and ABACON Capital GmbH, a family-owned investment firm focused on sustainable energy transition, new age mobility, deep tech, and real estate. The deal is expected to remove funding constraints associated with a public ownership model.[65]

Blackstone is a New York-based alternative investment management company. It is one of the largest PE investors in infrastructure assets, including digital infrastructure, energy transition infrastructure, transportation, as well as water and waste. It had $44 billion in assets under management and the total enterprise value at acquisition of companies in which it owned 30 per cent or more was $172 billion as of March 2024. The firm acquired a 19.9 per cent stake in Northern Indiana Public Service Company, or NIPSCO, for $2.16 billion together in January 2024 with the commitment of an additional $250 million in equity to fund ongoing capital requirements. NIPSCO serves 859,000 natural gas and 483,000 electricity customers in the northern third of Indiana. It targets to heavily invest in the energy transition, chiefly by building renewable energy generation capacity to replace coal-fired power plants. It will also modernise its gas and electric transmission distribution systems which it views as critical to the energy transition. NIPSCO is 80.1 per cent owned by NiSource, an energy company listed on the New York Stock Exchange, which has strong energy transition ambitions. It plans to invest $4 billion so it may reach net-zero GHG emissions by 2040.[66]

Canadian PE firm Brookfield is a major investor in clean energy, with approximately 33 GW of operational assets globally in hydro, wind, solar, distributed energy, and sustainable solutions such as CCS, green hydrogen, and nuclear power. The firm had $102 billion in assets under management and employs 4,000 people at over 7,000 power generation facilities. In June 2024, Brookfield announced plans to increase its renewable energy portfolio in India to over $10 billion within four years. The firm currently has around $3 billion of assets under management in India and controls a 25 GW portfolio across operating, under-construction, and late-stage projects. Brookfield is exploring mergers and acquisitions in the renewable energy space, as well as opportunities in EVs and green hydrogen. In 2023, the firm signed an agreement with Avaada to provide up to $1 billion in financing for the company's green hydrogen and green ammonia ventures in India. Avaada Group is an integrated energy platform whose businesses include making solar cells, modules, and electrolysers, as well as renewable power generation, green hydrogen, and green ammonia production. Its flagship company, Avaada Energy, developed 4 GW between 2019 and 2023 and targets 11 GW by 2026 and 30 GW by 2030. Also in 2023, Brookfield said it would invest up to $360 million to acquire a 55 per cent stake in CleanMax, a Mumbai-based renewable platform in the commercial and industrial segment in India. The funding will allow CleanMax to increase its capacity from 800 MW to 1,000 MW per year and reach a 5 GW level by 2026 or 2027 from 2 GW in 2024.[67]

In all three examples, the PE firms have come in to help the target company to scale up in size. Sometimes, they also bring in additional investors thus diversifying the funding sources for the companies.

The indirect investors

Indirect investors are financial institutions that typically invest capital on behalf of third parties or facilitate investments as intermediaries (financial services providers). They commonly do not directly invest in an energy transition opportunity but rather buy and sell the equity or debt of such projects. Brokerages, hedge funds, institutional fund management, investment banks, mutual funds, and wealth management can be included in this category. Among these, brokerages and investment banks are more like financial services providers. Another feature is that sometimes these institutions are diversified financial services providers, as they offer many different financial services all under one single umbrella institution-wise. One such institution is Goldman Sachs. It is consistently ranked as one of the biggest in the world revenue-wise in general (top 60), and one of the biggest investment banks (top 6) in particular. It offers all of the financial services in the five categories mentioned and more, including private equity. About 65 per cent of net revenues in 2024 came from its global banking and markets activities which include, for example, fixed-income and equities trading. Another 30 per cent came from asset and wealth management activities.[68] So there is much overlap with this type of financial institutions. Among the five different types of indirect investors, capital-wise institutional asset managers may have the greatest impact on climate finance given that a portion of global assets under management of over $100 trillion[69] can be channelled to climate action related investments (see Figure 9.9).

The world's six largest institutional asset managers had a staggering total of almost $40 trillion in assets under management (see Figure 9.10). They include BlackRock Asset Management with $11.6 trillion, Vanguard Asset Management with $10.1 trillion, Fidelity Investments Asset Management with $5.9 trillion, State Street Investment Management with $4.7 trillion, J.P. Morgan Asset Management with $3.7 trillion, and Goldman Sachs Asset Management with $2.9 trillion. They invest the assets of public institutions, corporations, individuals, and others in equities, fixed-income securities, real estate, alternative investments, including commodities, hedge funds, or private equity, and also manage investment vehicles such as mutual funds and exchange-traded funds.[70]

COMPANY	AUM ($ TRILLIONS)	SOURCE
BlackRock Asset Management	11.6	Q4 2024 10-K filing
Vanguard Asset Management	10.1	30 April 2025
Fidelity Investments Asset Management	5.9	2024 Annual Report
State Street Investment Management	4.7	2024 Annual Report
J.P. Morgan Asset Management	3.7	31 March 2025
Goldman Sachs Asset Management	2.9	31 December 2024

Figure 9.9 Assets under management of six largest asset managers

Source: Author (June 2025) using data from individual firms.

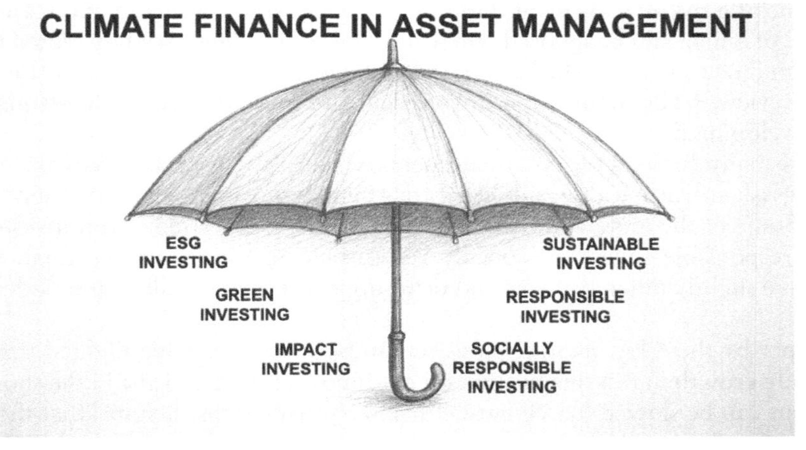

Figure 9.10 Climate finance in asset management

Source: Author, original chart design (June 2025); Background image from OpenAI, https://chat.openai.com accessed 25 June 2025.

The relationship between institutional asset management firms and the energy transition is multifaceted. Each of these firms offers a great variety of financial services. They can aim to have a net-zero portfolio by 2050, meaning that an institutional asset management firm has $100 worth of equities or bonds in oil and gas companies, they could invest $100 or more in net-zero companies such as a solar farm operator or an EV manufacturer. The massive financial muscles that these firms have can also influence companies in constructing vigorous transition plans. If they have funds that invest in private equity, they can direct capital towards projects or companies with energy transition assets. The firms can adopt net-zero policies voluntarily or could be forced to do so by regulatory bodies. This is complex too. For example, their public bonds and equities business would be supervised by the securities regulator but not their real estate or private equity business, for example.

In general, the big firms in Europe, such as Credit Agricole or UBS Group, have been more proactive, and are aligned with the regulators there. In the United States, firms have been less proactive, though those with international business would have to consider net-zero issues. The stance of the big six US asset managers in recent years has oscillated between strong and weak climate aspirations and action. In fact, as of June 2025, the major US asset managers had retreated from their climate action pledges while European institutions held their ground. One of the biggest upsets was the largest asset management firm in the world, BlackRock, leading the exit of the Net Zero Asset Managers initiative in January. This was a time when most large US fund managers decided to lower their environmental profile. BlackRock has stated that given a majority of global clients had committed to net zero, joining organisations such as Net Zero Asset Managers Initiative was logical. 'However, our memberships in some of these organisations have caused confusion regarding BlackRock's practises and subjected us to legal inquiries from various public officials', said BlackRock in a letter to clients, quotes Reuters.[71]

Such high-profile retreat announcement will not hold in the long term. All asset managers face the challenge that the capital markets are slowly-but-surely moving towards increasingly recognising that there is mounting pressure for greater climate action. 'These pressures include risk management duties, meeting consumer demand and regulatory scrutiny – none of which can be ignored, whoever the US president may be'. Noted the CEO of environmental organisation Market Forces Will van de Pol, in an op-ed for the Australian Financial Review.[72] The momentum towards climate-positive investing is strong, though it is still a developing field.

There are many different types of investments which aim to generate financial returns while considering risk mitigation alongside generating climate-positive or environmental-conscious investing. Some of the more common labels include ESG investing, green investing, impact investing, responsible investing, socially responsible investing, or sustainable investing. They all have slightly different focus and definitions, yet they can all be put under one single umbrella.

One paper by the CFA Institute Research and Policy Centre highlighted that there has been a steady growth in responsible investment funds but that, at least in the short term, the development can be slowed by regulation in some jurisdictions. It states that the assets and net inflows of such funds have been growing globally over the past ten years. Total net assets in this category, as defined by data and analytics firm Lipper, surged 2.7 times globally, to \$5,974.6 billion in 2022 from \$2,215.6 billion in 2012, with the market share rising 120 basis points during the period to 15.4 per cent from 14.2 per cent. The Centre's report notes that the motivations and strategy preferences for investing in these funds vary among retail and institutional investors in different regions. However, the growth has only marginally outpaced that of non-responsible investment funds, and retail assets continue to dominate institutional assets globally. The complex regulatory environment for responsible investment funds may also affect the growth of institutional assets and potentially deter investment firms from increasing their investments in climate-related products. Rising demand for personalisation in the investment process and the interests of younger investors will likely affect the market for responsible investment funds in the coming years. However, the paper underscores that the analysis has limitations, such as not accounting for assets held in segregated mandates or private market funds, in the assessment of the level of assets held in responsible investment funds overall. The contrasting regulatory environments around the world for responsible investment funds also create inconsistencies regarding the reporting and disclosure of ESG-related data. A general lack of clarity surrounding the terminology for 'responsible investment funds' makes these inconsistencies worse.[73]

As policy, corporate, and financial-market action on decarbonisation continue to rise, asset managers must consider the net-zero alignment of their investments. The policy momentum is accelerating worldwide, and climate-related transition, physical, and litigation risks are real and can significantly impact companies in which investment managers buy shares or bonds. However, this is not without challenges. Responsible Investor, a media outlet specialising in sustainable finance, discussed the usefulness and impact of net-zero targets set by investors to help shift the economy towards achieving the objectives of the Paris Agreement by 2050.[74] Specialist magazine Responsible Investor found that less than 50 per cent of investors surveyed sought external advice before making their net-zero pledges, and only 52 per cent of investors believed they could meet their net-zero goals without divestment. Some investors have expressed concerns about the feasibility of meeting net-zero targets, and Responsible Investor explored the legal implications of net-zero commitments, with a climate lawyer suggesting that funds may not be off-the-hook if they fail to meet their targets due to a lack of supportive policy environment. Overall, the podcast highlighted the challenges and complexities surrounding net-zero targets and their impact on the wider economy. The dilemma for most asset managers is that they need to generate financial returns, and if they do not invest in or divest from hard-to-abate sectors such as oil and gas or steel, they run the risk of underperforming or not generating returns. The challenge is that they should not invest to force companies to transition, but if the wider economy has not transitioned, they will limit the assets they can invest in and endanger their returns. Over the short term, three to five years, asset managers may shift their net-zero target from being a 'commitment' to an 'ambition', with the trajectory remaining the same but the pace slowing.

Notes

1 African Development Bank, *South Africa's Largest Renewable Energy Project Redstone CSP Achieves First Debt Draw Down* (African Development Bank Group 11 February 2022) <https://www.afdb.org/en/news-and-events/press-releases/south-africas-largest-renewable-energy-project-redstone-csp-achieves-first-debt-draw-down-49098> accessed 21 March 2025.

2 J Li and others, 'Green Credit Efficiency of Commercial Banks in China: Evidence from a Multi-Period Leader-Follower Model with Preference' [2024] International Review of Financial Analysis 103604.

3 UK Government, 'Tenfold Expansion in Chargepoints by 2030 as Government Drives EV Revolution' (GOV.UK 25 March 2022) <https://www.gov.uk/government/news/tenfold-expansion-in-chargepoints-by-2030-as-government-drives-ev-revolution#:~:text=The%20UK%20> accessed 14 June 2024.

4 United States Department of Transportation, 'President Biden, USDOT and USDOE Announce $5 Billion over Five Years for National EV Charging Network, Made Possible by Bipartisan Infrastructure Law | FHWA' (highways.dot.gov 10 February 2022) <https://highways.dot.gov/newsroom/president-biden-usdot-and-usdoe-announce-5-billion-over-five-years-national-ev-charging> accessed 14 June 2024.

5 US Department of Energy, 'Biden-Harris Administration Announces More than $104 Million to Advance Net-Zero Projects at Federal Facilities' (Energy.gov 24 January 2024) <https://www.energy.gov/articles/biden-harris-administration-announces-more-104-million-advance-net-zero-projects-federal> accessed 14 June 2024.

6 C Paas-Lang (ed), 'The Federal Government Promised to Plant Two Billion Trees. How's That Going?' (www.cbc.ca 30 March 2024) <https://www.cbc.ca/newsinteractives/features/two-billion-trees> accessed 14 June 2024.

7 CCS Norway, *Status June 2023, Longship* (CCS Norway 8 August 2023) <https://ccsnorway.com/status-june-2023-longship/> accessed 14 June 2024.

8 Ministry of Housing and Urban Affairs, 'Home Page | Smartcities' (Smartcities.gov.in June 2024) <https://smartcities.gov.in/> accessed 14 June 2024.

9 World Economic Forum, *Sustainable Financing of Cities: 4 Success Factors from India's Smart City Mission Experience* (World Economic Forum 10 July 2023) <https://www.weforum.org/agenda/2023/07/sustainable-financing-of-cities-india-s-smart-city-mission-shows-way-forward/> accessed 14 June 2024.

10 Monetary Authority of Singapore, 'Public-Private Partnerships to Mobilise Capital for Net Zero Transition' (www.mas.gov.sg 4 October 2022) <https://www.mas.gov.sg/news/media-releases/2022/public-private-partnerships-to-mobilise-capital-for-net-zero-transition> accessed 14 June 2024.

11 E Ng and M Choi, 'Hong Kong to Launch Subsidy Scheme for Green Fintech Start-Ups, Official Says' *South China Morning Post* (25 January 2024) <https://www.scmp.com/business/banking-finance/article/3249781/hong-kong-launch-subsidy-scheme-green-fintech-start-ups-bolster-sustainability-data-acumen-official> accessed 14 June 2024.

12 P Liu, *Green Fintech Map Launch Showcases Hong Kong's Edge in Sustainable Finance* (HK Green Finance Association 4 March 2024) <https://www.hkgreenfinance.org/green-fintech-map-launch-showcases-hong-kongs-edge-in-sustainable-finance/> accessed 14 June 2024.

13 US EPA, *Renewable Electricity Production Tax Credit Information* (US EPA 28 August 2020) <https://www.epa.gov/lmop/renewable-electricity-production-tax-credit-information#:~:text=The%20renewable%20electricity%20production%20tax> accessed 15 June 2024.

14 PV Magazine, 'Indian Government Approves $9 Billion Rebate Scheme for Residential PV' *PV Magazine International* (1 March 2024) <https://www.pv-magazine.com/2024/03/01/india-government-approves-9-billion-rebate-scheme-for-residential-pv/> accessed 15 June 2024.

15 I Ukpanah (ed), 'Heat Pump Statistics 2024: Market Size, Trends, and Predictions' (GreenMatch.co.uk 25 April 2024) <https://www.greenmatch.co.uk/heat-pumps/statistics> accessed 16 June 2024.

16 The ten banks are the African Development Bank, the Asian Development Bank, the Asian Infrastructure Investment Bank, the Council of Europe Development Bank, the European Bank for Reconstruction and Development, the European Investment Bank, the Inter-American Development Bank Group, the Islamic Development Bank, the New Development Bank, and the World Bank Group.

17 Asian Development Bank, 'COP28 Multilateral Development Banks (MDB) Joint Statement' (www.adb.org 3 December 2023) <https://www.adb.org/news/cop28-multilateral-development-banks-mdb-joint-statement> accessed 19 June 2024.

18 M Jones, 'Top Development Banks, Funds Set Up "Debt-For-Nature" Task Force' *Reuters* (4 December 2023) <https://www.reuters.com/sustainability/sustainable-finance-reporting/top-development-banks-funds-set-up-debt-for-nature-task-force-2023-12-04/> accessed 21 June 2024.

19 N Owen, *Belize: Swapping Debt for Nature* (IMF 4 May 2022) <https://www.imf.org/en/News/Articles/2022/05/03/CF-Belize-swapping-debt-for-nature> accessed 21 June 2024.

20 M Jones and R Campos, 'Ecuador Seals Record Debt-For-Nature Swap with Galapagos Bond' *Reuters* (9 May 2023) <https://www.reuters.com/world/americas/ecuador-seals-record-debt-for-nature-swap-with-galapagos-bond-2023-05-09/> accessed 21 June 2024.

21 D Schubiger, *SUSI Partners Holds Final Close for Southeast Asia Energy Transition Fund – SUSI Partners* (SUSI Partners 15 June 2023) <https://www.susi-partners.com/en/2023/06/susi-partners-holds-final-close-for-southeast-asia-energy-transition-fund/> accessed 21 June 2024.

22 PV Europe, 'Financing – BayWa R.e. And Susi Partners Cooperate in Southeast Asia' (www.pveurope.eu 13 September 2023) <https://www.pveurope.eu/markets/financing-baywa-re-and-susi-partners-cooperate-southeast-asia> accessed 21 June 2024.

23 Global Energy Alliance for People and Planet, *AIIB and GEAPP Enter $1 Billion Investment Partnership to Fund the Energy Transition in Asia and Beyond* (Global Energy Alliance for

People and Planet 8 November 2022) <https://energyalliance.org/aiib-and-geapp-enter-1-billion-investment-partnership-to-fund-the-energy-transition-in-asia-and-beyond/> accessed 22 June 2024.

24 Recourse, 'Smoke and Mirrors? New Report Analyses AIIB's Updated Energy Sector Strategy One Year on' *Recourse* (11 December 2023) <https://re-course.org/newsupdates/smoke-and-mirrors-new-report-analyses-aiibs-updated-energy-sector-strategy-one-year-on/> accessed 22 June 2024.

25 Inter-American Investment Corporation, 'IDB Invest Boosts Argentina's Lithium Production to Promote Green Energy Transition in Latin America and the Caribbean | IDB Invest' (idbinvest.org 14 December 2023) <https://idbinvest.org/en/news-media/idb-invest-boosts-argentinas-lithium-production-promote-green-energy-transition-latin> accessed 22 June 2024.

26 C Pöthig, 'Approximately EUR 1 Billion for the Energy Transition in India: KfW Supports Indo-German Solar Energy Partnership | KfW' (www.kfw.de 20 December 2023) <https://www.kfw.de/About-KfW/Newsroom/Latest-News/Pressemitteilungen-Details_791360.html> accessed 22 June 2024.

27 CDP, 'CDP Financial Services Disclosure Report 2022 – CDP' (www.cdp.net August 2023) <https://www.cdp.net/en/research/global-reports/financial-services-disclosure-report-2022> accessed 23 June 2024.

28 NewClimate Institute, *From Rhetoric to Reality: Investigating Financial Institutions' Net Zero Portfolio Commitments Report* (NewClimate Institute 2023) <https://newclimate.org/sites/default/files/2024-01/from_rhetoric_to_reality_investigating_financial_institutions_net_zero_portfolio_commitments.pdf> accessed 23 June 2024.

29 K Bryan, 'Investment Banks Squabble over Carbon Footprint of Underwriting Deals' *Financial Times* (7 July 2023) <https://www.ft.com/content/ca549b24-ece5-46c2-85fb-5fe1aa24d296> accessed 23 June 2024.

30 Q Wang, '做好科技金融大文章 服務科技和產業創新-理論-中國共產黨新聞網' (theory.people.com.cn 24 June 2024) <http://theory.people.com.cn/BIG5/n1/2024/0624/c40531–40262509.html> accessed 25 June 2024.

31 Source: J Zhang, S Ziying, and C Nedopil Wang, 'New Report: China Green Finance Status and Trends 2023–2024' (3 April 2024) <https://greenfdc.org/China-green-finance-status-and-trends-2023-2024/> accessed 25 June 2024.

32 ICBC, *Corporate Social Responsibility Report (ESG Report) 2024* (Industrial and Commercial Bank of China Ltd 28 March 2024) <https://v.icbc.com.cn/userfiles/resources/icbcltd/download/2025/esg2024en.pdf> accessed 29 June 2025.

33 European Central Bank, 'Climate Change and the ECB' (www.ecb.europa.eu 30 January 2024) <https://ecb.europa.eu/ecb/climate/html/index.en.html> accessed 27 June 2024.

34 Moody's, 'ECB to Expand Climate Change Work in 2024–2025' (www.moodys.com 23 February 2024) <https://www.moodys.com/web/en/us/insights/regulatory-news/ecb-to-expand-climate-change-work-in-2024-2025.html> accessed 27 June 2024.

35 Frank Elderson, 'Making Banks Resilient to Climate and Environmental Risks – Good Practices to Overcome the Remaining Stumbling Blocks' (331st European Banking Federation Executive Committee Meeting, 14 March 2024) <https://www.bankingsupervision.europa.eu/press/speeches/date/2024/html/ssm.sp240314~da639a526a.en.html> accessed 27 June 2024.

36 Greenpeace International, *EU Banks Have Poured €256 Billion into Sectors that Threaten Nature and Climate* (Greenpeace International 26 March 2024) <https://www.greenpeace.org/international/press-release/66013/eu-banks-have-poured-e256-billion-into-sectors-that-threaten-nature-and-climate/> accessed 27 June 2024.

37 Prudential Regulation Authority, 'Financial Risks from Climate Change' (www.prarulebook.co.uk 27 June 2024) <https://www.prarulebook.co.uk/guidance/supervisory-statements/ss03-19-enhancing-banks-and-insurers-approaches-to-managing-the-financial-risks-from-climate-change/2-financial-risks-from-climate-change/24-06-2024?p=1> accessed 27 June 2024.

38 M Costa, *BoE's Prudential Regulator to Assess Bank Progress on Climate Risk Plans* (Green Central Banking 23 April 2024) <https://greencentralbanking.com/2024/04/23/bank-of-england-pra-bank-progress-on-climate-risk-plans/> accessed 27 June 2024.

39 BNP Paribas, *Climate Report: The Bank for a Changing World* (BNP Paribas 2024) <https://cdn-group.bnpparibas.com/uploads/file/bnp_paribas_2023_climate_report.pdf> accessed 28 June 2024.

40 BNP Paribas, *Energy Transition and Climate Action, BNP Paribas* (BNP Paribas 2024) <https://group.bnpparibas/en/our-commitments/transitions/energy-transition-and-climate-action> accessed 28 June 2024.

41 HSBC, *HSBC Holdings Plc Annual Report and Accounts 2023* (HSBC Holdings plc 2024) <https://www.hsbc.com/-/files/hsbc/investors/hsbc-results/2023/annual/pdfs/hsbc-holdings-plc/240226-annual-report-and-accounts–2023.pdf?download=1> accessed 28 June 2024.

42 Federal Reserve Board, *Agencies Issue Principles for Climate-Related Financial Risk Management for Large Financial Institutions* (Board of Governors of the Federal Reserve System 24 October 2023) <https://www.federalreserve.gov/newsevents/pressreleases/bcreg20231024b.htm> accessed 28 June 2024.

43 JPMorgan Chase & Co., *Climate Report* (JPMorgan Chase & Co 2023) <https://www.jpmorganchase.com/content/dam/jpmc/jpmorgan-chase-and-co/documents/Climate-Report-2023.pdf> accessed 29 June 2024; and Citigroup, *2023 Citi Climate Report* (Citigroup Inc 2024) <https://www.citigroup.com/rcs/citigpa/storage/public/2023-Citi-Climate-Report.pdf> accessed 29 June 2024.

44 Bank of America, *Bank of America 2023 Annual Report* (Bank of America 2024) <https://investor.bankofamerica.com/annual-reports-and-proxy-statements> accessed 29 June 2024.

45 As You So, *Bank of America: Report on Climate Transition Planning* (Resolutions 6 November 2023) <https://www.asyousow.org/resolutions/2023/11/06-bank-of-america-report-on-climate-transition-planning> accessed 28 June 2024.

46 H Tabuchi, 'Bank of America Pledged to Stop Financing Coal. Now It's Backtracking' *The New York Times* (3 February 2024) <https://www.nytimes.com/2024/02/03/climate/bank-of-america-esg.html> accessed 29 June 2024.

47 G Steele, *US Block on Basel Risks Derailing Global Measures on Climate Risk* (Green Central Banking 27 June 2024) <https://greencentralbanking.com/2024/06/27/us-basel-block-climate-risk-graham-steele/> accessed 29 June 2024.

48 K Lee, *Japan's Climate Scenario Analysis Set to Include Financed Emissions* (Green Central Banking 15 May 2024) <https://greencentralbanking.com/2024/05/15/japans-climate-scenario-analysis-set-to-include-financed-emissions/> accessed 29 June 2024.

49 Mitsubishi UFJ Financial Group, *MUFG Climate Report 2024* (Mitsubishi UFJ Financial Group 2024) <https://www.mufg.jp/dam/csr/report/progress/climate2024_en.pdf> accessed 30 June 2024.

50 Sumitomo Mitsui, *Efforts for Social Value Creation in SMBC Group* (Sumitomo Mitsui Financial Group 2024) <https://www.smfg.co.jp/english/investor/financial/small/pdf/20240529esg_pre01e.pdf> accessed 30 June 2024.

51 The Taskforce on Nature-related Financial Disclosures, 'TNFD Adopters' (tnfd.global 2024) <https://tnfd.global/engage/tnfd-adopters/> accessed 30 June 2024.

52 The Alliance for Green Commercial Banks, 'Decarbonizing Heavy Industry: Scaling Low-Carbon Iron and Steel (Speaker: Sophie Lu, Global Head of Heavy Industry Decarbonisation and Climate Transition, HSBC)' (www.allianceforgreencommercialbanks.org 26 June 2024) <https://www.allianceforgreencommercialbanks.org/training/decarbonizing-heavy-industry-scaling-low-carbon-iron-and-steel> accessed 2 July 2024.

53 A Marsh and H Suzuki, 'MUFG Leaves Climate Group as Japanese Banks Join Wall Street Exits' *The Japan Times* (20 March 2025) <https://www.japantimes.co.jp/business/2025/03/20/companies/mufg-leaves-climate-group/> accessed 21 March 2025.

54 The Actuary, 'Rise in Pension Funds Committing to Net Zero' *The Actuary* (13 December 2023) <https://www.theactuary.com/2023/12/13/rise-pension-funds-committing-net-zero> accessed 6 July 2024.

55 Norton Rose Fulbright, *Insurance Foresight* (Norton Rose Fulbright 2024) <https://engage.nortonrosefulbright.com/66/33669/uploads/0183117-emea-brochure-insurance-foresight-v3.pdf?-intIaContactId=pNoV%2b9xImykrZyhXC5LJKg%3d%3d&intExternalSystemId=1> accessed 7 July 2024.

56 K Wells, 'Re/Insurance Industry Players Back New Initiative Launched at COP28 – Reinsurance News' (ReinsuranceNe.ws 4 December 2023) <https://www.reinsurancene.ws/re-insurance-industry-players-back-new-initiative-launched-at-cop28/> accessed 19 June 2024.

57 All data sourced from the institution's website <https://www.calstrs.com/> accessed 30 June 2025.
58 Caisse de Dépôt et Placement du Québec, *2024 Sustainable Investing Report: CDPQ Exceeds Its Climate Targets | La Caisse* (La Caisse de Dépôt et Placement du Québec 7 April 2025) <https://www.lacaisse.com/en/news/pressreleases/2024-sustainable-investing-report-cdpq-exceeds-its-climate-targets> accessed 30 June 2025.
59 S Shah, *10 Pension Funds with Climate Investing Allocations* (New Private Markets 10 April 2024) <https://www.newprivatemarkets.com/10-pension-funds-with-climate-investing-allocations/> accessed 7 July 2024.
60 C McDonnell, 'Pension Funds and Fossil Fuel Phase-Out: Historical Developments and Limitations of Pension Climate Strategies' (2024) 24 International Environmental Agreements: Politics, Law and Economics 169 <https://link.springer.com/article/10.1007/s10784-024-09626-0#citeas> accessed 7 July 2024.
61 J Chen, 'Private Equity Definition' *Investopedia* (20 March 2022) <https://www.investopedia.com/terms/p/privateequity.asp> accessed 2 July 2024.
62 KA Vidal and A Sabater, *Global Private Equity Deal Activity Plunges in 2023* (S&P Global 2024) <https://www.spglobal.com/marketintelligence/en/news-insights/latest-news-headlines/global-private-equity-deal-activity-plunges-in-2023-80032940> accessed 2 July 2024.
63 J Smyth, 'Can Private Equity Accelerate the Green Transition?' *Financial Times* (30 May 2024) <https://www.ft.com/content/8cc8095d-aa9a-4598-9624-544d7aff9bf5> accessed 2 July 2024.
64 S Shah, *Blackstone Raises $1bn in Six Months for Energy Transition IV* (New Private Markets 23 April 2024) <https://www.newprivatemarkets.com/blackstone-raises-1bn-in-six-months-for-energy-transition-iv/> accessed 2 July 2024.
65 A Gonzalez, E-V Farr, and I Binnie, 'Partners Considers Sale of German Renewables Firm VSB, Sources Say' *Reuters* (8 March 2024) <https://www.reuters.com/markets/deals/partners-considers-sale-german-renewables-firm-vsb-sources-say-2024-03-08/> accessed 30 June 2025. Reuters Staff, 'Elbe BidCo Signs Delisting Agreement with Encavis' *Reuters* (6 December 2024) <https://www.reuters.com/business/energy/elbe-bidco-signs-delisting-agreement-with-encavis-2024-12-06/> accessed 30 June 2025.
66 Reuters Staff, 'NiSource to Sell $2.15 Billion Stake in Indiana Unit to Blackstone' *Reuters* (20 June 2023) <https://www.reuters.com/markets/deals/nisource-sells-stake-nipsco-215-bln-blackstone-2023-06-20/> accessed 30 June 2025.
67 R Sharma, *Brookfield-Backed Avaada Refinances USD 145m* (ION Analytics 21 March 2025) <https://ionanalytics.com/insights/uncategory/brookfield-backed-avaada-refinances-usd-145m/> accessed 30 June 2025.
68 Goldman Sachs, 'Full Year and Fourth Quarter 2024 Earnings Results' (2025) <https://www.goldmansachs.com/pressroom/press-releases/current/pdfs/2024-q4-results.pdf> accessed 1 July 2025.
69 PricewaterhouseCoopers, *One in Six Asset and Wealth Management Companies Will Be Swallowed Up or Fall by the Wayside in the Next Five Years: PwC Global Asset & Wealth Management Survey* (PwC 10 July 2023) <https://www.pwc.com/gx/en/news-room/press-releases/2023/pwc-2023-global-asset-and-wealth-management-survey.html> accessed 7 July 2024.
70 ADV Ratings, 'World's Top Asset Managers 2019' (Advratings.com 31 March 2024) <https://www.advratings.com/top-asset-management-firms> accessed 3 July 2024.
71 R Kerber, 'BlackRock Quits Climate Group as Wall Street Lowers Environmental Profile' *Reuters* (9 January 2025) <https://www.reuters.com/sustainability/blackrock-quits-climate-group-wall-streets-latest-environmental-step-back-2025-01-09/> accessed 2 July 2025.
72 W van de Pol, 'Climate Initiative Investors Still Have a Responsibility to Cut Emissions despite BlackRock's Net Zero Exit' *Australian Financial Review* (14 January 2025) <https://www.afr.com/policy/energy-and-climate/climate-heat-is-still-on-investors-despite-blackrock-s-net-zero-exit-20250114-p5l461> accessed 2 July 2025.
73 J Report, 'Responsible Investment Funds Build Consistent Market Presence' (2024) <https://rpc.cfainstitute.org/-/media/documents/article/industry-research/responsible-investment-funds.pdf> accessed 7 July 2024.
74 PEI Group, 'The Responsible Investor Podcast' (26 June 2024) <https://www.responsible-investor.com/podcast/> accessed 11 July 2024.

Chapter 10

The growth in climate finance instruments

Aims:

- The function, intended purposes, and historical development of key climate finance instruments.
- Identifying the most appropriate financial instrument(s) for specific climate projects.
- Advantages, limitations, and potential implementation barriers of climate finance mechanisms.

Green capital flows are central to financing clean energy projects and solutions, and these flows occur in various forms of financing mechanisms and instruments. A prominent advocate for green finance has been Mark Carney, who has served as an investment banker, central banker, politician, and now Canada's Prime Minister. In 2016, while he was Governor of the Bank of England, Carney noted,

> Green finance is a major opportunity. By ensuring that capital flows finance long-term projects in countries where growth is most carbon-intensive, financial stability can be promoted. By absorbing excess global savings, equilibrium interest rates can be raised, enhancing macroeconomic stability. And by allocating capital to green technologies, the prospects for an environmentally sustainable recovery in global growth will increase.[1]

The previous chapter examined the capital providers and methods of financing the energy transition, such as loans and capital directed towards net-zero goals by asset managers. This chapter focuses on financial instruments, which can be broadly categorised into three baskets: fixed-income-related instruments, environmental commodities-related instruments, and other innovative climate financing tools.

Financing the transition through debt instruments

Profiling sustainable finance fixed-income instruments

There are a variety of types of sustainable finance fixed-income instruments, sometimes referred to as climate or sustainable debt instruments, which are used to raise capital for climate and environment-related projects or solutions. They include blue bonds,

DOI: 10.4324/9781003666509-13

catastrophe bonds, climate bonds, green bonds, green infrastructure bonds, green sukuk, sustainability-linked bonds, and transition bonds. The different labels indicate the use of proceeds of the bond.[2]

Blue Bonds: Raise capital for marine and ocean-based projects with positive environmental, economic, and climate benefits.
Catastrophe (Cat) Bonds: Transfer natural disaster risks from insurers and reinsurers to other operators, decreasing their exposure.
Climate Bonds: Raise finance for climate change solutions, such as mitigation or adaptation projects.
Green Bonds: Fund projects or solutions with positive environmental and climate benefits.
Green Sukuk: Islamic bond to fund environmentally sustainable infrastructure projects complying with Shariah law, which prohibits interest and favours profit sharing.
Sustainability-Linked Bonds: Issued with specific sustainability performance targets and a 'step-up' clause if targets are missed, increasing the interest paid by the bond.
Transition Bonds: Issued by high GHG emission companies to raise capital for shifting to greener business activities.

Any organisation, including sovereign governments, can issue debt instruments to fund climate-positive projects and solutions. The issuer must follow several steps, typically with the assistance of an investment bank like JPMorgan or Goldman Sachs. However, the issuing entity must clearly understand the classification of the economic activity, project, or solution within the net-zero emissions context. This understanding helps avoid reputational risks, such as greenwashing accusations, or legal action, including lawsuits from stakeholders or fines from regulatory bodies.

The complexity of this process can be illustrated through the Climate Bonds Standard and Certification Scheme by the Climate Bonds Initiative. It is a voluntary scheme meant to raise confidence of investors and others in the climate credentials of a green debt instrument. The scheme is today globally adopted by bond issuers, investors, and the financial markets at large.

Its labelling scheme applies to various debt instruments, not just fixed-income instruments, and showcases the classification challenges instruments may face. It was established to ensure consistency with the Paris Agreement and allows stakeholders to identify and prioritise low-carbon and climate-resilient investments and avoid greenwashing. The Climate Bonds Taxonomy, a guide for eco-friendly assets and projects, assists these groups in identifying key investments for a low-carbon economy. It uses a traffic light system which specifies eligible assets and projects based on the latest climate science and a multi-stakeholder approach. Institutional investors increasingly support climate change action but lack tools to ensure significant impact, especially for debt-based investments. Developed using recent climate science and expert input, it helps entities identify assets compatible with a net-zero trajectory by 2050. Sector-specific working groups collaborate to identify assets and projects aligned with a net-zero goal. The updated Taxonomy incorporates all this research and includes Sector Criteria for financing eligibility with climate-certified bonds and loans.

The Climate Bonds Initiative provides a detailed data methodology and approach. It cannot be reproduced, as it is protected by copyright. However, the materials are available from the organisation for internal and non-commercial purposes and can be accessed by contacting the Climate Bonds Initiative (https://www.climatebonds.net/data-insights/market-data/green-bond-dataset-methodology).

	ALIGNED GREEN DEBT	ALIGNED SOCIAL DEBT	ALIGNED SUSTAINABILITY DEBT	ALIGNED SLB (includes the aligned, strongly aligned, and aligning categories from Climate Bonds SLB Dataset)	ALIGNED GSS+
Market size in 2024[1] (bn)	$672.0	$167.6	$206.3	$7.9	**$1,053.8**
Market size in 2023[2] (bn)	$614.0	$153.5	$156.5	$22.8	**$946.8**
Change (2024 vs 2023)	*9.4%*	*9.2%*	*31.8%*	*-65.4%*	***11.3%***
Number of issuers	948	203	264	20	
Number of instruments	3,242	5,324	1,741	24	
Number of countries	66	36	49	13	
Number of currencies	38	30	36	7	

Figure 10.1 Climate Bonds Initiative aligned GSS bonds scorecard

Notes: (1) Data for the year to 31 December 2024; (2) data for the year to 31 December 2023.

Source: Clodagh M, Harrison C and Sharma D, 'Sustainable Debt Global State of the Market 2024' (Climate Bonds Initiative May 2025). Available at: https://www.climatebonds.net/files/reports/cbi_sotm23_02h.pdf accessed 30 June 2025.

It is difficult to capture using publicly available data the amount of capital specifically directed to climate-focused debt instruments, including green bonds, loans, repos, commercial paper, and revolving credit facilities. The distribution of this type of information has unfortunately not yet been democratised. However, the 'Sustainable Debt Global State of the Market 2024' report by the Climate Bonds Initiative[3] produces a meaningful amount of detail on the size of the various bond markets.

The reports highlight that about $5.7 trillion of aligned green, social, and sustainability (GSS) bonds had been issued cumulatively up to the end of 2024 (see Figure 10.1). The most popular of these instruments are green bonds with a total value of over $3.3 trillion. Social bonds amounted to about $1.1 trillion, sustainability-focused ones accounted for $47.2 billion, and sustainability-linked bonds reached $51 billion. Looking at the 2024 year-over-year increase, green bonds issuance increased 11 per cent in total. The issuance of green and social ones was up 9 per cent each, while that of sustainability-linked bonds decreased 65 per cent. Of note, country and currency diversity is also increasing. Green bonds came from 66 different countries in 38 currencies, for example.

Case studies

A sovereign transition bond, a corporate green bond, and a corporate sustainability-linked bond are examined to better illustrate the nature of sustainable finance fixed-income instruments.

First issuance of a transition bond

Japan held the world's first sovereign climate transition bond issuance. Known as 'GX bonds', these transition bonds aim at financing activities that do not narrowly qualify as 'green' but are expected to help decarbonise. In Japan's case, to help the nation with its goal of cutting GHG emissions to zero by 2050.

The government plans to sell 20 trillion yen ($135 billion) worth of climate bonds with maturities of five to ten years in several tranches. The first two, amounting to 800 billion yen ($5.4 billion) each, were successfully sold in February 2024. Another 1.4 trillion yen

($9.5 billion) worth should be sold in 2025. About 55.5 per cent of the proceeds will go towards research and development of technologies supporting industrial and energy transition. Another 44.5 per cent will be for subsidy programmes directed to such sectors as semiconductors, electricity, storage batteries, and energy-efficiency measures in buildings. About 39 per cent will be allocated for green activities, including R&D for Perovskite Solar Cells and wind, and subsidies for low-carbon transport and batteries. The remaining 18 per cent will be for R&D for the utilisation of hydrogen in the steelmaking process and the decarbonisation of the thermal process. None of the proceeds will go towards funding for gas-fired power generation. Japan's GX bonds were certified by the Climate Bonds Initiative and are part of a plan by government to encourage public and private investments of 150 trillion yen ($1.01 trillion) for ten years from 2024 in advanced, sustainable technologies that support national emissions reduction.[4] The Japanese government hopes that the 20 trillion yen worth of GX bonds would attract 50 trillion yen ($338 billion) in investments from the private sector over the next some small ten years.

First issuance of a nuclear project bond

Constellation Energy Corp is an electricity generator based in the US state of Maryland. It operates nuclear, hydro, wind, and solar generation facilities, supplying over 16 million homes and businesses across the country. The Fortune 200 company and largest producer of carbon-free energy in the United States announced the first corporate green bond in the country that can be used to finance nuclear energy projects in March 2024. The $900 million, 30-year term offering will be used for investments such as maintenance, expansion, and life extensions of Constellation's clean, reliable nuclear power generation. The green bond offering is based on a new green financing framework developed by Constellation, and proceeds can be used to finance other green projects such as nuclear uprates (raising power output), clean hydrogen production, energy storage systems, wind repowering, and carbon-free energy solutions for commercial customers.[5] ESG data, research, and ratings provider Morningstar Sustainalytics endorsed the issuance stating that the Constellation Energy's green financing framework was 'credible and impactful and aligns with the four core components of the Green Bond Principles 2021 and the Green Loan Principles 2023'.[6]

First issuance of a sustainability-linked bond

Sustainability-linked bonds are bonds where the proceeds are not just earmarked for green or sustainable purposes but also are linked to the performance of certain key performance indicators in achieving pre-defined sustainability performance targets. Italian utility ENEL, one of the largest in the world, is a producer and distributor of electricity and supplier of gas and is active in over 30 countries. It launched the world's first sustainability-linked bond in September 2019, which was oversubscribed and allowed the utility to issue the bond at a price lower than a conventional bond without the sustainability element. The bond stipulated that should ENEL not achieve its sustainability target, the coupon paid to bondholders would increase by 25 basis points as a penalty. ENEL raised a further €2.5 billion by issuing another such bond linked to the UN SDGs.[7] In April 2024, it was announced that ENEL had failed to meet one of its sustainability performance targets, which triggered a 25-basis-point step up in the coupon rate for the affected bonds. This failure was a watershed moment for ENEL and the sustainability-linked debt market and could help to restore confidence in the sustainability-linked bond format, according to a report by financial services provider Sustainable Fitch.[8]

Financing the transition through environmental commodities

Environmental commodities are a relatively new alternative tool to finance the energy transition. Environmental commodities have been around for some time but have become more prevalent since the Paris Agreement. Within the commodities space, they can be categorised as clean energy-based non-tangible energy credits. The value of the energy commodities market has become quite substantial, and the momentum of the past few years indicates that it will continue to expand rapidly. However, because it is still a young type of commodity, the rules and regulations continue to change and evolve. The main driver has been, and will continue to be, government efforts to cut GHG emissions and promote clean energy. There are several types of energy commodities, and new types will surely be created over the next few years. The more common ones include carbon credits, carbon offsets, and renewable energy certificates, commonly referred to as RECs, which have many subtypes, such as solar renewable energy certificates and white certificates, for example. The three products are different in terms of application, rules, and regulation, yet they are all related as tools for capital raising with the funds used to promote sustainable development and reduce GHG emissions.

First and foremost, carbon taxes must be distinguished from carbon credits or offsets (see Figure 10.2). The first difference is that typically a carbon tax itself cannot be traded. Both tools are central to driving emitters to think about their emissions more carefully. However, a carbon tax directly sets a price on carbon by defining a tax rate on GHG emissions or the carbon content of fossil fuels, defines the World Bank. Also, there is no market

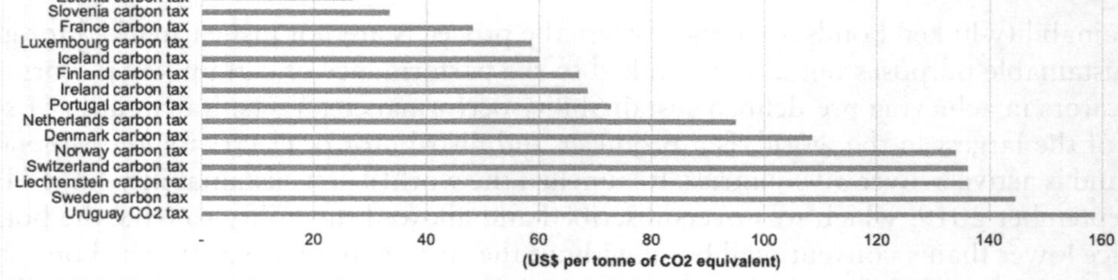

Figure 10.2 Carbon tax around the world 2025

Source: Data retrieved by author from World Bank, 'State and Trends of Carbon Pricing Dashboard' (Carbon Pricing Dashboard 30 June 2025). Available at: https://carbonpricingdashboard.worldbank.org/ accessed 30 June 2025.

determination of the carbon price. It is not overly difficult to establish carbon tax schemes for polluters. There were 43 jurisdictions around the world that have implemented some form of national carbon tax as of June 2025,[9] according to the World Bank. Some – the European Nordic countries – were early adopters with regulation implemented in the early 1990s. In the major regions, the most notable nations which do not have national carbon taxes schemes are India in Asia, Italy in Europe, and the United States in North America. The schemes still have some way to mature. The rates vary greatly among different countries in Europe. They were as high as €145 ($170) per tonne of CO_2e in Sweden, and as low as €0.10 ($0.12) in Poland.[10]

Carbon credits and offsets

When discussing the concept of intangible commodities, it is crucial to consider whether they can be classified as assets or not. The idea of trading carbon as a commodity was first explored in the United States. Some argue that the concept of carbon offsets also originated in the United States, with law and economics scholar Ronald H. Coase first alluding to it in his article, 'The Problem of Social Cost' published in October 1960.[11] Coase began the article with an excellent example, stating:

> The standard example is of a factory that produces smoke, which has harmful effects on those occupying neighbouring properties. The economic analysis of such a situation usually proceeds in terms of a divergence between the private and social product of the factory.

He added that

> most economists thought it would be desirable to make the factory owner liable for the damage caused to those injured by the smoke, or alternatively, to place a tax on the factory owner varying with the amount of smoke produced and equivalent in money terms to the damage it would cause.[12]

Carbon schemes can be complicated. Carbon credits allow the owner to emit a certain amount of CO_2 or other GHG emissions. Usually, one credit equals one tonne of CO_2 or CO_2-equivalent in other GHG emissions. The concept itself is simple. For example, a steel manufacturing facility, which emits CO_2, is allocated an allowance permitting the facility to continue to pollute up to a certain limit, which is periodically reduced. If it cannot stop emitting, it can buy credits from a facility which has been able to reduce its emissions. These are called cap-and-trade programmes. There are two main types of mechanisms: a compliance market and a voluntary one. The latter are also known as carbon offsets and have existed for nearly three decades. Throughout their history, carbon markets have seen great upheavals and changes. Yet, they have generally progressively evolved into robust and reliable markets.

Overall compliance mechanisms covered 14.7 gigatons of CO_2 equivalent in 2025, representing 28 per cent of the global GHG emissions; 5 from carbon taxes and 23 per cent from emissions trading systems (see Figure 10.3). The highest emissions coverage by carbon taxes or emissions trading systems in absolute terms was China, Western Europe, and the United States.[13]

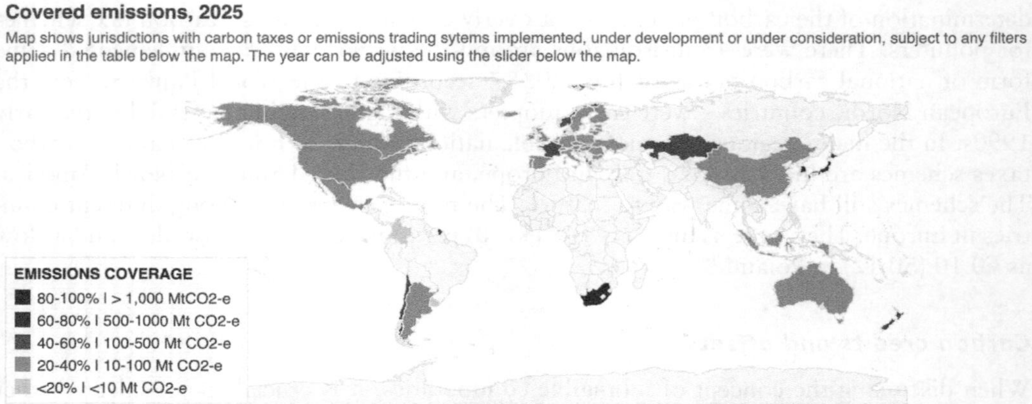

Figure 10.3 Covered emissions, 2025 (The World Bank Group)

Source: The World Bank Group, 'GHG Emissions Coverage' (The World Bank Group). Available at: https://carbonpricingdashboard.worldbank.org/compliance/coverage accessed 12 September 2025.

Renewable Energy Certificates (RECs)

RECs are market-based instruments that represent the non-power benefits of one MWh of energy generated from a renewable energy source. RECs allow organisations to claim the use of renewable energy and reduce Scope 2 emissions.[14] RECs can be bundled with the underlying electricity or sold separately as unbundled RECs. While some organisations could be sceptical of unbundled RECs, they can still help support the clean energy transition by directing funds towards renewable energy projects and improving the overall mix of renewable versus fossil fuel energy in an electricity grid. RECs can come from a variety of renewable energy sources, such as solar, wind, hydropower, biomass, or geothermal projects. Specific certification programmes ensure the authenticity of renewable energy projects and avoid problems like double-counting emissions benefits. RECs are used in the United States and Canada, while other countries use similar instruments called energy attribute certificates, such as guarantees of origin in Europe and international renewable energy certificates in over 50 countries. Organisations can purchase RECs from reputable sources, such as certified green power providers.[15]

Regional differences

There are significant regional disparities in carbon finance. Several factors drive these differences. They include different stages of economic and financial markets development, levels of policy support and regulatory frameworks maturity, varying degrees in the flows of clean technologies and solutions as well as capital, the industrial composition in a country or a specific region, and the level of international cooperation and maturity of the market mechanism. The progress of these factors has been positive over the past few years as shown in the growing adoption of carbon financing around the world. However, the progress has taken place at different speeds. The momentum will continue in the coming years, although various hurdles will also affect the speed of development. Hurdles faced include geopolitical upheavals, a possible global economic slowdown, and the effects of a decoupling between the world's two largest economies, China and the United States.

Carbon financing: North America versus Europe

The actual creation of a market where institutions or individuals could transact carbon credits or carbon offsets took hold in 1997 with the signing of the Kyoto Protocol. However, it was not until 2005 that the first major, and today's deepest, carbon market was established, the European Union Emissions Trading System (EU ETS; see Figure 10.4). While the United States may have first had the idea, the nation today significantly lags such jurisdictions as China and Europe, as it has not yet been able to create a national carbon market. Only the state of California has a formal cap-and-trade scheme. The United States did try to build a voluntary carbon credit market, but the transaction volume pales compared to that of a fully fledged compliance market.

No reliable or consistent numbers as to the amount traded in the compliance and the voluntary markets are easily available. This is likely due to different entities using different denominators in their methodologies. Yet the difference between the two types of carbon markets is hundreds of billions versus hundreds of millions. Still, to give an approximate realm as to the difference, one can quote a study by ResearchAndMarkets.com, a research firm, which estimated that the value of the global compliance carbon market was over $900 billion in 2022 and that by 2028, it would increase to about $2.7 trillion.[16] Ecosystem Marketplace, another research firm, said that in 2022 the transaction value of the global voluntary market is just under $2 billion.[17] Another research firm, Market Research Intellect, put the market size for voluntary carbon offsets $2.7 billion for 2023.[18] It is important to note that the actual revenue is smaller. For example, the World Bank put the government revenue from emissions trading schemes at $67 billion in 2022.[19]

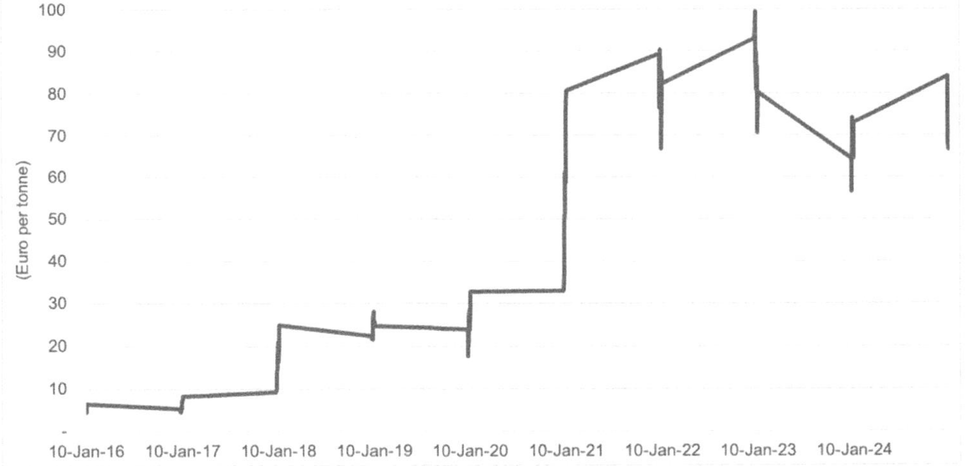

Figure 10.4 European Union Allowance Yearly Futures historical data

Note: Average monthly price starting 1 October 2016.

Source: Investing.com, 'European Union Allowance (EUA) Yearly Futures Historical Prices - Investing.com' (Investing.com 12 September 2025). Available at: https://www.investing.com/commodities/european-union-allowance-eua-year-futures-historical-data accessed 12 September 2025.

The EU ETS 2 is a new carbon emissions trading system that will operate separately from the existing EU ETS and cover CO_2 emissions from surface transport, buildings, and smaller industries not currently covered. It aims to complement the European Green Deal and bring down CO_2 emissions from transport and buildings by 42 per cent by 2030. The system will regulate upstream providers of transport fuels and building operators, rather than end consumers, and will require regulated companies to hold a GHG emissions permit and monitor and report their CO_2 emissions. Allowances will be bought at auctions, and companies must surrender enough allowances to match their annual verified CO_2 emissions or face fines. The price of carbon will be determined by supply and demand, with certain price safeguards in place. Revenues from carbon auctions will be used to support vulnerable households and climate action measures. Monitoring and reporting will begin in 2025, and the system will become fully operational in 2027, with the possibility of postponement until 2028 in case of high oil or gas prices in 2026.[20]

China: becoming world's biggest market

China is the world's biggest emitter of CO_2. It is estimated that China emitted almost three times as much as the second largest emitter, the United States, and well over three times that of the third largest emitter, India, in 2024. Once fully developed, the Chinese emissions trading market will significantly outsize any other in the world in terms of coverage of carbon emissions. The development of the compliance market, and later that of the voluntary market, progressed very slowly over the past few decades. The authorities took an experimental and precautious approach, wanting to avoid some of the challenges other markets had faced, especially the EU. Since the launch of the national market in 2021, the pace of development has accelerated.

Today, the national carbon market system comprises a mandatory market, the national carbon emissions trading market, and a voluntary one, the national voluntary GHG emission reduction trading market. Each has its own focus and operates independently. At the same time, they are complementary and interconnected. These markets are still at an early stage of development, though they are rapidly evolving.

China was an early participant in the global carbon credits market. In the early 2000s, the country ratified the Kyoto Protocol and became a major host to Clean Development Mechanism projects which generated Certified Emissions Reductions. These carbon credits were sold to European and other developed nations, funding clean energy projects in China in exchange for carbon offsets. This allowed the country to start gaining carbon trading expertise, though there was yet no domestic market framework.

China's carbon market has developed significantly in the past two decades. China started to seriously talk about the environmental cost of pollution[21] towards the end of the 10th Five-Year Plan period (2001–2005). It started planning for a national carbon trading platform in the following plan, the 11th Five-Year Plan (2006–2010). In October 2011, during the 12th Five-Year Plan (2011–2015), the National Development and Reform Commission issued the landmark NDRC Document No. 2601 [2011] titled 'Notice on Carrying out Carbon Emissions Trading Pilot Work'.[22] During the pilot phase, seven carbon trading pilot compliance markets were established in seven provinces and provincial-status cities. They included Beijing, Guangdong, Shanghai, Shenzhen, and Tianjin launched in 2013, and then Chongqing and Hubei in 2014. An eighth, Fujian, was added in 2016. These were a solid foundation for the national carbon market.

The first compliance cycle of the national carbon market was officially launched on 1 January 2021. In May, the Ministry of Ecology and Environment issued several new rules to further regulate the registration, trading, and settlement activities of carbon emission rights nationwide. On 16 July 2021, the national carbon trading was officially launched on the Shanghai Environment and Energy Exchange, involving more than 2,162 companies in the power generation industry with an emission quota of about 4.5 billion tons, amounting to 40 per cent of the total national carbon emissions.[23] On the third anniversary of the launch of the national carbon emissions trading market on 15 July 2024, the Ministry of Ecology and Environment said that the cumulative trading of carbon emission quotas was over 460 million tons for a total of almost nearly 27 billion yuan ($3.8 billion).[24] On the day of launch, the price ranged between 48.00 and 52.80 yuan ($6.7–$7.4) per tonne, the lowest price was on 38.50–42.75 yuan ($5.4–$6.0) per tonne on 26 October 2021 and the highest on 102.19–104 yuan ($14.33–$14.58) per tonne on 29 April 2024.[25] The national carbon market transacted 188 million metric tonnes of CO_2 equivalent in 2024 for a total turnover of 18 billion yuan ($2.5 billion). Another 55 billion had been traded in the first quarter of 2025. Since the market's inception in 2021, cumulative trading amounted to 700 million tonnes for a total value of 50 billion yuan ($7 billion).

Trading in the GHG emissions voluntary emissions reduction market, known as the China Certified Emissions Reductions (CCERs) scheme, started in 2012. It peaked in 2015 when the pilots integrated CCERs. Issuance was halted in 2017 as there were issues with the pricing and trading volume of CCER projects which led to a temporary suspension of new project approvals from March 2017. Still, the CCERs already issued could continue to be traded. Authorities have continued in their efforts to address these and other challenges and to further develop the carbon market, such as the establishment of a national CCER trading centre and the solicitation of methodological suggestions for voluntary GHG emission reduction projects.[26] In October 2023, the Ministry of Ecology and Environment and the State Administration for Market Regulation revived the voluntary market when they issued new measures. The CCERs scheme reforms focus included the project types (such as afforestation, solar thermal power, offshore wind power, and mangrove restoration), the trading platform, and the methodologies used. Less than five months later, 9.5 million metric tonnes of CO_2 equivalent were issued by nine offshore wind farms and a solar thermal project. This particular issuance is a major step in the advancement of the nation's carbon markets, noted financial data and analytics firm S&P Global, with the next step being the Integration of the voluntary market with the national emissions trading one, which would massively enhance liquidity.[27]

The Chinese compliance and voluntary carbon markets are still at a transitional phase. They will see a lot of fine-tuning over the coming months and years. The regulatory framework will become more sophisticated as more sectors, such as steel and cement, are included and as transactions gain pace in the short term. Monitoring, reporting, and verification system for carbon emissions has massively improved over the past few years but will need to be improved further. These and other challenges should be overcome as regulators gain more experience which will allow for the introduction of more diversified trading products, including carbon futures, which will in turn enhance market liquidity and drive greater participation from financial institutions.

Among the many hurdles, perhaps the steepest one is that the nation wants to move from an intensity-based cap to an absolute cap, similar to the EU, by 2030.[28] The adoption plan of a cap-and-trade system would include the participation of hard-to-abate industrial sectors, such as aluminium and chemicals, by 2027. This means gathering data for industries which may not necessarily have historical emissions data, dealing with regional economic differences (wealthy Guangdong versus less poor Guanxi, for example), and many other hurdles. Well, the trajectory is reasonably clear, the tightrope between economic stability and climate ambitions could mean some potential delays in implementation.

Some small, developed nations are pioneers: the case of Singapore

The small city state of Singapore has worked hard for over two decades to become a key global trading hub for energy commodities. Today, it is one of the largest commodity trading hubs for oil and liquefied natural gas, for example. In the past few years, it has also strived to become Asia's renewable energy hub. One of the many endeavours has been in the carbon markets.

The country's business and investment planning agency, the Economic Development Board, projected that a carbon hub could potentially generate a gross value of S$5.6 billion ($4.4 billion) to its economy by 2050. The city-state already has over 100 carbon service providers offering services like carbon monitoring, credit verification, and climate risk analysis. The foundation was laid in 2019 when it introduced a carbon tax, the first in Southeast Asia, among other initiatives.[29] It already has two voluntary carbon marketplaces and exchange platforms, Climate Impact X and AirCarbon Exchange, as well as a carbon credit certification and registration body, the Asia Carbon Institute.

Singapore's distinctive approach has been a convincing involvement and leadership on the part of government agencies, the construction of a relatively innovative regulatory framework, the sturdy encouragement of public–private partnerships, and an intense effort to work with high-quality globally recognised carbon credits.

Other innovative climate financing tools

Innovation can be synonymous with climate finance given this field of finance is still relatively young and fast-developing. There are a number of innovations which have been scaled up. One example is thematic bonds, such as green or blue bonds. Emerging instruments or mechanisms include new forms of credits such as transition credits, biodiversity credits, and other forms of credits or mechanisms such as blended finance. It is crucial to be aware of these new products so that the financing of a climate solution, a project, or a company's climate-focused activities can be optimised and maximised.

Transition credits

Transition credits have appeared in the climate finance discussion recently. So far, they are not widely used. The Rocky Mountain Institute, a respected think tank, highlighted the potential of such credits while Singapore is one of the first countries in the world to seriously look into this option.

A report by the Rocky Mountain Institute released in March 2024 discussed that transition credits may well be fit for purpose. It highlighted that two of the world's carbon standards had started work on transition credits. Verra and Gold Standard had released methodologies for generating voluntary carbon credits to support the early retirement (or phase out) and replacement of coal plants with renewable energy. The methodologies want to ensure the integrity and quality of these credits. They consider factors such as additionality, emissions leakage, and socio-economic impacts. The institute report said that the US Department of State, as well as the Bezos Earth Fund and the Rockefeller Foundation, two philanthropies, had presented a core framework for the Energy Transition Accelerator, an initiative aimed at accelerating the shift away from fossil fuels, to support a jurisdictional, power-sector-wide crediting approach. Five pilots were announced at COP28. Two in the Philippines and one each in Chile, the Dominican Republic, and Nigeria. Some corporations, consultancies, and financial institutions are supporting the large-scale power sector transformation. The Bank of America, Boston Consulting Group, Mastercard, McDonald's, Morgan Stanley, PepsiCo, Salesforce, Standard Chartered Bank, and Schneider Electric signed Letters of Intent to support such schemes. The Institute emphasised that the development of transition credits would depend on demand from buyers which will be driven by the level of the success of the initial pilots and the ability to demonstrate their climate and socio-economic impacts.[30]

In 2023, Singapore began studying the possibility of purchasing transition credits generated from the early retirement of coal-fired power plants and their replacement with cleaner energy sources. These credits would be used to meet Singapore's climate targets and may also be purchased by companies subjected to Singapore's carbon tax to offset up to 5 per cent of their taxable emissions from 2024. The de facto central bank, the Monetary Authority of Singapore, produced a working paper with global consultancy McKinsey & Company titled 'Accelerating the early retirement of coal-fired power plants through carbon credits'[31] in September 2023. It explored the creation of transition credits to improve the economic viability of the early phase out of coal-fired power plants (CFPPs). The working paper focuses on the generation of carbon credits, or transition credits, from such CFPPs phase out and their replacement with renewable energy. The use of such credits could increase the economic viability and scalability of early retirement transactions. The paper clearly recognised the complexity of transaction process flow and interdependencies. It also highlighted that the voluntary carbon market is still a maturing one, and transition credits would face close scrutiny due to their association with coal. It proposes an end-to-end approach that examines the key elements needed to effectively retire a CFPP early using transition credits. The four key areas are the economics of early retirement, carbon credits as an instrument for early retirement, financing early retirement transactions, and early retirement project development and integrity. The report also provided suggestions on how to interact with capital providers, carbon credit off-takers, power off-takers, and renewable energy asset owners. Another area of discussion is the likely price of such credits. Early estimates by some experts put the price at $14 per credit. Others, such as the CEO of Climate Impact X, a Singapore-based carbon credits global marketplace and exchange, estimated that they would need to be priced at a minimum of $30 per credit.[32]

Biodiversity credits

Biodiversity credits are also currently not yet common. Yet, this type of credits, which are sometimes referred to as biodiversity offsets or conservation credits, have a few more actual examples than transition credits.

The focus of these credits is on financial activities which can deliver net positive biodiversity gains. One credit can be equal to a certain amount of land conserved or restored over a specific period of time. Private companies can purchase these credits to meet their own biodiversity- or nature-based commitments. The World Resources Institute, a US-based nonprofit research organisation, noted that the biodiversity market mechanisms are often structured around the 'mitigation hierarchy', namely that companies should avoid creating negative environmental impacts as far as possible, decrease the extent of environmental impacts that cannot be avoided, and only when every attempt has been made to do these two steps, rely on other tools like market-based credits to offset their impact or see a net gain.[33]

Examples of biodiversity credits include programmes such as the Koala Credits in Australia, the Habitat and Species Conservation Banking in the United States, and the Biodiversity Offsets in England.

The Koala Biodiversity Species Credits programme in the Australian state of New South Wales involves developers paying for the loss of koala habitat (see Figure 10.5). It requires them to purchase credits that fund koala conservation efforts. The state of New South Wales publishes a Biodiversity Credits Market Sales Dashboard where the price of koala and other species credits can be monitored. The cost for purchasing these credits is determined through individual negotiations between the landholder and the buyer. At a minimum, the negotiated price should cover the expenses associated with maintaining the stewardship site; an area of land that is managed by a landholder or land manager for the purpose of conservation. Looking at data on the dashboard over the four years to July 2024, only 24 koala credit price points are displayed. Prices ranged from a low of A$176.50 ($115.7) to a high of A$1,507.60 ($988), with the median price being about A$430 ($282).

This programme could potentially be used by the current Labor Party-led federal government to address the country's extinction crisis. Some critics question the motivation for private investors to participate in these markets and argue that serious market intervention is required to deliver significant private capital. Some suggest that the government should create demand by buying the credits directly or forcing businesses to invest in them. While the

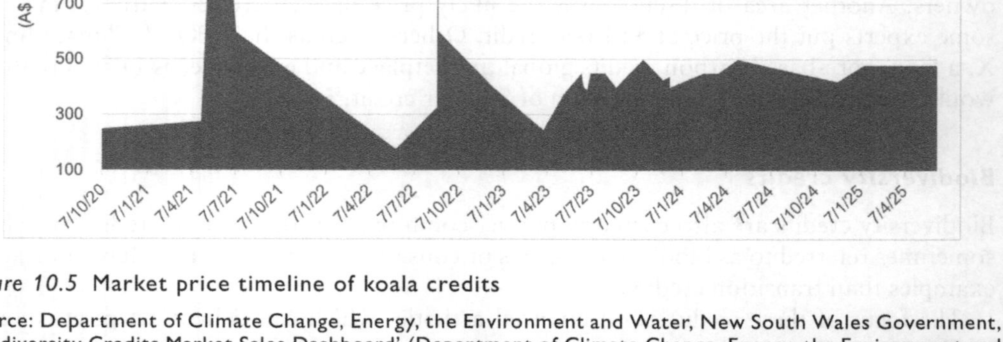

Figure 10.5 Market price timeline of koala credits

Source: Department of Climate Change, Energy, the Environment and Water, New South Wales Government, 'Biodiversity Credits Market Sales Dashboard' (Department of Climate Change, Energy, the Environment and Water, New South Wales Government 2025). Available at: https://app.powerbi.com/view?r=eyJrljoiZWI3M-mZhMTctZGVjNi00ZTdlLTkwZTEtOGY4NWNhYjc3M2RiliwidCI6Ijk2ZWY4ODIxLTJhMzktNDcxYy1iODIhLTY3YjA4MzNkZDNiOSJ9 accessed 2 July 2025.

government has not indicated any intention to force businesses to invest in nature, nearly 200 countries, including Australia, recently agreed to move towards requiring large, transnational companies and financial institutions to disclose their impacts on biodiversity.[34]

In the United States, Species Conservation Banking and Habitat Conservation Banking are strategies used to offset environmental impacts of development. Species Conservation Banking aims to protect and manage habitats for specific endangered, threatened, or at-risk species. Habitat Conservation Banking focuses on preserving and managing habitats that support a wide range of species. Both approaches involve creating conservation banks and selling credits to developers for regulatory compliance, albeit the two strategies differ in their targets and scope. Both of these strategies have been established for several decades. Species Conservation Banking was first established in California in 1986, for example.[35] Seemingly, the market for the credits is even thinner than the biodiversity credits market in Australia, despite the fact that when well-managed, investing in conservation banking can generate economic benefits. One study released in 2021 examined the costs and revenue data of 26 habitat conservation banks in California demonstrating that 14 out of the 26 had generated positive financial returns.[36]

England launched a biodiversity credit scheme in early 2024, known as the Biodiversity Net Gain. It mandates that all new road and housebuilding projects achieve a 10 per cent net gain in biodiversity or habitat. This requirement became law under the Town and Country Planning Act. The scheme aims to make developers think about minimising and mitigating the ecosystem impact of new developments, with the potential to restore numerous habitats. Internationally, England's approach is considered one of the most ambitious, with other countries like Sweden, Singapore, Scotland, and Wales expressing interest in adopting similar models. However, the success of the Biodiversity Net Gain hinges on effective regulation, monitoring, and enforcement, which have historically been challenges in environmental policies in the United Kingdom and elsewhere. Additionally, the scheme's reliance on off-site habitat restoration, often on farmland, faces uncertainties due to the nascent market and potential lack of farmer participation. While the legislation is a significant step, it currently excludes the environmental impact of construction materials and their processing. The growing interest from private players and the international community highlights the scheme's potential, but its success will depend on robust implementation and potential future expansions to address broader impacts, notes an article in the Guardian.[37]

Other types of credits

Another innovative type of credits is Carbon Dioxide Removal credits. They are generated from carbon dioxide removal projects that actively extract CO_2 from the atmosphere and store it permanently in natural sinks – such as soil, oceans, or forests – or through technological processes like direct air capture. Removal credits physically reduce atmospheric CO_2 levels, making them essential for achieving net-zero goals, unlike traditional carbon offsets, which compensate for emissions by preventing future CO_2 release. The Science Based Targets initiative mandates that, starting in 2030, only carbon removal credits will count as valid offsets for hard-to-abate emissions. Organisations can buy this type of credits to meet sustainability targets and comply with evolving carbon accounting standards.[38] One example is a deal secured in July 2024 with tech giant Microsoft by 1PointFive, a CCS, utilisation, and sequestration company. It will sell 500,000 metric tonnes of carbon dioxide removal credits to Microsoft over six years. The transaction was the largest single purchase of CDR credits enabled by direct air capture technology. 1PointFive's first industrial-scale

DAC facility under construction in Texas will ensure the captured CO_2 is securely stored through subsurface saline sequestration, rather than being used for oil and gas production.[39]

Blended finance

An increasingly important area for evaluating the sources of climate finance is blended finance. The concept shares some similarities with Public–Private Partnerships (PPPs). The latter typically involves a contract between a public entity and a private one to finance, build, and operate a project, typically an infrastructure project such as a highway or a port. Blended finance has several definitions. One is provided by the OECD, which argues it is a 'strategic use of development finance for the mobilisation of additional finance towards sustainable development in developing countries'.[40] Some of the providers of blended finance include multilateral development banks, international financial institutions, climate funds, private sector partners, philanthropic entities, and government entities (see Figure 10.6).

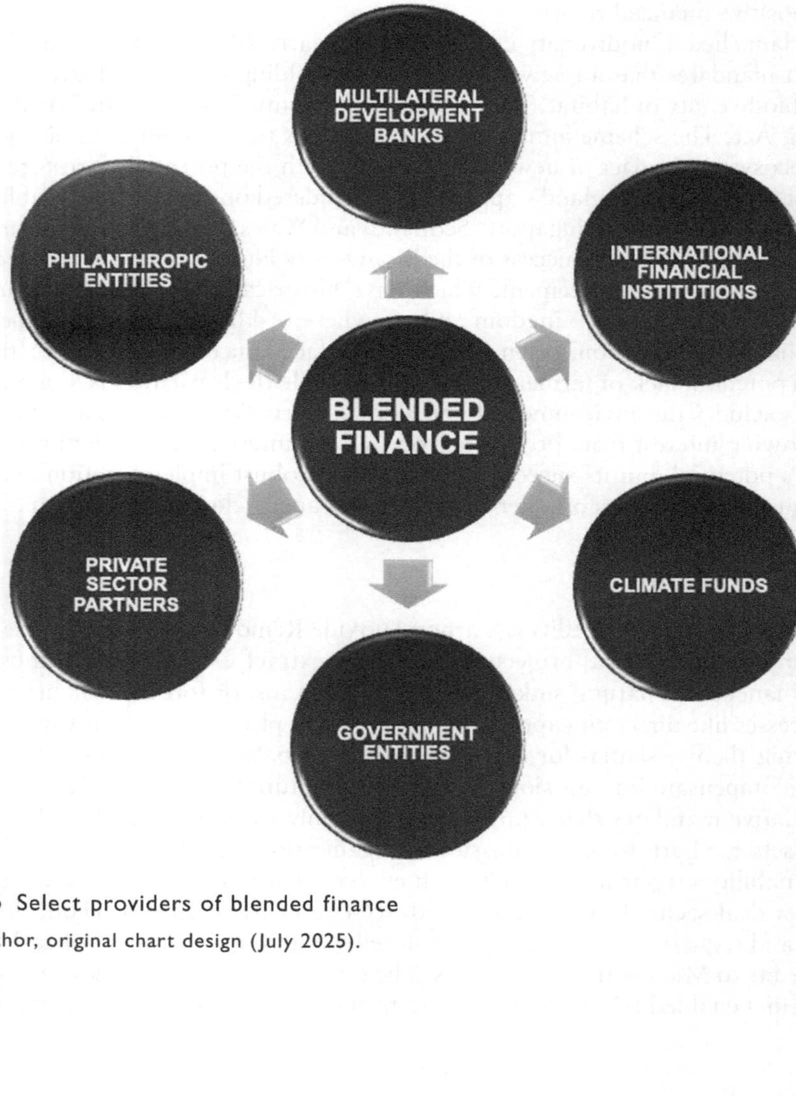

Figure 10.6 Select providers of blended finance

Source: Author, original chart design (July 2025).

International legal practice Hogan Lovells[41] noted in a short report that while blended finance is not a new concept, it has enjoyed a revival in recent years. It is seen as a way to mobilise large-scale private capital flows to achieve the UN SDGs. Hogan Lovells adds that blended finance involves using public capital, including philanthropic finance, to catalyse private sector investment by reducing risks associated with the investment and enhancing financial returns for private investors. The goal is to use the minimum amount of concessional capital to attract private sector investment that might not have otherwise occurred. Blended finance has been revolutionising public sector investment by providing potential returns on public funding that can be reinvested. It uses catalytic capital from public or philanthropic sources to increase private sector investment in developing countries. Structures vary and can be implemented under multiple potential frameworks. Global network for blended finance Convergence identified four key structural models: concessional or equity/first-loss capital, credit enhancement, technical assistance funding, and grants.[42]

Like most innovative and evolving climate finance approaches and instruments, blended finance faces several challenges. Hogan Lovells notes that barriers to private investment for climate, sustainable development, and nature include complex and bespoke transactions, conflicting expectations and documentary requirements, and a lack of commonly accepted terms and documentation. Recommendations to increase volume include standardising transaction structures, understanding the needs of key private capital investment allocators, and establishing blended finance as a large-scale climate, sustainability, and nature financing vehicle. Blended finance structures also face regulatory and other challenges, such as navigating an increasingly complex regulatory landscape affecting blended finance, tax systems not designed for blended finance structures, and compliance issues with regulations like the EU Alternative Investment Fund Management Directive and the EU Securitisation Regulation. The report concludes that the market for blended finance in the climate and nature context remains nascent, and teething issues are expected as participants focus on scaling a few structures that will become standard. Nevertheless, blended finance is likely to become an increasingly important way to mobilise private sector funds to mitigate and adapt to climate change and finance the conservation and restoration of nature.

Blended finance for sustainability has many successful examples. The United Nations Environment Programme Finance Initiative highlights two notable cases.[43] In 2022, the First Abu Dhabi Bank led the financing of a 500 MW wind project in Uzbekistan, the largest renewable energy project in Central Asia by the end of 2023. The bank acted as the green loan coordinator, structuring a $102 million green loan facility backed by Etihad Credit Insurance, with additional funding of over $175 million from four development finance institutions. Another significant example is the 2023 'Debt-for-Nature' transaction in Gabon, involving the Government of Gabon, The Nature Conservancy, and Bank of America. This $500 million refinancing of Gabon's sovereign debt freed up $125 million for ocean conservation, supporting the country's goal to protect 30 per cent of its lands and waters by 2030. The transaction benefited from political risk insurance provided by the US International Development Finance Corporation, which resulted in an Aa2 investment-grade rating, attracting investors and enabling longer-duration debt with lower interest payments. This innovative approach also established a conservation fund to ensure continued funding for conservation efforts even after the bonds are repaid.

Managing risk: the financial sector and business

Various aspects of climate finance from the perspective of the financial sector have been examined in this chapter. A final critical area to consider is the symbiotic relationship between the sector and businesses. From a revenue perspective, corporates are one of the principal sources of business for the financial sector. Consequently, the financial sector is heavily exposed to climate risks faced by corporations. Moreover, the combined economic and financial impacts associated with climate change may result in considerable future losses for a financial institution, potentially reducing its capacity to provide financial services to corporations.

Climate change poses a clear and present danger to a variety of businesses across a range of industries, regardless of their size. This includes sectors from agriculture to electronics manufacturing to infrastructure projects. Only in recent years have some businesses begun to address the different types of physical, transition, or liability risks they face. Physical risks could result in the loss or damage to a company's assets. Transition risks could lead to the loss of an entire customer base. Liability risks may result in heavy regulatory fines or lawsuits. Climate change can be existentially threatening for many industries, and corporates must find ways to mitigate the impact of these risks. It is fundamental for the financial sector to work closely with businesses to help them mitigate climate-related risks. There are a variety of ways this can be achieved. Some have been mentioned in the discussion of the various climate finance actors but are worth highlighting again in this context. Financial institutions can help and work with businesses in at least five physical, transition, and liability risk areas: risk scenario analysis, business advisory, climate financing, insurance, and business portfolio management (see Figure 10.7).

Most medium- to large-size financial institutions will have in place internal climate risk modelling capabilities. These can help businesses with physical, transition, and liability risks analysis. Some will have developed these internally and can provide to businesses advanced risk modelling and analytics so that businesses may better understand and, importantly, quantify their exposure to climate-driven physical risks. Some institutions may have opted to use third-party systems. Providers include financial services companies such as Moody's and S&P Global, accounting and consulting firms like EY or KPMG, and technology companies or software solutions providers such as IBM and SAS. There are also multitude of companies focused on climate risk modelling and analytics including Aon, Climate X, and Jupiter Intelligence.

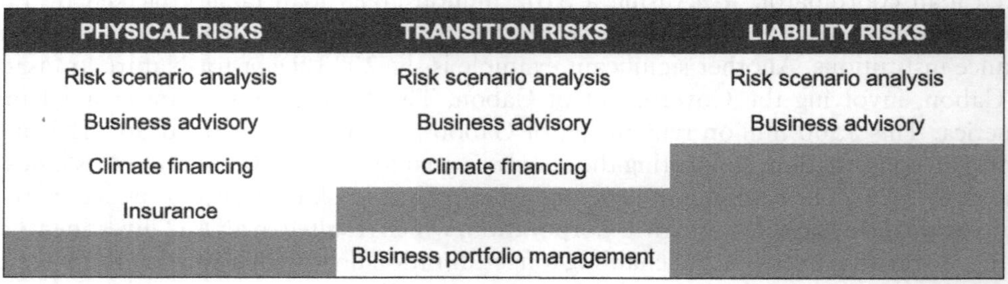

Figure 10.7 Climate risk areas intersection for financial institutions and businesses

Source: Author, original chart design (July 2024).

The modelling and analytics platforms collect data from a wide variety of sources, including sensors, satellite images, ocean temperatures, atmospheric conditions, land types and uses, and population dynamics. They can create models monitoring as well as simulating the impact of various aspects of climate change. All the analytics platforms used by financial institutions, whether developed internally or by third parties, will have different degrees of sophistication. Yet, the analyses can help corporates in a great variety of sectors when they do not have their own systems. Typically, the analytical systems will have to include efficient and timely modelling of risk management, the creation of scenarios and what-if analysis, risk simulation and forecasting, as well as stress test capabilities.

Assessing the financial risks of climate change is complex as the effects of multiple climate pathways over several decades must be assessed and while there could be lack of historical data. Also, uncertainty over a long horizon makes it more difficult to specify meaningful scenarios, develop good models, and interpret them. Even though it is challenging to predict a specific cash flow number several decades from now, financial institutions can still perform scenario-based risk analysis or stress testing to assess the climate exposure in the portfolio and link global temperature rises and other climate-related factors to macroeconomic aspects. This can help translate the impacts into direct effects on credit risk in their portfolios using existing credit risk management frameworks.[44]

Another area where financial institutions can help in supporting businesses in addressing climate-related risks is with their advisory services where institutions can proactively assist with physical, transition, and liability risks. Most medium- to large-size financial institutions already have structures in place to provide advisory services for their clients. It is in the interest of the financial institutions to ensure that their business clients minimise risk as any form of risk could, at best, hinder the growth of the business and, at worst, force the company into bankruptcy. There are many areas financial institutions can effectively participate from the advisory perspective: they can help with the development and implementation of business continuity plans, engage with policymakers to shape regulations supporting their clients' transition plans, and engage with stakeholders, such as investors or customers, regarding climate issues jointly with their business clients. If the client has a strong risk mitigation profile, it will be able to more easily undertake capital raising activities and the like.

Financial institutions can help and support their clients with the raising of green capital which could be deployed by the business for its transition planning as well as physical and transition risks mitigation. Capital raised from the issuance of green, sustainability-linked, and transition bonds as well as green loans would go towards the financing of projects which would make the business more resilient to physical risks, for example. The financial institution can support a business through helping to quantify the business' climate risks as well as provide support to the business in adhering to climate-related requirements like those of the Task Force on Climate Related Finance Disclosures.

Financial institutions that are insurers or have an insurance arm can help with climate-related physical risk. They can provide specific insurance products which could cover extreme weather events, sea level rises, unseasonal drought, and other climate-related physical risks. At the same time, several experts argue that Insurance companies are already heavily exposed to climate risk. US international law firm Skadden, Arps, Slate, Meagher & Flom, also known as Skadden, correctly noted that insurers are most likely currently over-exposed to climate risk. Their historical models were not designed to predict uncertain events such as natural disasters that can be exacerbated by climate change. While they could respond by underwriting and offering policies to consumers who would suffer without such safeguards, determining how to do so is not easy. Skadden notes that the European Insurance and Occupational Pensions Authority had reported that the EU insurance market is at an early stage in its journey to increase resilience to global warming. Insurers face two issues: if they price premiums too low, they may fail to take climate risk into account, leading to under-pricing and losses, but if they price premiums too high, businesses and consumers may not be able to afford them and may go uninsured. Skadden also remarks that the UK Prudential Regulation Authority is set to run a dynamic general insurance stress test in 2025 to assess the domestic insurance industry's resilience to climate-related losses, and insurers should use the findings to inform their approach to the market. Insurers can also adopt climate-specific stress testing to inform their pricing and make portfolio adjustments and use predictive analytics such as geospatial tools to make more detailed assessments of where wider protection could be needed. Insurers can also collaborate with governments to create agreements on how to apportion risks between public and private institutions and work with third parties to devise risk-transfer solutions that offer wider and more significant protection for consumers across the market.[45]

Finally, financial institutions can also engage with their business clients in the optimisation of their business portfolio to mitigate climate-related transition risks. A simple illustration would be a company which manufactures leather goods. The company's emissions start at the slaughterhouse section of the leather supply chain, and would include the energy use in tanneries, chemical outputs and their emissions, transportation, and the like. As part of its transition plan, the company could at the initial stage decide to build renewable energy generation capacity so it may use clean energy as well as purchase electric vehicles. A financial institution could provide green loans for these initiatives. In other cases, a company could stop producing products with high carbon footprints. There are of course immensely more complex business situations which would require a gradual approach to divestment. For example, a known gas company could simply stop producing oil and gas, but if it were to do so overnight, it would stop existing.

Notes

1 M Carney, 'Resolving the Climate Paradox' (Arthur Burns Memorial Lecture, 22 September 2016) <https://www.fsb.org/uploads/Resolving-the-climate-paradox.pdf> accessed 22 March 2025.

2 The definitions are sourced from finance-related organisations including Amundi Asset Management, BNP Paribas, CFA Institute, Climate Bonds Initiative, International Capital Market Association, International Monetary Fund, Nasdaq, S&P Global, Schroders Investment Management, Union Bancaire Privée, and the World Bank Group.

3 M Clodagh, C Harrison, and D Sharma, *Sustainable Debt Global State of the Market 2024* (Climate Bonds Initiative May 2025) <https://www.climatebonds.net/files/reports/cbi_sotm23_02h.pdf> accessed 30 June 2025.

4 Climate Bonds Initiative, *Briefing Note: Japan's Climate Transition Bond* (Climate Bonds Initiative 2024) <https://www.climatebonds.net/files/reports/japan-transition-bond-briefing-note-14022024.pdf> accessed 14 July 2024; S Take, 'Japan Hopes Climate Transition Bonds Draw More Foreign Investors' *Nikkei Asia* (27 February 2024) <https://asia.nikkei.com/Business/Markets/Japan-hopes-climate-transition-bonds-draw-more-foreign-investors> accessed 14 July 2024.

5 Constellation Energy Corp, 'Constellation Offers Nation's First Corporate Green Bond for Nuclear Energy' (Constellationenergy.com 2024) <https://www.constellationenergy.com/newsroom/2024/Constellation-Offers-Nations-First-Corporate-Green-Bond-for-Nuclear-Energy.html> accessed 2 July 2025.

6 Sustainalytics, 'Constellation Energy Green Financing Framework Second-Party Opinion (2024)' (sustainalytics.com 2024) <https://www.sustainalytics.com/corporate-solutions/sustainable-finance-

and-lending/published-projects/project/constellation-energy-corporation/constellation-energy-green-financing-framework-second-party-opinion-(2024)/constellation-energy-green-financing-framework-second-party-opinion-(2024)> accessed 2 July 2025.

7 Norton Rose Fulbright, 'Sustainability-Linked Bonds' (2020) <https://www.nortonrosefulbright.com/en/knowledge/publications/8a104da8/sustainability-linked-bonds> accessed 14 July 2024.

8 Sustainable Fitch, 'Sustainable Fitch: SLB Market Entering next Phase Following Enel's Missed Targets' (Sustainablefitch.com 29 April 2024) <https://www.sustainablefitch.com/corporate-finance/sustainable-fitch-slb-market-entering-next-phase-following-enels-missed-targets-29-04-2024> accessed 14 July 2024.

9 World Bank, *State and Trends of Carbon Pricing Dashboard* (Carbon Pricing Dashboard 30 June 2025) <https://carbonpricingdashboard.worldbank.org/> accessed 30 June 2025.

10 A Mengden, *Carbon Taxes in Europe* (Tax Foundation 5 September 2023) <https://taxfoundation.org/data/all/eu/carbon-taxes-in-europe-2023/> accessed 25 March 2024; Deloitte Conseil, *Energy Efficiency in Europe: The Levers to Deliver the Potential* (Deloitte Conseil 2016) <https://www2.deloitte.com/content/dam/Deloitte/global/Documents/Energy-and-Resources/energy-efficiency-in-europe.pdf> accessed 11 May 2024.

11 RH Coase, 'The Problem of Social Cost' (1960) 3 The Journal of Law and Economics 1.

12 RH Coase, 'The Problem of Social Cost' (1960) 3 The Journal of Law and Economics 1.

13 World Bank, *State and Trends of Carbon Pricing Dashboard* (Carbon Pricing Dashboard 30 June 2025) <https://carbonpricingdashboard.worldbank.org/> accessed 30 June 2025.

14 Scope 1 emissions: come directly from an organisation's activities, like burning fuels in boilers, furnaces, or company vehicles. Scope 2 emissions: are indirect and are caused by the electricity, steam, heat, or cooling one buys. Although the emissions themselves happen at the power plant, they are counted in the organisation's footprint because the energy use creates a demand for them.

15 3Degrees, *What are Renewable Energy Certificates (RECs)?* (3Degrees 4 December 2023) <https://3degreesinc.com/resources/what-are-renewable-energy-certificates-recs/> accessed 15 July 2024.

16 ResearchAndMarkets.com, 'Global Carbon Credit Market 2023–2028: Growing Coverage of Carbon Pricing Initiatives Fuels the Sector – ResearchAndMarkets.com' (www.businesswire.com 20 April 2023) <https://www.businesswire.com/news/home/20230420005830/en/Global-Carbon-Credit-Market-2023-2028-Growing-Coverage-of-Carbon-Pricing-Initiatives-Fuels-the-Sector-ResearchAndMarkets.com> accessed 26 March 2024.

17 Ecosystem Marketplace, *State of the Voluntary Carbon Markets 2023 Finds VCM Demand Concentrating around Pricier, High-Integrity Credits* (Ecosystem Marketplace 28 November 2023) <https://www.ecosystemmarketplace.com/articles/new-state-of-the-voluntary-carbon-markets-2023-finds-vcm-demand-concentrating-around-pricier-high-integrity-credits/> accessed 26 March 2024.

18 Market Research Intellect, *Voluntary Carbon Offsets Market Size, Trends and Projections* (Market Research Intellect | Market Analysis and Research Reports March 2024) <https://www.marketresearchintellect.com/product/global-voluntary-carbon-offsets-market-size-and-forecast/> accessed 26 March 2024.

19 World Bank, *Instrument Detail* (Carbon Pricing Dashboard 30 October 2023) <https://dev-rad-carbon-pricing.pantheonsite.io/compliance/instrument-detail> accessed 25 March 2024.

20 Redshaw Advisors, 'Here Are 8 Things You Should Know' (www.linkedin.com 11 April 2024) <https://www.linkedin.com/pulse/here-8-things-you-should-know-redshaw-advisors-ltd-qbgae/> accessed 15 July 2024.

21 Reuters Staff, 'China Silences Green GDP Study, Report Says' *Reuters* (9 August 2007) <https://www.reuters.com/article/economy/China-silences-green-gdp-study-report-says-idUSPEK219981/> accessed 3 July 2025.

22 国家发展改革委办公厅，'《关于开展碳排放权交易试点工作的通知》(发改办气候(2011)2601号）_跨境碳定价工具' (Sh.gov.cn 2020) <https://fgw.sh.gov.cn/ys-gjmy-1.1.2.2.1/20240313/de453165b7d64c3887740751da562396.html> accessed 3 July 2025.

23 高金智库，上海高级金融学院，'中国碳市场发展历程、问题及建议 | 高金智库-腾讯新闻' (view.inews.qq.com 10 August 2023) <https://view.inews.qq.com/k/20230810A06O5F00?no-redirect=1&web_channel=wap&openApp=false> accessed 16 July 2024.

24 Yi Carbon Home, '全国碳市场累计成交268.65亿元，企业建议增加碳金融产品' (m.tanpaifang.com 8 July 2024) <http://m.tanpaifang.com/article/107224.html> accessed 16 July 2024.

25 China Environment and Energy Trading Network, *Comprehensive Price Trend of National Carbon Market* (CNEEEX 15 July 2024) <https://www.cneeex.com/zhhq/quotshown.html> accessed 16 July 2024.

26 高金智库, 上海高级金融学院 (n 24).

27 I Yin, *China Completes First Issuance of Domestic Voluntary Carbon Credit CCERs* (S&P Global Commodity Insights 6 March 2025) <https://www.spglobal.com/commodity-insights/en/news-research/latest-news/energy-transition/030625-China-completes-first-issuance-of-domestic-voluntary-carbon-credit-ccers> accessed 3 July 2025.

28 I Yin, *China Signals Shift to Absolute Compliance Carbon Market Cap by 2030* (S&P Global Commodity Insights 1 July 2025) <https://www.spglobal.com/commodity-insights/en/news-research/latest-news/energy-transition/070125-China-signals-shift-to-absolute-compliance-carbon-market-cap-by-2030> accessed 3 July 2025.

29 S Ong, 'How Singapore is Positioning Itself as Asia's Carbon Hub' *Reuters* (6 November 2023) <https://www.reuters.com/sustainability/sustainable-finance-reporting/how-singapore-is-positioning-itself-asias-carbon-hub-2023-11-06/> accessed 16 July 2024.

30 E Slater and others, *Transition Credits Are Gearing up to Support Global Energy Transformation* (Rocky Mountain Institute 2024) <https://rmi.org/transition-credits-are-gearing-up-to-support-global-energy-transformation/> accessed 16 July 2024.

31 Monetary Authority of Singapore and McKinsey & Company, *Accelerating the Early Retirement of Coal-Fired Power Plants through Carbon Credits* (The Monetary Authority of Singapore and McKinsey & Company 2023) <https://www.mas.gov.sg/-/media/mas-media-library/publications/monographs-or-information-paper/sg/accelerating-the-early-retirement-of-coal-fired-power-plants-through-carbon-credits-september-2023.pdf> accessed 16 July 2024.

32 J Lim, 'Transition Credits Need to Be at Least US$30 to Close Coal Phase-out Financing Gap: CIX' *The Business Times* (17 April 2024) <https://www.businesstimes.com.sg/esg/transition-credits-need-be-least-us-30-close-coal-phase-out-financing-gap-cix> accessed 21 July 2024.

33 R Rao, E Choi, and RP Czebiniak, *Can 'Biodiversity Credits' Boost Conservation?* (World Resources Institute 2024) <https://www.wri.org/insights/biodiversity-credits-explained> accessed 21 July 2024.

34 M Slezak, 'How Much Money is a Koala's Home Worth? In Several States, There's a Market That Can Tell You' *ABC News* (9 January 2023) <https://www.abc.net.au/news/2023-01-10/labor-environmental-biodiversity-credits-investment-critics/101804974> accessed 23 July 2024.

35 MJ Carreras Gamarra and TP Toombs, 'Thirty Years of Species Conservation Banking in the U.S.: Comparing Policy to Practice' (2017) 214 Biological Conservation 6 <https://www.conservationfund.org/wp-content/uploads/2023/08/CarrerasGamarra__Toombs-_2017_cons_banking__draft_ESA_mitigation_policy.pdf> accessed 24 July 2024.

36 J Poudel and R Pokharel, 'Financial Analysis of Habitat Conservation Banking in California' (2021) 13 Sustainability 12441 <https://www.mdpi.com/2071-1050/13/22/12441> accessed 24 July 2024.

37 P Weston, 'England Brings in Biodiversity Rules to Force Builders to Compensate for Loss of Nature' *The Guardian* (12 February 2024) <https://www.theguardian.com/environment/2024/feb/12/england-brings-in-biodiversity-net-gain-rules-to-force-builders-to-compensate-for-loss-of-nature#:~:text=England%20is%20launching%20a%20biodiversity> accessed 24 July 2024.

38 CarbonBetter, *Carbon Dioxide Removal (CDR) vs. Other Carbon Credits* (CarbonBetter 14 March 2023) <https://carbonbetter.com/story/carbon-removal/> accessed 22 March 2025.

39 1PointFive, *1PointFive Announces Agreement to Sell 500,000 Metric Tons of Direct…* (1PointFive 9 July 2024) <https://www.1pointfive.com/news/1pointfive-and-microsoft-announce-agreement-for-direct-air-capture-cdr-credits> accessed 22 March 2025.

40 OECD, *Making Blended Finance Work for the Sustainable Development Goals* (OECD 2018) <https://www.oecd.org/en/publications/2018/01/making-blended-finance-work-for-the-sustainable-development-goals_g1g88c68.html> accessed 24 July 2024.

41 E Julier and B Widdup, *Blended Finance: Combining Public and Private Funding to Meet Sustainable Financing Needs* (Hogan Lovells International LLP 2024) <https://www.engage.hoganlovells.com/knowledgeservices/insights-and-analysis/blended-finance-combining-public-and-private-funding-to-meet-sustainable-financing-needs?ts=1719899221503> accessed 8 July 2024.

42 E Julier and B Widdup, *Blended Finance: Combining Public and Private Funding to Meet Sustainable Financing Needs* (Hogan Lovells International LLP 2024) <https://www.engage.hoganlovells.com/knowledgeservices/insights-and-analysis/blended-finance-combining-public-and-private-funding-to-meet-sustainable-financing-needs?ts=1719899221503> accessed 8 July 2024.

43 UN Environment Programme FI, *Blended Finance Case Studies* (United Nations Environment Programme – Finance Initiative December 2023) <https://www.unepfi.org/industries/banking/blended-finance-case-studies/> accessed 24 July 2024.

44 SAS, 'The Business Risks of Climate Change: Where Technology and Nature Meet' (*SAS Blogs*, 21 April 2021) <https://blogs.sas.com/content/sascom/2021/04/21/climate-change-business-risk/?utm_source=LinkedIn&utm_medium=social-voicestorm&utm_content=7eeb5506-d9db-495c-9ddb-39d3f20e5678> accessed 25 July 2024.

45 R Chaplin, M Pahuja, and F Ryan, *Climate Change and Its Undeniable Impact on Insurance: How to Respond? | Insights | Skadden, Arps, Slate, Meagher & Flom LLP* (Skadden, Arps, Slate, Meagher & Flom LLP 2023) <https://www.skadden.com/insights/publications/2023/12/2024-insights/corporate-trends/climate-change-and-its-undeniable-impact> accessed 25 July 2024.

Chapter 11

Climate finance regulation

The twists and turns of the rules of game

Aims:

- Challenges climate finance and the fragmented, varying global and jurisdictional rules.
- The impediments created by insufficient data and inadequate reporting mechanisms.
- Business' greenwashing problem and the need for accountability and transparency.

Climate finance cannot function effectively without clear rules and regulations. However, as of June 2025, these rules remain highly complex and sometimes contradictory, whether they apply nationally or internationally. Ursula von der Leyen, President of the European Commission, discussed a subset of these rules – those governing sustainability reporting for corporations – and said,

> We are introducing our first proposal for far-reaching simplification. EU companies will benefit from streamlined rules on sustainable finance reporting, sustainability due diligence, and taxonomy. This will ease the burden on businesses while keeping us firmly on track towards our decarbonisation goals.[1]

Yet, she added, 'And more simplification is on the way', acknowledging that significant work remains. Today, the climate finance world would propose alphabet soup sentences which are not easily accessible to many and make a complex topic more difficult. A hypothetical example would be

> the IPCC-endorsed TCFD framework, backed by the UNFCCC and the GFANZ, encourages NGFS-aligned FIs to leverage SBTi-validated emissions targets while navigating the Regulation (EU) 2020/852 requirements, measuring climate-related risks through ISSB standards, aligning with CDP reporting, implementing TNFD recommendations, and tracking progress via SBTi metrics, all while coordinating with the IFC, GBP, and PRI.

Gaining a broad understanding of the rules and regulations related to climate finance is essential, as they significantly influence the sector. However, grasping these concepts presents several challenges. First is moving the goal post problem. The regulatory landscape is constantly evolving, with many regulations still in development and potentially superseding existing ones. Second, the sheer volume of regulations makes navigation difficult for experts

DOI: 10.4324/9781003666509-14

FRAGMENTED REGULATION	DATA & REPORTING ISSUES	GREENWASHING
International inconsistencies	Insufficient data availability	Lack of rigorous accountability
Varying rules across jurisdictions	Inadequate reporting mechanisms	Misleading sustainability claims
	Variable data quality	

Figure 11.1 Three critical climate and sustainable finance regulatory challenges

Source: Author, original chart design (July 2025).

and even more so for non-specialists. Additionally, regulations vary in scope, with some being international and others specific to countries or regions. Furthermore, overlapping or contradictory areas often exist. To clarify what these regulations aim to address, key examples are reviewed. Finally, the critical issue of greenwashing at both financial institutions and corporate levels is examined.

Rules, guidelines, and structures governing climate and sustainable finance encounter significant challenges that undermine their effectiveness. Among these obstacles, three critical issues warrant deeper examination. First, the regulatory landscape is highly fragmented, both internationally and across different jurisdictions. Second, the persistent problem of insufficient data and inadequate reporting mechanisms further complicates sustainable finance efforts, compounded by the variable quality of data and reporting. Third, greenwashing, exacerbated by the lack of rigorous accountability mechanisms, remains a particularly pernicious issue within the sustainable finance ecosystem. These interconnected challenges underscore the urgent need for more comprehensive, standardised, and transparent approaches to climate and sustainable finance regulation (see Figure 11.1).

Regulatory complexity and fragmentation

Objectives of climate finance regulation: is it really needed?

By a significant margin, the primary challenge in climate finance regulation is the complexity and fragmentation of the incredible multitude of guidelines, frameworks, rules, and structures. Observers not familiar with climate finance could be surprised, if not shocked, by the number of rules and regulations that are being developed, or revised, or applied. But this has been true for financial markets in general since laws and regulations for the financial sector were introduced centuries ago. For several hundreds of years, regulators have constructed and frequently revised rules that would ensure the fairness, integrity, and stability of financial markets. Over the past few years, some of the existing rules are being adapted to cope with a new set of circumstances caused by climate change, sustainability goals, the energy transition, and the like. Brand new rules have also been adopted.

The current domestic and international climate finance regulatory systems have a wide variety of objectives. Some of the key, interrelated goals include transparency, risk management, standardisation, incentives, alignment, as well as the Just Transition.

Transparency and disclosure must be provided by financial market participants at an adequate level and under all circumstances. This is imperative so that market participants can make well-informed investment, lending, and other decisions. It is also crucial for market integrity. A significant amount of regulatory compliance is directed towards ensuring that market participants supply sufficient transparency. Climate-related disclosures are a relatively new area in the financial field. In the past few years, there has been a progressive improvement in disclosure requirements as both regulators and institutions have come to understand the kind of information that needs to be supplied. However, it is a field which is still at the development stage. This means that market participants need to adopt new methodologies to collect and disclose climate-related information. Data related to materiality and climate risk, for example. At the same time, they must work towards meeting new or updated regulations. The struggle by financial institutions in Europe is an example which may well illustrate the complexity of the task.

The European Central Bank released the results of the 2022 supervisory assessment of climate-related and environmental risks disclosures of institutions it supervises in April 2023. It was the bank's third such review. The assessment was a supervisory priority for the period from 2023 through 2025 and was based on a guide on climate-related and environmental risks it had released. The review covered 103 significant institutions – those whose total value of assets exceeds €30 billion ($35 billion) and 28 less significant institutions, as well as benchmarking the disclosures of 12 globally systemically important banks established outside the EU. The outcome was that the majority of significant institutions disclosed basic information for most expectations, with improvements observed in 2022. However, only 34 per cent of banks disclosed information on all categories. The bank said that the quality of disclosures remained low and that most of the information disclosed was more qualitative and generic in nature. While some institutions disclosed relevant information, the overall level of disclosures demonstrated that their level of preparedness was low. While keeping the names of the financial institutions anonymous, the European Central Bank also identified that a group of them persistently lagged behind in their disclosures, with six banks assessed as insufficient in all categories. The bank noted that the disclosures of the largest European banks outperformed global peers when assessed against the bank's standards. A sample of less significant institutions from four countries was also assessed. Disclosure by 80 per cent of them was inadequate or somewhat inadequate in disclosing climate-related and environmental risks.[2]

This example is of particular importance to illustrate the current level of climate-related transparency. Financial institutions are probably one of the most tightly regulated and scrutinised actors. It is simple to extrapolate that if financial institutions, especially the large ones, fall short of meeting requirements, the picture for corporations in other sectors must surely be worse. Still, it is a new and evolving field, and progress has already been made over the past few years. Bodies such as the European Central Bank will ensure that we will progressively see better transparency and disclosure in the coming years.

When considering risk, it is crucial for financial institutions, corporations, and other entities to have established systems to identify, disclose, manage, and mitigate climate-related risks, including physical, transition, and liability risks. This is essential for numerous reasons, not least to meet regulatory requirements. Moreover, failure to address these climate-related risks could jeopardise their very existence. In recent years, there have been some examples of the negative financial impact on companies. In 2015, Volkswagen Group, one of the world's largest car manufacturers, was found hiding excessive levels of toxic diesel emissions. In 2020, it disclosed that the diesel cheating scandal had cost the company €31.3 billion ($37 billion) in fines and settlements.[3] In 2016, Peabody Energy Corp, then one of the world's largest coal producers, declared US bankruptcy protection. It was driven by the fall in prices of coal and other fossil fuels as well as environmental pressures.[4] In 2019, the United States' Pacific Gas and Electric Co., one the largest utilities in California, also declared US bankruptcy protection after its equipment sparked deadly wildfires in the state costing the company an estimated tens of billions of dollars at the time.[5] A 2022 settlement alone amounted to $117 million. It was placed into a victim's trust which by that time had already paid out nearly $5 billion.[6]

Standardisation is another crucial, interconnected objective. To monitor climate finance progress, ensure accountability, and stimulate investments, strong measurement frameworks are essential, as highlighted by the International Organisation for Standardisation, an independent standards development body. The organisation reports that significant work is underway to enhance the transparency, consistency, and comparability of climate finance reporting. It stresses that international standards play a pivotal role in attracting and managing climate finance. They ensure transparency, reliability, and accountability in financial flows and help measure, report, and verify the environmental impact of climate-related investments.[7] While there is progress, more efforts are needed because the current state of climate finance accounting is chaotic. The multitude of voluntary initiatives, labels, and standards underscores the urgent need for globally accepted climate finance accounting standards. The immaturity of these has opened the doors to bad actors as well as greenwashing, which is a key challenge to climate action.

In climate finance, financial incentives is a well-established approach. The most common incentives are those implemented to support low- or zero-carbon transition projects and solutions, such as clean energy generation or energy efficiency. Historically, these incentives have been country-specific, with climate finance incentives tailored to individual countries or even specific industries. Due to varying and sometimes conflicting domestic agendas and priorities, developing an efficient and effective international regulatory system for incentives may take years, if not decades. Nevertheless, there are areas of progress, particularly concerning carbon. Even the IMF has advocated for substantial incentives-driven policy shifts to mobilise capital. The IMF suggests that a central component could be a robust carbon price, increasing to a global average of at least $85 per tonne by 2030. This would create broad incentives to reduce carbon-intensive energy use, transition to cleaner sources, and invest in green technologies.[8]

Regulatory alignment is another critical goal for climate finance regulation. To be effective, a nation's climate finance regulation must, at least in part, align with international standards. This alignment should be achieved in several ways. Climate finance regulation should be consistent with the objectives and principles of global climate action, such as those outlined in the Paris Agreement. Regulations should be conformed to internationally recognised best practices to ensure their effectiveness and credibility. Regulation must balance and align the interests of both developed economies and emerging markets, acknowledging their differing capacities, needs, and priorities. Achieving such alignment is a complex task, as evidenced by the challenges faced during various COP meetings. However, nations have made progress in finding common ground, and more agreements are expected in the coming years. Notable examples of areas where some consensus has been reached include the Paris Agreement, corporate disclosure standards, and green bond standards.

The final key objective is the Just Transition, a concept that emphasises the need for the energy transition to be fair and inclusive. The UN defines the Just Transition as a shift that ensures no one is left behind or disadvantaged in the move to low-carbon, environmentally sustainable economies and societies.[9] This is not merely a high-level concept; it is practical and is already being implemented. Germany's Energiewende ambitious energy transition plan serves as an example. It aims to achieve secure, sustainable, and affordable energy while phasing out both nuclear and coal power generation. Energiewende has substantial social and economic impacts, particularly for workers and communities in energy-producing regions. The Transatlantic Climate Bridge, a consortium of climate and energy think tanks, consultancies, an NGOs, wrote[10] that eliminating coal from Germany's energy supplies is socially challenging. This is because the coal sector has historically been crucial to the country's economic recovery and national pride. The transition of Germany's traditional coal mining region of the Ruhr area in North Rhine-Westphalia, which began in the late 1960s and ended in 2018, is considered successful due to massive public investments and an inclusive approach that allowed for social dialogue and economic diversification. However, some believe the transition has not been optimal, as noted by the Transatlantic Climate Bridge. Germany's Coal Commission, established in 2018, developed a phase-out plan by 2038, but it has been criticised for being too generous to coal companies and lacking in procedural and distributional justice. The consortium suggests that Germany could learn from Canada's example by dividing decision-making roles among different government bodies to strengthen procedural justice and increase social investment. The Just Transition, like many other areas in climate business and finance, is still developing and evolving, and related actions are progressively improving, although the road has been bumpy.

Climate finance rules and regulations: navigating the complex labyrinth

The players: a crowded field

The astounding complexity of climate and sustainable finance regulations, standards, and reporting is largely due to the involvement of numerous organisations operating at global, regional, national, and even local levels. This complexity is compounded by the fact that these bodies often work in parallel, of times with overlapping mandates but differing approaches. The complete list of such organisations is extensive, numbering in the dozens. Within this fragmented landscape, it is useful to briefly compare 16 of the most influential organisations, currently shaping climate finance regulation (see Figure 11.2). Some of them have already been mentioned elsewhere in the book but it is worth putting them under one umbrella.

The Financial Stability Board (FSB), the International Organisation of Securities Commissions (IOSCO), and the Basel Committee on Banking Supervision are the three major standard-setting bodies in the world. Additionally, three key bodies operate under or are related to the United Nations: the UN Framework Convention on Climate Change (UNFCCC), the UN Environment Programme Finance Initiative (UNEP FI), and the UN-convened International Sustainability Standards Board (ISSB). Key multilateral development organisations involved include the World Bank Group, the International Monetary Fund (IMF), and the Organisation for Economic Cooperation and Development (OECD). Among the many private sector and multi-stakeholder initiatives are the International Capital Market Association (ICMA), the Climate Bonds Initiative (CBI), the Network for Greening the Financial System (NGFS), the Global Reporting Initiative (GRI), and the Sustainability Accounting Standards Board (SASB). Finally, some regional bodies exert significant global influence, such as the European Commission and the International Platform on Sustainable Finance (IPSF).

	ORGANISATION	PRIMARY FOCUS	REGULATORY APPROACH	KEY INSTRUMENTS / FRAMEWORKS	GEOGRAPHIC SCOPE	STAKEHOLDER FOCUS	INTEGRATION WITH FINANCIAL SYSTEM
International Standard-Setting Bodies	Financial Stability Board (FSB)	Financial stability risks from climate change	Recommendation-based	Task Force on Climate-related Financial Disclosures (TCFD)	Global (G20 focus)	Financial institutions, investors, regulators	High - central to mainstream financial risk assessment
	International Organization of Securities Commissions (IOSCO)	Securities markets regulation	Coordination of securities regulators	Sustainability-related disclosure recommendations	Global	Securities markets, investors, issuers	High - directly influences securities regulation worldwide
	Basel Committee on Banking Supervision	Banking regulation	Prudential standards	Climate risk management principles for banks	Global	Banks, banking supervisors	High - core to banking system regulation
United Nations	UN Framework Convention on Climate Change (UNFCCC)	International climate policy	Treaty-based commitments	Paris Agreement climate finance provisions	Global	Governments, multilateral institutions	Medium - influences policy but less direct financial regulation
	UN Environment Programme Finance Initiative (UNEP FI)	Financial sector sustainability practices	Voluntary principles and commitments	Principles for Responsible Banking, Net-Zero Banking Alliance	Global	Banks, insurers, investors	Medium - voluntary but with growing membership
	International Sustainability Standards Board (ISSB)	Sustainability reporting standards	Global baseline standards	IFRS Sustainability Disclosure Standards	Global	Public companies, investors	High - designed for global adoption by securities regulators
Multilateral Development Organisations	World Bank Group	Climate finance and development	Financing criteria and methodologies	Climate finance tracking, green bonds	Global (development focus)	Governments, development institutions	Medium - influential for public finance
	International Monetary Fund (IMF)	Macroeconomic and financial stability	Financial sector assessments	Climate Macroeconomic Assessment Program	Global	Governments, central banks	Medium-High - growing integration with financial stability work
	Organisation for Economic Co-operation and Development (OECD)	Economic policy frameworks	Guidelines and standards	Green finance taxonomies, ESG investing standards	Global (developed nations focus)	Governments, policymakers	Medium - policy guidance rather than direct regulation
Private Sector Initiatives	International Capital Market Association (ICMA)	Capital markets standards	Voluntary principles	Green Bond Principles, Social Bond Guidelines	Global	Bond issuers, investors	Medium-High - de facto standards for sustainable debt
	Climate Bonds Initiative (CBI)	Green bond standards	Certification scheme	Climate Bonds Standard & Certification Scheme	Global	Green bond market participants	Medium - voluntary certification system
	Network for Greening the Financial System (NGFS)	Central banking and supervision	Knowledge sharing, best practices	Climate scenarios, supervisory guidelines	Global (member countries)	Central banks, financial supervisors	High - direct influence on supervisory approaches
	Global Reporting Initiative (GRI)	Sustainability reporting	Comprehensive reporting standard	GRI Standards	Global	Broad range of organizations	Medium - traditionally focused beyond just financial materiality
	Sustainability Accounting Standards Board (SASB)	Industry-specific standards	Financial materiality focus	SASB Standards (now part of IFRS)	Global (US origins)	Investors, companies	High - focused on financially material sustainability issues
Regional Bodies with Global Influence	European Commission	Comprehensive sustainable finance regulation	Mandatory regulation	EU Taxonomy, SFDR, CSRD	European (with global influence)	EU financial market participants	Very High - mandatory requirements affecting global participants
	International Platform on Sustainable Finance (IPSF)	Regulatory coordination	Policy dialogue	Common Ground Taxonomy	Global (member jurisdictions)	Policymakers, regulators	Medium - coordination rather than direct regulation

Figure 11.2 Climate and sustainable finance regulation global organisations

Notes: The complexity and fragmentation of the global regulatory landscape for sustainable finance are understandable given the enormous scale of the challenge and the vast number of stakeholders involved, reaching tens of thousands. Nevertheless, the development of frameworks, regulations, rules, and standards follows an evolutionary path. It took at least a decade to establish the 1997 Kyoto Protocol and roughly two more decades to reach the 2015 Paris Agreement. These processes demand time. While climate action has generally increased over the years, the trajectory has not followed a straight line. Significant domestic and global political events have caused disruptions, such as the United States repeatedly entering, withdrawing, re-entering, and withdrawing again from the Paris Agreement.[11]

Source: Author (July 2025) using data from the websites of the mentioned organisations.

Despite these challenges, regulatory achievements have accumulated, including notable successes in convergence and harmonisation. The International Sustainability Standards Board (ISSB) offers a prime example of this progress. The FSB announced in July 2023 that the TCFD had successfully completed its work, culminating in the ISSB Standards. Consequently, the TCFD was disbanded in October 2023, having achieved its objectives. It meant that a global approach to sustainability reporting became a little simpler and more streamlined. The ISSB consolidated two previously separate frameworks – the Sustainability Accounting Standards Board (SASB) and the TCFD – into a unified system called International Financial Reporting Standards (IFRS) S1 and S2. The integration created a consistent global baseline that companies can follow when disclosing sustainability information, allowing them clearer guidance and reduced complexity in their reporting processes. At the same time, investors gained the ability to make more meaningful comparisons between companies. The new standards address both general sustainability-related financial information (S1) and specific climate-related risks and opportunities (S2), working with regional requirements rather than competing with them, representing significant step towards more coherent, comparable, and useful sustainability reporting worldwide.[12]

The regulatory milestones and their acceleration

Over the past four decades or so, there has been a vast array of climate-related rules, regulations, and frameworks. Notably, the pace of development has accelerated since the signing of the Paris Agreement in 2015. Among the many milestone documents, eight exemplify the tremendous progress in this area. These include the United Nations Framework Convention on Climate Change (UNFCCC), the Kyoto Protocol, the Principles for Responsible Investment (PRI), the Sustainability Accounting Standards Board (SASB), the Paris Agreement, the Task Force on Climate-related Financial Disclosures (TCFD), the EU Taxonomy Regulation, the International Sustainability Standards Board (ISSB), and the EU Corporate Sustainability Reporting Directive (CSRD) (see Figure 11.3).

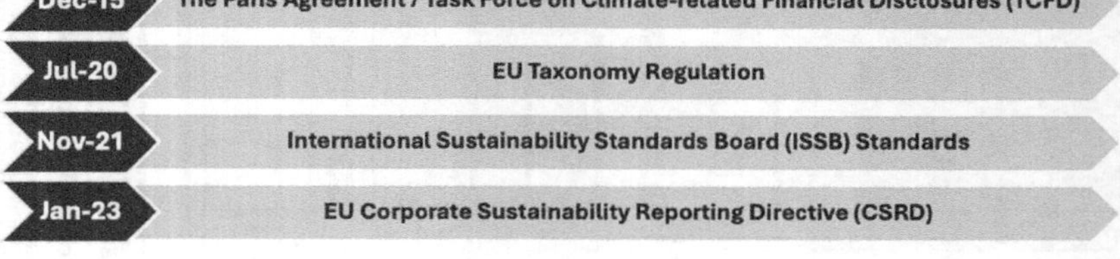

Figure 11.3 Historical sustainability-related regulation milestones

Notes: (*) Approximate month and year, accurate date not available.

Source: Author, original chart design (July 2025) using data of regulatory bodies websites.

UNITED NATIONS FRAMEWORK CONVENTION ON CLIMATE CHANGE (UNFCCC)

Signed in 1992, the United Nations Framework Convention on Climate Change, as the foundation for international climate negotiations, enabled landmark agreements such as the Kyoto Protocol (1997) and the Paris Agreement (2015). The Convention has widespread support, with 197 states committing to address climate change and to regularly report their progress.[13]

THE KYOTO PROTOCOL

Adopted in December 1997, this international treaty aims to reduce GHG emissions. Since entering force in 2005, the protocol has targeted a 5.2 per cent reduction of six GHGs below 1990 levels across 41 countries plus the EU during the 2008–2012 commitment period. Many consider it the most significant environmental treaty ever negotiated.[14]

PRINCIPLES FOR RESPONSIBLE INVESTMENT (PRI)

In early 2005, the UN invited leading financial investors to develop the Principles for Responsible Investment. A 20-person investor group from institutions across 12 countries worked alongside 70 experts from investment, intergovernmental organisations, and civil society. PRI is now one of the foremost advocates for responsible investment, helping investors understand the implications of ESG factors and incorporate these considerations into their investment and ownership decisions.[15]

SUSTAINABILITY ACCOUNTING STANDARDS BOARD (SASB)

Founded in 2011, SASB helps businesses communicate sustainability information to investors through industry-specific standards. These standards cover 77 industries and identify risks and opportunities that may affect a company's financial performance, including cash flows, access to finance, and capital costs. In August 2022, the International Sustainability Standards Board (ISSB) of the International Financial Reporting Standards (IFRS) Foundation assumed responsibility for SASB Standards, which provide a framework for measuring ESG factors beyond traditional financial disclosures.[16]

THE PARIS AGREEMENT AND TASK FORCE ON CLIMATE-RELATED FINANCIAL DISCLOSURES (TCFD)

Adopted in December 2015, the Paris Agreement aims to improve upon the Kyoto Protocol by further reducing GHG emissions. 195 countries had signed this international treaty. The agreement entered into force on 4 November 2016.[17] The Financial Stability Board created the Task Force on Climate-related Financial Disclosures (TCFD) in 2015. This development came as financial leaders increasingly recognised climate risk's potential impact on financial systems. It was particularly relevant given the number of countries which committed to significant climate action under the Paris Agreement that year. The TCFD addressed the need for greater transparency by developing voluntary, consistent climate-related financial risk disclosure guidelines for companies, publishing its final recommendations in 2017.[18]

EU TAXONOMY REGULATION

The EU taxonomy is fundamental to the European sustainable finance framework and provides a critical market transparency tool. It directs investments towards economic activities key for the transition, aligning with European Green Deal objectives. This classification system defines criteria for economic activities that support a net-zero trajectory by 2050 and broader environmental goals. The Taxonomy Regulation took effect on 12 July 2020 and establishes four overarching conditions that economic activities must meet to qualify as environmentally sustainable.[19]

EU CORPORATE SUSTAINABILITY REPORTING DIRECTIVE (CSRD)

The Non-Financial Reporting Directive (NFRD), introduced in 2014, marked a significant step in the EU's effort to enhance ESG transparency by requiring large companies to disclose their approaches to ESG challenges. However, the NFRD soon faced criticism for its limited scope and disclosure requirements. In response, the European Commission proposed the Corporate Sustainability Reporting Directive (CSRD) on 21 April 2021 to strengthen the existing regulatory framework. The new directive enforces stricter eligibility criteria, expanding coverage from 11,700 companies under NFRD to approximately 50,000 EU companies, with phased implementation beginning January 2024.[20]

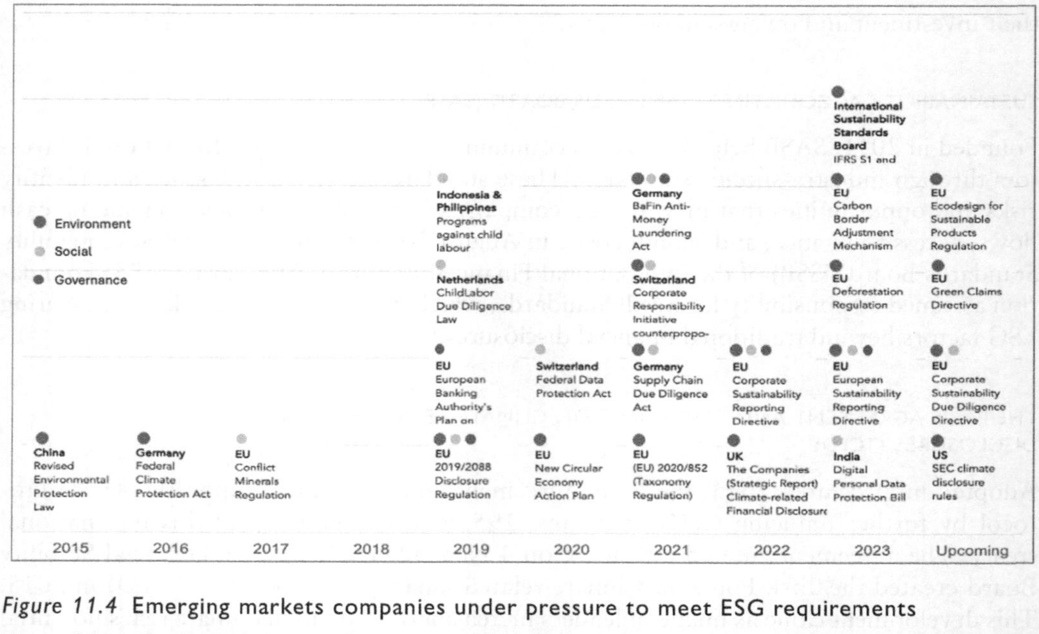

Figure 11.4 Emerging markets companies under pressure to meet ESG requirements

Notes: Switzerland's Ordinance on Reporting on Non-Financial Matters went into effect on 1 January 2023. The EU is considering whether to adopt the Swiss measure.

Source: Tansan B, 'Why Emerging Markets Need to Prepare for the EU's New Climate and ESG Regulations' (Tim Figures and others eds, BCG Global 6 November 2023). Available at: https://www.bcg.com/publications/2023/how-emerging-markets-can-prepare-for-the-new-esg-regulations accessed 2 April 2024.

INTERNATIONAL SUSTAINABILITY STANDARDS BOARD (ISSB) STANDARDS

On 3 November 2021, the IFRS Foundation announced the creation of the International Sustainability Standards Board (ISSB). This new body aims to formulate a baseline for sustainability disclosures that meet investor needs. The ISSB operates alongside the International Accounting Standards Board and incorporates the existing Climate Disclosure Standards Board and Value Reporting Foundation. This consolidation helps address the fragmentation of reporting standard bodies while ensuring appropriate expertise within the organisation.[21]

Naturally, there are numerous additional laws, directives, and bills. Figure 11.4 offers a snapshot of the vast number of documents that have been published and the timeline.

The information scarcity dilemma: data gaps and inadequate reporting

The second critical challenge to regulatory frameworks is the issue of data gaps and inadequate reporting, which affects regulatory bodies, financial institutions, investors, and others. The Global Innovation Lab for Climate Finance, an investor-led public-private initiative focused on developing climate finance solutions, highlights that insufficient data makes it difficult to differentiate between actual and perceived risks in climate-related sectors. This uncertainty can deter investors from supporting transition projects and solutions. The Lab emphasises that improving data quality and standardising reporting are crucial for attracting investment in climate finance.[22]

Organisations often find it challenging to gather, authenticate, and convey detailed environmental impact assessments. This difficulty impedes stakeholders' capacity to accurately assess the sustainability of investments, calculate carbon footprints, and track advancements towards environmental goals. In the absence of strong and consistent reporting standards, investors and regulators are restricted in making well-informed decisions and evaluating the true environmental performance of financial entities.

The reporting of climate finance data for corporations comprises two principal broad baskets of data. One is physical data, such as corporations reporting on their exposure to climate risk like extreme weather events. The second is corporation-specific data such as their emissions.

Physical climate risk data includes information on how a corporation is exposed to climate-related risks, such as extreme weather events – including droughts, floods, storms, wildfires, and long-term climate changes – including rising sea levels and changing precipitation patterns, as well as other environmental factors that may disrupt operations, supply chains, or financial stability.

A study by S Rapach and others titled 'A Taxonomy of Earth Observation Data for Sustainable Finance'[23] explores well the physical climate risk related data issue. It explores how Earth Observation data can support sustainable finance by providing critical environmental insights. Earth Observation is information from satellites or airborne sensors monitoring the surface and atmosphere of the Earth. It categorises different types of Earth Observation data relevant to financial decision-making, particularly in assessing climate risks, environmental impacts, and corporate sustainability performance. The paper highlights how Earth Observation data can complement traditional financial and corporate disclosures to

	DATA TYPE
PHYSICAL CLIMATE RISK	Earth Observation data helps assess exposure to climate hazards like extreme weather events, flooding, wildfires, and rising sea levels. This information is crucial for financial institutions to evaluate investment risks in different geographic areas.
CARBON AND EMISSIONS	Satellite-based measurements can track GHG emissions, deforestation, and industrial pollution. This supports corporate reporting on Scope 1, 2, and 3 emissions and helps verify the accuracy of self-reported data.
LAND AND BIODIVERSITY MONITORING	Earth Observation data is essential for tracking land use changes, deforestation, and biodiversity loss. It plays a role in assessing companies' environmental impacts, particularly in agriculture, mining, and real estate sectors.
WATER AND OCEAN	Monitoring water quality, ocean acidification, and coastal erosion can inform financial risks related to resource-intensive industries like agriculture and energy.
SOCIOECONOMIC AND INFRASTRUCTURE	Earth Observation can provide insights into urbanisation trends, energy infrastructure, and population density, which impact investment strategies and sustainability assessments.

Figure 11.5 Types of data necessary for sustainable finance

Source: Rapach S and others, 'A Taxonomy of Earth Observation Data for Sustainable Finance' (2023) 6 Journal of Climate Finance 100029Available at: https://www.sciencedirect.com/science/article/pii/S2949728023000251?via%3Dihub accessed 27 March 2025.

enhance transparency and accountability in sustainable finance. The authors identified five different datasets needed for sustainable finance (see Figure 11.5).

Corporate-specific emissions and environmental impact data comprise information on a company's GHG gas emissions. These are usually categorised into: Scope 1 emissions, which are direct emissions from owned or controlled sources; Scope 2 emissions, which are indirect emissions from purchased electricity, steam, heating, and cooling, for example, and Scope 3 emissions, which are all other indirect emissions in the company's value chain, such as supplier emissions, business travel, and product use. Different industries approach emissions reporting in different ways. Corporate environmental impact measurement is complex and contains much variability.

For example, tech giant Apple Inc.'s 2024 Environmental Progress Report, covering fiscal year 2023, demonstrates a comprehensive approach to emissions tracking. For Scope 1, the company tracks gross emissions from natural gas, diesel, propane, from fleet vehicles, as well as from process emissions (from the R&D process). For Scope 2, it includes electricity, as well as steam, heating, and cooling. For Scope 3, it tracks business travel, employee commute, and corporate carbon offsets. It monitors product life-cycle emissions which comprise manufacturing (purchased goods and services), product transportation (upstream and downstream), product use (use of sold products), end-of-life treatment, and product carbon offsets. Apple said that it had reduced overall emissions by more than 55 per cent (2015 baseline year) and that it was still carbon-neutral for its corporate operations, something achieved in 2020. It had retained its ambitious goal for 2030 to be carbon-neutral for its entire carbon footprint. This includes reducing its Scopes 1, 2, and 3 upstream and downstream emissions first by 75 per cent before balancing remaining emissions with high-quality carbon removals.[24]

Apart from physical climate-related data and data specific to the corporation, there are several other baskets of information that are needed for corporations to supply to their stakeholders. Among these, three examples are transition risk-related, financial performance and ESG integration data, and nature and biodiversity impact data.

Transition risk data includes financial risks and opportunities linked to transitioning to a low-carbon economy, such as regulatory changes (including carbon taxes, emissions trading schemes), market shifts (including consumer preferences for green products), and technological innovations (including clean energy, CCS).

Some corporations also report financial performance and ESG integration data, focused on explaining how sustainability and climate risks or opportunities are factored into financial performance, investment strategies, and overall ESG integration. It can include green bonds, sustainability-linked loans, or ESG-related investments, as well as climate-related disclosures in financial statements, such as those following TCFD or ISSB standards.

Nature and biodiversity impact data are something that companies are increasingly reporting. It includes, for example, deforestation, water usage, biodiversity loss, and frameworks like the Taskforce on Nature-related Financial Disclosures.

Greenwashing and accountability: challenges for financial institutions and corporations

The second critical challenge to regulatory frameworks is greenwashing. One of the broader definitions of greenwashing is that it involves presenting inaccurate or deceptive information which creates a misleading impression that a company's products are more environmentally friendly than they truly are. This deceptive practice includes making unfounded claims to convince consumers that products have a greater positive environmental impact than is accurate. Additionally, greenwashing can occur when a company highlights minor sustainable features of a product to distract from its broader environmentally harmful activities. This tactic often employs environmental imagery, misleading labels, and the concealment of trade-offs.

Determining what constitutes greenwashing is not straightforward. The inaccurate or deceptive information can be voluntary or accidental. It is crucial to analyse this issue, as some bad actors may take advantage of greenwashing. This can be highly damaging, including undermining the credibility of climate finance. One analytical approach is to evaluate a sample list of high-profile examples while considering that some regulators are not yet fluent on greenwashing issues, albeit globally the problem has been recognised and is gradually improving.

One set of examples comes from Australia. The integrated corporate, markets, financial services, and consumer credit regulator, the Australian Securities and Investments Commission (ASIC), ruled on several greenwashing cases. Three cases, as of March 2025, led to fines amounting to almost A$35 million ($22.9 million). The Federal Court imposed an A$11.3 million ($7.4 million) penalty on Mercer Superannuation for misleading consumers about their 'Sustainable Plus' investment options. The court found that Mercer falsely claimed to exclude investments in industries like alcohol, gambling, and fossil fuels. Mercer admitted to greenwashing and was also ordered to publish an adverse publicity notice and cover ASIC's costs. The same court ordered Vanguard Investments Australia to pay a penalty of A$12.9 million ($8.5 million) for making misleading claims about the ESG exclusionary screens of its Ethically Conscious Global Aggregate Bond Index Fund. The court found that Vanguard made false or misleading statements, marking the highest penalty for greenwashing in Australia in March 2025. In a third case, the Australian Securities and Investments Commission sued superannuation fund Active Super trustee LGSS for greenwashing, arguing that the firm invested in areas it claimed to exclude for ESG reasons.

The court found that Active Super had made misleading representations and fined them A$10.5 million ($6.9 million).

In the United Kingdom, the Advertising Standards Authority (ASA) banned a LinkedIn advertisement by Lloyds Bank that highlighted its role in financing the low-carbon transition through clean energy initiatives. The ASA found the ad misleading because it omitted crucial information about Lloyds Bank's continued significant financing of activities that contribute to carbon emissions. The specific LinkedIn post featured the text 'What are we doing to help accelerate the transition to a low-carbon economy?' alongside imagery of wind turbines and solar panels. Adfree Cities, a campaign organisation, challenged the ad in May 2024, arguing it constituted greenwashing by not disclosing the full extent of Lloyds' environmental impact. While Lloyds Bank contended that its claims were factually accurate and it had provided 'balancing information' elsewhere, the ASA disagreed. The regulator concluded that the ad's focus on clean energy projects created the impression that a substantial portion of Lloyds' investments was directed towards renewable energy. This was deemed misleading because Lloyds' financed emissions in 2022 amounted to 32.8 million tonnes of CO_2e, indicating a significant contribution to GHG emissions that was not reflected in the advertisement. As a result of the ruling, Lloyds Bank was instructed to refrain from displaying the ad in its current form and to ensure that future advertisements featuring environmental claims do not mislead consumers by omitting significant information about the company's overall environmental impact.

The company South Pole, a leading carbon project developer, faced a significant scandal in 2023 concerning its Kariba REDD+ project in Zimbabwe. This project, aimed at forest conservation, generated carbon credits that were sold to major corporations like Gucci, Nestlé, and Volkswagen. The scandal arose from allegations and evidence suggesting that South Pole vastly overstated the climate benefits of these carbon credits, by a factor of at least five, according to media reports and internal whistleblowers. Investigations revealed flaws in the project's accounting and difficulties in tracking the financial flows, with a significant portion of the revenue seemingly returning to South Pole and its partner. The greenwashing element is central to this case. By purchasing these potentially inflated carbon credits, the buyers were able to make claims about reducing their environmental impact. However, if the underlying carbon savings from the Kariba project were significantly overestimated, these claims become misleading, constituting greenwashing. These companies risked being labelled as 'greenwashers' themselves due to their reliance on these credits. The controversy highlights the broader issues within the voluntary carbon market, particularly concerning the quality and verification of carbon credits, and the potential for companies to use them to present a greener image without making substantial reductions in their own emissions. The case has led to increased scrutiny of carbon credit projects and the methodologies used for their calculation and certification.

In recent years, there have been many regulatory and market responses to greenwashing. An investigation by Climate Fund Managers revealed that executives earned millions by investing taxpayers' money in renewable energy projects. While these investments are crucial for the transition to a low-carbon economy, the high fees and bonuses paid to executives raise concerns about the distribution of benefits. This case highlights the need for greater transparency and accountability in climate finance. Another study found that 40 per cent of European funds marketed as sustainable invest in companies that derive significant revenue from fossil fuels. This discrepancy between claims and reality underscores the need for stricter regulations and more transparent reporting standards. The European Securities and Markets Authority is working to address this issue by implementing new guidelines that will restrict the use of terms like 'green' and 'sustainable' in fund names. Finally, the Science Based Targets initiative (SBTi) is considering relaxing its standards to allow companies to use carbon credits to offset their emissions. This move has sparked outrage among scientists and environmental advocates, who argue that such a change would undermine the integrity of climate targets. This debate also highlights yet another debate, the tension between corporate interests and scientific recommendations in setting environmental standards.

The increasing scrutiny on greenwashing has significant implications for financial institutions and corporations. Companies that engage in greenwashing face reputational risks that can lead to loss of customer trust and investor confidence. As consumers and investors become more environmentally conscious, the stakes for authentic sustainability initiatives are higher than ever. Regulators are stepping up their efforts to hold companies accountable for their environmental claims. Financial institutions must ensure their sustainability initiatives are genuine and transparent to avoid penalties and legal actions. Finally, the integrity of the carbon market and climate finance depends on the accuracy and reliability of environmental claims. Greenwashing undermines this integrity, making it crucial for companies to adhere to strict standards and regulations.

Greenwashing poses a significant challenge to the credibility of climate finance in general and sustainability initiatives in particular. As regulators and consumers become more vigilant, companies will be prioritising transparency and authenticity in their environmental claims. The high-profile cases and regulatory actions discussed highlight the need for continued improvements in the standards and accountability mechanisms.

Notes

1 European Commission, *Commission Simplifies Rules on Sustainability and EU Investments, Delivering over €6 Billion in Administrative Relief* (European Commission 26 February 2025) <https://ec.europa.eu/commission/presscorner/detail/en/ip_25_614> accessed 22 March 2025.
2 European Central Bank, *The Importance of Being Transparent: A Review of Climate-Related and Environmental Risks Disclosures Practices and Trends* (European Central Bank 2023) <https://www.bankingsupervision.europa.eu/ecb/pub/pdf/ssm.theimportanceofbeingtransparent042023~1f0f816b85.en.pdf> accessed 3 August 2024.
3 E Taylor, 'Volkswagen Says Diesel Scandal Has Cost It 31.3 Billion Euros' *Reuters* (17 March 2020) <https://www.reuters.com/article/business/volkswagen-says-diesel-scandal-has-cost-it-313-billion-euros-idUSKBN2141JA/> accessed 3 August 2024.
4 M Scott, 'Peabody Bankruptcy Offers Stark Warning to Oil and Gas Groups of Risks of Ignoring Climate Change' *Forbes* (14 April 2016) <https://www.forbes.com/sites/mikescott/2016/04/14/peabody-bankruptcy-offers-stark-warning-to-oil-and-gas-groups-of-risks-of-ignoring-climate-change/> accessed 3 August 2024.
5 J Christie, 'PG&E Puts Cost of Judge's Wildfire Plan at up to $150 Billion' *Reuters* (24 January 2019) <https://www.reuters.com/article/world/pg-e-puts-cost-of-judge-s-wildfire-plan-at-up-to-150-billion-idUSKCN1PI0CF/> accessed 3 August 2024.
6 J Stempel, 'PG&E Officials Reach $117 Mln Settlement over California Wildfires' *Reuters* (29 September 2022) <https://www.reuters.com/markets/commodities/pge-officials-reach-117-million-settlement-over-california-wildfires-2022-09-29/> accessed 3 August 2024.
7 International Organization for Standardization, *Climate Finance: The Key to a Sustainable Future* (ISO 2024) <https://www.iso.org/climate-change/climate-finance> accessed 4 August 2024.
8 S Black, F Jaumotte, and P Ananthakrishnan, 'World Needs More Policy Ambition, Private Funds, and Innovation to Meet Climate Goals' (*IMF Blog*, 27 November 2023) <https://www.imf.org/en/Blogs/Articles/2023/11/27/world-needs-more-policy-ambition-private-funds-and-innovation-to-meet-climate-goals> accessed 4 August 2024.

9 UN Committee for Development Policy, *Just Transition* (UN Committee for Development Policy 2023) <https://www.un.org/development/desa/dpad/wp-content/uploads/sites/45/CDP-excerpt-2023-1.pdf> accessed 4 August 2024.
10 R Bordon, 'Achieving Justice in Germany's Energy Transition | Transatlantic Climate Bridge' (theclimatebridge.org 2024) <https://theclimatebridge.org/achieving-justice-germanys-energy-transition> accessed 6 August 2024.
11 IFRS Foundation, 'IFRS – ISSB and TCFD' (www.ifrs.org 2024) <https://www.ifrs.org/sustainability/tcfd/> accessed 23 March 2025.
12 A Nieves, *From SASB and TCFD to ISSB: Simplifying Sustainability Reporting* (Sustainable Investment Group 13 May 2024) <https://sigearth.com/from-sasb-and-tcfd-to-issb-simplifying-sustainability-reporting/> accessed 23 March 2025.
13 London School of Economics, *What is the UN Framework Convention on Climate Change (UNFCCC)?* (Grantham Research Institute on Climate Change and the Environment 24 October 2022) <https://www.lse.ac.uk/granthaminstitute/explainers/what-is-the-un-framework-convention-on-climate-change-unfccc/> accessed 23 March 2025.
14 The Editors of Encyclopaedia Britannica, 'The Kyoto Protocol', *Encyclopedia Britannica* (14 Spring 2025) <https://www.britannica.com/topic/United-Nations-Framework-Convention-on-Climate-Change> accessed 23 March 2025.
15 PRI, *About the PRI* (PRI 2024) <https://www.unpri.org/about-us/about-the-pri> accessed 23 March 2025.
16 SASB, *About Us* (SASB 2024) <https://sasb.ifrs.org/about/> accessed 23 March 2025.
17 Encyclopædia Britannica, 'Paris Agreement | Summary & Facts', *Encyclopædia Britannica* (2019) <https://www.britannica.com/topic/Paris-Agreement-2015> accessed 23 March 2025.
18 ASIC, 'Historical Development of Climate-Related Financial Disclosures | ASIC' (Asic.gov.au 2022) <https://asic.gov.au/regulatory-resources/sustainability-reporting/historical-development-of-climate-related-financial-disclosures/> accessed 23 March 2025.
19 European Commission, *EU Taxonomy for Sustainable Activities* (European Commission 2024) <https://finance.ec.europa.eu/sustainable-finance/tools-and-standards/eu-taxonomy-sustainable-activities_en> accessed 23 March 2025.
20 C Branquart, 'The Evolution of NFRD to CSRD' (Greenomy.io 28 October 2014) <https://www.greenomy.io/blog/evolution-nfrd-csrd> accessed 23 March 2025.
21 M Baker, *Birth of a Standard: Where the ISSB Came from and What It Will Do* (Euromoney 5 November 2021) <https://www.euromoney.com/article/29a2t1n0x3f40blljhlvk/esg/birth-of-a-standard-where-the-issb-came-from-and-what-it-will-do> accessed 23 March 2025.
22 B Broché (ed), 'Emerging Trends, Challenges, and Opportunities in Climate Finance' (Climatefinancelab.org 17 September 2024) <https://www.climatefinancelab.org/news/trends-in-climate-finance/#more> accessed 27 March 2025.
23 S Rapach and others, 'A Taxonomy of Earth Observation Data for Sustainable Finance' (2023) 6 Journal of Climate Finance 100029 <https://www.sciencedirect.com/science/article/pii/S2949728023000251?via%3Dihub> accessed 27 March 2025.
24 Apple Inc., *Environmental Progress Report 2024* (Apple 2024) <https://www.apple.com/environment/pdf/Apple_Environmental_Progress_Report_2024.pdf> accessed 27 March 2025.

Section IV

The business of transition

Chapter 12

Transition shift of corporates

Navigating dynamics

Aims:

- Governance, business, technology, and finance sectors catalysts driving corporate change.
- Businesses responding to, and shaping, sustainability pressures.
- Asia, Europe, and North America corporations implementing sustainability strategies.

The catalysts of change

Imagine a fossil fuel company suddenly under all forms of pressure to decarbonise. Pressure from new regulations, from stakeholders, and from civil society. It is nothing less than a colossal task. Yet there are many companies that have successfully done it and many more in the process of shifting away from highly polluting fuel sources. German utility E.ON, one of the largest in Europe, has made such a journey. The company transitioned away from conventional generation to a business model comprising clean generation, smart networks, and customer solutions, including digital solutions. It managed to reduce its carbon emissions to just 2 million metric tonnes in 2024 from 76.8 million ten years earlier. It targets Scope 1 emissions reductions of 50 per cent to 75 per cent by 2030 and to reach net zero by 2040. The energy transition is driving change at E.ON and other companies through at least four drivers: government and compliance, technology, finance, and business operations. These areas interact dynamically. In some occurrences, these drivers push companies to transform, while at other times they are shaped by corporate actions. Regulations create mandatory shifts, technological innovations make clean energy more viable and provide new solutions, financial considerations provide new investment pathways, and business strategies seek competitive advantages. Companies are both responding to and spearheading these changes, creating a complex, interactive process of energy transformation.

Within the four categories, 12 specific elements can be singled out (see Figure 12.1). The list is by no means exhaustive, but these 12 catalysts of change are representative of the pressure points that businesses face in enacting or planning their transition-related strategies.

Some of these catalysts of change were discussed at varying depths in previous sections. A brief synopsis of each as well as real-world snapshots of how they are manifested is helpful in framing this fourth section. Importantly, there may be some overlap with some of the

DOI: 10.4324/9781003666509-16

GOVERNANCE & REGULATORY ADHERENCE	TECHNOLOGY CLEAN ENERGY SOLUTIONS	FINANCE CLIMATE FINANCE	BUSINESS MARKET DYNAMICS
(ESG, CSR)	*(EE)*	*(sustainable finance, green financing, financial incentives)*	*(growth opportunities, consumer demand, data and analytics)*
Hitachi (Japan)	Swire Properties (Hong Kong, China)	Sydney Airport Holdings (Australia)	Panasonic Holdings (Japan)
BASF (Germany)	CTP Group (Netherlands)	Volkswagen (Germany)	Schneider Electric (France)
General Motors (US)	Walmart (US)	Verizon Communications (US)	NextEra Energy (US)
STAKEHOLDERS' CONSIDERATIONS *(consumers, shareholders, investors)*	**ELECTRIFICATION**	**COST CONTROLS**	**CIRCULAR ECONOMY**
Sony Group (Japan)	Komatsu (Japan)	Samsung Electronics (South Korea)	Lenovo Group (Hong Kong, China)
Airbus (France)	A.P. Møller - Mærsk (Denmark)	Unilever (UK)	Michelin Group (France)
Ford Motor (US)	Prologis (US)	Magna International (Canada)	Steelcase (US)
SUSTAINABILITY PLEDGES *(corporate, policy, targets, decarbonisation)*	**INNOVATION & RESEARCH**	**RISK MANAGEMENT**	**SUPPLY CHAIN SUSTAINABILITY**
Toyota Motor (Japan)	Tata Steel (India)	Singapore Telecommunications (Singapore)	Huawei Technologies (China)
Ørsted (Denmark)	Siemens (Germany)	Nestlé (Switzerland)	Danone (France)
Microsoft (US)	Apple (US)	Salesforce (US)	Cisco Systems (US)

Figure 12.1 Corporations and businesses driving energy transition elements

Source: Author, original chart design (February 2025).

catalysts. For example, clean energy solutions may include electrification or there maybe crossovers with circular economy actions and supply chain sustainability.

Governance and compliance transition catalysts

Regulatory adherence

One cannot overly emphasise the regulatory challenges that are faced by companies. The hurdles include the high level of regulatory complexity as well as the evolutionary nature of the rules and regulations which are constantly evolving. The regulatory pressure on companies to meet corporate governance standards and ensure they are accountable for their environmental and social impact has existed for decades. Corporate Social Responsibility (CSR) has been a concept for over 70 years. Environmental, Social, and Governance (ESG) principles became mainstream over 20 years ago. Rules have slowly evolved, and more recently new regulations have emerged, encouraging companies to consider transitioning. In the United States, the world's largest capital market, a vocal school of thought argues that considering ESG factors leads to lower returns on capital, something that has not yet been unequivocally proven. This perspective has temporarily influenced the approach of many US companies both domestically and internationally. However, when viewed from a multi-year or multi-decade perspective, the trajectory is clear. Financial markets, consumers, and other stakeholders, at a minimum, increasingly care about a company's environmental impact, internal governance, and the related risks to their business. These concerns will certainly not only persist but also intensify in the medium to long term.

REPORT TYPE	CSR REPORT	ESG REPORT	SUSTAINABILITY REPORT	ANNUAL REPORT
Temporal focus	Past	Present	Past, present, future	Past, present, future
General topics	Environment, ethics, philanthropy, economic	Environment, social, governance	Environment, social, governance	Financial
Audience	Broad, including employees, investors, local community	Mainly investors	Broad, including employees, investors, customers	Broad, including shareholders, potential investors, employees, customers

Figure 12.2 Sustainability reporting types

Source: Szweda K, 'ESG, CSR, Sustainability Reporting – What's the Difference?' (Connect Earth23 December 2022). Available at: https://connect.earth/esg-csr-sustainability-reporting-whats-the-difference/ accessed 10 February 2025.

Sustainability reporting occurs in different types and formats. Broadly speaking, it is done via CSR, ESG, sustainability, and annual reports. The four reporting types address slightly different topics and audiences (see Figure 12.2).

A survey on sustainability reporting by accounting firm KPMG in 2024[1] highlights the continued dominance of the Global Reporting Initiative Standards (see Figure 12.3) as the leading framework for sustainability reporting worldwide. The survey examined 5,800 companies across 58 countries. It found that 77 per cent of the world's largest companies (G250) and 71 per cent of national top companies (N100) use GRI Standards. This widespread adoption underscores GRI's universal applicability and acceptance, with regional adoption rates varying significantly. Taiwan leads with 100 per cent adoption, followed by Singapore at 97 per cent, while Pakistan and Estonia have the lowest rates. As the sustainability reporting landscape evolves, companies are increasingly integrating other frameworks, such as SASB Standards, alongside GRI. The move towards mandatory ESG reporting, particularly with the EU's Corporate Sustainability Reporting Directive (CSRD), is influencing reporting practices, but GRI's position remains strong. Looking ahead, GRI is expected to play a crucial role as sustainability reporting transitions from voluntary to mandatory requirements in many jurisdictions.

Examples of companies which are advancing their regulatory adherence in response to climate action include Hitachi, BASF, and General Motors.

REGULATORY ADHERENCE: ASIA

Japan's Hitachi Ltd is both a service provider and a manufacturer. Hitachi targets carbon neutrality at its factories and offices by fiscal 2030 (to 31 March 2031) and for its value chain by fiscal 2050. It endorsed TCFD disclosure in 2018. The motivation was probably that it sources almost two-thirds of its revenues from international markets. It reported that its TCFD disclosure was top-ranked by third parties, including by Japanese equity investment management institutions the highest ranking that any selected company had received. Hitachi has a broad range of businesses globally, each with their own set of risks and opportunities which it monitors very closely. In business planning and strategy, it looks at climate-related risks from a variety of angles. Its assessment is categorised by short-, medium-, and long-term time spans, the latter being up to fiscal 2050. For each of the periods and businesses, a rating of minor to major impact is gauged, 'major' is defined as 'sufficient to disrupt business or cause it to substantially decrease or increase'.[2]

	GRI	ESRS		ISSB	Consolidated into ISSB		
		Pre-Omnibus	Post-Omnibus		Integrated Reporting Framework	SASB Standards	TCFD
Type of Guidance	Standards	Standards	Standards	Standards	Framework	Standards	Guidelines
Application	Voluntary	Mandatory for large companies, 250+ employees, EUR 50 M turnover, or EUR 25 M balance sheet total, and listed SMES	Mandatory for largest companies, >1000 employees, EUR 50 M turnover, or EUR 25 M balance sheet total, and listed SMES exempted Companies no longer subject to CSRD can opt for voluntary reporting based on simplified standards (similar to VSME standards)	Subject to national jurisdiction adoption	Voluntary	Voluntary	Voluntary
Coverage	Global	European Union EU Large Public Interest: FY24 EU Other Large Undertakings: FY25 EU-listed SMEs: FY26 Non-EU countries as of FY28 net turnover EUR 150 M, EU branch with > 40 M, or listed on an EU market	European Union EU Large Public Interest: FY24 EU Other Large Undertakings: FY27 EU-listed SMEs: FY28 Non-EU countries as of FY28 net turnover EUR 450 M, EU branch with > 50 M, or listed on an EU market	Global	Global	US-focused originally, applicable globally as part of ISSB standards	Global
Topics	Economic, environmental, and social activities and impacts	Environmental, social and governance	Environmental, social and governance (with fewer mostly quantitative metrics) (forthcoming)	General Sustainability, Climate, Other topics to be added (biodiversity and human capital in next two years)	Six capitals: financial, manufactured, intellectual, human, social, natural	Environment, social capital, human capital, business model & innovation, leadership & governance	Climate-related risks, opportunities, financial impacts, and scenario analysis
Sector Specific	Yes	Yes (forthcoming)	No (eliminated)	No	No	Yes (77 sectors)	Yes
Target Audience	All stakeholders	All stakeholders	All stakeholders	Investors	Providers of financial capital	Investors	Investors
Building Blocks		TCFD, GRI, CDP	TCFD, GRI, CDP	TCFD, SASB, CDSB			
Materiality type	Impact materiality	Double-materiality (financial + impact materiality)	Retained	Single materiality (financial materiality)	Single materiality (financial materiality)	Single materiality (financial materiality)	Single materiality (financial materiality)
Materiality definition	Aspects that reflect the organization's significant economic, environmental, and social impacts; or that substantively influence the assessments and decisions of stakeholders	Impact on people or the environment and financial effects on undertaking over the short-, medium- and long-term time horizons	Retained	Information is material if omitting, misstating or obscuring that information could reasonably be expected to influence decisions that the primary users of general-purpose financial reporting	Matter that could substantively affect the organization's ability to create value in the short, medium, or long term.	A fact is material if there is a substantial likelihood that a reasonable investor would view its omission or misstatement as having significantly altered the total mix of information.	Public companies' legal obligation to disclose information in their financial filings- including material climate-related information.
Assurance	No assurance requirement	Limited assurance remains, with plans to transition to reasonable assurance	Limited assurance remains, reasonable assurance requirement removed	No assurance requirement but designed to make companies assurance ready	No assurance requirement	No assurance requirement	No assurance requirement

Figure 12.3 Comparison of main sustainability frameworks and standards

Source: IFC, 'Comprendre Les Cadres de Référence Pour l'Établissement Des Rapports Mondiaux | IFC beyond the Balance Sheet' (Ifcbeyondthebalancesheet.org 2024). Available at: https://www.ifcbeyondthebalancesheet.org/fr/understanding-global-reporting-frameworks accessed 7 July 2025.

REGULATORY ADHERENCE: EUROPE

Germany's BASF SE is a leading global industrial company generating almost half of its revenues from too-hard-to-abate sectors, chemicals, and materials. The group lowered GHG emissions by half between 1990 and 2018. They target a further 25 per cent drop by 2030 from the 2018 level and reach net zero by 2050. BASF has adopted integrated reporting by combining both financial and sustainability reporting. BASF stresses that the sustainability-related information meets all of the disclosure requirements of the European Sustainability Reporting Standards. The company is keen to supply sustainability-related information in a clear and easy-to-understand manner in its annual report. For example, it produces a value creation flow chart which shows inputs, business model, output, outcomes, and impact, clearly underlining sustainability measures at each stage.[3]

REGULATORY ADHERENCE: NORTH AMERICA

US automotive manufacturing giant General Motors Company aims to turn carbon-neutral in its global products and operations by 2040, with an interim 2035 objective of a 72 per cent emissions cut relative to a 2018 baseline. It seems that the company has prepared an infrastructure for sustainability reporting. A sustainability report was published in April 2024, covering the 2023 fiscal year, which spelled out GM's sustainability reporting based on GRI standards and contained a response to Sustainability Accounting Standards Board requirements.[4] GM was also an early supporter of the SEC's proposed climate disclosure rules, which were dropped in February 2025. As of mid-2025, the company had yet to update its sustainability data.

Stakeholders' considerations

Another catalyst of change is stakeholders' considerations. The considerations or pressure points come from consumers (who represent market demand) as well as from investors and shareholders, governments and regulators, employees, supply chain and related business partners, and from NGOs, communities, and society (see Figure 12.4).

Consumers play an increasingly pivotal role in shaping corporate sustainability through their purchasing decisions and expectations. Many favour environmentally friendly products and are willing to pay a premium for sustainable alternatives. Brand reputation is often linked

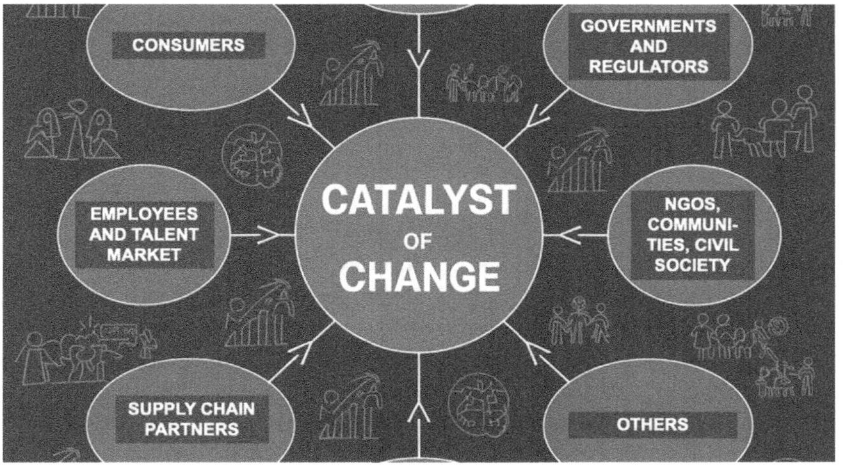

Figure 12.4 Key catalysts of corporate transformation

Source: Author, original chart design (February 2025); background image created using Ideogram AI.

to environmental performance, with growing demand for transparency regarding corporate ecological impact. Companies face intense scrutiny and risk boycotts for misleading green claims, compelling them to balance sustainability investments with cost competitiveness.

Investors and shareholders are reshaping corporate strategies by prioritising climate-related financial risks and opportunities. Many now assess businesses against ESG criteria, insisting on detailed climate risk disclosures and credible transition plans. Many institutional investors have or plan to decarbonise their portfolio and redirect capital towards sustainable corporations (or corporations which have plans to become sustainable). Shareholder activism is gaining momentum, with investors filing climate-related resolutions and seeking safeguards against stranded asset risks. Also, to secure green financing, companies must demonstrate tangible progress on their sustainability commitments.

Governments and regulators are accelerating corporate transformation through progressively stringent environmental legislation and reporting obligations. Many businesses must navigate carbon pricing schemes, emissions caps, and mandatory climate risk disclosures, such as the EU's CSRD. While regulatory frameworks impose compliance costs, they also provide incentives and support to ease the transition.

Employees are emerging as influential advocates for corporate sustainability, particularly as younger generations prioritise environmental responsibility in their career choices. Internal activism is emerging all over the world, with employees pushing for more ambitious climate policies. Managing workforce transitions sensitively is crucial, particularly in hard-to-abate industries, where retraining programmes can mitigate job displacement.

Supply chains and business partners are themselves under increasing pressure to reduce their carbon footprint (Scope 3 emissions) and comply with stricter environmental standards. Businesses must support suppliers in their transition efforts, strengthen supply chain resilience, and manage the financial and operational challenges posed by climate-related risks. Industry-wide collaboration and the adoption of greener logistics solutions are slowly becoming key priorities.

Finally, NGOs, activists, and community groups also exert significant influence on corporate environmental behaviour through public campaigns, legal challenges, and media exposure. These organisations hold businesses accountable for their environmental impact, particularly in relation to marginalised communities. Different approaches exist, ranging from some taking adversarial approach, to others trying to collaborate with companies to advance sustainable practices.

Examples of companies that are working towards advancing stakeholder considerations in response to climate action include Sony, Airbus, and Ford.

STAKEHOLDERS' CONSIDERATIONS: ASIA

The sustainability report of the Japanese technology and entertainment conglomerate Sony Group Corp spells out a variety of goals and communication methods for stakeholder engagement. These show that the company invests significant time in stakeholder dialogue. Given the business is consumer-centric, it tries to offer a variety of platforms to engage with customers including contact points for reporting product problems, surveys, trade shows, seminars, as well as dedicated area on its portal website. Closely related to this are a myriad of events and initiatives for local communities, as well as activities with NGOs and similar organisations. It contributed about 5 billion yen ($34 million) in social contribution engagement initiatives including education, arts and culture, and emergency relief.[5]

STAKEHOLDERS' CONSIDERATIONS: EUROPE

Almost all of the revenues of French aerospace giant Airbus SE are from selling products and services to a leading hard-to-abate industry, aviation. Its net-zero goals are a 63 per cent reduction against 2015 by 2030 and neutrality by 2050. Management said it is highly committed to the 2050 target as it sees climate as both a financial and a business risk, yet innovation and technology will be key to reach the target.[6] The company has extensive engagements with stakeholders, including consumers, suppliers, and shareholders and integrates their expectations via double materiality (the assessment of ESG issues' impact on financial performance and the company's impact on the environment and society). Similar to Sony, it undertakes extensive stakeholder engagement including interviews, surveys, and workshops. Such activities gave the group the idea to invest in the development of hydrogen-powered aircraft and sustainable aviation fuels.[7]

STAKEHOLDERS' CONSIDERATIONS: NORTH AMERICA

US automaker Ford Motor Co seeks to reduce Scopes 1 to 3 emissions 50 per cent by 2030 and 100 per cent by 2050. It previously produced a separate sustainability report which spelt out an array of stakeholder engagement practices. It created lines of communication with all internal and external stakeholders throughout its value chain. This ranged from upstream – mining and processors and parts fabrication – all the way to dealers and customers as well as recyclers. It even created a dedicated role for community engagement so it could improve communication in communities where it has manufacturing operations.[8] Its 2024 annual report combined financial reporting and sustainability considerations which shows a decline in the amount of information available compared to previous reports. This is possibly due to some domestic political pressures.

Sustainability pledges

How are sustainability pledges, including corporate sustainability policies, sustainability targets, decarbonisation aims, and related initiatives, important for the broader energy transition and for the specific transition of corporations? Is there a practical approach or are there several?

Businesses are driving the energy transition through a wide variety of sustainability pledges. These pledges extend far beyond merely declaring carbon footprint reduction goals or net-zero targets. In recent years, there has been an increasing trend where corporations are integrating sustainability considerations into their short-term and long-term business plans and strategies. There has been, in recent years, a notable rise in the adoption of climate-related risk management, which includes regulatory changes, the physical impacts of climate change, and reputational risks. Examples of corporations that illustrate how sustainability is becoming a core component of their strategic direction in the energy transition are abundant, including Toyota, Ørsted, and Microsoft.

SUSTAINABILITY PLEDGES: ASIA

The sustainability journey of Japanese car manufacturer Toyota Motor Corp began in the 1960s when it implemented some early initiatives related to pollution control infill efficiency.

The company launched the first mass-produced hybrid vehicle in the world, the Prius, in 1997. The company's environmental challenge 2015 aimed at carbon neutrality throughout the entire life cycle with vehicles was announced in the 2000s. While the company has not been aggressive in the electric vehicle market segment, its strategy is to raise the manufacturing of four types of eco-friendly cars: conventional hybrids which use more gasoline than electricity, plug-in hybrids which use more electricity than gas, hydrogen-powered fuel cell vehicles, and pure electric vehicles. Internal combustion engine vehicles will continue to be produced but will be gradually phased out over time.[9]

SUSTAINABILITY PLEDGES: EUROPE

The company Danish Oil and Natural Gas changed its name to Dong Energy in the early 2000s and to Ørsted A/S in 2017. Each change marked a transition to its business. The major Strategic shift was transitioning from oil and gas to renewables. It has pledged to reach Scopes 1 to 3 carbon neutrality by 2040. In 2024, 97 per cent of energy generation was from renewable power, including 41 per cent from offshore wind, 26 per cent from onshore wind, and 22 per cent from sustainable biomass. Sustainability pledges are not limited to their energy mix. The company is committed to developing, constructing, and operating its assets in a sustainable way, for example, already meeting its commitment to not sending to landfills any waste from wind turbine blades or solar PV panels. It has also committed to innovation in renewable technologies such as wind, solar, and energy storage solutions.[10]

SUSTAINABILITY PLEDGES: NORTH AMERICA

The US software and technology global giant Microsoft Corp also started its sustainability journey early, in the 2000s. Then, it had announced efforts towards energy efficiency and carbon offsetting. It turned carbon-neutral internally through internal carbon pricing in 2012. It secured Science Based Target Initiative certification for its carbon targets in 2019. Its goal is to eliminate all direct emissions and reach 100 per cent renewables usage by 2030. Another ambition is to remove all historical emissions by 2050, backed by a $1 billion Climate Innovation Fund. To back its pledges, it is investing in clean energy generation, AI-driven climate solutions as well as carbon removal technologies. In addition, it has made other environmental pledges. It is keen on water conservation, waste production, and biodiversity, the latter specifically through replenishing more water than it consumes and protecting more land than it uses.[11]

Technology transition catalysts

Clean energy solutions

Investing in clean energy related solutions has been a natural catalyst for energy and transport companies. Yet, companies in many other sectors as part of their climate and transition planning have also looked at energy transition projects and solutions. These include a wide range of initiatives which could include using green hydrogen for industrial processes, adding on-site renewable energy assets such as solar panels, adopting digital energy platforms such as energy management solutions, energy efficiency activities such as retrofitting and building upgrades, or circular economy programmes such as using waste-to-energy technology. Examples of companies which are not in the energy or transportation sectors adopting clean energy related solutions include Swire, CTP Group, and Walmart.

CLEAN ENERGY SOLUTIONS: ASIA

Hong Kong's Swire Properties Ltd develops and manages commercial, retail, hotel, and residential properties in Hong Kong, Chinese Mainland, Southeast Asia, and the United States. It was the first real estate developer to set a 2050 carbon neutrality goal in Hong Kong. Clean energy solutions is one of the initiatives to achieve the target. It has adopted a variety of energy efficiency measures for its existing portfolio and for new buildings. It upgraded air conditioning systems with electrically commutated motor plug fan, resulting in significant energy reduction. The building operations were digitalised through the use of smart energy management platforms and digital twins[12] systems. To raise the amount of clean energy consumption, it has adopted some on-site renewables generation and raised procurement. It also invested in energy storage at some sites. In 2024, about 60 per cent of electricity consumption in its Chinese Mainland portfolio was renewables.[13]

CLEAN ENERGY SOLUTIONS: EUROPE

Dutch company CTP NV is an owner, developer, and manager of logistics and industrial real estate, the largest in Europe by lettable area. Like Swire Properties, the company uses clean energy technologies and solutions to reach carbon neutrality by 2050 and even strives to become carbon negative. It strives to introduce energy efficiency solutions to its portfolio. CTP too has introduced smart building management which has included advanced energy and lighting management systems, including installing autonomous sensors, remote metering, low-consumption LED lighting, and heat pumps. CTP is also building a clean energy generation and storage portfolio which has become a small but growing revenue stream. An on-site solar power initiative resulted in 138 MW in 2024, with a target of 400 MW by 2026. This will be complemented by some wind power as well as energy storage systems.[14]

CLEAN ENERGY SOLUTIONS: NORTH AMERICA

Giant US retailer Walmart Inc seeks to reach net zero across its global operations by 2040. It aims at supplying 100 per cent of all of its facilities with renewable energy from wind, solar, and other clean energy sources by 2035. It had reached 48 per cent by the end of 2023, close to its 2025 interim goal of 50 per cent. The sourcing will be both from its own facilities as well as from direct procurement. It targets to add about 1 GW in clean energy generation, including solar and storage. It will cut emissions to zero from all of its vehicle fleet by 2040. It also aims at using low-impact refrigerants for cooling and electrified equipment for heating at all of its facilities by 2040. Also on the energy efficiency front, the company introduced AI-powered energy optimisation tools which adjust power usage in real time.[15]

Electrification

Similar to clean energy generation and solutions, electrification may often be associated primarily with energy companies and land transportation businesses. In fact, it is a strategy being adopted by many non-energy companies to reduce their carbon footprints. This trend is evident across various sectors and regions. Three companies exemplify this approach: Komatsu, A.P. Moller-Maersk, and Prologis. These companies share common strategies in their electrification efforts despite operating in different industries and geographical areas. They focus on electrifying core equipment and operations, as well as developing the necessary charging and energy infrastructure. This approach not only reduces their direct emissions but also contributes to the broader transition towards a net-zero global economy.

ELECTRIFICATION: ASIA

Japanese construction equipment manufacturer Komatsu Ltd is a leading heavy equipment manufacturer, including for the construction and mining sectors all over the world. Komatsu targets carbon neutrality by 2050 and is leading industry electrification transition from diesel-powered machinery to electric and hybrid solutions through some pioneering initiatives. The company developed battery-electric and hybrid hydraulic excavators for construction and mining operations and is electrifying its large mining trucks which traditionally relied on diesel power. It is also working with several strategic partners on fast-charging solutions for its electric heavy machinery, with the aim to make these more practical and efficient for daily operations. In the batteries sector, Komatsu acquired American Battery Solution Inc in late 2023. In the mining sectors, it formed an alliance with several of its customers, including BHP, Rio Tinto, and Grupo México.[16] These electrification efforts will significantly impact decarbonisation in the construction and mining sectors, two high-carbon-emitting, hard-to-abate sectors.

ELECTRIFICATION: EUROPE

The Danish company A.P. Møller – Mærsk A/S is one of the largest shipping companies in the world. It aims at achieving carbon neutrality across its value chain by 2040, targeting a 96 per cent cut in Scopes 1 and 2 emissions, and 90 per cent for Scope 3 emissions, from a 2022 base year. Part of its plan is a comprehensive electrification strategy. It has been piloting electrification options at its ports and for its trucking fleet. The network of terminals owned and operated by Mærsk have high GHG emissions from the generation of purchased electricity, so it is transitioning to renewable energy from on-site, including solar PV, and off-site solutions and swapping fossil-fuel container handling equipment with electric ones. This transition may take some time due to the lower priced diesel-powered equipment. At its ports in Egypt, Jordan, and Spain, Mærsk is testing battery-electric container handling equipment, as part of a $60 million pilot programme.[17]

ELECTRIFICATION: NORTH AMERICA

San Francisco-based Prologis Inc is a real estate investment trust focused on logistics aiming at carbon neutrality across Scopes 1 to 3 by 2040. Like Mærsk, clean energy procurement for its facilities like solar on-demand power infrastructure, and the electrification of transport, including vehicle charging, are two priorities. The company's solar and energy storage installed capacity was 626 MW at the end of 2024 and it kept its target of 1 GW by the end of 2025, almost five times more than its 252 MW in 2029. It used electric heat pumps for heating and cooling instead of natural gas-powered climate control systems where practicable. Clean transportation-wise, it had completed the largest heavy-duty truck charging hub in North America in partnership with Performance Team, a Maersk company, capable of charging 300 EV truck daily using a 9 MW microgrid with 18 MWh of battery storage and hydrogen-ready generators. It also had realised 16.1 million kilometres of fleet charging service in 2023 and 2024.[18]

Innovation and research

Corporate innovation and R&D are crucial for the energy transition and corporate transformation for several reasons. Innovation and research efforts drive technological advancements by developing new clean energy technologies and solutions, improving existing ones, and making them more efficient and cost-effective. As the energy sector shifts, companies need to innovate to maintain or grow their market share in a changing technological landscape. Innovation also helps address challenges by overcoming barriers to a zero-carbon energy sector, such as improving energy efficiency, developing renewable energy technologies, or advancing digital solutions, including AI-related tools and services.

Investments in innovation and R&D can lead to cost reductions in clean technologies, making them more competitive with polluting conventional energy sources. This is crucial to companies adapting to policy changes and responding to new regulations aimed at curbing climate change. Companies investing in clean energy R&D are also more likely to attract funding from investors and other stakeholders, further enhancing their ability to innovate.

Also, innovation and R&D help solve specific industry problems by developing solutions for cement, chemicals, steel, and other hard-to-abate sectors that may rely on disruptive technologies not yet economically viable. It also creates new business opportunities through the creation of new products, services, and business models aligned with the energy transition. Innovation also contributes to improving environmental performance by reducing GHG emissions and enhancing environmental quality. Finally, corporate innovation and R&D efforts often foster collaboration with start-ups, research institutions, and other companies, accelerating the pace of innovation across industries. Examples of corporations focused on innovation and R&D as part of their transition include Tata Steel, Siemens, and Apple.

INNOVATION AND RESEARCH: ASIA

The Indian steelmaking giant Tata Steel Ltd adopted a goal to be net zero by 2045 across all of its operations globally. Innovation at its India operations in the short term, up to 2030, includes operating modular scrap-based Electric Arc Furnace plants, which are today not yet commonly used, as well as developing low Technology Readiness Level technologies (i.e., early stage technologies) together with academia and manufacturers. Long term, up to 2045, Tata Steel will drive several initiatives. It will add new and different ironmaking approaches such as hydrogen or natural gas Direct Reduced Iron, an alternative to the more traditional blast furnace process. It will expand gas injection into the blast furnaces to reduce coal and coke, scale up the HIsarna technology,[19] and further advance Carbon Capture Usage and Storage (CCUS) pilot projects. It wants to use green hydrogen across the steel value chain. Finally, it wants to develop value-added products which use the captured carbon.[20]

INNOVATION AND RESEARCH: EUROPE

German industrial technology conglomerate Siemens AG serves industry, infrastructure, mobility, and healthcare. The group intends for its own operations to reach carbon neutrality in 2030 and for its whole value chain by 2050. The company spent about 8 per cent of revenue amounting to €6.3 billion on innovation in three areas in 2024: decarbonisation and energy efficiency, resource efficiency and circularity, and people centricity and society. Examples in the first two areas include innovative building technologies for energy efficiency, predictive maintenance systems, new materials to reduce electricity consumption by railroads, software systems and processes for low-voltage grid monitoring and outage management which increase the capacity of existing grids, and automated battery recycling. Its achievements are numerous.[21]

INNOVATION AND RESEARCH: NORTH AMERICA

US technology giant Apple Inc. achieved carbon neutrality for its global corporate operations in 2020 and targets that for its entire value chain by 2030. Because of the latter target, the company is highly focused on exploring innovative approaches related to recycling and renewable materials, clean energy, and lower carbon shipping. The company has made good progress in finding innovative ways to source and use recycling and renewable materials. By the end of 2025, 100 per cent of the gold, tin, cobalt, and rare earth elements it uses will be recycled. Its in-house disassembly robot, Daisy, and recycling machine, Dave, assist in the recovery and recycling of tungsten from the Taptic Engine (the custom vibration and haptic feedback system) of Apple products. It also puts a lot of effort in the discovery of new, safer chemistries and better dyes. Apple not only targets 100 per cent clean electricity for its whole value chain by 2030 but also invests in reducing GHG emissions through process innovation as well as measures to cut energy consumption across its facilities.[22]

Finance transition catalysts

The third category in the catalysts of change which are drivers or pressures faced by businesses in their transition-related strategies is finance. The three elements in this category include climate finance tools, cost benefits, and risk management.

The transition to sustainable energy solutions requires vast amounts of capital. The financial sector faces growing pressures, both internal and external, to adopt environmentally responsible practices and account for climate risks in their portfolios. At the same time, corporations feel increasing pressure from financial institutions to integrate sustainability and climate resilience into their operational strategies. In turn, the strategic climate initiatives and transition efforts of corporations influence the financial sector's own sustainability objectives and risk assessments. This creates a synergistic relationship – a virtuous cycle – where finance drives corporate sustainability and climate risk management, which then strengthens the financial sector's commitment to environmentally sound practices, as financial institutions must build structures and add resources towards addressing this change on the part of corporates.

Climate finance approaches

Similar to the other categories, there are hundreds of examples of companies successfully adopting climate finance policies, tools, and products, including those related to sustainable finance, green finance, and other financial incentives, to advance their transition plans and strategies. Examples of such corporations include Sydney Airport, Volkswagen, and Verizon.

CLIMATE FINANCE APPROACHES: ASIA

Australian airport infrastructure operator Sydney Airport Holdings Ltd aims for carbon neutrality by 2030, with a 6 per cent cut in Scopes 1 and 2 in 2023 and plans to secure 100 per cent renewable electricity by January 2025, the company said in 2023. The group's climate finance activities include a sustainability-linked loan and a placement. The group successfully secured a sustainability-linked loan of A$1.4 billion ($0.9 billion) in May 2019 with three-to-five-year maturities. At the time, it was the first syndicated sustainability-linked loan in Australia, the largest transaction of its kind in the Asia Pacific region, and the largest such loan by an airport worldwide. The two-way pricing sustainability linkage meant that the bank debt facility margin would increase or decrease depending on the sustainability performance of Sydney Airport.[23] It was also successfully completed. In February 2020, a sustainability-linked US Private Placement, or USPP, a type of privately placed bond not registered with the US Securities and Exchange Commission and exempt from regulatory requirements applied to publicly issued bonds. The sustainability-linked tranche was one of five tranches and amounted to A$100 million ($66 million) with a 20-year tenor. At the time, it was the world's first sustainability-linked issuance with two-way pricing.[24]

CLIMATE FINANCE APPROACHES: EUROPE

German automotive manufacturing leader Volkswagen AG has committed to reach carbon neutrality by 2050 at the latest. Volkswagen has been successful at leveraging climate finance strategies, sustainable finance tools, and green financial instruments. It successfully issued two green bonds worth €2 billion ($2.3 billion) with terms of 8 and 12 years, and coupons of 0.875 per cent and 1.250 per cent in 2020. Since then, Volkswagen AG and subsidiaries, including Volkswagen Leasing, Volkswagen International Finance, and Volkswagen Bank, financial services arms, issued a number of green and hybrid bonds.[25] The group also concluded several sustainability-linked loans. The first loan tied to achieving sustainability was for €1.8 billion ($2.1 billion) with the interest rate on the three-year loans been depended on the Volkswagen Group achieving its CO_2 fleet emission targets in Europe.[26]

CLIMATE FINANCE APPROACHES: NORTH AMERICA

US telecommunications giant Verizon Communications Inc.'s net-zero target is set for 2050, comprising Scopes 1 to 3 emissions. Verizon is one of the largest US corporate green bond issuers. It has stated that its green bond issuance is essential to its efforts to reach its carbon neutrality targets. The company had issued six green bonds amounting to about $6 billion between 2019 and the end of 2024. The bonds' proceeds were chiefly for financing, in whole or in part, long-term renewable energy purchase agreements (REPAs) for new renewable energy projects. The company had an ESG Risk Rating of 'low risk' by Morningstar Sustainalytics, an ESG data, research, and ratings provider.[27]

Cost controls

All over the world, there are firms that employ climate initiatives, transition plans, and sustainability targets for the purpose of reducing operational costs. They look at achieving this by slashing energy expenditure, enhancing resource efficiency, and reducing regulatory risks. Investments in renewables, energy-efficient infrastructure, and waste reduction programmes may yield long-term savings on utilities and materials, for example. At the same time, supply chain optimisations and circular economy practices can lower procurement and production expenses. These efforts also help mitigate climate change related risks, leading to further medium- to long-term cost savings. Examples of corporations using transition strategies to reduce expenses include Samsung Electronics, Unilever, and Magna International.

COST CONTROLS: ASIA

South Korean electronics giant Samsung Electronics Co Ltd wants to become carbon-neutral by 2050. Its components division Device Solutions (DS) and its products division Device eXperience (DX) have slightly different targets. The DS division intends to reach net-zero Scopes 1 and 2 emissions by 2050. The DX division intends to achieve net zero for Scopes 1 and 2 by 2030 and for all of its value chain by 2050. The company's major strategy to reduce expenses and benefit from lower emissions is through energy efficiency and water efficiency. These initiatives have produced many successes. For example, at its data centres, it has been installing energy efficiency systems, such as open-type cooling towers and variable-type air handling units, has upgraded the uninterruptible power supply systems with higher efficiency models, and has been implementing immersion cooling technology to maximise the cooling efficiency of its equipment. To conserve water, the company installed water-saving facilities, treated wastewater, and expanded greywater reuse, as well as using groundwater and rainwater for landscaping and everyday purposes at its business sites.[28]

COST CONTROLS: EUROPE

Anglo-Dutch consumer goods giant Unilever NV has set a net-zero goal for the whole value chain by 2039. Unilever saved €1.2 billion ($1.4 billion) through sustainable sourcing and eco-efficient factory practices. Indian subsidiary Hindustan Unilever worked on water conservation, plastic waste management, and sustainable sourcing strategies. Hindustan Unilever cut water consumption in its operations by 54 per cent, versus the 2008 baseline, and created a cumulative water conservation potential of approximately 1.3 trillion litres across India. The subsidiary facilitated the safe disposal of over 150,000 tons of plastic waste since 2018 and continues to collect and dispose of more plastic waste than it uses in packaging. Also in India, it set up a partnership with infrastructure investor Brookfield for a 45 MW off-site solar project expected to create a cost saving of about 25 per cent over 20 years.[29]

COST CONTROLS: NORTH AMERICA

Canadian automotive parts manufacturer Magna International Inc, one of the largest companies in the country, targets to achieve carbon neutrality by 2050. Magna aims at cutting costs by implementing energy-efficient manufacturing processes, including a reduction in energy consumption, waste reduction programmes, and using recycled materials in production. Examples include smarter lighting systems and optimised facility shutdown procedures across its 341 divisions lowering electricity consumption by 5 per cent and C$36 million ($26 million) in cost avoidance in 2024, the second consecutive year it achieved such 5 per cent reduction. In 2024, it started its Energy Cost Optimisation programme with a goal of C$50 million ($36 million) annual savings by the end of 2050 through operational efficiency, downtime energy usage, and on-site renewables. For example, four initiatives realised about C$36 ($26 million) in annual savings. It minimised equipment working in passive mode at a Mexican division, eliminated leaks in paint-shop spray booths at a Chinese division, replaced a gas heating system with a heat pump at a French division, and installed an 11.2 MW on-site solar facility in Austria.[30]

Risk management and financial risk reduction

Many medium to large businesses have dedicated staff responsible for overseeing risk management. This is considered good corporate governance and is closely monitored by stakeholders, including financial lending institutions. Such staff would handle the identification, assessment, prioritisation, and mitigation of risks affecting the company.

An increasingly critical area of risk management is climate-related. For businesses that have already integrated climate action into their strategic plans, managing climate risks is a priority. In fact, proactive climate action enhances their ability to mitigate climate-related risks. The breakdown of Earth's systems is leading to reduced corporate profitability, damage to fixed assets, and disruptions to supply chains and communities, according to the World Economic Forum, a global advocacy and think tank NGO. It calculates that companies that fail to adapt to climate risks could see earnings decline by up to 7 per cent by 2035.[31]

To equip senior management with the necessary skills to navigate these challenges, there are executive training programmes at many universities with courses on corporate climate change risk management. Example of one such programme at the Yale School of Management helps leaders assess the impact of climate-related trends on their businesses within different climate scenarios. It provides guidance on defining the company's role in transitioning to a low-carbon economy and developing strategies to address emerging climate risks and regulatory changes. It also teaches how to evaluate accounting frameworks to measure both a company's carbon footprint and its positive environmental impact. Businesses also receive support in formulating carbon credit strategies.[32]

Examples of companies aiming at enhancing climate risk management include Singapore Telecom, Nestlé, and Salesforce.

RISK MANAGEMENT AND FINANCIAL RISK REDUCTION: ASIA

Singapore's leading telecommunications company Singapore Telecommunications Ltd intends to reach Scopes 1 to 3 carbon neutrality by 2045. Singtel has a comprehensive climate risk management approach and had invested about S$337 million ($262 million) in fiscal 2025 (to March 2025) in climate mitigation and adaptation efforts to address climate risks. The company has a Risk, Sustainability, and Technology Committee which supervises the whole Group's sustainability strategy and adaptation to address climate risks. It also has a group-level body, group risk and compliance, which reviews and updates the risk register and also conducts biannual risk assessments, including sustainability and climate-related risks, to ensure that plans and mitigation measures are in place to manage the risks. Each

RISK	RISK DESCRIPTION
Riverine flooding *Expected time horizon: Across all horizons*	Increased frequency and intensity of rainfall alter the frequency and intensity of river flooding, which can damage low-lying equipment and infrastructure assets.
Surface water flooding *Expected time horizon: Short to medium term*	Increased frequency of extreme rainfall leading to floods including flash flooding, which can damage low-lying equipment and infrastructure assets.
Extreme heat *Expected time horizon: Short to medium term*	New extremes of high temperatures, more frequent hot days and longer-lasting heatwaves, which can result in the loss of use or failure of equipment and infrastructure.
Coastal inundation *Expected time horizon: Long term*	Rising sea levels and higher incidence of extreme sea events including sea water flooding due to high tides, low air pressure and waves, which can damage coastal assets.
Bushfires *Expected time horizon: Short term*	Increased incidence of fire weather due to confluence of days with higher temperatures, high wind speeds and drier conditions. Flames and heat from burning vegetation can damage equipment and infrastructure.

PHYSICAL RISK SCENARIO	ASSUMPTIONS
RCP* 2.6 *Warming limited to 2°C (above pre-industrial levels) by 2100*	• 1.5°C policy ambition • Immediate policy reaction • Fast technology change • Medium use of carbon dioxide removal • Medium variation in regional policy
RCP* 8.5 Warming *Warming exceeds 4°C (above pre-industrial levels) by 2100*	• 4°C+ policy ambition • No policy reaction • Slow technology change • Low use of carbon dioxide removal • Low variation in regional policy

** = Representative Concentration Pathway scenarios, Intergovernmental Panel on Climate Change, 5th Assessment Report*

Figure 12.5 Singapore Telecommunications' material physical risks

Source: Singapore Telecommunications Limited, 'Sustainability Report 2025: Singtel28 - the Growth Trail', (Singapore Telecommunications Ltd 2022. Available at: https://www.singtel.com/about-us/sustainability/sustainability-reports/2025 accessed 12 July 2025.

of the Group's operating Businesses is responsible for maintaining its own risk register and action plans. For example, its Australian subsidiary is accountable for assessing the potential impact on network infrastructure from natural disaster risks such as cyclones, floods, or bush fires. Singtel uses its own Enterprise Risk Management (ERM) rating and applies ERM methodologies to assess the impact and likelihood of identified risks which then allows the Group to assess and prioritise material sustainability and climate-related risks consistently across all of its business. Finally, it conducts climate scenario analysis to appraise the potential financial implications of climate-related risks.[33] Figure 12.5 illustrates some practical examples of risks that some of its business units may face.

RISK MANAGEMENT AND FINANCIAL RISK REDUCTION: EUROPE

Swiss food and beverage giant Nestlé SA's aim is to halve GHG emissions by 2030 and reach carbon neutrality for Scopes 1 to 3 by 2050. The company has aligned its sustainability disclosures with the EU Corporate Sustainability Reporting Directive and the European Sustainability Reporting Standards. However, Nestlé does not provide much detail and illustrations of the climate risks it faces apart from the obvious; given it is involved in food and beverage, extreme weather events have an immediate impact on the costs of its raw materials. Nestlé does state that its Sustainability Committee is responsible for reviewing responses to climate change and other environmental issues and that risk assessment is embedded in its Enterprise Risk Management. In its last Non-Financial Statements Report (February 2025), it highlighted that in 2023 it had used scenario-based modelling to identify climate-related impact risks over the medium term, five years, and the long term (10–20 years). One example of the type of action it has taken is the implementation of the Nestlé Agriculture Framework, a regenerative agriculture programme designed to enhance farm resilience and, in turn, mitigate climate risk for key ingredients.[34]

RISK MANAGEMENT AND FINANCIAL RISK REDUCTION: NORTH AMERICA

US cloud software company Salesforce Inc is one of the few companies in the world to have achieved carbon neutrality across its whole value chain as well as procuring 100 per cent of its energy consumption from renewable energy. Climate risk management principally focuses on risks to its infrastructure and operations, including the potential impact on its supply chain. The company chiefly operates through its own and third-party data centres. Climate impacts could include power price volatility and power availability during this transition to low-carbon grids, in addition to expenses for water or cooling equipment. To mitigate such risks, Salesforce prioritises resilience through strategic sites selection as well as backup plans for those facilities. The company also implements a robust supplier audit and risk assessment, as extreme weather events could damage infrastructure, delay shipments, and cause shortages of critical components. Importantly, the company also works on preventing climate impact on its most important asset, its customers. For this, it provides technology solutions to help to accelerate the transition of its customers.[35]

Business-related transition catalysts

The fourth and last category is the business-related catalysts of change. These catalysts comprise the drivers or pressures on the business operations of companies. They include how the energy transition affects market forces impacting a company, how circular economy considerations affect their strategies, and how the transition may impact the sustainability of their supply chains.

Market dynamics

Climate and the transition impact the market in which a company operates in a variety of ways. Some of the effects include increasing or reducing growth opportunities, changing consumer demand, altering the use of data and analytics, and even fostering industry collaboration. Companies such as Panasonic, Schneider Electric, and NextEra Energy provide examples of how business operations may be affected by changing market dynamics caused by climate and the transition.

MARKET DYNAMICS: ASIA

The 100-year-plus Panasonic Holdings Corp is a Japanese multinational supplier of innovative technologies and solutions for consumer electronics, communications, energy, and other sectors with a target to achieve net zero for Scopes 1 and 2 by 2030 and for Scope

3 by 2050. The transition has positively boosted some existing business lines. Businesses including significantly enhanced EV battery production, energy efficiency equipment like air-to-water heat pumps, Eneloop-branded ready-to-use rechargeable batteries pre-charged with solar energy, carbon-neutral automotive systems at global sites, and smart technologies for sustainable city projects in Japan and in Europe. New business-wise, Panasonic entered green hydrogen production devices using surplus solar power, pure hydrogen fuel cells for distributed energy solutions, as well as circular economy ventures (refurbishment, recycling-oriented manufacturing).[36]

MARKET DYNAMICS: EUROPE

The almost 190-year-old French industrial technology specialist, including digital automation and energy management, Schneider Electric SE has committed to turn its entire value chain to net zero by 2050. The transition helps Schneider raise sales at several existing business lines. They include energy management solutions (driven by increased demand for electrification and digitalisation), renewable energy sourcing, leveraging green tariffs, power purchase agreements, on-site generation, decarbonisation services, including supply chain emissions reduction through the Zero Carbon Project, energy efficiency products and software, and sustainable building solutions, enhanced by AI and automation for smarter homes and urban infrastructure. In terms of new business, Schneider has newly been able to expand its sustainability consulting services and become a provider of circular economy solutions as well as tax credit transfer agreements in the United States to facilitate corporate investments in clean energy technologies.[37]

MARKET DYNAMICS: NORTH AMERICA

US energy company NextEra Energy Inc, whose history goes back to 100 years, adopted a goal to become carbon-emissions-free by 2045, through zero-carbon-emissions resources and energy storage. The global transition enables NextEra Energy to expand some of its existing businesses. These include expanding its solar and wind power generation capacity, increasing investments in transmission and distribution infrastructure, which are needed to support renewable energy growth, expanding its retail energy services through NextEra Energy Services, such as offering customised clean energy solution, and possibly boosting its nuclear power operations, such as potentially restarting the Duane Arnold nuclear plant in Iowa. For new businesses, the company is looking at hydrogen production initiatives, battery storage facilities, and other energy storage solutions, and is exploring partnering with GE Vernova for natural gas-fired power generation targeting AI data centres and other large users.[38]

Circular economy

The circular economy is a well-recognised model of production and consumption. The European Parliament defines the circular economy as involving ‘sharing, listing, reusing, repairing, refurbishing, and recycling existing materials and products as long as possible’ so that the life cycle of such products can be extended while, at the same time, waste is reduced to a minimum.[39] While some observers view it as not a productive use of resources for corporations, actually by encouraging sustainable practises, the circular economy can help corporations reduce costs and, in some situations, generate new income streams. Lenovo, Michelin, and Steelcase are three very different examples of the positive effects the circular economy may have.

CIRCULAR ECONOMY: ASIA

Chinese multinational technology company Lenovo Group Ltd wants to reach carbon neutrality throughout its supply chain by 2050. Carbon neutrality strategies help Lenovo to raise revenues at existing business lines and provide potential new revenue streams. It has adopted a variety of circular economy programmes which strive to maximise the value and potential reuse of excess, returned, and obsolete products and parts across its business and manufacturing operations, repair network, and channel partners. Improving the energy efficiency of its notebook computers, desktop computers, servers, and smartphones could raise the attractiveness of the product for some customers, especially business users. In addition to expanding the use of recycled materials in laptops, monitors, and servers, it is designing devices for easier repair and refurbishment, which should cut Lenovo's expenses.[40]

CIRCULAR ECONOMY: EUROPE

The objective of French tyre manufacturer Michelin Group is to achieve net-zero emissions by 2050. Michelin says that it applies circular economy principles throughout its operations and business using its 4Rs approach: Reduce, Reuse, Recycle, Renew. Michelin develops tyres that increase the battery range of EVs. Another is investing in recycling to repurpose waste into tyres. The group sees transport decarbonisation as a great business opportunity and much of its efforts are towards remaining a leader in this space and has allocated a budget of €1.2 billion ($1.4 billion) for this purpose. It has nine R&D centres around the world staffed with over 6,000 people.[41]

CIRCULAR ECONOMY: NORTH AMERICA

Steelcase Inc. is a US designer and manufacturer of furniture with a global reach. It set a net-zero objective for Scopes 1 to 3 for 2050, with an interim target of a 50 per cent cut versus fiscal 2020. The company stated that it has a long history of sustainable design. It works on the whole product life cycle. From the acquisition of materials to end-of-use solutions. It has created the Steelcase Sustainable Design Framework focused on reducing its carbon footprint, design for circularity, and the responsible choice and use of materials. It is using fewer packaging materials and replacing what is used with sustainable materials, including recycled ones. It is investing in energy efficiency and renewable energy projects, and has scaled back payback expectations for these initiatives to four years from two. Similar to China's Lenovo, it is also looking to remanufacture products into a like-new-state for resale.[42]

Supply chain sustainability

The management of supply chain sustainability has already changed the way a great many companies operate around the world. The due diligence of supply chain sustainability is complex. It is easier for a company to control its own internal process, such as raw materials acquisition, than to monitor those of third parties. Companies must devote more effort to building a greener supply chain. For example, they need to establish periodic supplier sustainability audits to ensure compliance with environmental standards. They may also need to organise supplier sustainability conferences and training. Three examples of companies which have fully integrated supply chain sustainability processes are Huawei, Danone, and Cisco.

SUPPLY CHAIN SUSTAINABILITY: ASIA

Chinese multinational technology and telecommunications company Huawei Technologies Co Ltd is aiming to reach carbon neutrality by 2040. Huawei has intensified its supply chain sustainability measures in recent years. The company's major production hub is in China, but it also has manufacturing and assembly presence in other locations around the world including Brazil, Europe, India, and Southeast Asia. The company published two important policies to ensure a sustainable value chain. One is a supplier code of conduct which mandates suppliers' compliance with all environmental regulations, minimise pollution, manage hazardous substances, and, critically, reduce GHG emissions. The other is on mineral supply chain which stresses Huawei's pledge for the responsible procurement of tin, tantalum, tungsten, gold, cobalt, and other minerals it uses in its products and compels suppliers to conduct source tracing and due diligence for the mineral products they use. To ensure compliance, Huawei conducts regular supplier, numbering over 10,000, sustainability audits. It applies a risk rating (high to low) and assesses if those with a 'high' rating should be made not eligible to supply the company. Huawei also supports suppliers in their carbon emissions reduction by assisting them with energy efficiency and clean energy adoption measures. Huawei will even pay premium prices to suppliers offering higher quality to motivate them to improve their sustainability performance.[43]

SUPPLY CHAIN SUSTAINABILITY: EUROPE

French multinational food company Danone SA has a net-zero target for Scopes 1 to 3 by 2050. Danone is another company with a complex supply network which comprises 400,000 farmers, 57,000 suppliers, 170 factories, and 400 distribution centres all over the world. The company is shifting to a pull-based supply chain model (production driven by customer orders) from a push-based one (production based on forecasted demand). The transition will reduce waste and excess inventory by producing goods based on actual demand. The company's supply chain sustainability revolves around regenerative agriculture (boosting soil health, improving biodiversity, and preserving water resources), energy efficiency, better water resources management, optimising logistics (including decarbonising transport), and increasing eco-friendly (circular and low-carbon) packaging to cut carbon emissions by 30 per cent by 2030.[44]

SUPPLY CHAIN SUSTAINABILITY: NORTH AMERICA

US multinational technology conglomerate Cisco Systems Inc wants to achieve net zero across its value chain by 2040. Similar to Huawei, Cisco has put in place a policy for the sustainable sourcing of minerals. It closely works with suppliers on resources conservation and transitioning to a circular economy. It has engaged in a variety of industry initiatives to create standards for suppliers to foster sustainability improvements. Also similar to Huawei, Cisco closely audits the sustainability practices of its suppliers. It will work with suppliers found to be non-conformant to Cisco's policies to develop, implement, and monitor Corrective Action Plans. The company has become one of the best-in-class for the manufacture of goods in a sustainable and responsible manner. Its sustainability-related report (the Purpose Report) has been in the top two in Gartner's Supply Chain Top 25 for five consecutive years through fiscal 2024 (to July 2024).[45]

Notes

1 J McCalla-Leacy and J-H Gnändiger, *The Move to Mandatory Reporting: Executive Summary* (KPMG International 2024) <https://assets.kpmg.com/content/dam/kpmgsites/xx/pdf/2024/11/the-move-to-mandatory-reporting-executive-summary.pdf.coredownload.inline.pdf> accessed 10 February 2025.
2 Hitachi, 'Climate-Related Financial Information Disclosure (Based on TCFD Recommendations): Sustainability Report: Hitachi' (Hitachi.com 2025) <https://www.hitachi.com/sustainability/report/environmental/tcfd.html> accessed 8 July 2025.
3 BASF, *BASF Group Annual Report 2024* (BASF 2025) <https://report.basf.com/2024/en/> accessed 8 July 2025.
4 General Motors, *2023 Sustainability Report: Journey to Zero* (General Motors 2024) <https://www.gm.com/content/dam/company/docs/us/en/gmcom/company/GM_2023_SR.pdf#page=2> accessed 8 July 2025.
5 Sony Group Corporation, *The Sustainability Report 2024* (Sony Group Corporation 2024) <https://www.sony.com/en/SonyInfo/csr_report/> accessed 8 July 2025.
6 J Daleo, 'Airbus CEO: Aviation Net Zero by 2050 Goals May Be at Risk' *FLYING Magazine* (24 March 2025) <https://www.flyingmag.com/airbus-ceo-aviation-net-zero-by-2050-goals-may-be-at-risk/> accessed 9 July 2025.
7 Airbus, 'Airbus: Pioneering Sustainable Aerospace' (2025) <https://www.airbus.com/sites/g/files/jlcbta136/files/2025-04/2025_Airbus_Pioneering_sustainable_aerospace_publication.pdf> accessed 9 July 2025; Airbus, 'Airbus Annual Report 2024: Innovation in Action' (2025) <https://www.airbus.com/sites/g/files/jlcbta136/files/2025-04/Airbus%20Annual%20Report%202024.pdf> accessed 9 July 2025.
8 Ford Motor Company, 'On the Road to Better Helping Build a Better World Integrated Sustainability and Financial Report 2024' (2024) <https://corporate.ford.com/content/dam/corporate/us/en-us/documents/reports/2024-integrated-sustainability-and-financial-report.pdf> accessed 9 July 2025; Ford Motor Company, '2024 Annual Report Ford Motor Company' (2024) <https://s205.q4cdn.com/882619693/files/doc_financials/2024/ar/Ford-2024-Annual-Report.pdf> accessed 9 July 2025.
9 Toyota Motor Corporation, *Sustainability | Toyota Motor Corporation Official Global Website* (Toyota Motor Corporation Official Global Website 2025) [online] <https://global.toyota/en/sustainability/> accessed 16 February 2025.
10 Ørsted A/S, 'Q4 & FY2024 Investor Presentation' (Windows.net 2025) [online] <https://getvisual.blob.core.windows.net/v3-all-job-pdfs/2609-Orsted_Investor_Presentation_-_Q4_2024.pdf> accessed 17 February 2025.
11 Microsoft, *Our Sustainability Journey | Microsoft CSR* (Microsoft 2025) [online] <https://www.microsoft.com/en-us/corporate-responsibility/sustainability-journey> accessed 17 February 2025.
12 The digital model of a physical process, product, project, or system for the purposes of simulation testing, monitoring, and maintenance prior to building process, product, project, or system, such as a new EV model or an infrastructure project.
13 Swire Properties Ltd, *2024 Annual Report* (Swire Properties Ltd 2025) <https://ir.swireproperties.com/en/ir/reports/ar2024.pdf> accessed 10 July 2025; Swire Properties Limited, *Performance (Environment)* (Swire Properties 2025) [online] <https://www.swireproperties.com/en/sustainable-development/performance-environment/> accessed 17 February 2025.

14 S Spataru and S Garg, 'Sustainalytics Second Party Opinion Overall Assessment Contribution to SDGs' (2025) <https://ctp.eu/files/2025/06/CTP-N.V.-Green-Bond-Framework-Second-Party-Opinion.pdf> accessed 10 July 2025; CTP N.V., *CTP NV Annual Report 2024* (CTP NV 2025) <https://ctp.eu/files/2025/03/CTP-N.V.-AR–2024.pdf> accessed 10 July 2025.
15 Walmart, *Climate Change* (Corporate – US 2023) [online] <https://corporate.walmart.com/purpose/sustainability/planet/climate-change> accessed 17 February 2025; Walmart, 'Energy' (2025) [online] <https://www.walmartsustainabilityhub.com/project-gigaton/energy> accessed 17 February 2025.
16 Komatsu, 'Home | Komatsu' (www.komatsu.com 2025) [online] <https://www.komatsu.com/en/> accessed 19 February 2025.
17 Mærsk, 'Decarbonising Terminals' (www.maersk.com 2025) <https://www.maersk.com/sustainability/our-esg-priorities/climate-change/decarbonising-port-terminals> accessed 11 July 2025; Maersk, *Decarbonising Our Global Operations All the Way* (Maersk 2024) [online] <https://investor.maersk.com/static-files/ba893ee6-706f-48ad-9514-a12e5c67419e> accessed 19 February 2025.
18 Prologis, '2024–25 Global Impact & Sustainability Report' (2025) <https://prologis.getbynder.com/m/4e832274a5346909/original/Prologis-2024-25-Global-Impact-Sustainability-Report.pdf> accessed 11 July 2025.
19 A new steelmaking method that simplifies traditional processes. Unlike blast furnaces, which need specially processed iron ore and coal, HIsarna can use raw, powdered materials. It directly turns iron ore and coal powder into liquid pig iron, removing extra steps. This makes steel production easier and potentially more efficient. Source: Tata Steel, 'HISARNA: Building a Sustainable Steel Industry' (2020) <https://products.tatasteelnederland.com/sites/producttsn/files/tata-steel-europe-factsheet-hisarna.pdf> accessed 23 February 2025.
20 Tata Steel, 'Tata Steel Annual Report 2023–2024' (Tatasteel.com 2023) <https://www.tatasteel.com/investors/integrated-report-2023-24/climate-change-report.html> accessed 11 July 2025.
21 Siemens, *Sustainability at Siemens – Scaling Sustainability Impact* (Siemens AG 2025) <https://assets.new.siemens.com/siemens/assets/api/uuid:32371798-2ab8-44ca-82b0-450900622ce3/Sustainability-at-Siemens.pdf> accessed 11 July 2025.
22 Apple, 'Environmental Progress Report' (2025) <https://www.apple.com/environment/pdf/Apple_Environmental_Progress_Report_2025.pdf> accessed 11 July 2025.
23 BNP Paribas, *Sydney Airport Hits the Skies with Pioneering Sustainable Loan – BNP Paribas CIB* (BNP Paribas CIB 28 June 2019) <https://cib.bnpparibas/sydney-airport-hits-the-skies-with-pioneering-sustainable-loan/> accessed 12 July 2025.
24 MUFG, *MUFG Partners with Sydney Airport to Deliver World's First ESG-Linked US Private Placement* (MUFG EMEA 20 February 2020) <https://www.mufgemea.com/media/mufg-partners-with-sydney-airport-to-deliver-world-s-first-esg-linked-us-private-placement/> accessed 12 July 2025; M Zaunmayr, 'Australian Corporates Push the Boundaries of Sustainable Funding' *KangaNews* (2020) <https://www.kanganews.com/news/11589-australian-corporates-push-the-boundaries-of-sustainable-funding> accessed 12 July 2025.
25 Volkswagen, *Volkswagen Successfully Places First Green Bonds with a Volume of € 2 Billion* (Volkswagen Group 16 September 2020) <https://www.volkswagen-group.com/en/press-releases/volkswagen-successfully-places-first-green-bonds-with-a-volume-of-2-billion-16716> accessed 12 July 2025.
26 Volkswagen Group, *Volkswagen Group Ties Loan to Sustainability Target for the First Time* (Volkswagen Group 7 December 2021) <https://www.volkswagen-group.com/en/press-releases/olkswagen-group-ties-loan-to-sustainability-target-for-the-first-time-16800> accessed 12 July 2025.
27 Verizon, 'Green Bond Impact Report' (2025) <https://www.verizon.com/about/sites/default/files/Verizon-green-bond-impact-report-february-2025.pdf> accessed 2 March 2025.
28 Samsung Electronics, *A Journey towards a Sustainable Future Samsung Electronics Sustainability Report 2024* (Samsung Electronics Co Ltd 2024) <https://www.samsung.com/global/sustainability/media/pdf/Samsung_Electronics_Sustainability_Report_2024_ENG.pdf> accessed 2 March 2025; Samsung SDS, 'Samsung SDS's Journey to Reducing Greenhouse Gas Emissions | Impact News | ESG NEWS | Samsung SDS' (Samsungsds.com 21 April 2025) <https://www.samsungsds.com/en/sustainability-news/reducing-greenhouse-gas-emissions.html> accessed 12 July 2025.

29 N Singal, 'Unilever Saved €1.2 Billion of Cost due to Sustainable Sourcing, Eco-Efficiencies at Factories' *Business Today* (13 November 2021) <https://www.businesstoday.in/latest/corporate/story/unilever-saved-eu12-billion-of-cost-due-to-sustainable-sourcing-eco-efficiencies-at-factories-312105-2021-11-13> accessed 2 March 2025; Unilever PLC, *Unilever Solar Electricity Deal Powers Renewable Energy Use in India* (Unilever 26 February 2025) <https://www.unilever.com/news/news-search/2025/unilever-solar-electricity-deal-powers-renewable-energy-use-in-india/> accessed 12 July 2025.

30 Magna International Inc, 'FY 2024 Sustainability Report' (2025) <https://www.magna.com/docs/default-source/financial-reports-public-filings/tax-other-reports/101227_magna_sustainabilityreport_fy2024_final_cda.pdf?sfvrsn=76c40972_11> accessed 12 July 2025.

31 G Einhorn, T Siddall, and World Economic Forum, *10 Ways Businesses Can Build Resilience to Climate Hazards* (World Economic Forum 11 December 2024) <https://www.weforum.org/stories/2024/12/ways-business-leaders-build-resilience-climate-hazards/> accessed 28 March 2025.

32 Yale School of Management, 'Corporate Climate Change Risk Management Online Program' (Yale.edu 28 October 2024) <https://som.yale.edu/executive-education/for-individuals/leadership/corporate-climate-change-risk-management> accessed 28 March 2025.

33 Singtel, *Sustainability Report 2025: Singtel28 – the Growth Trail* (Singapore Telecommunications Ltd 2022) <https://www.singtel.com/about-us/sustainability/sustainability-reports/2025> accessed 12 July 2025.

34 Nestlé, *Non-Financial Statement 2024* (Nestle 2025) <https://www.nestle.com/sites/default/files/2025-02/non-financial-statement-2024.pdf> accessed 12 July 2025.

35 Salesforce Inc, *Salesforce Achieves Net Zero across Its Value Chain and 100% Renewable Energy* (Salesforce 21 September 2021) <https://www.salesforce.com/au/news/press-releases/2021/09/21/salesforce-achieves-net-zero-across-its-full-value-chain/> accessed 12 July 2025; Salesforce, *FY25 Stakeholder Impact Report* (Salesforce Inc 2025) <https://www.salesforce.com/en-us/wp-content/uploads/sites/4/documents/white-papers/salesforce-fy25-stakeholder-impact-report.pdf> accessed 13 July 2025.

36 Panasonic, *Official Website* <https://www.panasonic.com> accessed 13 July 2025.

37 Schneider Electric, *Official Website* <https://www.se.com/ww/en/> accessed 13 July 2025.

38 NextEra Energy, *Official Website* <https://www.nexteraenergy.com/home.html> accessed 13 July 2025; L Kearney, 'NextEra Advances toward Iowa Nuclear Plant Restart' *Reuters* (24 January 2025) <https://www.reuters.com/business/energy/nextera-advances-toward-iowa-nuclear-plant-restart-2025-01-24/> accessed 13 July 2025; Reuters Staff, 'US Renewable Power Producer NextEra Energy Expanding Gas-Fired Generation' *Reuters* (24 January 2025) <https://www.reuters.com/business/energy/nextera-energy-posts-lower-fourth-quarter-profit-2025-01-24/> accessed 13 July 2025.

39 European Parliament, *Circular Economy: Definition, Importance and Benefits* (European Parliament 24 May 2023) <https://www.europarl.europa.eu/topics/en/article/20151201STO05603/circular-economy-definition-importance-and-benefits> accessed 13 July 2025.

40 Lenovo, *2024/25 Environmental, Social and Governance Report – Lenovo Group Limited* (Lenovo Group Limited 2025) <https://doc.irasia.com/listco/hk/lenovo/annual/2025/esr.pdf> accessed 13 July 2025.

41 Michelin, *Official Website* <https://www.michelin.com/en/> accessed 13 July 2025.

42 Steelcase, *The Power of Possibility: A Net-Zero Future Needs Us All* (Steelcase 2024) <https://www.steelcase.com/content/uploads/2024/06/Steelcase_Net-Zero-Transition-Plan.pdf> accessed 13 July 2025.

43 Huawei, *Official Website* (Huawei Technologies Co Ltd) <https://www.huawei.com/en/sustainability/sustainability-report> accessed 14 July 2025.

44 A Scott, 'From Push to Pull: Danone's Supply Chain Journey' (Supplychain360.io 19 August 2024) <https://supplychain360.io/danone-shifts-to-pull-based-supply-chain-model/> accessed 14 July 2025; Danone, *Official Website* <https://www.danone.com/> accessed 14 July 2025.

45 Cisco, 'Supply Chain Sustainability | CISCO ESG Reporting Hub' (www.cisco.com April 2025) <https://www.cisco.com/c/m/en_us/about/csr/esg-hub/supply-chain/sustainability.html> accessed 14 July 2025.

Chapter 13

Businesses and the transition

On the right trajectory

Aims:

- Sectoral impacts from transition and physical risks.
- Impact of the energy transition on individual sectors.
- Strategic levers and corporate action pathways: corporate clean energy purchasing.

It is easier for some companies than others to transition. A software company with limited physical assets will be able to transition to carbon neutrality much faster than a business in a hard-to-abate industry. ENN Energy Holdings is a Chinese company set up in the early 1990s in the northern city of Langfang which at the time had a population of less than one million, relatively small by China's standards. For about three decades, the company built a natural gas supply distribution business (see Figure 13.1). By the end of 2024, ENN had become a significant private company. It had revenues of 110 billion yuan ($15.4 billion) and had sold 33.8 billion cubic metres (1.19 trillion cubic feet) of natural gas to over 31 million households – similar to the whole of the United Kingdom, and over a quarter of a million commercial and industrial customers. In the late 2010s, management decided to take some early transition steps. It set up a new unit focused on clean energy generation, services, and solutions called Integrated Energy Business. The unit is focused on providing clean energy solutions such as renewables, energy storage, energy efficiency, and other low-carbon solutions, while leveraging digital technologies. In just five years, the new Integrated Energy Business segment contributed about 14 per cent, or over 15 billion yuan (S2.1 billion), to the company's revenues and is expected to continue to grow rapidly.

ENN's dynamic shift is an example that even companies in hard-to-abate industries can set a path for a progressive long-term transition. Understanding how corporations operate, invest, and create value in the global transition to net zero and an operationally and economically sustainable future can be examined through two separate lenses. First, understanding the addressable market and sector impact, particularly in transition-exposed sectors. Second is understanding the strategic levers and corporate action pathways. Corporate renewable energy purchasing serves as a case study to illustrate the latter concept.

Transition and businesses: impact on sectors

There is a distinct and tight correlation between the financial sector and corporations as financial institutions rely on securing business from corporations and corporations need

DOI: 10.4324/9781003666509-17

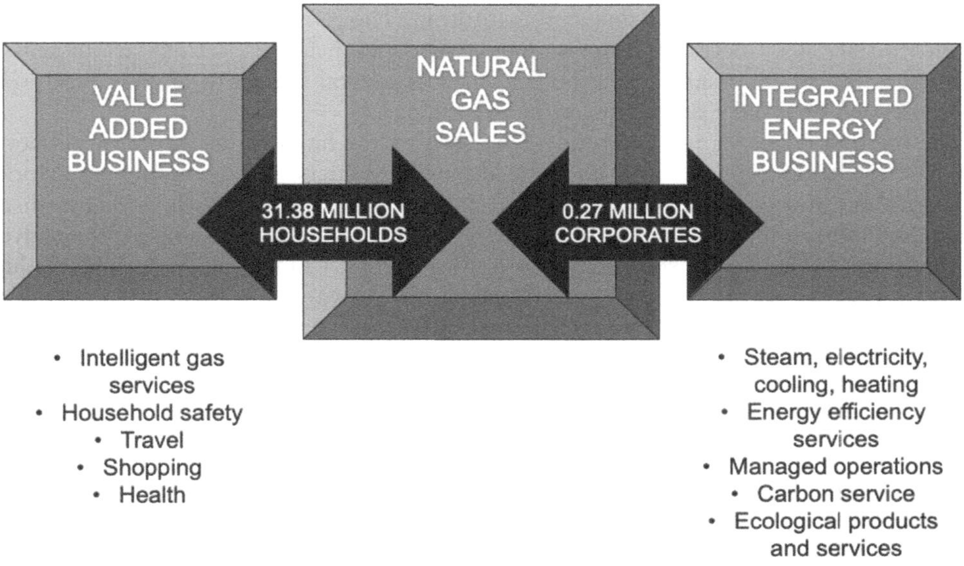

Figure 13.1 ENN Energy business growth focus

Source: ENN Energy Holdings Limited, 'ENN Energy 2024 Annual Results Presentation' (ENN Energy Holdings Limited 2025). Available at: https://doc.irasia.com/listco/hk/ennenergy/cpresent/pre250326.pdf accessed 17 July 2025.

the financial institutions for funding. From the financial sector's perspective, it is critical to consistently and continuously assess how clients are affected by the transition to net zero. Financial institutions principally focus on two types of climate risk, transition and physical risks. How are climate transition and physical risks defined? Why does the financial sector chiefly focus on these two types of climate risks? Which sectors are most or least impacted by these risks? What are some of the specific risks?

Broad sector impact

Climate-related transition risks are created by transitioning away from a high-carbon economy to a low-carbon one. An organisation must manage the process, adapting to internal and external pressures. During this process, the entity will have to successfully overcome a variety of changes in the space it operates. Changes in such areas as laws and regulations, market expectations and preferences, or technology. The company must adjust the way it conducts its business internally and externally. The uncertainty produced by the transition generates risks for the company as well as for the financial institution working with the company. Climate-related physical risks revolve around the physical impacts of climate change on the operations or physical assets of a business. They include extreme weather events as well as long-term variations in climate patterns. Climate change-related events can cause operational disruptions, physical damage, or property losses. An entity affected by such events faces financial loss or increased operational and financial costs, including borrowing costs and insurance expenses.

Financial institutions prioritise climate transition and physical risks in their assessment as they directly affect the financial performance and stability of a business. Such a threat to the business' creditworthiness, asset valuations, and investment returns in turn creates a material financial risk to the financial institution. The risks are both material and measurable and are also increasingly quantifiable. Also, financial institutions are increasingly under scrutiny by their supervising bodies, such as central banks, to have in place robust transition and physical risk assessment methodologies.

The methodologies can be internally generated by the financial institutions, or they can purchase the data from one of the many third-party providers such as Bloomberg, Moody's, Morningstar's Sustainalytics, or S&P Global. It is the same for corporations. They must formulate scenarios and set metrics for their planning. They can do it in-house if they have the resource capacity or purchase the data from third parties. Climate risk assessment is highly complex. It is a great interplay of a very large number of variables in a range of disciplines. They comprise environmental, financial, legal, market, technological, and many other factors. Also, many of the factors may be shifting and evolving with time and the assessment must be forward-looking in nature, further increasing layers of complexity. The added complexity for financial institutions is that specific sub-industries will comprise factors which are not applicable to other sub-industries.

There are a variety of approaches to selecting relevant sectors. None is perfect as they all have some strengths or weaknesses. One standard sector segmentation is the Global Industry Classification Standard, jointly developed by MSCI and S&P. The Global Industry Classification Standard is an 11-sector classification system, as of January 2025, mainly used for listed equities. The 11-sector classification includes 25 industry groups which include 74 industries which in turn include 163 sub-industries. The standards omit some economic sectors, such as agriculture, government, and services, for example. Despite these omissions, the Standard is widely used and respected. It is highly suited for snapshot-type analysis, such as determining which sectors are most impacted and which ones the least impacted, as examined next.

SECTOR	TRANSITION RISK IMPACT LEVEL	PHYSICAL RISK IMPACT LEVEL
ENERGY	HIGH	MEDIUM-HIGH
UTILITIES	MEDIUM-HIGH	MEDIUM-HIGH
CONSUMER STAPLES	LOW-MEDIUM	MEDIUM-HIGH
INDUSTRIALS	MEDIUM-HIGH	HIGH
MATERIALS	HIGH	MEDIUM
CONSUMER DISCRETIONARY	LOW-MEDIUM	LOW-MEDIUM
REAL ESTATE	MEDIUM-HIGH	HIGH
COMMUNICATION SERVICES	LOW	LOW-MEDIUM
INFORMATION TECHNOLOGY	LOW	LOW-MEDIUM
FINANCIALS	MEDIUM	LOW-MEDIUM
HEALTHCARE	LOW-MEDIUM	LOW-MEDIUM

MEDIUM-HIGH / HIGH
MEDIUM
LOW / LOW-MEDIUM

Figure 13.2 Sectoral climate risk assessment under a 2°C scenario by 2050

Source: Author (July 2025). Data aggregated from Bank of England, European Central Bank, Intergovernmental Panel on Climate Change, International Monetary Fund, MSCI, Network for Greening the Financial System, Organisation for Economic Co-operation and Development, S&P Global, Task Force on Climate-related Financial Disclosures, UNEP Finance Initiative, US Environmental Protection Agency, World Bank, and World Resources Institute.

Figure 13.2 is a sectoral climate risk assessment under a 2°C scenario by 2050 of just the 11 sectors to provide a broad view on the assessment. Transition-related risks and physical ones are assigned 'High', 'Medium', and 'Low'. As a great variety of sources was used, including the European Central Bank, the International Monetary Fund, MSCI, and many others, some of the ratings have been turned into ranges, such as medium-to-high or low-to-medium.

The broad summary is that four sectors have a 'high' level of transition and physical risk impact from climate change, including energy, industrials, materials, and utilities. Also ranked 'high' are real estate for transition risk and consumer staples for physical risk. Three sectors are rated 'medium' for both types of risks, including consumer discretionary, financials, and healthcare. Also rated 'medium' for transmission risk is consumer staples while for 'medium' physical risk communication services, information technology, and real estate are included. Finally, communication services and information technologies are rated 'low' for transition risk. Interestingly, none of the sources used rate any of the 11 sectors as having 'low' physical risk.

Transition and physical risks sector impact

When it comes to examining transition and physical risks to each of the 11 industries, there are some commonalities as well as industry-specific risks. Industries providing products may be exposed to carbon-related costs as a transition risk, for example. Facilities owning industries, be it a factory or a manufacturing plant, may be exposed to disruptions or damages from extreme weather events as a type of physical risk. So while there may be some overlap among the 11 industries, it is a value-added exercise to look at the risks for each of the 11 industries.

Energy

Transition risk: High. The profitability of the fossil fuel business could decline as operational costs could rise from carbon pricing mechanisms, emissions trading costs, or tighter regulatory standards in general. Regulation of the markets could make fossil fuel assets stranded and economically unviable. Fossil fuel cost competitiveness could be eroded by cheaper clean energy alternatives. High emissions activities could face legal or reputational risks as well as decarbonisation pressures from stakeholders.

Physical risk: Medium-High. Critical energy infrastructure, such as offshore platforms or refineries, could be damaged by extreme weather events such as storms and floods. Drought and water stress could affect the operations of thermal energy facilities. Coastal flooding and the rise of sea levels could impact offshore, nearshore, and coastal facilities. Higher temperatures could reduce the efficiency of equipment, such as operational heat stress.

Utilities

Transition risk: Medium-High. Fossil fuel generation could face regulatory pressure to decarbonise, to phase down or phase out assets, or increased compliance costs, including carbon pricing. Power network operators may face enhanced requirements to modernise their grid infrastructure. Distributed energy resources facilities, including microgrids, could disrupt markets or displace the traditional utility business model.

Physical risk: Medium-High. Extreme weather events could damage electric power generation, or transmission and distribution infrastructure droughts could impact fossil fuel power generation plants. Similar to the energy sector, coastal facilities could be affected by coastal flooding.

Consumer staples

Transition risk: Low-Medium. Higher supply chain costs, including carbon pricing, from the adoption of sustainable practices. Shift of consumer preference in favour of sustainable products. Rise in regulatory pressure and in regulatory compliance cost on emissions, ingredients, packaging, and the like. Reputational risks from unsustainable practices.

Physical risk: Low-Medium. Extreme weather may disrupt the food supply chain in a variety of ways, such as impacting crop yields and other agriculture-related disruptions, and transportation logistics. Beverage production, food processing, and agricultural raw material availability can be affected by water scarcity.

Industrials

Transition risk: Medium-High. Energy-intensive operations may face increasing carbon-related costs, particularly heavy industries. Regulatory requirements may force these industries to invest in equipment upgrades, process modifications, energy efficiency, on-site clean energy generation, and the like. They may have to adopt new technologies or processes which could disrupt their operations. Supply chains could be disrupted due to decarbonisation-related obligations. Revenues from a traditional high carbon industrial offering could decrease and sustainable competitors could gain market share.

Physical risk: High. Floods, storms, wildfires, and other extreme weather events could affect, or damage, facilities, especially those located in coastal areas. Heat stress could raise cooling costs or affect operations in other ways. Water-intensive manufacturing will suffer from water scarcity.

Materials

Transition risk: High. Carbon-related costs will rise for hard-to-abate industries such as chemicals, cement, or steel. Facilities unable to meet the stricter standards may become stranded assets. Operations will have to address tighter restrictions on emissions and waste. Supply chains will have to be adjusted to include more sustainable materials and processes.

Physical risk: Medium. Extreme weather events endanger facilities, such as damage from floods and in mining facilities. Water scarcity would put some limits on mineral, chemical, and other types of materials processing. Industrial infrastructures and supply chains could face disruptions or damage.

Consumer discretionary

Transition risk: Low-Medium. The sales volume and pattern of traditional products may be impacted by a shift in consumer demand towards sustainable products. Progressively stricter regulatory restrictions could affect product design and manufacturing.

Sustainability obligations may raise supply chain costs, and as the business transitions it may be increasingly exposed to reputational risks, including greenwashing concerns. Specific to the automotive industry, over the next one or two decades, a massive shift – from internal combustion engines to electric mobility – in the product they saw would have to take place.

Physical risk: Low-Medium. Extreme weather events could disrupt or damage supply chains, warehouses, distribution centres, retail facilities, and the like. Climate events impact the tourism and hospitality sectors. Temperature sharply differing from the seasonal average will affect product demand.

Real estate

Transition risk: Medium-High. Businesses may face higher construction or retrofit costs from regulatory mandates for green building certifications, including energy efficiency requirements, or carbon pricing. Buildings unable to meet low or zero-carbon requirements may become stranded assets.

Physical risk: High. Extreme climate events may not only damage properties but also reduce their desirability and insurability. Such events may also cause infrastructure stress, which could manifest as weakening foundations and subsidence, causing permanent structural damage. The events would negatively affect property valuations and deter investment.

Communication services

Transition risk: Low. Businesses will face significant transition costs as they must adapt existing technological and digital infrastructure, including data centres, to regulatory-mandated low or zero-carbon standards. Potentially, part of the infrastructure may become obsolete. Businesses must invest in on-site clean power generation or structure corporate clean energy procurement. They will also be challenged in monitoring suppliers' and service providers' carbon footprints.

Physical risk: Low-Medium. Increased or added investment to ensure the technological and digital infrastructure is climate resilient. Undersea and on-land cable, wireless transmission towers, data centres, and other assets are vulnerable to extreme weather events.

Information technology

Transition risk: Low. Higher operating expense from carbon footprint reduction and e-waste compliance. Added costs from making information technology hardware energy-efficient, low to zero carbon, and sustainable.

Physical risk: Low-Medium. Components supply disruptions from global supply chains. Climate events affecting power supply which in turn would negatively impact cloud services, the operations of data centres, and other information technology infrastructure.

Financials

Transition risk: Medium. Exposure to stranded assets of clients in hard-to-abate industries. Regulatory, litigation, or reputational risks for financing emissions – financing clients whose business generates high emissions.

Physical risk: Low-Medium. Insurance losses from claims from climate-related damage. Decline in the value of collateral and assets, or even credit losses, from clients negatively impacted by extreme climate events.

Healthcare

Transition risk: Low-Medium. Expenses incurred in transitioning energy-intensive medical equipment or equipment for the manufacture of pharmaceuticals and medical devices. Higher supply chain costs from the shift to sustainable sourcing.

Physical risk: Low-Medium. Extreme temperatures creating infrastructure stress, including the storage of medical supplies, medical equipment, or pharmaceuticals.

Climate opportunities

The transition to net zero of course also provides companies in sectors in the 11 industries with a vast array of opportunities, both in the short and long term. Four subsectors, among the many, provide a snapshot of the potential (Figure 13.3).

In the services and solutions providers category, there are many businesses that actually didn't even exist a few years ago. Others have just become more complex as they have adopted digitalisation. They include behavioural energy optimisation, carbon accounting, decarbonisation advisory, clean energy financing and advisory, demand response aggregators, energy efficiency, energy management, energy-as-a-service (EAAS), green power procurement, smart grid solutions, and virtual power plant (VPP). All of these solution providers play a critical role in strengthening the benefits of clean energy. For example, energy management platforms and smart grid technology companies optimise energy use, integrate distributed energy, and implement demand response. This leads to more reliable, cost-effective, and efficient systems.

The energy-related owners and operators category includes such areas as Carbon Capture, Utilisation and Storage, distribution networks, energy storage infrastructure, EV

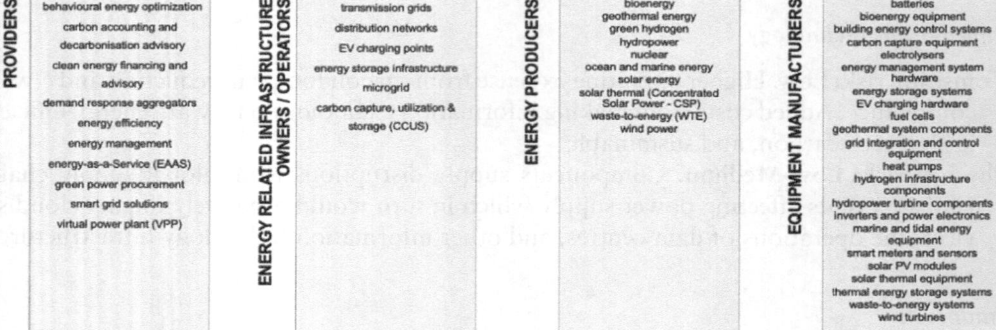

Figure 13.3 Sample of sectors benefiting from the energy transition

Source: Author, original chart design (July 2025).

charging points, microgrids, and transmission grids. The modernisation and expansion of energy infrastructure are absolutely critical to the transition to low carbon. This has opened vast opportunities to a variety of infrastructure owners and operators not limited to the traditional transmission and distribution network businesses. A striking example is the surge in EV adoption which has demanded extensive public and private investments in charging networks. This has also fuelled investment opportunities in data analytics and digital services related to the EV charging infrastructure.

The energy producers segment includes segments such as bioenergy, geothermal energy, green hydrogen, hydropower, nuclear, ocean and marine energy, solar energy, solar thermal (Concentrated Solar Power – CSP), waste-to-energy (WTE), and wind power. As illustrated several times, the global shift from fossil fuels to clean energy has boosted the growth and provided vast opportunities to clean energy producers. What is regarded as conventional clean energy, solar, and wind power should continue to account for the bulk of additional capacity, at least through 2025. Businesses in this segment have greatly benefited from energy demand from a variety of sources including corporations and municipalities who have committed to decarbonise. One estimate puts the value of the global renewable energy market at over $1.2 trillion in 2023.

Finally, the clean energy equipment manufacturers category includes a vast array of sectors such as batteries, bioenergy equipment, building energy control systems, CCS equipment, electrolysers, energy management system hardware, energy storage systems, EV charging hardware, fuel cells, geothermal system components, grid integration and control equipment, heat pumps, hydrogen infrastructure components, hydropower turbine components, inverters and power electronics, marine and tidal energy equipment, smart meters and sensors, solar PV modules, solar thermal equipment, thermal energy storage systems, waste-to-energy systems, and wind turbines. The growth in the other above-mentioned subsectors has opened the door to a flood of opportunities for clean energy related equipment manufacturers. In some cases, the attraction to the business has caused over-investment in some segments, especially in China. For example, estimates by the China Association of Automobile Manufacturers and some analysts put the number of Chinese companies producing and selling electric vehicles at over 100 as of June 2025. Although the top manufacturers control the lion's share of the market, with the top three accounting for well over 50 per cent.

Corporate clean energy procurement

There are many strategies that businesses may enact to lower their carbon footprints. The most common approaches revolve around using energy from clean sources instead of fossil fuel ones. Three of the most common and widely used strategies are self-generation, power purchases, and carbon credits (Figure 13.4).

For the self-generation strategy, the business can procure the energy from its own on-site clean energy generation facilities. It can install at its own premises energy sources including rooftop solar PV, ground-mounted solar PV, wind turbines, and other renewable generation technologies as well as using energy storage. The facility may be operated by the business itself or by a third party, but the business retains full ownership.

For the power purchase strategy, the business can directly purchase the energy from a clean energy generation facility owned by a third-party through Corporate Power Purchase Agreements (CPPAs). Some businesses may also invest some capital into the third-party

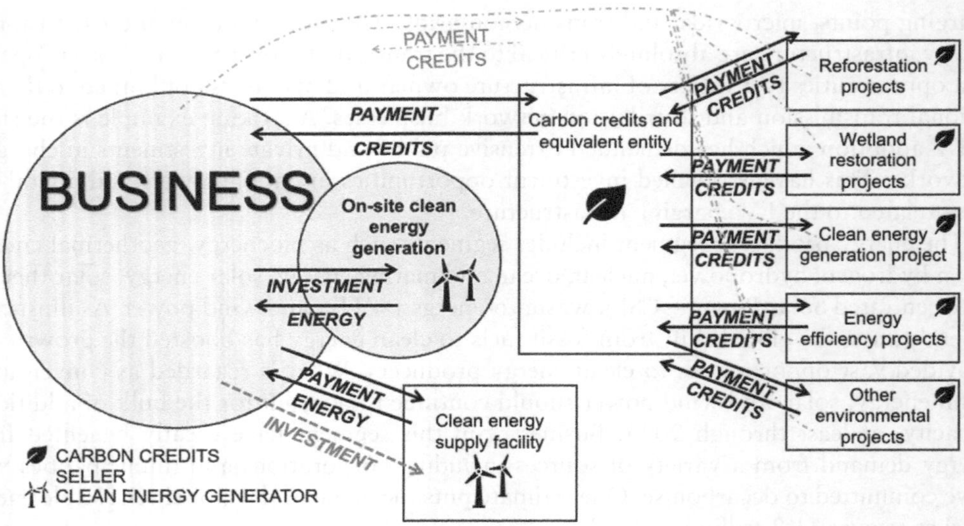

Figure 13.4 Corporate clean energy procurement possibilities
Source: Author, original chart design (July 2025).

clean energy generation facility. A derivative strategy, or financial variant, of CPPAs are Virtual Power Purchase Agreements (VPPAs). This financial transaction involves the buyer buying a certain amount of the production output of the clean energy generation facility, but the output is not consumed by the buyer, rather the output is sold onto the wholesale market.

For the carbon offsets strategy, in order for the business to reduce or completely offset its own carbon footprint, it can purchase carbon credits, or equivalent (such as Renewable Energy Credits or RECs) through a third-party entity selling such credits. This third-party entity purchases the credits from carbon offsetting project, including reforestation, wetland restoration, clean energy generation, energy efficiency, or other environmental projects. Some businesses, especially large corporations and multinationals, may also directly purchase carbon credits, or equivalent, from an environmental project.

These corporate procurement strategies are a critical element of support to the energy transition. They direct capital to the clean energy generation ecosystem, including equipment manufacturers, energy producers, and service providers. Demand response aggregators, an example of a service provider, coordinate and sell reduced energy use by arranging with users to lower their demand during peak times. All three of the corporate procurement strategies have been growing exponentially in terms of volume and value over the past few years. Having discussed the various forms and mechanics of corporate power and carbon credits purchasing, the direct procurement of clean energy can be examined in more detail as a brief case study.

Corporate power purchase agreements

The two most common ways businesses shift to using clean energy for their operations from fossil fuels are by generating the energy themselves or by purchasing the energy from a third party.

An increasing number of companies are opting to build, own, and operate their own clean energy generation solutions. The capacity of such generation will depend on the space available on-site, or in some cases, near-site – using the premises of an adjacent business. There are typically one or more motivations for such investment. The company may want to fully or partially guarantee the supply of energy. It can also build more capacity than it needs, so that the energy surplus can be sold to the power grid or other parties, creating a new revenue stream. Another motivation could be for cost savings because the price of the energy supply available is too expensive, or if the price is too volatile which hinders the company's mid- to long-term cost planning. A model sometimes used is for a company to build and own the facility but assign its operation to another party at a fee. Finally, the clean energy output can reduce the company's own carbon footprint.

In Asia, an example of self-generation clean energy investment is by French multinational Sidel, a global market leader in packaging solutions for various materials. Sidel installed a 2.1 MW solar PV system on the rooftop of its Beijing plant. This on-site clean energy facility is expected to generate about 4.4 GWh of electricity annually. The output will be able to meet about 60 per cent of the plant's daily operational electricity requirements. The company also said that the facility had adopted a 'self-consumption with surplus feed-in' model. This involves the Beijing facility feeding back to the municipal grid 35 per cent of the power produced using the smart power grid network, including digital metering. The amount of power fed back is deducted from the amount of power sold to the plant.[1]

In Europe, an example of an on-site facility is by digital transformation of energy management and automation by the French multinational Schneider Electric. At a new manufacturing facility in Scarborough in the United Kingdom, Schneider said in September 2024 that it had built an advanced rooftop solar energy system occupying 50 per cent of the facility's roof and supplying 30 per cent of its energy needs. Schneider also adopted other energy reduction strategies at the Scarborough facility, such as intelligent building management systems, which will improve energy efficiency and reduce the amount of energy consumed.[2]

In North America, one similar investment is by Google for its Google Bay View Campus real estate project in Mountain View, California, completed in 2022. The facility includes an on-site solar rooftop array made up of 90,000 silver solar panels across four buildings with an installed capacity of about 7 MW. The solar PV system meets about 40 per cent of Bay View's electricity requirements.[3]

One of the many tools for businesses to transition is corporate power purchase agreements or corporate PPAs. They offer many advantages for both buyers and sellers of clean energy. The buyer will have an assured amount of green energy with the fixed price ensuring cost certainty. The seller will have a secure offtake for its output translating into assured cash flows and higher project bankability. Corporate PPAs are contractual arrangements between an energy generation facility and a business. In the context of the energy transition, the source of the electricity from the energy generation facility is clean energy. Key contractual terms in PPAs include the volume of energy to be purchased, the price, and the delivery risk (see Figure 13.5). PPAs broadly come in three different separate formats.[4]

The most common format is the Physical PPA, sometimes called Sleeved PPA, Direct PPA, Back-to-Back PPA, and Wheeling PPA. Physical PPA may have accounted for as much as 50 per cent of Corporate PPAs in 2024 according to some reports. It involves a direct, long-term contract for the delivery of energy between the power generation facility and the corporate buyer. The purchaser commits to buying the energy at a set price throughout the term of the contract, which is typically between 10 and 20 years. In most cases, an

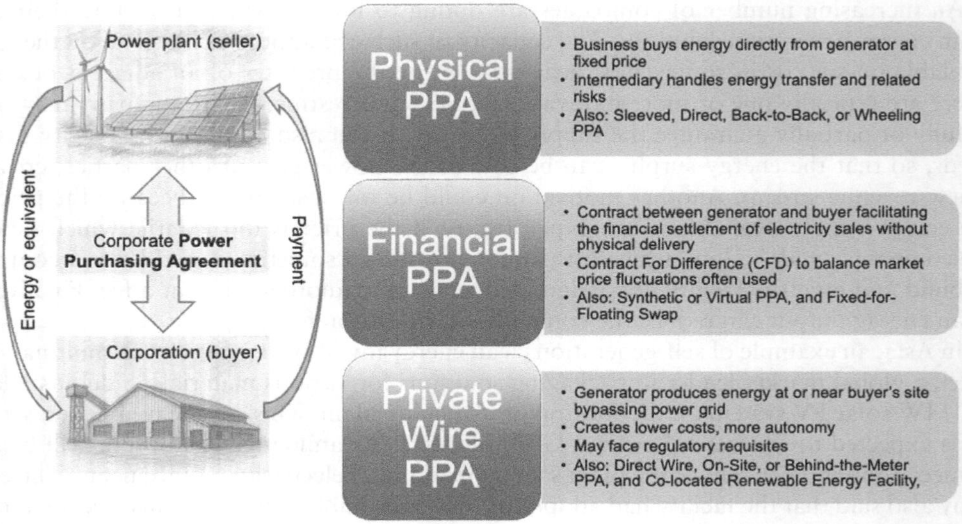

Figure 13.5 Types of corporate power purchasing agreements

Source: Author, original chart design (July 2025). Source of background image OpenAI, https://chat.openai.com accessed. Basis of physical, financial and private wire PPA details: DLA Piper, 'Corporate Power Purchase Agreements' (Dlapiper.com 2025). Available at: https://intelligence.dlapiper.com/corporateppa/ accessed 27 July 2025.

intermediary is needed, usually the electricity grid network, to ensure the transfer of the energy from the seller to the buyer. This process is commonly known as a 'sleeving arrangement'. The intermediary ensures that the energy from the seller is integrated into the buyer's existing supply as well as making sure that any additional electricity requirement is met. The price is commonly fixed given that the cost of production of the clean energy is not much exposed to fluctuations. Sometimes the contract includes some form of price indexation which can be constructed in a variety of ways such as, for example, having a certain percentage of the price, say 20 per cent, rising at a rate of the annual national inflation rate.[5]

Another format is the Financial PPA, also known as Synthetic PPA, Virtual PPA, and Fixed-for-Floating Swap. This kind of non-physical PPA could have been responsible for over 40 per cent of transaction in 2024, based on various reports. Financial PPAs do not involve the physical delivery of energy. The output from the clean energy facility is sold to the grid network. The pricing is based on one of the two approaches. One is by the difference between the agreed strike price and the prevailing market rates. The other is at the market price less a discount. The Fixed-for-Floating Swap involves a Contract-for-Difference. In such contracts, both parties make payments to each other depending on whether the market price ends up higher or lower than what the two originally agreed. Financial PPAs help with sidestepping complicated arrangements of physical energy exchange.[6]

The third format is the Private Wire PPA, which can also be referred to as Direct Wire PPA, On-Site PPA, Behind-the-Meter PPA, and Co-located Renewable Energy Facility. These PPAs comprise clean energy facilities located at, or near, the site of operations of the buyer with a direct electric power wired connection. It means that the energy is consumed on-site, bypassing the electric power grid. The challenge to such agreements is whether there is a suitable amount of space for the clean energy facility at the site, going through whatever planning constraints may exist in the buyer's particular jurisdiction, such as regulatory environmental requirements, for example. The major benefit of Private Wire PPAs is that the corporation buying the energy can utilise its own property to supply its operations.[7]

Advancing corporate clean energy procurement

Corporate clean energy procurement is increasingly being adopted by companies as part of their net-zero commitments strategies. The number of deals and overall kWh amount is growing at a healthy pace, and the momentum will steadily grow in the coming years. Calculating data compiled by research firm BloombergNEF,[8] corporate power purchase agreement volumes increased at a compound annual growth rate of about 27 per cent in the five years to 2023 (see Figure 13.6). The annual rate for markets outside the Americas was 39 per cent while that of the Americas was 18 per cent. The share of the total from the Americas was higher than that of other markets in the first four years, averaging at about 66 per cent. In 2023, the share of other markets overtook that of the Americas for the first time in the period, reaching 55 per cent or over 25 GW. This trend will accelerate in the next few years, especially given the Trump administration's lack of enthusiasm for clean energy projects.

An important element for the growth of corporate clean energy procurement is on-the-ground advocacy. This advocacy involves active engagement and support from the local level up. It is about ensuring that there is strong three-way cooperation between governments, financial institutions, and corporations. Perhaps nowhere is this more important than in the Asia Pacific region, given its size and because corporate clean energy procurement in this region has lagged Europe and North America. Various entities, such as NGOs and industry associations, are putting in efforts to accelerate the adoption of procurement

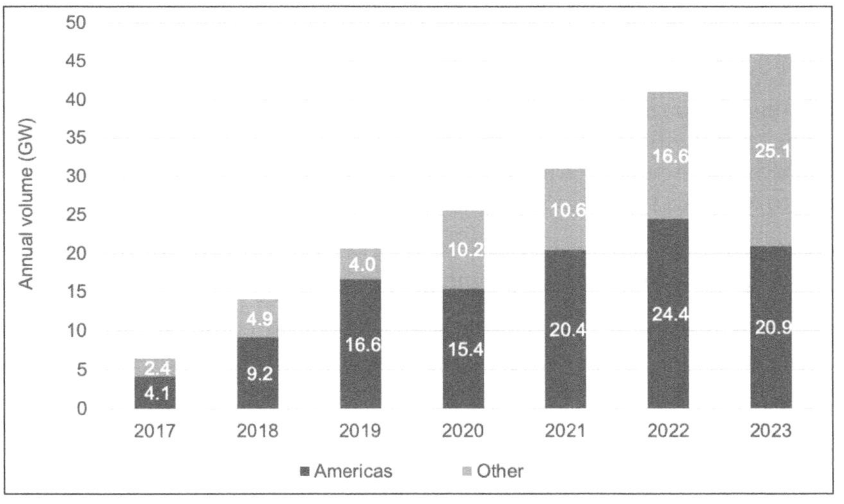

Figure 13.6 Corporate power purchase agreement volumes, by region

Notes: Chart is for off-site, publicly disclosed deals only and may be subject to change as more information is made publicly available. Capacity is in GW DC.

Source: BloombergNEF, 'Corporate Clean Power Buying Grew 12 per cent to New Record in 2023, according to BloombergNEF' (BloombergNEF 13 February 2024). Available at: https://about.bnef.com/blog/corporate-clean-power-buying-grew-12-to-new-record-in-2023-according-to-bloombergnef/ accessed 16 March 2024.

schemes all over the world. The role of these entities is fundamental to ensuring that the three-way conversation is effective and that their work should be understood and supported.

One such organisation is the Asia Clean Energy Coalition, or ASEC, which focuses on the whole Asia Pacific region. It was launched at the COP 27 in November 2022 by three nonprofit organisations: The Climate Group, the Global Wind Energy Council, and the World Energy Resource Institute. The three organisations work in various ways with business, finance, governments, and others on sustainable and governance conduct on various areas of climate change, renewable energy, sustainability practices, or others. Founding members involved tech companies like Amazon, Apple, Cisco, Google, and Meta, energy utilities including Enel Green Power, Iberdrola, Mainstream Renewable Power, Ørsted, and Sembcorp, as well as consumer products companies, such as Ingka Group (the largest IKEA franchisee), Nike, and Samsung Electronics.[9]

ACEC was the only regional platform dedicated to corporate renewable energy procurement as of March 2024, according to Programme Director Suji Kang.[10] Kang highlighted that the type of procurement differs among countries. Some have one or more of the different mechanisms found in the United States or Europe, and they are well implemented. Some have none as yet. For example, in Southeast Asia, CPPAs are only available in Singapore. Kang also underlined that corporations in general are ramping up their decarbonisation efforts leading to higher demand for high-quality clean energy projects. This is a challenge. The supply of such projects is limited, for some, the output price is too high, and there is often a convoluted regulatory environment.[11] These are some of the reasons for organisations such as ACEC being crucial to the development of corporate clean energy procurement.

Part of the work is to produce expert analysis reports around the policy priorities identified by ACEC's members. The analysis and the data offer governments tools to craft policy. The NGO had five priority markets, Indonesia, Japan, Korea, Singapore, and Vietnam, as of March 2024. In Indonesia, for example, expanding the procurement options available, which are currently limited to RECs and rooftop solar, is being explored with authorities. In Japan, ACEC is working on further optimising the regulatory environment, including offshore wind zoning and renewable energy prices issues. In Korea, it is working on unlocking renewable energy potential in general and also on enhancing the green premium programme and PPAs. The work includes setting up high-level round tables so that all stakeholders may discuss how to advance the various issues.[12]

One view of corporates decarbonising strategy: Google

Corporates decarbonising through purchasing clean energy could be illustrated through the experience of tech giant Alphabet, the parent company of Google. Alphabet is a massive and thus complex company by many measures. It posted revenues in excess of $350 billion in 2024, and its stock market capitalisation averaged over $2.1 trillion in the first half of 2025. Google started its clean energy procurement journey in 2010. It was not quite a pioneer but definitely one of the most ambitious companies of its size. It has set for itself a goal to have carbon-free energy 24 hours a day by 2030. Google said that it was one of the first companies with an objective to match 100 per cent of the global annual energy consumption with energy from clean sources. Specifically, its objective is not one of using procurement plus offsetting. It is one of having all of its operations globally powered by carbon-free energy sources within each grid where it has a presence every hour of every day.

The company stressed that such hourly matching is complex and technically challenging work when compared to annual matching. In 2023 alone, the tech giant signed about 4 GW worth of agreements for clean energy. For the same year, the company kept its carbon-free energy use at 64 per cent on an hourly basis across all of its data centres and offices, as well as over 90 per cent in ten grid regions.[13]

Focusing on only Google's Asia Pacific region procurement activities, the company has said that it has tailored its clean energy strategy to the very different market structures and specific resources availability. A critical approach has been to address a series of region-specific energy transition-related challenges. The challenges include the many diverse grid networks, country-specific ways to access to clean energy procurement, and the collection and transparency of the data, as granular data is essential to advance the energy transition. Google has devoted a great amount of effort in advocacy, communication, and education. For example, it co-authored a report 'The Role of High Impact Utility Green Tariffs, Expanding Clean Energy Procurement Options in the Asia Pacific Region' together with two industry groups, the Clean Energy Buyers Association and the Asia Clean Energy Coalition. The report analysed utility green tariffs as a voluntary programme which would enable businesses to purchase clean energy and associated energy attribute certificates directly from the electric power utilities. This would offer price stability and encourage new projects with transparent and flexible pricing.

Google has already announced long-term power purchase agreements for about 275 MW of new clean energy capacity across several different jurisdictions, including Australia, India, Japan, and Singapore. It has stayed away from a one-size-fits-all approach that it believes is ineffective. The company adopts specific solutions for each of the different energy markets which have different regulatory environments and resource landscapes. For example, in Australia and India, Google operates cloud regions rather than only in data centres. There the company set up multiparty and multi-project agreements for solar-wind hybrid generation plants and other clean energy sources. This approach enables the developers of the projects to secure the financing they need because of Google's long-term part purchase commitments. In Japan, Google found that there is a limited amount of land to build ground-mounted solar systems. The company aggregates 60 MW of clean energy from a number of small-scale solar projects. The projects maybe from repurposed golf courses as well as parking lots. In Singapore, it has signed an offtake commitment with a first-of-its-kind sustainable biomass power plant which processes waste wood and includes pilot Carbon Capture, Utilisation and Storage technology. In Taiwan, Google made a capital investment together with NGP (a BlackRock portfolio company) to support the development of a 1 GW pipeline of new solar projects.

Notes

1 Sidel, *Sidel Parma Site Boosts Sustainability with Cutting-Edge Solar Panel Installation* (Sidel 2023) <https://www.sidel.com/media/dryaxk1c/press-release-solar-panels-26062023.pdf> accessed 25 July 2025.

2 Schneider Electric, *Schneider Electric to Invest £42 Million in New Manufacturing Site in North Yorkshire* (Schneider Electric 9 September 2024) <https://www.se.com/uk/en/about-us/newsroom/news/press-releases/schneider-electric-to-invest-%C2%A342-million-in-new-manufacturing-site-in-north-yorkshire-66db07d60c7ec5dc0d0ceb11> accessed 25 July 2025.

3 Google, 'Https://Realestate.withgoogle.com/Bayview/' (Withgoogle.com May 2022) <https://realestate.withgoogle.com/bayview/#/solutions/dragonscale-solar> accessed 25 July 2025.

4 DLA Piper, 'Corporate Power Purchase Agreements' (Dlapiper.com 2025) <https://intelligence.dlapiper.com/corporateppa/> accessed 27 July 2025.
5 DLA Piper, 'Corporate Power Purchase Agreements' (Dlapiper.com 2025) <https://intelligence.dlapiper.com/corporateppa/> accessed 27 July 2025.
6 DLA Piper, 'Corporate Power Purchase Agreements' (Dlapiper.com 2025) <https://intelligence.dlapiper.com/corporateppa/> accessed 27 July 2025.
7 DLA Piper, 'Corporate Power Purchase Agreements' (Dlapiper.com 2025) <https://intelligence.dlapiper.com/corporateppa/> accessed 27 July 2025.
8 BloombergNEF, 'Corporate Clean Power Buying Grew 12 per cent to New Record in 2023, according to BloombergNEF' *BloombergNEF* (13 February 2024) <https://about.bnef.com/blog/corporate-clean-power-buying-grew-12-to-new-record-in-2023-according-to-bloombergnef/> accessed 16 March 2024.
9 Asia Clean Energy Coalition, 'The Coalition – Asia Clean Energy Coalition Media Site' (asiacleanenergycoalition.com) <https://asiacleanenergycoalition.com/en/the-coalition.html> accessed 17 March 2024.
10 The Asia Climate Finance Podcast, 'Ep42 Boosting Corporate Clean Energy Purchases in Asia, Ft Suji Kang (Asia Clean Energy Coalition)' (www.buzzsprout.com 14 March 2024) <https://www.buzzsprout.com/1951932/episodes/14683672-ep42-boosting-corporate-clean-energy-purchases-in-asia-ft-suji-kang-asia-clean-energy-coalition> accessed 17 March 2024.
11 The Asia Climate Finance Podcast, 'Ep42 Boosting Corporate Clean Energy Purchases in Asia, Ft Suji Kang (Asia Clean Energy Coalition)' (www.buzzsprout.com 14 March 2024) <https://www.buzzsprout.com/1951932/episodes/14683672-ep42-boosting-corporate-clean-energy-purchases-in-asia-ft-suji-kang-asia-clean-energy-coalition> accessed 17 March 2024.
12 The Asia Climate Finance Podcast, 'Ep42 Boosting Corporate Clean Energy Purchases in Asia, Ft Suji Kang (Asia Clean Energy Coalition)' (www.buzzsprout.com 14 March 2024) <https://www.buzzsprout.com/1951932/episodes/14683672-ep42-boosting-corporate-clean-energy-purchases-in-asia-ft-suji-kang-asia-clean-energy-coalition> accessed 17 March 2024.
13 The Asia Climate Finance Podcast, 'Ep58 A Corporate Leader Driving Asia's Energy Transition, ft. Giorgio Fortunato, Google' (www.buzzsprout.com 13 January 2025) <https://theasiaclimatefinancepodcast.buzzsprout.com/1951932/episodes/16378414-ep58-a-corporate-leader-driving-asias-energy-transition-ft-giorgio-fortunato-google> accessed 27 July 2025.

Chapter 14

The real world of corporate transition

> **Aims:**
>
> - Companies incorporation of climate considerations into their operational and strategic plans.
> - Transition paths and strategies though three case studies in utility, financial, and ICT sectors.
> - Wider impacts and implications of corporate transitions on other economic sectors and the economy.

Companies all over the world are incorporating climate elements to their operational plans and business strategies. The motivations range from simply having to follow local regulations, to being risk averse to corporations with visionary senior leadership wanting to be ahead of the curve and wanting to be among the first to grab opportunities created by the global transition to net zero. To illustrate the variety of approaches three sectors are closely examined. First is the electric power utility sector because of its large contribution to GHG emissions and because of the central role the sector plays in supporting one of the mega trends created by the transition, electrification. The company selected for an in depth sector case study is Italian multinational utility Enel. The second sector chosen is financial services and banking. Its GHG emissions impact is minimal. At the same time, its role in financing the transition is central given its position of great influence on its corporate clients. The institution selected is the Industrial and Construction Bank of China, the world's largest bank by assets, headquartered in the world's second largest economy. The third and last sector is the information and technology sector. The ICT sector also is not a major emitter, but digitalisation is a key enabler of the transition leading the sector to be instrumental for change. The corporate case study is Google, one of the largest companies in the sector and a one of the world's leading technology companies driving the transition from a digital perspective.

Electric power utility sector

Sector profile

The electric power utility sector is the largest GHG emissions contributor in the world by a significant margin. The share of global emissions from electric power generation is

DOI: 10.4324/9781003666509-18

estimated to be between 25 and 30 per cent, a broad range as different organisations have different calculation methodologies. Sector emissions are driven by the large contribution from power generation from fossil fuel sources. These fuels accounted for about 59.2 per cent of all electricity output worldwide in 2024 according to independent think tank Ember.[1] Thermal coal was responsible for 34.1 per cent in total, while natural gas made up 22.4 per cent of the total, and other fossil fuels, chiefly oil, had a 2.8 per cent share. The amount in 2024 was 7.3 percentage points lower than that of 2015 when the contribution was 66.5 per cent, a percentage which has been progressively declining since 2013, with the exception of 2021, calculates Ember (see Figure 14.1).

One approach to evaluating the transition path and future trajectory of companies in the electric power utility sector is to analyse publicly listed entities. These utilities have to report details of their climate strategies, depending on the jurisdiction. However, there is one notable aspect to the utility sector that limits a comprehensive picture. There is a significant proportion of operating companies around the world, potentially up to half, that are not listed publicly, many of them state-owned. In some cases, one may get a glimpse of these non-listed utilities through a listed subsidiary. For example, Huaneng Power International, listed on the Hong Kong and Shanghai stock exchanges, had a total installed power generation capacity of 145.1 GW as at the end of 2024. It represented 54 per cent of China Huaneng Group, its unlisted parent, whose total capacity was 269.3 GW. In effect, public access to detailed insights is limited to 54 per cent of the group's transition trajectory.

The total stock market capitalisation of the top 15 electric power utility companies was $1.1 trillion. Seven of the 15 were headquartered in the United States (see Figure 14.2). The remainder are based in China, France, Germany, India, Italy, Saudi Arabia, Spain, and the UAE. All 15 electric power companies have carbon neutrality pledges. Among the 15, only two have net-zero targets beyond 2050. China Yangtze Power's objective is aligned with that of the Chinese government which is looking at carbon neutrality before 2060. India's NTPC is also aligned with the national target which is currently 2070. All of these top 15 utilities have publicly declared sustainability pledges. Importantly, all of the companies own and operate clean energy generation facilities in their asset portfolio and have plans to further invest in more such facilities. Typically there is a good level of transparency as their initiatives are typically easily found on their respective websites, for example.

FUEL TYPE	Terawatt-hours (2024)	Percentage (2024)	*Percentage (2015)*
Coal	10,542	34.1	*38.7*
Gas	6,892	22.3	*23.1*
Other fossil	875	2.8	*4.7*
Fossill fuel sub total	**18,308**	**59.2**	***66.5***
Hydro	4,408	14.3	*16.2*
Nuclear	2,778	9.0	*10.6*
Wind	2,503	8.1	*3.5*
Solar	2,129	6.9	*1.1*
Bioenergy	700	2.3	*2.0*
Other renewables	89	0.3	*0.3*
Clean energy sub total	**12,607**	**40.8**	***33.5***
Power generation total	**30,914**	**100.0**	***100.0***

Figure 14.1 Global electric power generation

Source: Ember, 'Electricity Data Explorer | Ember' (Ember 5 June 2025). Available at https://ember-energy.org/data/electricity-data-explorer/?chart=single_year&metric=pct_share accessed 9 August 2025.

ELECTRIC POWER UTILITY	STOCK SYMBOL	COUNTRY OF INCORPORATION	CAPITALISATION ($, billion)	NET ZERO TARGET (yes/no + year)	SUSTAINABILITY OBJECTIVES (yes/no)	CLEAN ENERGY FACILITIES (yes/no)
NextEra Energy, Inc	NEE	United States	144,974	Yes, 2045	Yes	Yes
Iberdrola, SA	IBE.MC	Spain	117,567	Yes, 2040	Yes	Yes
Constellation Energy Corp	CEG	United States	106,803	Yes, 2040	Yes	Yes
The Southern Co	SO	United States	104,494	Yes, 2050	Yes	Yes
Duke Energy Corp	DUK	United States	95,533	Yes, 2050	Yes	Yes
China Yangtze Power Co, Ltd	600900.SS	China	94,967	N/A (China 2060)	Yes	Yes
Enel SpA	ENEL.MI	Italy	90,365	Yes, 2040	Yes	Yes
ENGIE SA	ENGI.PA	France	53,648	Yes, 2045	Yes	Yes
Dominion Energy, Inc	D	United States	51,517	Yes, 2050	Yes	Yes
EON SE	EOAN.DE	Germany	48,195	Yes, 2040	Yes	Yes
ACWA Power Co SJSC	2082.SR	Saudi Arabia	44,931	Yes, 2050	Yes	Yes
Xcel Energy Inc	XEL	United States	42,375	Yes, 2050	Yes	Yes
Entergy Corp	ETR	United States	40,029	Yes, 2050	Yes	Yes
NTPC Ltd	NTPC.NS	India	36,790	N/A (India 2070)	Yes	Yes
Dubai Electricity and Water Authority PJSC	DEWA.AE	United Arab Emirates	37,164	Yes, 2050 (UAE)	Yes	Yes
Total market capitilisation of top 15			**1,109,353**			

Figure 14.2 Electric power utility sector decarbonisation

Notes: N/A = The company's principal shareholder is the national government. Although the company itself has not publicly declared a net-zero target, its respective government has: China has committed to carbon neutrality by 2060, and India by 2070. It is therefore reasonable to infer that the company aligns with the national objective.

Source: Author (August 2025).

The electric power utility companies' climate strategies and decarbonisation have significant cross-sectoral influence on other economic sectors. Three examples of such impact are lower-cost power, industry decarbonisation-wide, and power grid stability.

Lower-cost, stable-price power

In many power markets, today electricity from solar and wind sold to commercial and industrial users can be cheaper than that from fossil fuels, including the cost of transmitting and distributing the power. In some regions where these mainstream clean energy sources have an increasingly dominating position in the local electric power grid, unit cost of power to consumers can be 10 per cent or cheaper.

One of many examples is Spain and Portugal. The two Iberian power markets have strong clean energy profiles and some of the cheapest cost of renewable energy and green hydrogen production in the European region, consultancy McKinsey argues.[2] The abundant solar resource translated into solar power costs which are 20 to 25 per cent cheaper than in Central Europe. Wind and hydro resources are also well placed cost-wise. This results into a 15 to 20 per cent cost advantage in the production of green hydrogen compared to Central Europe. Also, the consultancy analysis concluded that Spanish electric power prices for industrial users were 20 per cent lower than the EU average, partly because of the mainstream renewable energy resource.

Also industrial users, such as an automotive manufacturing plant, can sign a long-term power purchasing agreement with a clean energy producer. Such plant would benefit from stable and predictable energy prices. It would avoid the many power price fluctuations from grids heavily using thermal coal or natural gas, two fuels whose price can fluctuate enormously.

Industry decarbonisation

Utilities' increasing production of clean energy is of great help and importance for the lowering of the carbon footprint of a variety of industries. These industries can avoid having to commit capital up front to invest in their own clean energy facilities. Producers of construction materials and other high-carbon emitters can lower their emissions when they use green energy instead of fossil fuel-based electricity, for example. One of many examples is pharmaceutical giant Pfizer who pledged carbon neutrality by 2030. One of Pfizer's strategies is to cut direct emissions 46 per cent and purchase 100 per cent of the electricity it consumes from renewable energy sources.[3] Decarbonisation from consuming clean energy is particularly important for the hard-to-abate industrial sectors such as chemicals, cement, and steel.

Power grid stability

It is important for power markets with a high percentage of renewable-energy production to have decentralised electric power grids. Renewable energy generation is typically not in one single concentrated area. Rather they are most often distributed in a variety of locations. Decentralisation of the power grid allows for an effective and efficient integration of clean energy resources and will be enhanced by being less dependent on a few large power plants. At the same time, it will boost the reliance and the reliability of the power supply. Decentralised grids also reduce transmission losses typically associated with long transmission lines. Such grids are more flexible and adaptable, especially if the clean energy is coupled with energy storage, to changing demand patterns, including sudden surges caused by unexpected temperature changes. Higher resilience and stable supply are of great value to electricity consumers, from hospitals to data centres.

Electric power utility sector transition journey case study: Enel

Italian utility Enel is an interesting case study in the electric power utility sector corporate transitioning. Among the 15 largest companies by market capitalisation, only two of them may be considered as multinational, France's ENGIE and Enel. The key difference between the two is that ENGIE's business has evolved from a traditional utility business model to a diversified energy and services company over the past few years. The business of the Italian multinational today extends significantly beyond electricity generation and into energy infrastructure and customer solutions. Enel's business model is more that of a vertically integrated utility, chiefly being involved in power generation, transmission and distribution, and gas distribution.

About 60 years ago, Enel was born as Italy's national vertically integrated electric power utility. In the 1990s Enel reduced its share of electric power generation within Italy following the liberalisation of the European power markets. Today, its asset base and operations go well beyond Italy. The home market accounted for 50.6 per cent of its earnings[4] of €11.5 billion ($13.4 billion), the Iberian Peninsula was 23 and the rest of the world, especially the Americas, made up for 26.6 per cent in the first six months of 2025 to June. Mostly from an installed capacity of almost 86 GW and sale of 93.3 TWh. The sale of power that it generated plus the trading of electricity accounted for 13.5 per cent of earnings, fees from transmission and distribution of electricity made-up for 38.1 per cent, the sale of electricity from clean energy sources was responsible for 29.3 per cent and its subsidiary Enel X was 19.1 per cent of the total.[5] Enel X offers customers energy supply, management solutions, and other value added services including demand response, energy storage, smart charging, and energy efficiency services.

Transition journey

PLANNING AND STRATEGIES

Enel had targeted Scope 3 carbon neutrality by 2050. It moved the objective forward to 2040 in late 2021 and has in place interim targets for 2030. The year 2040 is an aggressive target for Enel given its asset exposure to fossil fuels, including coal and gas fired power plants and its gas distribution business.

Enel categorises its targets into four sets: Power Generation, Integrated Power, Natural Gas, and Others. The aim for the Power Generation business unit is Scope 1 emissions cut of about 80 per cent versus its 2017 baseline to 72 grammes of CO_2-equivalent per kWh (g CO_2e/kWh) by 2030 and zero by 2040. For its Integrated Power business, Enel wants to reduce Scopes 1 and 3 emissions by about 78 per cent, also against its 2017 baseline, to 73 gCO_2e/kWh by 2030 and to zero by 2040. For Gas Retail, the Scope 3 objective is a cut of about 55 per cent to 10.3 gCO_2e/kWh by 2030 compared to 2017, and to net zero by 2040. The fourth set of targets are for Additional Emissions. The company has said that there is some uncertainty given 'several exogenous factors' which could ease the reduction. These include 'new carbon-free solutions in the supply chain at large-scale, and change of certain market conditions and policies to enable zero emissions business models'. Nevertheless, should there be residual emissions then the goal is a decrease of about 55 per cent to 10.4 metric tonnes of CO_2-equivalent (Mt CO_2e) against the 2017 baseline by 2030, and to less than 2.5 Mt CO_2e by 2040.[6]

The utility plans several short- and long-term strategies to achieve its carbon neutrality targets. The approaches include scaling up clean energy generation capacity, upgrading power grids, energy storage additions, and advanced demand management.

Booming clean energy capacity growth Enel is spending about €12 billion ($14 billion) to add about 12 GW of clean energy generation capacity between 2025 and 2027 (see Figure 14.3), according to its strategic plan released in late 2024.[7] About 48 per cent (5.7 GW) of the additional capacity will come from wind power, approximately 27 per cent (3.2 GW) from solar related technologies, about 19 per cent (2.3 GW) will be battery energy storage systems (BESS) while hydro will make up for the remaining 6 per cent (0.7 GW). The additions will raise total clean energy capacity to 76 GW by 2027 from 66 GW in 2024.

Enel had a renewable projects pipeline of 308 GW as of October 2024 (see Figure 14.4). The pipeline included 117 GW of projects at a mature stage of development, and 191 GW at an early stage. For the mature pipeline, solar and related accounted for 53 per cent (62 GW), wind for 28 per cent (33GW), and BESS for 19 per cent (22 GW). The company has not specified clean-energy installed capacity objectives for 2040, but the additional capacity will be substantial given that it will be phasing out thermal coal power generation by 2027,

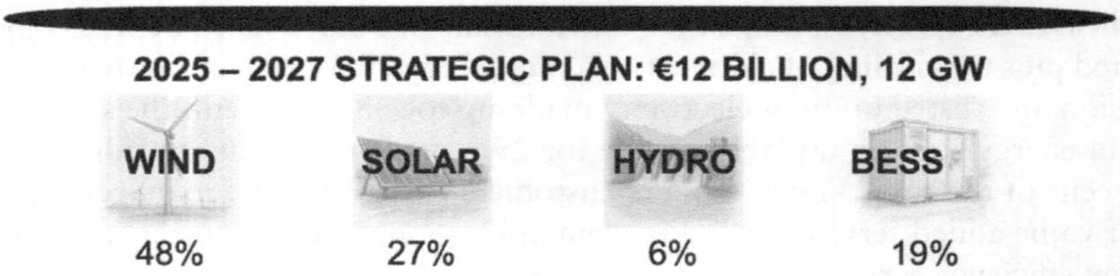

Figure 14.3 Enel's 2025–2027 strategic plan: generation

Source: Author, original chart design (August 2025). Source of data: Enel, 'Enel Capital Markets Day 2024 Presentation' (Enel SpA 2024). Available at https://www.enel.com/content/dam/enel-com/documenti/investitori/informazioni-finanziarie/2024/2025-2027-strategic-plan.pdf accessed 11 August 2025. Source of background image OpenAI, https://chat.openai.com accessed 11 August 2025.

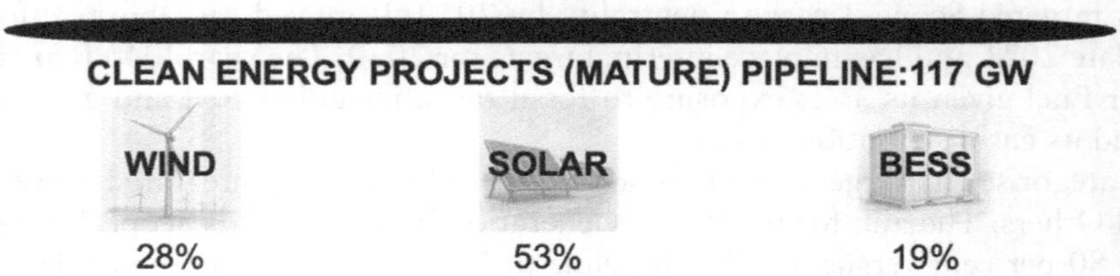

Figure 14.4 Enel's clean energy pipeline

Source: Author, original chart design (August 2025). Source of data: Enel, 'Enel Capital Markets Day 2024 Presentation' (Enel SpA 2024). Available at https://www.enel.com/content/dam/enel-com/documenti/investitori/informazioni-finanziarie/2024/2025-2027-strategic-plan.pdf accessed 11 August 2025. Source of background image OpenAI, https://chat.openai.com accessed 11 August 2025.

and plants using natural gas by 2040. Before publishing its 2025–2027 strategic plan, the utility had mentioned that it was hoping to add about 100 GW compared to the 2021 level, which translates into a total of 154 GW or so.

Upgrading to smart grids The second long-term strategy of Enel revolves around grid networks. The Italian multinational has allocated €26 billion, more than double the spending on clean energy generation. One of the objectives is to increase the resilience of its grids. The networks need to be physical climate risk ready. They must mitigate the impacts of extreme weather events such as intense rain and snow as well as severe air temperature fluctuations. Electric power lines, transformers and other transmission and distribution equipment must have risk prevention measures against wildfires as well. About 63 per cent of the grid capex will be towards maintenance, development and improvement for the quality and digitalisation of the grids. This will help to lower grid losses and the related GHG emissions. Enel will also be replacing existing distribution grid infrastructure components with SF6-free solution; SF6, or sulphur hexafluoride, is a synthetic, odourless potent GHG common the power industry to keep networks running safely and reliably.

The grid business has adopted the 4-R strategy. The first is 'risk prevention'. It involves procedures to lower the chance of losing particular elements of the grid during an event, such as a wildfire, and to reduce the impact of such event, including maintenance and raising resilience. The second is 'readiness', which involves the rapid identification of events which could perhaps turn critical, as well as ensuring coordination with local authorities, such as civil protection bodies. The third is 'response' which comprises evaluating the operational capacity to deal with emergencies caused by extreme events, including mobilising resources and performing remote operations. The fourth is 'recovery' which includes restoring power distribution to normal operating conditions following a service interruption caused by an extreme event.[8]

Investments to tackle the risk prevention, readiness, response, and recovery strategy will be towards modernisation and digitisation of its grids. In the short term (2025–2027), Enel plans to grow the amount of distributed generation by 3 per cent to 489 TWh and the number of smart meters 7 per cent to 49.5 million. About 66 per cent of its grid customers were digitalised in 2024. The goal is 70 per cent by 2027, and 100 per cent by 2030.[9]

Adding flexibility with energy storage, raising demand management Adding significant amounts of battery energy storage systems is critical for Enel as it will provide the company with more flexible or dispatchable capacity and reinforce its power grids. In the short term, Enel will invest €720 million ($844 million) and add 2.3 GW in battery energy storage systems.[10]

According to the IEA, demand management is about maintaining a balance in power-grid utilisation. The goal is to encourage consumers to use electricity when it is more readily available or when demand is lower, typically through incentives such as price changes. Advanced digital technologies can enhance this strategy by using interconnected devices. These advancements also help manage sudden changes in demand, such as those caused by extreme weather.[11]

Enel's investments in energy storage solutions and demand management play a crucial role as the company extends its renewable-energy capacity and modernises its networks. These strategies collaborate to stabilise the balance between electricity consumption and production, minimise the likelihood of power failures, and facilitate the integration of sustainable energy sources. They enhance the dependability and adaptability of the grid.

By mitigating peak demand, energy storage and demand coordination help circumvent the necessity for expensive new power facilities that would operate sporadically. This cost-effective approach benefits both grid operators and customers. Demand management also offers direct financial incentives to consumers, such as compensating them for reducing their electricity usage during specific periods of the day. Both technologies contribute to reducing GHG emissions. Energy storage enables increased utilisation of zero-emission clean energy sources, while demand management promotes a more flexible and efficient electricity consumption pattern.

STRUCTURAL AND OPERATIONAL SHIFTS, AND TANGIBLE PROGRESS

Managing a vertically integrated traditional utility structure is second nature for a company like Enel. It was established as a traditional utility and operated as such for several decades. Enacting structural and operational shifts to embrace transition is a mammoth task for a traditional utility. For example, Enel has been operating coal fired power plants for decades, a technology which is over 140 years old. While the production process has improved and the size of generators massively increased since the inception of the technology, the fundamental operational processes have not changed dramatically.

For a utility such as Enel to be suddenly asked to operate solar, wind and other clean-energy assets, relatively newer technologies, which have very different operational processes is a challenge. Emissions-free solar, wind and hydropower generation are subject to weather patterns. Even hydropower, generally considered as a reliable source of energy, can be negatively impacted by droughts or seasonal water shortages. Structural and operational changes driven by the energy transition are far from straightforward. Some of its changes include a highly extensive use of digital solutions, the repurposing or integration of assets, strategic alliances and innovation, and workforce changes.

Enel has significantly committed to digital transformation at a variety of levels. In its electric power generation business, the company has deployed a variety of digital solutions. It is automating and digitalising operational centres. In addition to automating process controls, it is using cloud and digital solutions to streamline the actual operation and maintenance of its power plants. For example, drones are used for remote inspections monitoring. It uses a digital, virtual replica of the power plant (known as the Digital Twins technology) to optimise performance, simulate operations, and undertake predictive maintenance. The utility deployed around 250 AI tools between 2021 and 2024 to reach foundational efficiencies, such as boosting energy efficiency by 5 per cent. For example, AI algorithms are used to evaluate operational data and estimate in the energy output and processes which increase the efficiency of solar, wind, hydro, in other power assets. These technologies also help Enel to improve benchmarking and real-time data sharing, resulting in lower CO_2 emissions from its IT operations. The digital solutions extend to supporting commercial and industrial customers with their electrification and residential users with their smart home integration.[12]

Another structural change is the repurposing of assets, particularly for clean energy. Through its majority owned subsidiary Endesa, the company set up a 4 MW/1.7 MWh backup power storage system at the Melilla power plant in Spain in 2022. The battery energy storage system uses 48 second-life batteries or disused EV batteries from Nissan vehicles with another 30 which are new. It is purposed to support the plant and also improve grid reliability.[13] Enel also launched a 2.5 MW/10 MWh storage system comprising 762 battery packs and modules including second-life batteries from several EV makers, including Mercedes-Benz, Nissan, and Stellantis in 2025. The storage system is located at Fiumicino Airport in Italy's capital city of Rome and is integrated to a large solar PV plant which feeds the airport.[14] A third example, also in Italy, is integrating a lithium-ion battery energy storage system of 4 MW/8 MWh to the Dossi 43.4 MW pumped storage hydropower plant in Bergamo in 2024, a plant which is over a century old.[15]

To further its transition objectives, Enel has formed a numerous number of partnerships and throughout the world. Several strategic alliances set up in the past two years or so can be assessed. It is currently in talks with Masdar, an Emirati state-owned renewable energy company, to jointly develop an energy storage facility in Italy. It formed joint venture with Ansaldo Energia and Leonardo to explore advanced nuclear technologies and market opportunities in Italy. Ansaldo Energia is a leading Italian power engineering firm specialising in turbines and generators for fossil and nuclear plants, while Leonardo is a multinational focused on aerospace, defence, and security technologies, including helicopters, aircraft, and cyber systems. It joined the pan-European AI-EFFECT Project, a consortium of 18 organisations, to study AI applications and integration across the region's energy sector. It is collaborating with Italian start-up Axyon AI to develop advanced predictive AI solutions for energy trading, aimed at improving market forecasts and reducing operational risks. In Taiwan, it is partnering with provider of wireless Internet-of-Things infrastructure EpiSensor, an Irish company, to develop a virtual power plant based on battery-swapping stations, supporting renewable energy integration and demand response. To enhance customer service for electric mobility in the United States and Canada, it has partnered with Spain's Atento. Atento is a global provider of Customer Relationship Management and Business Process Outsourcing services, known for its expertise in customer care, sales, and technical support, especially in Latin America.[16]

Another example of structural and operation shifts at Enel relates to its workforce and organisational make-up. This chiefly involves extensive reskilling and retraining. As it works to shut down its coal-fired power plants, by 2025 in Italy and by 2027 in the rest of the world, it is developing new skills for its work force to allow staff from these plants to adopt different roles in the clean energy sector. It also offers this to its contractors' employees, who, once trained, can work in the new renewables contract sector.[17] Enel also said that it is continually investing in 'developing the skills of its staff through training programs and up-skilling and re-skilling initiatives. This approach enables the company to remain at the forefront of technological innovation, maintain a competitive edge and successfully meet future challenges'. The shift will likely accelerate as the company digitalises further.[18]

Funding and financing the transition

Funding and financing are critical for Enel as it shifts its asset portfolio away from fossil fuels. It faces tens of billions of Euros in spending on clean energy resources, power grids, and digitalisation over the next decades. Enel has maintained a solid financial position in recent years and is especially cautious in retaining it. The company has maintained a good long-term debt credit rating from S&P, Moody's and Fitch, the three key credit agencies (see Figure 14.5) over the past five fiscal year. It only experienced a one-notch downgrade by S&P in 2023, to BBB – stable[19] from BBB+ – stable, over concerns that the company reduced its overall debt at a pace slower than expected that year as the group's asset disposals took more time than planned.[20]

SUSTAINABILITY-LINKED BONDS PIONEER

Enel has been one of the leaders in the issuance of Sustainability-Linked Bonds (SLBs). The company views itself as a leading actor in sustainable finance and believes that it has introduced key innovation in recent years. The company was an early issuer of bonds under the climate umbrella. The first was a green bond raising €1.25 billion ($147 billion) (see Figure 14.6). Enel at the time stated that the net proceeds raised from the issuance would be used to finance eligible green projects 'identified and/or to be identified in accordance with the Green Bond Principles 2016 published by the International Capital Market Association (ICMA)'. It specified that the eligible projects categories include, for example, 'the development, construction and repowering of renewable power plants; the development of transmission and distribution networks, and the implementation of smart grids and smart

FISCAL YEAR	S&P	MOODY'S	FITCH
2020 (to 31 Dec)	BBB+ - Stable	Baa1 - Stable	BBB+ - Stable
2021 (to 31 Dec)	BBB+ - Stable	Baa1 - Stable	BBB+ - Stable
2022 (to 31 Dec)	BBB+ - Negative	Baa1 - Negative	BBB+ - Stable
2023 (to 31 Dec)	BBB - Stable	Baa1 - Negative	BBB+ - Stable
2024 (to 31 Dec)	BBB - Stable	Baa1 - Stable	BBB+ - Stable
2025 (to 30 Jun)	BBB - Stable	Baa1 - Stable	BBB+ - Stable

Figure 14.5 Enel's long-term debt credit rating

Source: Author (August 2025) based on information from Enel, 'Consolidated Results Investor Presentation First Half 2025' (Enel 2025). Accessed at https://www.enel.com/investors/financials accessed 13 August 2025, as well as the investor presentations for fiscal 2020, 2021, 2022, 2023, and 2024.

BONDS	AMOUNT AND TYPE	ISSUE DATE	MATURITY DATE	COUPON (AT ISSUANCE)
1	EUR 1,250 mn Green Bond (EMTN)	Jan 2017 (placement)	16 Sep 2024	1.000%
2	EUR 1,250 mn Green Bond (EMTN)	2018 (placement)	16 Sep 2026	1.125%
3	EUR 1,000 mn Green Bond (EMTN)	2019 (placement)	21 Jul 2025	1.500%
4	USD 1,500 mn SDG-linked bond	10 Sep 2019 (settlement)	10 Sep 2024	2.65%*
5-8	USD 4,000 mn Multi-tranche SLB ($1,250 mn / $1,000 mn / $1,000 mn / $750 mn)	12 Jul 2021 (placement)	(12 Jul 2026 / 12 Jul 2028 / 12 Jul 2031 / 12 Jul 2041)	(1.375% / 1.875% / 2.250% / 2.875%)*
9-11	EUR 3,500 mn Triple-tranche SLB (€1,250 mn / €1,000 mn / €1,250 mn)	28 Sep 2021 (placement)	(28 Sep 2026 / 28 Sep 2029 / 28 Sep 2034)	(0.000% / 0.375% / 0.875%)*
12	GBP 750 mn SLB	11 Apr 2022	11 Apr 2029	2.875%*
13-16	USD 4,000 mn Multi-tranche SLB (Oct 2022: $750 mn / $1,000 mn / $1,250 mn / $1,000 mn)	14 Oct 2022	(14 Oct 2025 / 14 Oct 2027 / 14 Oct 2032 / 14 Oct 2052)	(6.800% / 7.100% / 7.500% / 7.750%)*
17-18	EUR 1,500 mn Dual-tranche SLB (Feb 2023: €750 mn / €750 mn)	20 Feb 2023	(20 Feb 2031 / 20 Feb 2043)	(4.000% / 4.500%)*
19-20	EUR 1,750 mn Dual-tranche SLB (Jan 2024: €750 mn / €1,000 mn)	23 Jan 2024	(23 Jul 2028 - short / 23 Jan 2035 - long)	(3.375% / 3.875%)*
21-22	USD 2,000 mn Dual-tranche SLB (Jun 2024: $1,250 mn / $750 mn)	26 Jun 2024	(26 Jun 2029 / 26 Jun 2034)	(5.125% / 5.500%)*
23-25	EUR 2,000 mn Triple-tranche SLB (Feb 2025: €750 mn / €750mn / €500 mn)	24 Feb 2024	(24 Feb 2028 / 24 Feb 2031 / 24 Feb 2036)	(2.625% / 3.000% / 3.500%)*

Figure 14.6 Partial list of climate bonds issued by Enel and group companies

Notes: * = performance linked coupon adjustment.

Source Author (August 2025). Data sourced from Enel Green Bond page, Enel Green Bond Reports, Enel SDG press release, Enel SLB materials, and various Enel press releases.

meters in the geographic areas' where Enel has operations.[21] Based on publicly available information as the end of 2024, the group issued climate bonds every year since 2019, except in 2020, given healthy investor appetite for its issuance, not including possible private placements. It raised about €12.25 billion ($14.4 billion) in Euro-denominated bonds, $11.5 billion in US-dollar-denominated bonds, and £750 million ($1.01 billion) in British Pounds-denominated bonds.

In 2019, Enel took the bold initiative to issue an innovative financial product. It was a general corporate purpose financing product which created financial incentives for the issuer to meet its sustainable business objectives. It raised $1.5 billion issuing an SDG-linked bond with a mid-term maturity, five years. It consisted in linking Enel's sustainability strategy to the 'terms of the general purpose debt'. The goal was to incentivise achieving predetermined Sustainability Performance Targets within a certain timeline. This SDG-linked bond marked the birth of the Sustainability-Linked bond market.[22] Counting one tranche as a single bond, the company issue no less than twenty Sustainability-Linked bonds between 2021 and 2024, based on publicly available information.

In March 2024, the company announced that it had failed to meet one of its Sustainability Performance Targets related to its 2023 emissions reduction target. It resulted in a 'step-up' or 'penalty trigger' of 25 basis points – 0.25 per cent above the set coupon rate for the Sustainability-Linked Bond – for ten bonds. Most analysts regarded this event as a boost for the Sustainability-Linked Bond market from a credibility perspective. In fact, Enel's Sustainability-Linked Bonds had a good reaction from the fixed-income markets as spreads tightened (i.e., the price of the bonds rose) 5–10 basis points, because of the credibility of the penalisation.[23]

ASSETS REBALANCING: DISPOSALS

Another active funding strategy has been raising funds through asset disposals. The company set a programme aimed at disposing of some of its non-core assets in its 2023 to 2025 strategic plan. The aim was to reinvest proceeds from the asset sale into clean energy, power grids, and digitalisation. The company at the time said that it expected that the disposal amount would have a positive impact on net financial debt estimated at about €11.5 billion ($13.5 billion) in 2023 and 2024. In early 2025 it announced that the disposal programme has been successfully completed. The sale of assets in Argentina, Peru, Eastern Europe, and elsewhere reduced Enel's debt burden, and opened the door for new decarbonisation-related opportunities.[24] This capital recycling approach will remain a viable option for Enel in future following the lessons that the group learned from the 2023 to 2024 disposal programme, The group held physical assets with a book value on its balance sheet of about €94 billion ($110 billion) as at the end of June 2025, though the disposal value would be subject to market valuation.

STRATEGIC PARTNERSHIPS AND CO-INVESTMENTS

Enel has set up a great variety of collaborative partnerships, strategic alliances and co-investment structures over the past few years. These have been a significant structural and operational shifts for the company. This approach has enabled Enel to amplify its opportunities identification and investment capabilities. Opportunities-wise, for example, Enel joined hands with Intesa Sanpaolo in 2022 to enter the fintech business. Intesa Sanpaolo is one of the largest banking groups in Europe with €1.4 trillion ($1.6 trillion) in customer financial assets as of June 2025. The two acquired shares in the Mooney Group, a payment firm for €1.6 billion ($1.9 billion). The acquisition will allow the two companies to leverage the Mooney Group's payment and banking extensive services for businesses and consumers. The then Enel CEO stated that the acquisition would help the company with digital payments by customers who increasingly use such payments for power bills and would support 'beyond commodity' services, such as electric mobility – charging solutions, emissions tracking and the like.[25] Another example is its expansion of investment capabilities by setting up alliances with financial institutions. In 2023, Enel sold 50 per cent of its Greek subsidiary to Macquarie Asset Management, raising €345 million ($404 million) in 2023. The joint venture company is expanding into storage and hybrid renewable energy projects, and other innovative solutions. Given the extensive clean energy foot printing of Macquarie Asset Management, such as its portfolio of over 30 energy transition-related portfolio companies, the firm is a valuable additional partner to Enel.[26]

SUSTAINABILITY-LINKED LOANS AND CREDIT LINES

Enel's decarbonisation and transition plans have also allowed the company to tap the green loans market. The company had secured a €10 billion ($11.7 billion) sustainability-linked revolving credit facility in 2021 from a consortium of financial institutions. The facility was expanded a further €3.5 billion ($4.1 billion) the following year, or a total of €13.5 billion

($15.8 billion). The main financing conditions of the facility are that the money must be linked to the Key Performance Indicator related to the Direct GHG Emissions intensity. The amount was targeted to be equal to, or lower than, 148 gCO_2s/kWh by 31 December 2023. This goal would determine a step-up or step-down mechanism – a premium or a discount to the borrowing rate.[27] The facility was renewed with a pool of 26 leading global financial institutions in 2025 with a €12 billion sustainability-linked credit facility with a five-year maturity.

Opportunities and challenges from the transition

The transition opens Enel to a great number of opportunities as well as new challenges. Some of the new opportunities include benefiting from the rapid growth of electrification, new revenues as well as cost optimisation from digital solutions, including AI, expanding revenue generation capacity from new clean energy generation facilities, and the revenue and financing benefits from growing sustainability credentials. At the same time, the utility must optimise the phasing-down or phasing-out of fossil fuel-based facilities, it has to manage higher expenses and capital expenditure risks caused by the transition, it must successfully navigate highly complex regulatory changes at a global level as well as specific evolutions at the local level, and it has to deal with many new technical challenges.

OPPORTUNITIES

Electrification growth. Electricity contributes less than one-fifth of primary energy consumption around the world. Its share will grow rapidly over the next a few years as most large economies raise the percentage of primary energy from electricity. One sector shifting rapidly, for example, is transport. Especially vehicle and rail transport. Enel is well placed to benefit from this growth, particularly in its existing key markets which have ambitious electrification targets.

Digitalisation. The breath-taking speed of the evolution of digital solutions, including AI, is a clear business growth opportunity for Enel. The digitalisation of its grids coupled with more advanced digital capabilities of its generation fleet should help the company in optimising operational expenses. Its digitalisation efforts also nurture new services that it can provide to its customers, from new behind-the-meter offerings to residential users, to advanced energy efficiency services to its commercial and industrial customers.

Clean energy markets. Enel is a leading clean energy developer and as markets grows at a brisk pace hundreds of gigawatts over the next few years. The utility will be expanding large-scale hydro, solar, storage, wind and other clean energy sources. These facilities will be supported by battery energy storage systems. The company's clean energy growth will also be helped by factors such as its deep local market knowledge, partnerships and alliances, solid supply chain management and focused and disciplined capex allocation.

Sustainability credentials: consumers and funding. The company has built strong sustainability credentials over the past six years or so. As it progressively shifts away its robust green credentials from fossil fuels, puts the company in a good position to entice new customers in the jurisdictions where it operates. Also its track record and transparency, for example, through its sustainability linked bonds, puts the company in pole position for green funding.

CHALLENGES

Fossil -fuel plants. The company is shutting down its coal fired power plants by 2027, and its gas fired ones in later years. The phasing-out or phasing-down of generation plants powered by fossil fuels is uniquely challenging for any owner. While the decision is up to the company, it is not solely dependent on its management, it must receive regulatory approvals whose timing is beyond the company's control. Another hurdle is that such plants are typically large in size and essential to the supply security of a particular area. It means that the company will have to first undertake comprehensive and careful planning. Enel will have to strategically add generation as well as create infrastructure capacity with great caution. Finally, among the many factors the company has to consider is managing the social and economic impacts, especially in communities which are dependent on the plants for livelihood.

Expenses and capex risks. Enel faces a series of different risks to its expenses and capital expenditure. Like all utilities, the group invests in heavy-capex, long-duration assets (built to operate for several decades), and is greatly exposed to interest-rate fluctuations. Given the tight decarbonisation timeline, it cannot delay expenditure by much and could be exposed to having to borrow when interest rates are high. This also applies to fund raising. There is a risk that because of unfavourable macroeconomic or geopolitical factors, the company may be unable to effectively secure funding when necessary. This concentrates risk on timely deployment and funding availability. Also, given the front-loaded investment for clean energy assets, the company is exposed to raw-material price fluctuations, including aluminium, copper, and steel prices. Enel's clean energy equipment suppliers are also exposed to securing rare earths, such as Dysprosium (Dy), critical for the reliable operation of EVs and turbines, and this raises the susceptibility of Enel's project costs and timelines to disruption.

Regulatory complexity. Enel operates in liberalised markets, where consumers can choose their suppliers, and regulated markets. This is one of the many regulatory complexities that the company faces in its transitioning. One of a multitude of risks globally, is that the company may face higher costs of fossil fuel-based generation and will require costly compliance mechanisms from evolving carbon tax or other energy tax directives around the world. Another global risk is that increasingly stringent climate reporting raises disclosure complexity and exposes Enel's reputation if its climate risk governance is deemed insufficient. There are also many local risks such as slow and fragmented permitting processes for clean energy projects in Italy, five-year tariff review cycles in Spain, the negative clean energy generation policies shift in the United States, or exposure to the sudden alteration of power purchasing agreements due to political and policy flux in Latin America.

Technical challenges. Enel's transition also faces many technical challenges. First, the company must address the technical and economic challenges of grid stability with clean energy integration. It must cautiously plan grid reinforcement and digitalisation to remove the risk of impact from the intermittent clean energy sources – such as solar generation day-time disruptions from the weather. It must consider introducing new climate technologies, such as marine energy and advanced battery energy storage system chemistries, but these may pose performance issues due to their lack of maturity. It must design generation and grid assets which can be resilient to extreme weather. It must also adapt to managing a rapidly growing electric mobility infrastructure involving tens of thousands of vehicle charging points. Among the many measures, this involves grid-reinforcement, the standardisation of power electronics, as well as new and sophisticated demand response.

Financial services and banking sector

Sector profile

The financial services and banking sector makes an ideal second case study. On the one hand, the sector's own GHG emissions are minimal in the global context. On the other hand, those of its clients are sizeable. Also, as discussed in detail in Part Three earlier, the sector is a key source of financing to corporates, making it a uniquely influential sector in the transition to net zero.

The sector's direct GHG emissions as a percentage of the world's total is not publicly readily available. One reputable source, the Central Banks and Supervisors Network for Greening the Financial System, affirmed that Scopes 1 and 2 emissions from financial services and banking institutions are 'negligible'.[28] Importantly, however, the global share rises to possibly 40 per cent or more when financed and facilitated emissions are included. These Scope 3 financed emissions are from companies that are funded or invested in by the financial institutions while facilitated emissions occur when the financial institution provides a service to its corporate client. Scope 3 calculations can be quite tricky. Even the Central Banks and Supervisors Network for Greening the Financial System admitted that the 'design and use of metrics to measure financed emissions can also be challenging for stakeholders, and methodologies are evolving', and that while the 'emissions of individual financial assets relate directly to the emissions from real-economy activities' and could be 'aggregated at the level of a financial portfolio . . . it comes with the challenge of accounting for double counting of Scope 3 value chain emissions'.[29]

Another dimension of the impact by the financial services and banking sector on the global transition and corporate behaviour lies in the way they lend or invest. Financial institutions are themselves working towards achieving long-term carbon neutrality targets internally and externally. Many institutions aim for their lending, investment or other portfolio to gradually shift to net zero. To achieve this, they can either not be involved at all with high carbon emitting companies, or they can work with such companies to support them in their own net-zero journey. As financial institutions increasingly apply climate parameters, they also have a great influence on corporate behaviour.

The financial services and banking sector is sizeable both in terms of total assets and stock market capitalisation. The largest 15 banking institutions in the world had total assets of $51.8 trillion as of 8 April 2025 (see Figure 14.6). The top 15 financial services and banking listed companies had a combined market capitalisation of almost $5 trillion, as of 3 August 2025 (see Figure 14.7). Each of largest eight had a market capitalisation of over a quarter of a trillion dollars. The largest of the financial services and banking institutions are based China and the United States, making up 12 of the top 15.

Most of these large financial services and banking institutions have established net-zero targets, generally with at 2050 goal. The exceptions are Visa and Mastercard which aim for 2040, and the four Chinese banks whose net-zero targets are aligned with a national goal, carbon neutrality by 2060 or earlier. Interestingly, all 15 had substantive sustainability objectives clearly stated in their financial or other reporting. Also all are aiming for portfolio

FINANCIAL SERVICES AND BANKING	STOCK SYMBOL	COUNTRY OF INCORPORATION	CAPITALISATION ($, billion)	NET ZERO TARGET (yes/no + year)	SUSTAINABILITY OBJECTIVES (yes/no)	PORTFOLIO DECARBONISATION (yes/no)
JPMorgan Chase & Co	JPM	United States	795,672	Yes, 2050	Yes	Yes
Visa Inc	V	United States	658,658	Yes, 2040	Yes	Yes
Mastercard Incorporated	MA	United States	507,159	Yes, 2040	Yes	Yes
Industrial and Commercial Bank of China Ltd	1398.HK	China	348,210	N/A (China 2060)	Yes	Yes
Bank of America Corp	BAC	United States	339,559	Yes, 2050	Yes	Yes
Agricultural Bank of China Ltd	601288.S S	China	300,384	Yes, 2050	Yes	Yes
China Construction Bank Corp	601939.S S	China	273,317	N/A (China 2060)	Yes	Yes
Wells Fargo & Co	WFC	United States	250,480	No	Yes	Yes
Bank of China Ltd	601988.S S	China	231,753	N/A (China 2060)	Yes	Yes
Morgan Stanley	MS	United States	222,266	Yes, 2050	Yes	Yes
The Goldman Sachs Group, Inc	GS	United States	217,725	Yes, 2050	Yes	Yes
HSBC Holdings plc	HSBC	United Kingdom	215,520	Yes, 2050	Yes	Yes
American Express Co	AXP	United States	204,777	Yes, 2050	Yes	No
HDFC Bank Ltd	HDB	India	196,892	N/A (India 2070)	Yes	Yes
Commonwealth Bank of Australia	CBA.AX	Australia	191,730	Yes, 2050	Yes	Yes
Total market capitilisation of top 15			**4,954,102**			

Figure 14.7 Financial services and banking sector decarbonisation

Notes: N/A = The company's principal shareholder is the national government. Although the company itself has not publicly declared a net-zero target, its respective government has: China has committed to carbon neutrality by 2060, and India by 2070. It is therefore reasonable to infer that the company aligns with the national objective.

Source: Author (August 2025).

decarbonisation, with the sole exception of Wells Fargo which has not as yet declared such target. The eight US-headquartered financial services and banking firms have been under pressure to downplay (or 'greenhush') their transition plans and business strategies given the unfavourable political atmosphere at home, especially under the Trump presidency, as of August 2025. However, their net zero, sustainability, and portfolio decarbonisation objectives have not been withdrawn, and are unlikely to be rescinded in the near future, given their past track record of commitments, as well as the more global nature of their business.

Financed and facilitated emissions: political and data challenges

Financed and facilitated emissions are a critical and complex topic for the financial services and banking sector. The calculation of financed emissions is complex, and methodologies are fast moving and evolving. There are many challenges, yet these hurdles are short term in nature. The challenges include significant data gaps as well as the quality of the data from the clients they serve. Something particularly difficult for financial institutions to handle given that they have no control over the way their clients collect data which is especially difficult for their small to medium enterprise clients who may not have the capability or capacity to collect such information. There are a variety of methodologies to approach the calculations, especially when it comes to different assets classes, and in some cases the jurisdiction. There is a lack of regulatory clarity with reporting requirements in general and by jurisdiction in particular, difficult challenge for those financial institutions with global portfolios. There are also many other challenging internal problems such as those related to compliance costs, lack of technical expertise, inconsistent metrics across industries, as well as potential legal, political, and reputational liabilities.[30]

An additional issue is facilitated emissions, which are emissions from off-balance-sheet financial services that financial institutions provide their clients. These are activities that facilitate capital-market transactions. Examples include the issuance of securities, securitisation, advisory services such as mergers and acquisitions advice, brokerage and trading services, another similar services. All these are categorised as Scope 3 emissions under the GHG protocol (Category 15: Investments). An example illustrating the challenges with financed and facilitated emissions is the recent upheaval with the various Net-Zero alliances.

Former UN Special Envoy on Climate Action and Finance and current Canadian prime minister Mark Carney together with US philanthropist Michael Bloomberg drove the creation of the Glasgow Financial Alliance for Net Zero (GFANZ) in April 2021. GFANZ is an umbrella organisation dedicated to mobilising capital and lowering obstacles to global transition investment. A key milestone is the measurement of portfolio alignment, the measuring of the alignment of investing, lending, and underwriting activities by financial institutions with the goal of carbon neutrality. Various specialised groups were separately established for different categories of the financial services and banking sector including the Net Zero Asset Managers, Assets Owner, Banking, Insurance, Financial Services Providers, and Investment Consultants alliances and initiatives. The financed and facilitated emissions assessment methodology has been critical to GFANZ's portfolio measurement. It plays a principal role in ensuring accountability, strategic alignment, and transparency among financial institutions.[31]

The history of GFANZ has been tumultuous partly due to political pressures and backlash, especially in the United States, and partly due to different approaches on target setting, reduced autonomy and flexibility, data collection, and methodology-setting struggles. This led to the exit of some major financial institutions, especially some large US-based ones as well as the dissolution of the Net Zero Insurance Alliance. This caused GFANZ to cut formal ties with several sector-specific alliances, and in January 2025 it restructured and adopted a new model. It has opened participation to attract a broader range of institutions, especially from developing countries, and reduce legal exposure and reputational risk for its members. However, its aims of capital mobilisation and facilitation to raise energy transition financing have remained intact.[32]

Despite the highly public upheaval, GFANZ Remains a strong and influential organisation with a bright long term future. There are still a great number of financial institutions that are still part of GFANZ and that are committed to ensuring GFANZ's success. The alliance's Principals Group continues to include CEOs from major financial institutions, even from those that have already exited coalitions. It is working hard on the development of forward-looking decarbonisation contribution methodologies and transition finance strategies. Also GFANZ's efforts are being indirectly supported by increasing adoption of mandatory financed emissions reporting in such places as Canada, the EU, Singapore, and other jurisdictions. Also factors such as advances in technology and automation are also helping with a variety of data issues. These are clear signs that GFANZ's many challenges may be short term in nature and that over the next five or ten years, methodologies and approaches will become harmonised.

Other influence factor on businesses

Financed and facilitated emissions link the financial services and banking sector with how businesses plan their transition to a carbon-neutral economy. Financial institutions influence corporate strategies in several ways. Four of the most direct influences are: capital allocation and financing (directing funding towards low or zero-carbon projects), risk management (helping clients prepare for and mitigate climate-related risks), regulatory influence (implementing new climate rules that will also affect clients), and product innovation (providing financial products such as green bonds or sustainability-linked loans). Alongside these high-impact factors, there are other medium- to low-impact ones including data expertise and advisory, stewardship and engagement, reputational aspects, and investor confidence. These are some of the many factors that shape how businesses respond to climate challenges and plan their transition.

Financial services and banking sector transition journey case study: ICBC

Many of the largest corporations in the financial services and banking sector would be interesting corporate-transition case studies. The Industrial and Commercial Bank of Chinese, commonly known as ICBC, is one of the more unique transition examples for several reasons including its size and profile, its treatment of sustainability, and its climate financing activities. It is not only massively influential in China but also internationally.

ICBC is the largest commercial bank in the world by assets which amounted to 51.55 trillion yuan ($7.2 trillion) based on International Financial Reporting Standards (IFRS) as of 31 March 2025. It is the largest of the 'big four' Chinese banks which include the Agricultural Bank of China (ABC) with 44.82 trillion yuan ($6.3 trillion), the China Construction Bank (CCB) with 42.37 trillion yuan ($5.9 trillion) lion, and the Bank of China (BOC) with 35.46 trillion yuan ($5 trillion), also based on IFRS as of 31 March 2025. For comparison, that of JPMorgan Chase & Co., the largest financial services and banking firm by market capitalisation, was $4.36 trillion, also as of 31 March 2025.

ICBC's assets are still relatively concentrated domestically, although the overseas portion is gradually growing. The overseas portion as a percentage of total assets has risen 3.6 percentage points in the past five years to 11.8 per cent as at the end of 2024 from 8.2 per cent at the end of 2020.[33] ICBC's dominant position in China means it can be the most prominent player in the world's second largest economy after the United States which also happens to be the largest energy transition market in the world. A market where in 2024 alone, $818 billion was invested, an increase of 20 per cent year over year, according to research firm BloombergNEF, an amount greater than that of the European Union, United Kingdom, and United States combined.[34]

The group is involved in all forms of financial services. The group's principal business verticals include corporate and retail commercial banking, insurance, asset management, wealth management, leasing, investment and financial services, financial assets investment, and custody and trust services (see Figure 14.8). Each of the business units is involved in providing climate and sustainable products and services.

As the Chinese government is the major shareholder of ICBC, the bank must concurrently navigate national policy directives, pursue market opportunities, and align with

ICBC PRINCIPAL BUSINESS VERTICALS

Commercial Banking	Leasing
Domestic and international corporate and retail banking.	*Tailored financial leasing services: main leasing business lines include aviation, shipping and large equipment.*
Insurance	**Investment and financial services**
ICBC-AXA Life Insurance, services include accident insurance, health insurance (medical, critical illness, pension / annuity products, traditional life insurance (whole life, term life, endowment, long-term care), universal life and investment-linked insurance (savings and investment components).	*Broad range of investment banking services including investment and financing advisory service, cross-border M&A, investment banking research service, bond issuance, new shares issuance and additional issuance, debt regrouping and financing and the like*
Asset management	**Financial assets investment**
ICBC UBS Asset Management (formerly ICBC Credit Suisse Asset Management), services include diversified products including funds and discretionary management accounts, asset management services for global investors including investment categories such as fixed income, equities, and indices.	*Investment and financing activities, including financing policies and environmental analysis, customer investment and financing capability diagnosis, investment and financing asset risk and income analysis, design of investment and financing plans and schemes, investment and financing maturity structure matching, and the like*
Wealth management	**Custody and trust**
Wealth management services, including tailored investment solutions and investment products, as well as time deposits, stock trading, foreign exchange, and the like.	*Basic custody services such as asset custody, capital clearing, accounting, asset valuation, investment supervision, and information disclosure, as well as the relevant value-added custody services such as providing comprehensive financial information, bond default warning, investment manager analysis, and the like.*

Figure 14.8 ICBC main business lines

Source: Author (August 2015). Information sourced from ICBC, 'Home-ICBC China' (Icbc.com.cn 2015). Available at https://www.icbc.com.cn/en/column/1438058319784067131.html accessed 20 August 2025, and ICBC, 'Industrial and Commercial Bank of China Limited' (www.icbc-ltd.com2025). Available at https://www.icbc-ltd.com/en/column/1438058319654043654.html accessed 20 August 2025.

international sustainability expectations. The nation formerly declared a 'dual carbon' goal in 2020, commonly called the 30/60 in China. It aims for C02 emissions to peak before 2030 and achieve carbon neutrality before 2060. Some experts believe that C02 emissions may have peaked in 2025, suggesting the 2060 goal is highly achievable. As a state-owned bank, ICBC's goals must be aligned with those of the nation. Domestically it must ready itself for this transition by actively financing energy transition-related projects. At the same time, this offers a unique revenue generating opportunity for the bank given the massive number of transition-related projects in the country. The bank has been working hard for many years to enhance its green credentials. The vast experience it is gaining in its home market means that it can comfortably meet international expectations. The bank has been putting great emphasis on ESG, progressively aligning to international standards. It is also aligned to TCFD and a signatory of the Principles for Responsible Banking (PRB). These efforts gained consistent recognition by various domestic and international awards, including from media organisations like The Asset, Euromoney and Xinhua.

ICBC climate finance activities are extensive, similar to best-in-class Western banking institutions. It has not, however, set clear climate strategy targets, especially Scope 3 carbon neutrality goals for its whole portfolio. Also, its latest sustainability report, released in March 2025, has no specific mention of financed and facilitated emissions. Yet, given its goals are aligned with the national development goals, one could infer that the target will fall sometime before 2060. It has been actively increasing green finance activities and has stated in the past that it does plans to release in future a road map for the gradual withdrawal from coal financing, for example.

Transition journey

PLANNING AND STRATEGIES

Own transitionI CBC has made advancing climate finance as one of the groups five strategic priorities, collectively known as the 'Five Priorities'; the others are technology finance, inclusive finance (extending services to undeserved groups), pension finance (especially retirement planning, and digital finance, it aims to involve green finance in every single key aspect of its operations, internally and externally. For its operations, the bank uses a 'comprehensive green finance system' which it includes in its strategic planning, policy guidance, product innovation, and research collaboration. Externally, the bank's green finance commitment is marketed to corporate clients and the greater public in general through a dedicated green finance brand 'ICBC Green Bank+'.[35]

ICBC's own transition is best-in-class in some areas while lagging behind some international peers in other areas. The bank has formally declared that it has fully recognised that its business faces climate-related risks, both physical and transition risks. It is addressing these risks in a variety of ways. A key strategy is to make every effort to track domestic and international climate change and green finance policy and regulation and through these efforts to develop into an 'internationally leading green bank' in the longer term. The bank has not yet spoken of its operational carbon neutrality by 2030. In documents in the past five years. Yet it is navigating the business progressively towards Scope 1 carbon neutrality. The bank said that for its own operations, it is 'steadily' promoting carbon footprint management, low-carbon outlets and green offices. One small but insightful example was the announcement that one of its branches in Fujian province, was formally verified as having reached carbon neutrality for its operations by a third party evaluation agency. This was achieved through carbon offsets using verified international carbon reduction projects in 2024.[36]

China's central bank, the People's Bank of China, together with other central government bodies, issued Important guidelines to all Chinese banks. The document released in late 2024 was titled 'Opinions on Leveraging Green Finance to Support the Beautiful China Initiative'. It required banks to improve their risk response abilities partly through establishing climate change related risk assessment and prediction models and using big data and other technologies to conduct climate disaster risk analysis. In addition, big data, AI, and other digital technologies will support such areas as 'carbon accounting, sustainable information disclosure, and green project identification'.[37] ICBC is one of the banks proactively adopting these guidelines. In Europe, ICBC launched an advanced ESG and sustainable finance risk management system to provide ESG insights, automate regulatory disclosures, and assess climate-related risks. The bank says that the system integrates 147 environmental data points for loans and uses business intelligence visualisation for monitoring. The idea is to ensure standardisation across all of its seven branches around Europe.[38]

The bank's senior leadership formed a Green Finance Committee to oversee ESG risk. This was an important development in the bank's own transition. The Committee oversees and manages the ESG risk management in financing activities, throughout the entire investment and financing lifecycle. It evaluates both the environmental risks of clients' industries and their environmental and social performance. Key risk areas include clients' environmental pollution prevention, energy conservation, and response to climate change and carbon emission control. It also assesses their handling of water resource conservation and flood prevention, as well as biodiversity and ecological protection. Much of the work is with the help of digital technologies. It has an enterprise-level intelligent risk control platform and now has an independently controllable large-scale AI model with hundreds of billions of parameters.[39]

Other corporate transition initiatives driven by digital technologies include a digital carbon accounting system for investments, financing as well as for the management of its internal carbon footprints. It set up in-house environmental assessment system known as the Eco-Protection Redline Risk Control Map system. The system is a geospatial tool developed by the group itself, aiming to assess, monitor, and manage environmental risks in its lending and investment activities, especially for projects close to or within ecologically sensitive areas in the country. The areas include nature reserves, critical biodiversity areas, key water source regions, and the like. Also, it has been exploring the construction of a climate-disaster risk-warning management system.[40]

Clients' transition ICBC and its peers play a critical executional role in advancing corporate transition in China. The bank has initiated a diverse range of green finance services and products, from green loans to issuing green bonds, for clients. At the same time, the design of these products includes parameters, such as eligibility criteria and reporting requirements, which help to encourage businesses to begin or hasten their climate transition.

While China is a centrally administered economy, the dual pressure for state-owned businesses is the delicate balance between profitability and meeting state-mandated targets, noting that some may argue that the order is state targets first and profitability second. As the nation set a goal to reach carbon neutrality before 2060. Public and private companies must abide by this national mandate. However, Chinese companies, especially private businesses, may opt to focus on profitability first and address transitioning later. As such, receiving extra motivation, and support, from ICBC and other banks is significant for incentivising the transition of Chinese corporates.

A report on one of the branches of the bank's green activities offers a practical view at the group's varied green-finance services and products range.[41] The climate finance work of the bank's branch in the southern Chinese metropolis of Guangzhou, with a population of about 15 million, was featured in the local newspaper Guangzhou Daily in late 2024. The article highlighted some of the branch's green finance activities in the first ten months of the year, a period which saw the balance of the branch's green loans rise 21 per cent to 240 billion yuan ($34 billion).

In late 2023, the branch identified an EV manufacturer that was exploring building a factory in Thailand. Given the company's green credential the branch deployed several business units of the group to support the company. The services included assisting with tax and foreign debt registration policies and address financial needs for overseas construction. The group also provided a credit-risk guarantee via risk participation as well as project financing loans for the construction of the facility. When this EV company sought a public capital increase, the bank worked with ICBC Investment to participate in the fund-raising through a debt-to-equity conversion which injected 1 billion yuan ($140 million) into the company.

In June 2024, Guangzhou announced local standards for climate investment and financing to clarify the evaluation principles for climate-friendly enterprises and projects, providing guidance for enterprises to adapt to climate change and pursue green, low-carbon development. The bank identified a financial leasing company which would meet these standards and managed to disburse a loan to the company of 10 million yuan ($1.4 million) in just two days. The ICBC Guangzhou branch recommended another business unit, ICBC Wealth Management, to invest 140 million yuan ($19.6 million) in the financial leasing company's issuance of China's first climate-friendly enterprise carbon-neutral green corporate bond.

Also in June 2024, the Guangzhou branch co-underwrote the issuance of 1.5 billion yuan ($210 million) in green medium-term notes for a local grid company. The five-year bond, with a coupon rate of just 2.17 per cent, raised funds entirely for climate-related grid technological transformation infrastructure projects. These projects aim at facilitating large-scale equipment updates, enabling energy conservation, carbon reduction, ultra-low emissions, digital transformation, and smart upgrades.

This green financing snapshot of activities led by the ICBC Guangzhou branch is but small highlight of the great variety of climate financing activities undertaken by the group as well as its integrated climate finance approach. It extends to a wide array of areas including ESG-linked lending, carbon finance – including carbon-linked (carbon emissions reduction) loans, emissions trading facilitation, and transition financing products. The group also provides support for climate tech innovators, including seawater desalination and smart meters, through green bonds and ESG investments.

STRUCTURAL AND OPERATIONAL SHIFTS, AND TANGIBLE PROGRESS

Much evidence of ICBC's structural as well as operational transition was partly demonstrated in the earlier section. Of particular importance is the fact that climate finance is one of five board level priorities. This has enabled the banking giant, with its 415,000 employees, to drive an increasingly integrated climate finance approach. The massive undertaking has been partly enabled by the investments in digital technologies and solutions. The technological advancements have facilitated this integration and is progressively improving many of the banks internal systems. One of the many examples is the adoption of the Central Banks and Supervisors Network tor Greening the Financial System climate risk stress scenarios approach, including the technical framework from The United Nations environment programme. The bank wide climate risk stress tests were undertaken by using data that the group collated about its customers, businesses and industries.[42]

The group's efforts have also been recognised by international third parties. For example, the bank's ESG rating measured by financial services firm MSCI was 'A' in 2022 and subsequently raised to 'AA' in 2023, the second highest rating out of seven. The 'AA' rating indicates that MSCI thinks that it is 'a company leading its industry in managing the most significant sustainability risks and opportunities'.[43]

One of the many benchmarks of the bank's climate-finance performance is the total balance of its green loans, based on the National Financial Regulatory Administration criteria which is China's primary finance regulator for the banking industry. The green-loans balance reached over 6 trillion yuan ($841 billion) in 2024 compared to just 1.8 trillion yuan ($252 billion) in 2020, a compound annual growth rate of over 34 per cent (see Figure 14.9). ICBC's green-loan and domestic green bonds cumulative balance was the largest disclosed figure for any Chinese bank to 2024.

By the end of 2024, ICBC had cumulatively issued 110 billion yuan ($15.4 billion) in domestic green bonds, again the largest cumulative amount reported by any single Chinese issuer.

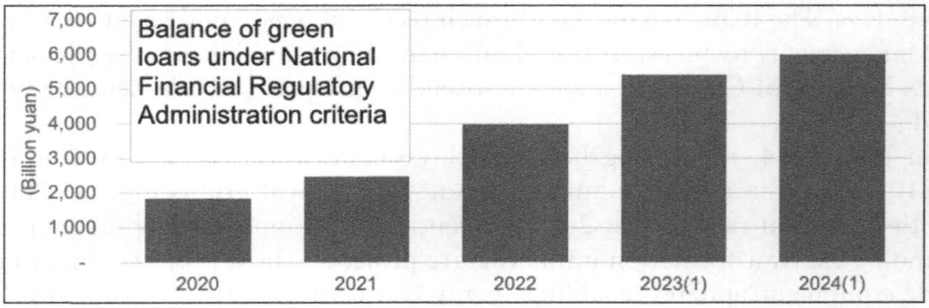

Figure 14.9 Balance of ICBC green loans under NFRA criteria

Notes: (1) ICBC only released a rounded number.

Source: Author (August 2025). Source of data: Industrial and Commercial Bank of China Limited, Annual Report 2020 (ICBC, 2021). Available at https://www.icbc-ltd.com/en/page/721858136553324554.html accessed 17 August 2025; Industrial and Commercial Bank of China Limited, Annual Report 2021 (ICBC, 2022). Available at https://www.icbc-ltd.com/en/page/721852240511139844.html accessed 17 August 2025; Industrial and Commercial Bank of China Limited, Annual Report 2022 (ICBC, 2023). Available at https://www.icbc-ltd.com/en/page/824694856168763392.html accessed 17 August 2025; Industrial and Commercial Bank of China Limited, Annual Report 2023 (ICBC, 2024). Available at https://www.icbc-ltd.com/en/page/957353942088728576.html accessed 17 August 2025; Industrial and Commercial Bank of China Limited, Consolidated Annual Report 2024 (ICBC, 2024). Available at https://v.icbc.com.cn/userfiles/Resources/ICBCLTD/download/2025/Announcement20250425_1.pdf accessed 17 August 2025.

Funding and financing the transition

The role of ICBC in funding and financing the transition to net zero can be examined through multiple perspectives. One is on-balance sheet financing for clients. The loans and investments are from ICBC's own balance sheet. These are counted as Scope 3 emissions. Another is underwriting green bonds, sustainability-linked instruments and other capital markets activities. Third is internal and operational decarbonisation targeting ICBC's own Scopes 1 and 2.

ICBC has been progressively increasing its financing for the green projects and activities of its clients from its own balance sheet and has become a leading player in the transition of many businesses, in China and abroad. These have taken many forms including loans, project financing, equity investments, and debt holdings. As mentioned, the amount of green loans on its balance sheet has been growing at about 34 per cent per year over the past four years (see Figure 14.10). Given that the group has been a major financing source for hard-to-abate industries, including coal-fired power plants, raising the amount of exposure to low- or zero-carbon industries is crucial for the banks reduction of financed emissions[44] (i.e., Scope 3).

The bank has been issuing a number of green bonds over the past few years. The use of proceeds from such issuance is to finance or refinance what it calls Eligible Green Assets geared to promoting environmental protection, sustainable economic development, and combatting climate change. Eligible Green Assets include such projects as renewable energy, clean transportation, energy efficiency, or sustainable water and wastewater. The bank stipulated that eligible green assets do not include fossil fuel related assets, nuclear and nuclear related assets, and some forms of biomass.

The bank issued its first overseas green note in 2017. By the end of 2024, the outstanding balance of overseas issuance amounted to almost $22 billion (see Figure 14.10). It issued its first domestic green bond in 2021, and the cumulative amount reached 110 billion yuan

Green bonds issuance (cumulative)	2020	2021	2022	2023	2024
Domestic issuance (billion Chinese yuan)	-	9.9	20.0	60.0	110.0
Domestic issuance (billion USD-equivalent)	-	1.4	2.8	8.4	15.3
Overseas issuance (billion USD)	9.8	13.1	15.7	19.9	21.7
Total	**9.8**	**14.4**	**18.5**	**28.3**	**37.0**

Figure 14.10 Balance of ICBC's green bonds issuance

Source: Author (August 2025). Source of data: Industrial and Commercial Bank of China Limited, Annual Report 2020 (ICBC, 2021). Available at https://www.icbc-ltd.com/en/page/721858136553324554.html accessed 17 August 2025; Industrial and Commercial Bank of China Limited, Annual Report 2021 (ICBC, 2022). Available at https://www.icbc-ltd.com/en/page/721852240511139844.html accessed 17 August 2025; Industrial and Commercial Bank of China Limited, Annual Report 2022 (ICBC, 2023). Available at https://www.icbc-ltd.com/en/page/824694856168763392.html accessed 17 August 2025; Industrial and Commercial Bank of China Limited, Annual Report 2023 (ICBC, 2024). Available at https://www.icbc-ltd.com/en/page/957353942088728576.html accessed 17 August 2025; Industrial and Commercial Bank of China Limited, Consolidated Annual Report 2024 (ICBC, 2024). Available at https://v.icbc.com.cn/userfiles/Resources/ICBCLTD/download/2025/Announcement20250425_1.pdf accessed 17 August 2025.

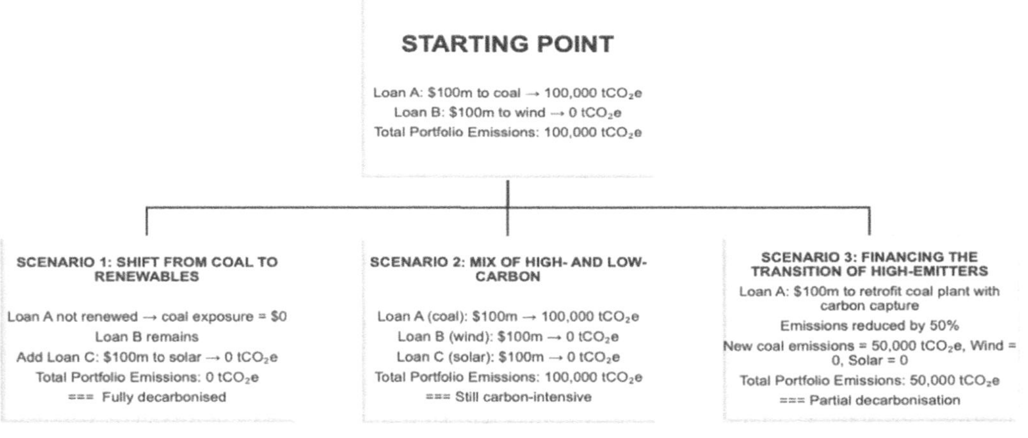

Figure 14.11 Combined flow chart: bank loan emissions scenarios

Source: Author, original chart design (August 2025).

($15.4 billion) in 2024. The total green bond issuance amounted to the equivalent of about $37 billion. Portfolio decarbonisation is, of course, not just about adding green assets, the objective is to reduce exposure to carbon intensive ones. Figure 14.11 illustrates a hypothetical approach of it means for a bank such as ICBC to decarbonise its portfolio.

The bank will also have to progressively reduce its exposure to facilitated emissions given its works with hard-to-abate industries. While facilitated emissions refer to emissions from capital market activities for clients in China and abroad. As of August 2025, there were not as yet any formal rules and guidelines addressing Facilitated Emissions for banks' portfolio. It is an evolving discussion in many jurisdictions and remains the subject of an ongoing active debate. Importantly, for financed emissions, the group does not require additional funding as the solution is how it balances the provision of its services.

The funding of its own internal, operational decarbonisation (Scopes 1 and 2) can comfortably be met from the group's own cash flows. The group has already been working on this for several years. For example, in 2023, which refers to the 2022 activities, it reported that it was intensifying energy conservation and carbon-emission reduction activities at its operations including at its technological, and building infrastructures, and its offices. It undertook, for example, the structural renovation of building enclosure, it replaced aging equipment, installed energy monitoring platforms, began to substitute its vehicle fleet to EVs, and enhanced green procurement. A year earlier, it was addressing its data centres to reduce their power consumption through improving natural cooling as well as lowering their water consumption.

Opportunities and challenges from the transition

ICBC is the leader in China's banking sector in terms of total assets, market share of loans and market share of deposits. Its size, experience in climate finance and ambition to retain its title as the nation's green and sustainable bank, naturally puts the group in pole position from benefitting the many opportunities created by China's decarbonisation drive. One of the many areas, for example, is the water conservation industry which is expected to reach one trillion yuan ($140 billion) by 2027.[45] In the coming years, all of the groups various businesses should have continued growth opportunities. It should see more income generation from green lending, from retaining its position as the lead under writer and book runner of domestic green bonds, from carbon finance trading and market meeting making, from transition finance advisory and M&A, from digital carbon accounting and risk management services for its clients, among the many areas. This also provides ICBC with great foundational experience to develop its climate-finance activities in overseas markets.

ICBC faces a broad set of challenges like banks elsewhere in the world. Domestically, its biggest challenge is its exposure to hard-to-abate industries, especially those involved in fossil fuels. This has many aspects. Its balance sheet has a high concentration in the coal industry. Some have estimated the exposure could be around one-tenth of its loan book. It will have to find ways to progressively lower this exposure. It is a complex and demanding task for the group. It will have to use a variety of solutions including, for example, green bond issuance for refinancing the early retirement of qualified power plants. The fossil-fuel exposure also opens the group to reputational risks which could impact its ESG rating, for example. Another important challenge is data. As in many other jurisdictions, especially in developing economies, ICBC's clients may not have adequate tools for Scope 1 data collection making it difficult for the group to assess its real exposure. While this is progressively improving near term it will remain a challenge. The main challenge in overseas markets will be expanding and growing its climate finance activities, especially as ESG related regulation becomes tighter and the geopolitical landscape becomes increasingly complex.

Information and communications technology sector

Sector profile

The emissions picture for the information and communications technology sector, or ICT, is complex. It is not a major contributor as estimates, quoted by the World Bank, put the sector's global share at a relatively wide range of between 1.5 per cent and 4 per cent. Part of the reason may be because it includes a wide variety of subsectors. Industries such as

INFORMATION AND COMMUNICATIONS TECHNOLOGY	STOCK SYMBOL	COUNTRY OF INCORPORATION	CAPITALISATIO N ($, billion)	NET ZERO TARGET (yes/no + year)	SUSTAINABILITY OBJECTIVES (yes/no)	CLEAN ENERGY INVESTMENTS (yes/no)
NVIDIA Corp	NVDA	United States	4,236,614	Yes, 2030	Yes	Yes
Microsoft Corp	MSFT	United States	3,895,799	Yes, 2030	Yes	Yes
Apple Inc	AAPL	United States	3,022,707	Yes, 2030	Yes	Yes
Alphabet Inc	GOOG	United States	2,290,949	Yes, 2030	Yes	Yes
Amazon.com, Inc	AMZN	United States	2,279,872	Yes, 2040	Yes	Yes
Meta Platforms, Inc	META	United States	1,884,130	Yes, 2030	Yes	Yes
Broadcom Inc	AVGO	United States	1,357,610	No	Yes	Yes
Taiwan Semiconductor Manufacturing Co Ltd	TSM	Taiwan	1,219,921	Yes, 2050	Yes	Yes
Tesla, Inc	TSLA	United States	976,118	Yes, 2040	Yes	Yes
Oracle Corp	ORCL	United States	686,534	Yes, 2050	Yes	Yes
Tencent Holdings Ltd	TCEHY	China	615,467	N/A (China 2060)	Yes	Yes
Netflix, Inc	NFLX	United States	492,319	Yes, 2030	Yes	Yes
Palantir Technologies Inc	PLTR	United States	364,063	Yes, 2024	Yes	Yes
SAP SE (Societas Europaea)	SAP	Germany	334,667	Yes, 2030	Yes	Yes
Samsung Electronics Co, Ltd	005930.KS	South Korea	325,854	Yes, 2050	Yes	Yes
Total market capitilisation of top 15			**23,982,625**			

Figure 14.12 Information and communications technology sector decarbonisation

Notes: N/A = the company's principal shareholder is the national government. Although the company itself has not publicly declared a net-zero target, its respective government has: China has committed to carbon neutrality by 2060. It is therefore reasonable to infer that the company aligns with the national objective.

Source: Author (August 2025). Share price and issued share data: CompaniesMarketcap.com, https://companiesmarketcap.com/accessed 3 August 2025). Net-zero targets, sustainability objectives, and clean energy facilities information drawn from each company's latest annual report, most recent sustainability or ESG disclosures, financial statements, and investor presentations.

data and cloud computing, hardware and infrastructure, information technology services and support, telecommunications, and software and applications development. At the same time the ICT sector includes some of the largest companies in the world in terms of stock market capitalisation. The total for the top 15 was nearly $24 trillion, as of 3 August 2025 (see Figure 14.12). The largest eight commanded a market capitalisation of more than $1 trillion. Most are familiar household names like Microsoft, Apple, Google's parent company Alphabet, Amazon, and WhatsApp and Facebook parent Meta; the number one is Nvidia, a chip designer whose major clients include many of the large tech firms.

Among the 15 companies, 14 have made carbon neutrality pledges. The only exception is Broadcom but even then, the company is not a complete laggard as it is working on Scopes 1 and 2 emissions cuts. Eight of the 15 companies have a set net-zero target year of 2030 or earlier, two aim for 2040, while the remaining four seek to turn net zero by 2050 or 2060. All 15 top ICT companies have publicly declared sustainability pledges, which for the most part or clear and transparent; these pledges can typically be found on the companies' website, in their respective sustainability or ESG reports, as well as in most of their financial statements. They all have already undertaken, and are in the process of undertaking, investments in clean-energy projects and solutions.

When it comes to corporate transitioning or decarbonising, for a multitude of reasons the ICT sector is significantly more influential and far reaching than its market size or GHG emissions share may indicate. Some of the factors include innovation, its role as an enabler, and growing energy demand.

Innovation

ICT companies are among the largest spenders on R&D in almost any industry (see Figure 14.13). The top five companies – NVIDIA, Microsoft, Apple, Alphabet, and Amazon – spent a staggering amount on a cumulative basis in their combined last three fiscal years, almost $600 billion; the five mostly have different fiscal year ends. R&D expenditure as an average percentage of revenue in the past three fiscal year ranged from 7.4 per cent of revenue for Apple to 14.8 per cent for Microsoft. This financial muscle enables the five companies to lead innovation thanks to the significant leverage they gain from capital expenditure on ICT, including in transition-related projects and solutions.

Some ICT companies focused on decarbonisation have successfully developed innovative solutions. They have actively invested in or deployed such solutions as AI for energy management, including for smart grids (Alphabet, for example), energy efficiency solutions (Microsoft, for example), optimisation of cooling systems for data centres (Alphabet, for example). As well as IoT devices for environmental purposes (Cisco, for example), digital twins for industrial decarbonisation (Nvidia, for example), AI-driven predictive maintenance (PXiSE, for example), and data-driven supply chain emissions tracking (Amazon, for example).

Enabler role

Many ICT companies are also major decarbonisation enablers. They play an important enabling role outside their immediate ecosystem. The innovative solutions that they developed are shared with third parties thus widening the decarbonisation scope. As all major ICT companies target Scope 3 GHG emissions reductions and carbon neutrality, some of the recipients of their innovative solutions are their suppliers, resulting in supply chain decarbonisation. This proactive approach makes them not only solid decarbonisation adopters but also has positioned them as catalysts for much broader systemic change.

Alphabet, Amazon, Apple and Microsoft are some of the companies which have aggressively adopted corporate clean energy strategies and are in part responsible for the progressive widespread adoption of corporate power-purchasing agreements. These companies have also proactively engaged with, trained and supported in a variety of ways their suppliers in green procurement, including clean energy procurement. They have led by example in terms of circularity adoption. Some of these companies, for example, have been extending the lifespan of their digital products or have been integrating eco-design principles into these products. These and other circular economy strategies have also been passed on to their supply chain players.

Company	Fiscal Year End	R&D expenditure ($, billion)			R&D / Revenue (%)		
		2022	2023	2024	2022	2023	2024
NVIDIA Corp	Jan	3.1	3.9	5.8	11.5	8.8	10.4
Microsoft Corp	Jun	26.2	32.7	38.3	13.2	15.4	15.7
Apple Inc	Sep	26.3	31.3	37.1	6.7	7.4	8.1
Alphabet Inc	Dec	39.5	44.3	51.5	14.0	13.7	14.3
Amazon.com, Inc	Dec	73.2	82.3	96.5	14.2	14.5	15.5

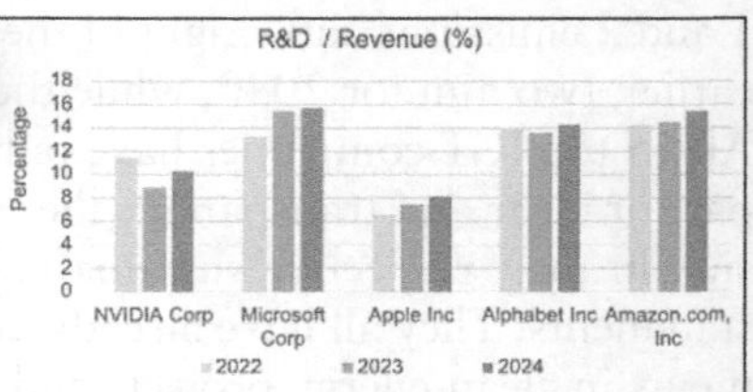

Figure 14.13 ICT companies R&D spending

Source: Company websites.

Energy demand

A third example of the important influence of companies in the ICT sector is that their business has also created new demand for energy. Internally this is mostly satisfied by the use, in some form, of clean energy physically or virtually – for example, using virtual power purchasing agreements, for example. This internal shift to clean energy has a cascading effect on the companies' supply chain participants. It is positive for decarbonisation as it promotes the development of clean energy generation facilities. At the same time the increase in digital solutions mean more electricity requirements. Energy consumption is boosted from cloud computing, data centres, smart grids, and IoT behind-the-meter products, for example.

The IEA projects that electric-power consumption from data centres will more than double by 2030 from 2022. It will amount to almost 1000 TWh, roughly equivalent to the whole electricity consumption in Japan currently. At the same time AI in the data centres can help a variety of sectors to reduce their energy through process optimisation (see Figure 14.14). For industrial users, it could save about 8 per cent. For the transport sector, it could reduce energy consumption 5 to 20 per cent. For buildings, savings could be as much as 10 per cent.[46]

Information and communications technology sector transition journey case study: Alphabet

Alphabet is one of the best-in-class examples of corporate transitioning in general, and in the ICT sector in particular. The company has a track record of being an early adopter and a pioneer of energy transition-related projects and solutions. It has significantly ambitious decarbonisation targets, is a unique sustainability enabler in its supply chain and beyond and has a high level of transparency.

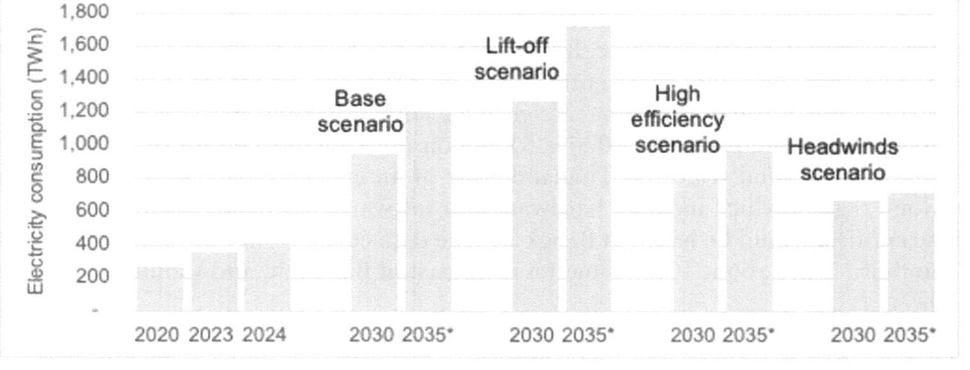

Figure 14.14 World data centres electricity consumption

Notes: (1) The 'Lift-Off Case' assumes stronger AI uptake and limited local constraints on datacentre buildout. (2) The 'High Efficiency Case' is driven by energy savings in both software and hardware. (3) * = 2035 numbers serve as exploratory scenarios given the high level of uncertainty around data centre demand growth. This is a work by the author derived from IEA material and the author is solely liable and responsible for this derived work. The derived work is not endorsed by the IEA in any manner.

Source: IEA, 'World Energy Outlook Special Report Energy and AI' (International Energy Agency 2025). Available at https://iea.blob.core.windows.net/assets/601eaec9-ba91-4623-819b-4ded331ec9e8/EnergyandAI.pdf and https://www.iea.org/data-and-statistics/data-product/energy-and-ai accessed 4 August 2025.

Alphabet is a US-based global technology conglomerate with over 50 per cent of its revenue generated from outside the United States. Alphabet's chief revenue contributors are the Google-branded parts of the business. Out of $181.2 billion in revenue, Google-branded businesses accounted for $180.4 billion in the first half of fiscal 2025 in June. Also, almost two-thirds of revenue is related to advertising.

The engine behind Google's revenue is its technical infrastructure, a key area investment for the company. Such includes servers and network equipment for computing, storage, networking requirements, and other related equipment. Apart from some office facilities, the company also owns, in some cases owns the land where its data centres are located. This makes the tech giant not an asset-light company. The balance sheet net value of property and equipment as of June 2025 was $203.3 billion. This is similar to Microsoft's $205 billion, smaller than Amazon's $297.6 billion, but larger than Apple's $48.5 billion,[47] a relatively asset light tech company.

Several examples in the Asia Pacific region illustrate more clearly the type and scope of Google's technical infrastructure investments.

The company opened its first data centre in Japan in Inzai City, Chiba, in 2023. This centre was part of a $730 million technical infrastructure investment which continued through 2024. In addition to the data centre and related facilities, the investment also included the Topaz subsea trans-Pacific fibre cable, connecting eastern Japan and Western Canada. Topaz's dual benefits are delivering low-latency – the transmission of data with minimum delay – for Google's various services as well as increasing capacity in the region.

Google is investing a total of S$6.7 billion ($5.2 billion) in four data centres in Singapore. This is a substantial increase from S$1.1 billion ($0.9 billion) in 2022, the company said in late 2024. Singapore is one of 11 countries with the company runs data centres. The data centres benefited from innovations in facility design and hardware which allow super computers to operate at higher temperatures which will require less energy for cooling. They would also include the use of recycled water, which can be reused multiple times, cutting CO_2 emissions by 10 per cent compared to air cooling. Google is using a new type of network switch that moves data with light, not electricity. It avoids the usual energy heavy signal conversion and cuts data centre electricity consumption by up to 40 per cent. This makes it a faster, greener way to handle growing computing and AI demands.[48]

The company announced in 2024 a $1 billion investment to establish its first regional data centre and cloud region in Thailand, part of an effort to increase its cloud services. The cloud region, which includes hardware and software to provide services to public and private entities, would be based in Bangkok. The data centres will be at an industrial estate in Chonburi, a city about 100 kilometres southeast of Bangkok, and should be operational by 2027.[49]

Also in 2024, Google announced yet another data centre investment in the Southeast Asia region. It is a large investment in Malaysia. Google plans to invest $2 billion to establish the first data centre and cloud region in the country. The data centre, which will be located in the Elmina Business Park, about 30 kilometres from the nation's capital of Kuala Lumpur. The new Malaysia-based data centre will be dedicated to boosting many Google services such as search, maps, workspace, as well as AI solutions.

Google will likely expand its footprint in the Asia Pacific region with more investments in data centres, based on unconfirmed media reports as of June 2025, possibly in India and in other countries.

Transition journey

PLANNING AND STRATEGIES

Alphabet's sustainability journey began early. It started when Larry Page and Sergey Brin founded Google, as Alphabet was then known, in 1998. Alphabet has often underlined that it was the first major company to turn carbon-neutral in 2007 (see Figure 14.15). This effectively meant accounting for and offsetting direct and indirect emissions. It began to purchase energy from clean energy sources in 2010, one of the early pioneers among large companies.

Seven years later, it reduced its reliance on carbon offsets and was able to fully match its total electricity use with corporate clean energy purchases. During this period, it tested a variety of strategies including one known as Renewable Energy Cheaper than Coal or RE<C, aimed at lowering the cost of energy from renewable sources below that from thermal coal. RE<C involved directly investing in mainstream renewable energy technologies, such as solar and wind, as well as start-ups. Alphabet gave up on the RE<C strategy in 2014 but continued to buy power from green sources. The company was probably a few years too early given that today solar and wind are cheaper than coal fired power generation in most major jurisdictions.

In 2020, Alphabet announced its 'moonshot' goal. This objective involves consuming carbon-free electricity every hour of the day at all its major facilities, principally the data centres and campuses all around the world. The mechanics are different from the annual matching exercise. The 24/7 ambition is complex and requires a great deal of background work. The first part is to ensure that it keeps on working on energy efficiency, making

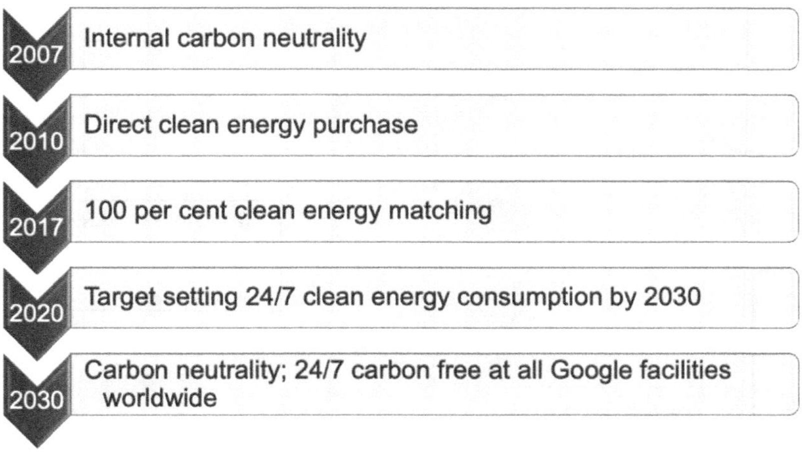

Figure 14.15 Google's journey to net zero

Source: Author (August 2025). Timeline sourced from Pichai S, 'Our Third Decade of Climate Action: Realizing a Carbon-Free Future' (Google 14 September 2020). Available at https://blog.google/outreach-initiatives/sustainability/our-third-decade-climate-action-realizing-carbon-free-future/ accessed 5 August 2025; Google, 'Google Environmental Report 2025' (2025). Available at https://www.gstatic.com/gumdrop/sustainability/google-2025-environmental-report.pdf accessed 5 August 2025.

its data centres as super-efficient as possible. The second part involves addressing how to address clean energy consumption from grids which are dominated by fossil fuels.[50]

Google's clean energy generation expansion in the Asia Pacific region illustrates the company's efforts to add new carbon-free energy. The region presents its own set of unique hurdles for Google and other clean-energy generation project developers. The challenges, among the many, include a lack of experience with corporate power-purchasing agreements, land constraints, evolving regulation, low availability of commercially scalable wind and solar resources, and high construction costs. Google has been expanding its generation capacity in the region at a healthy pace despite the many hurdles. In October 2024, the company announced long-term power purchase agreements for a total of 275 MW of new clean energy generation capacity, in addition to supporting the development of a 1 GW pipeline of new solar capacity in Taiwan (see Figure 14.16).

In Australia, Google announced an innovative power purchase agreement and collaboration with AirTrunk and OX2. In India, it is partnering with Adani Group and CleanMax on long-term collaborations. These partnerships add 186 MW of new clean energy to the Indian grid by 2026. CleanMax is developing a 125.4 MW hybrid renewable-energy project in India, with 66 MW of solar generation in Rajasthan and 59.4 MW of wind generation in Karnataka. This project is expected to begin commercial operations in late 2025. The Adani Group will supply energy from a new 30 MW solar-wind hybrid project located in Khavda, Gujarat, further expanding clean energy access in the region. In Japan, Google signed two solar power purchases, the first for the company in Japan. It is partnering with Itochu's Clean Energy Connect and Shizen Energy, these initiatives will add 60 MW of new solar energy capacity to the Japanese grid. In Singapore, the company has a significant

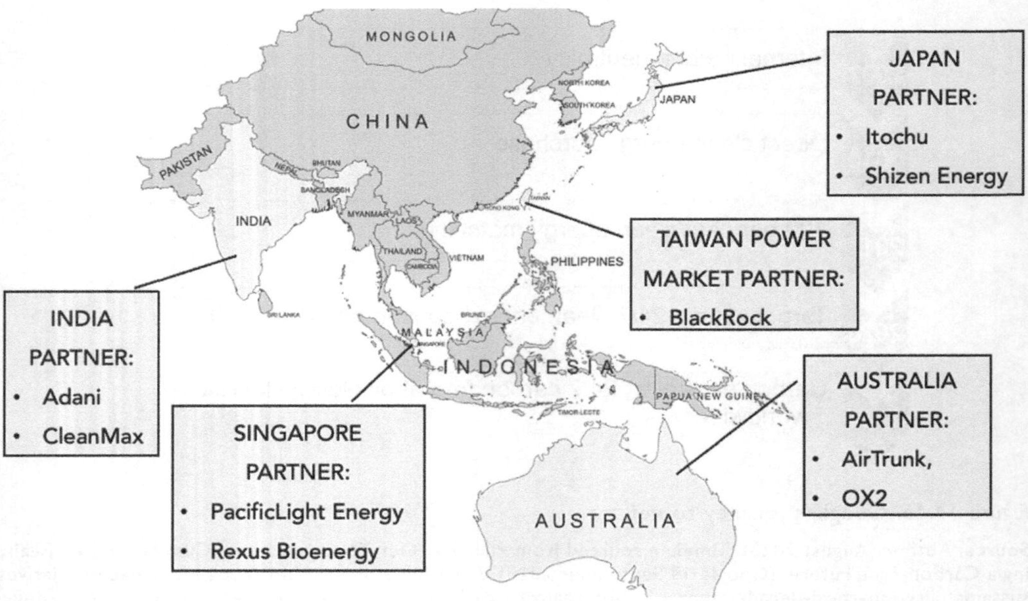

Figure 14.16 Google's clean energy generation expansion in Asia Pacific

Source: Author (August 2025). Data information from various media announcements by Google and media articles. Map created using MapChart (https://www.mapchart.net/).

long-term collaboration with PacificLight Energy and Rexus Bioenergy. This partnership enables PacificLight to offtake renewable energy generated from Rexus Bioenergy's waste Wood-to-Energy plant and supply the output directly to Google's operations. In Taiwan, it announced its partnership with BlackRock's Climate Infrastructure business to support 1 GW of new solar capacity.[51]

Another part is a strategy involving carbon-intelligent computing. This is a platform dedicated to moving flexible tasks across time and location. It allows the data centres to consume more energy from clean energy sources when they are more abundant. The company will favour at any particular time regions with cleaner grid networks and at the same time, optimise media processing efforts. This processing encodes, analyses and processes millions of multimedia files such as videos uploaded to YouTube, for example, which 'can technically run in many places'. According to Google, the

> global carbon-intelligent computing platform will increasingly reserve and use hourly compute capacity on the [cleanest] grids available worldwide for these compute jobs – meaning it moves as much energy consumption as possible to times and places where energy is cleaner, minimizing carbon-intensive energy consumption.[52]

STRUCTURAL AND OPERATIONAL SHIFTS AND TANGIBLE PROGRESS

Alphabet is a massive organisation in terms of business size, geographical footprint, and businesses. Collecting data and reducing GHG emissions are complex and demanding tasks. Disclosure is rapidly improving but based in the analysis of the past five years it is still lacking, making it challenging to judge progress. Nevertheless, looking at the 2024 data's year on year change, there is some evidence that most data points are improving, apart from Scope 3 emissions (see Figure 14.17). There have been reductions in data-centre energy emissions as well as Scopes 1 and 2 emissions. At the same time, clean energy purchased, enabled GHG emissions reductions and water replenishment have increased.

Year	Data Centre Energy Emissions (tCO2e)	Water Replenished (Billion Gallons / % of Freshwater Consumption)	Clean Energy Purchased (GW)	Enabled GHG Emissions Reductions (tCO2e)	Scope 1 Emissions ('000 tCO2e)	Scope 2 Emissions (Market-Based, '000 tCO2e)tCO2e)	Scope 3 Emissions ('000 tCO2e)
2024	2,717,000*	4.5 / 64%	8.00	26,000	73	3,059	12,053
2023	3,085,000**	1.0 / 18%	4.00	2,900	78	3,500	10,800
2022	Not Available	0.4 / 6%	2.80	1,200	70	3,200	9,500
2021	Not Available	Not Available	2.60	Not Available	65	2,900	8,700
2020	Not Available	Not Available	2.50	Not Available	60	2,800	8,200

Figure 14.17 Google's environmental profile

Notes: * Reduced by 12 per cent from 2023; ** Estimated; Data Centre Energy Emissions: Exact figures for 2023 are estimated based on the 12 per cent reduction reported in 2024 (3,059,100 tCO_2e Scope 2 in 2024 implies ~3,085,000 tCO_2e in 2023). Earlier years lack specific data centre emissions breakdowns in the reports; Water Replenishment: Data for 2020 and 2021 are not explicitly detailed in the reports; Google announced its 120 per cent replenishment goal in 2021 but did not provide annual figures until 2022; Clean Energy Purchased: Figures reflect power purchase agreements (PPAs) and targeted renewable energy investments, as reported annually; Enabled GHG Emissions Reductions: Data for 2020 and 2021 are not specified, as Google began reporting enabled emissions (e.g., via fuel-efficient routing) more prominently from 2022; Emissions (Scopes 1, 2, and 3): Values for 2020–2022 are approximated from Google's 2023 report and earlier sustainability disclosures, as exact figures vary slightly across sources due to methodology updates; All data is sourced from Google's Environmental Reports (2020–2025) or related sustainability pages.

Funding and financing the transition

Google has been funding and financing energy transition, sustainability, and decarbonisation projects and solutions in a variety of means. The company has used internal funding, has issued that instruments, has set up joint ventures or joint investments with a variety of actors and has even used the venture capital approach.

STRONG INTERNAL FUNDING

In terms of balance sheet and internal funding, at the parent level, it has been generating strong positive free cash flows, giving the group significant financial muscle. In the five fiscal years to December 2024, annual free cash flows rose at a healthy pace, except in 2022. They rose to $67 billion in 2021 from about $43 billion in 2020. They fell back to about $60 billion in 2022 and then rose to $69 billion in 2023 and to $73 billion in 2024. The company's annual capital expenditure also increased during the same period, more than doubling to about $53 billion in 2024 from a little over $22 billion in 2020. Investments have focused on data centres, technical infrastructure, offices, related facilities, and AI-related expenditure. All these buckets had some form of decarbonisation-related investments. The company has commented on its sustainable office design and construction. This ranges from using renewable materials to using smart controls to reduce energy use.[53]

SUSTAINABILITY BOND ISSUANCE EXPERIENCE

Alphabet has a proven track record for the issuance of sustainability fixed income. Given the company's scope to issue more such fixed-income notes in the future. In August 2020, the company raised about $5.8 billion in sustainability-related notes. This is the largest fixed-income sustainability insurance in the United States as of August 2025. The three notes had maturities of 5, 10, and 30 years. In the prospectus, the company said that the use of net proceeds, about $5.68 billion, would go mainly towards the financing of at least four types of projects. The first type is the construction, development, acquisition, maintenance, and operation of clean energy generation projects, some including energy storage. Another is the design, construction, and improvements of office spaces with the aim to make them into third-party certified green buildings. The third type of expenditure is into energy-efficient facilities and infrastructure, such as lowering the power usage effectiveness at its data centres. A final type is investing in the procurement, maintenance, and operation chiefly of EVs including the installation of EV charging stations.[54]

COLLABORATION AND JOINT INVESTMENTS

Alphabet has been incredibly active in signing corporate power-purchasing agreements, one of the most prolific in the world. It had signed over 170 such agreements amounting to more than 22 GW of clean energy, between 2010 and 2024. They include 17.3 GW in North America, about 4.5 GW in Europe, approximately 0.4 GW in Latin America, and around 0.3 GW in the Asia Pacific region.[55] These are not actual physical investments, but they greatly facilitate the construction operation of the clean energy facility. It gives investors and lenders a higher level of certainty as to the future cash flows of the project, particularly important given the capital-intensive and long duration asset nature of these clean energy generation projects. One of many examples is the agreement with Kairos Power LLC to buy 500 MW of energy through a long-term corporate power-purchasing agreement, from several Small Nuclear Reactors of 50–75 MW each from 2030.[56] Small Modular Reactors are a very new technology so Google will be supporting its development.

The company has also been willing to jointly invest with developers of clean energy projects. An important strategy given that it reduces the company's overall capital commitment when compared to building ones on facilities. Google made an equity investment in 2024 in clean-energy power-projects developer Intersect Power LLC. In the strategic partnership with Intersect Power, Google will purchase energy from $20 billion worth of energy parks to be built by Intersect Power in the United States, with the first phase becoming operational in 2026 and be fully complete in 2027. These parks will be co-located with data centres and include clean-energy generation, including solar and wind power, as well as energy storage.[57]

Google has also shown to leverage its own balance sheet to invest into companies involved in clean energy technology end solutions. It made an equity investment in 2021 in Commonwealth Fusion Systems, a company which is developing a fusion-energy facility – a form of energy generation from the heat from nuclear fusion reactors – which is expected to come on stream in the United States in the early 2030s.[58] Another example is its investment in Energy Dome S.p.A. in 2025. The Italian company specialises in long-duration battery technology. Energy Dome's CO_2 Battery technology, the company says, allows the system to store the electric power in an energy and cost-efficient way.[59]

Another approach has been to join hands with financial investors, particularly private equity firms that are significant actors in investments in clean energy projects. The partnerships include some of the industry's biggest names including BlackRock, Brookfield, and TPG. For example, for its equity investment into Intersect Power, Google partnered with an arm of TPG, a financial investor with almost $270 billion in assets under management. The TPG platform that invested into Intersect Power, called TPG Rise Climate, is a multi-strategy investor with dedicated pools of capital across private equity, transition infrastructure, and the like. This climate-investing dedicated platform has been investing for almost a decade into growth companies in such areas as energy transition, green mobility, sustainable materials and products, sustainable fuels, and carbon solutions.[60]

Google's multipronged funding and financing approach to transition-related projects and solutions is not unique to the company and is well proven. However, Google is a company at the top of its league. This is thanks to its strong free cash flow generation – enabling Google to fund growth, pay debt, and attract investors, for example – as seen in the most recent five fiscal years to December 2024. It also thanks to the extensive network of partners it has built over the past few years. This financial and networking capacity and capability allow Google to invest in a great variety of projects while at the same time lowering its carbon footprint and working towards its 24/7 carbon-free energy objective.

Opportunities and challenges from the transition

The transition creates new business and investment opportunities as well as new risks and challenges. For Google, some of the new prospects relate to climate data, data-centres optimisation, formidable alliances and branding and sustainable finance among many. Some of the new short- and long-term hurdles include dirty power grids, capital allocation, stranded asset risk, and managing suppliers.

OPPORTUNITIES

Climate data. Google is one of the few companies well-positioned to leverage the data opportunity offered by the global movement towards carbon neutrality. The tech giant's broad and deep ever-growing expertise in data analytics combined with the rapid and continuous improvement of Ai tools, could make Google a leader in processing and utilising data related to climate, decarbonisation, clean energy transition. This data could range from grid-network management to climate modelling to the provision of decarbonisation solutions for businesses and other entities via Google Cloud. This leading role could make the company a top software-as-a-service solutions provider in green data for other businesses, governments, and others.

Data centres optimisation. Google is one of a few companies extensively building data centres, which increasingly use clean energy. It is continuously working on optimising the data centres. It seeks to raise their quality and power while at the same time reduce the operational expenses, including energy costs. This data-centres optimisation in their efficiency and sustainability makes the company's data services highly cost-competitive, allowing Google to retain clients and expand market share.

Formidable alliances. Google has established in recent years a powerful network of partnerships and alliances with a variety of financial institutions, such as private equity firms, and commercial businesses, including clean energy technologies companies. By continuously nurturing this wide-ranging network allows Google to create new investment and expansion opportunities. For example, it could undertake more investments in energy parks that comprise data centres and clean energy facilities. These alliances will allow Google to both de-risk some of the large-scale and capital extensive projects, while at the same time it can build more data centres and increase its market share.

Branding and sustainable finance. Another opportunity lies with Google's green branding and sustainability objectives, which can attract sustainable capital. The company's aggressive targets are a key competitive advantage in attracting such capital given the exponential growth of sustainable finance. Google's goal to reach full carbon neutrality by 2030, including Scope 3 emissions, puts the company in a leading position among ICT sector companies. The 24/7 carbon-free energy pledge and net-zero promise by 2030 are particularly appealing to financial investors and lending institutions. Its verifiable green pedigree should make Google a top candidate for a variety of sustainable instruments, from green bonds to sustainability-linked loans, as the momentum of sustainable capital continues to accelerate.

CHALLENGES

Dirty power grids. Google must actively manage its grid fuel exposure worldwide. This is a major challenge for the company as it aims to achieve 24/7 carbon-free energy globally. Some grids have plentiful supply of clean energy. Others may only have a limited amount, giving the company no guarantee it can source clean power. For example, in India, Indonesia, or Vietnam and other large developing economies in Asia, the dominant fuels in the grids are dirty fossil ones, predominantly thermal coal. As such, securing green energy may be a long-term, systemic risk for the company as the grid's fuel need to progressively shift from dirty to clean power sources.

Capital allocation. To retain market competitiveness or market share, there is a risk Google may have to accelerate capital spending on initiatives not directly associated with sustainability or clean energy, such as investments on AI. These capital requirements can compete internally with capital needs for clean-energy generation. In turn this could slow down Google's 24/7 carbon-free energy ambitions, resulting in the company missing its 2030 goal.

Stranded asset risk. The fast pace of innovation and change in the clean technology space at time can be surprising. A risk for Google, and for other companies investing in clean technologies, is for the technology to be overtaken by a newer one. This would force the company's own technology to become obsolete and the asset to become stranded. This is especially true in the clean technology space as it is a fast-moving and ever-evolving one. For example, a solar power plant or a new battery storage facility could lose their economic value before the end of their useful life.

Managing suppliers. Another challenge true for Google but also for most companies is to ensure that all suppliers and other partners who must reduce carbon emissions to achieve carbon neutrality by 2050. The challenge is that Google must manage that from afar, it cannot do so internally unless it is a shareholder of a particular facility. Also, it has limited control over its suppliers' own suppliers. An added difficulty is that it may be forced to suddenly shift suppliers because of geopolitical reasons.

Notes

1 Ember, *Electricity Data Explorer* (Ember 5 June 2025) <https://ember-energy.org/data/electricity-data-explorer/?chart=single_year&metric=pct_share> accessed 9 August 2025.
2 A Anacleto and others, *The Iberian Green Industrial Opportunity: Seizing the Moment* (McKinsey & Company 23 July 2024) <https://www.mckinsey.com/industries/electric-power-and-natural-gas/our-insights/the-iberian-green-industrial-opportunity-seizing-the-moment> accessed 9 August 2025.
3 D Jimenez, *Cutting the Carbon Footprint of Pharma's Supply Chain* (Pharmaceutical Technology 9 February 2022) <https://www.pharmaceutical-technology.com/features/cutting-carbon-footprint-pharma-supply-chain/> accessed 9 August 2025.
4 Earnings = Ordinary Earnings Before Interest, Taxes, Depreciation, and Amortisation (EBITDA). The item 'Services & Other adjustment' amounting to negative €93 million (negative \$109 million). In the first half of the 2025 fiscal year to 30 June 2025, is allocated proportionally by the author based on each business line's or region's share of the total EBITDA before adjustment.
5 Enel, *First Half 2025 Consolidated Results Presentation* (Enel SpA 2025) <https://www.enel.com/content/dam/enel-com/documenti/investitori/informazioni-finanziarie/2025/trimestrali/1h-2025-risultati.pdf> accessed 10 August 2025.
6 Enel, *2024 GHG Inventory: Build the Future through Sustainable Power* (Enel SpA 2024) <https://www.enel.com/investors/sustainability/strategy-sustainable-progress/net-zero> accessed 10 August 2025.
7 Enel, *Enel Capital Markets Day 2024 Presentation* (Enel SpA 2024) <https://www.enel.com/content/dam/enel-com/documenti/investitori/informazioni-finanziarie/2024/2025-2027-strategic-plan.pdf> accessed 11 August 2025.
8 Enel, *Enel Integrated Annual Report 2024: Build the Future through Sustainable* (Enel SpA 2025) <https://www.enel.com/content/dam/enel-com/documenti/investitori/informazioni-finanziarie/2024/annuali/en/integrated-annual-report_2024.pdf> accessed 11 August 2025.
9 Enel, *Enel Integrated Annual Report 2024: Build the Future through Sustainable* (Enel SpA 2025) <https://www.enel.com/content/dam/enel-com/documenti/investitori/informazioni-finanziarie/2024/annuali/en/integrated-annual-report_2024.pdf> accessed 11 August 2025.
10 M Hall, *Enel Plans 2.3 GW of Battery Energy Storage through 2027 – Energy Storage* (Energy Storage 19 November 2024) <https://www.ess-news.com/2024/11/19/enel-plans-2-3-gw-of-battery-energy-storage-through-2027/> accessed 11 August 2025.
11 E Bertoli, *Demand Response* (IEA 11 July 2023) <https://www.iea.org/energy-system/energy-efficiency-and-demand/demand-response> accessed 11 August 2025.

12 E Eren, 'Enel AI Initiatives for 2025: Key Projects, Strategies and Partnerships' (Enkiai.com 5 August 2025) <https://enkiai.com/enel-ai-initiatives-for-2025-key-projects-strategies-and-partnerships> accessed 12 August 2025.

13 C Murray, *Enel Repurposes EV Batteries for 4MW Backup Power at Plant* (Energy Storage 22 March 2022) <https://www.energy-storage.news/enel-repurposes-ev-batteries-for-4mw-backup-power-at-plant/> accessed 12 August 2025.

14 M Hall, *Enel Inagurates 10 MWh Second-Life Battery Project at Italian Airport* (Energy Storage 4 June 2025) <https://www.ess-news.com/2025/06/04/enel-inagurates-10-mwh-second-life-battery-project-at-italian-airport/> accessed 12 August 2025.

15 P Sánchez Molina, 'Enel to Retrofit Battery Storage at Century-Old Pumped Hydro Storage Plant' *PV Magazine International* (20 December 2024) <https://www.pv-magazine.com/2024/12/20/enel-to-retrofit-battery-storage-at-century-old-pumped-hydro-storage-plant/> accessed 12 August 2025.

16 E Eren, 'Enel AI Initiatives for 2025: Key Projects, Strategies and Partnerships' (Enkiai.com 5 August 2025) <https://enkiai.com/enel-ai-initiatives-for-2025-key-projects-strategies-and-partnerships> accessed 12 August 2025.

17 Enel, 'Here's How We're Working towards a Just Transition' (Enelgreenpower.com 12 July 2022) <https://www.enelgreenpower.com/stories/articles/2022/07/just-transition-reskilling-workers> accessed 12 August 2025.

18 Enel, 'Enel's Innovation through AI' (Enel.com 11 July 2024) <https://www.enel.com/media/word-from/news/2024/07/ai-future-on-the-road-to-innovation> accessed 12 August 2025.

19 A BBB rating from S&P means that the company is assessed as 'moderately safe' and as a borrower with a low risk of default. The 'stable' part of the rating implies that S&P expects the rating to remain unchanged near term. In the S&P ratings scale, AA- to AAA means very attractive high grade rating. A- to A+ is for attractive, upper medium grade, BBB- to BBB+ is equal to neutral, lower investment grade. Enel's long-term debt credit rating is comfortable within investment grade.

20 S&P Global, 'Italian Energy Giant Enel SpA and Subsidiary Ende | S&P Global Ratings' (Spglobal.com 5 December 2023) <https://www.spglobal.com/ratings/en/regulatory/article/-/view/sourceId/12938598> accessed 13 August 2025.

21 Enel, 'Enel Group Launches Its First Green Bond Totalling 1,250 Million Euros on European Market' (Enel.com 9 January 2017) <https://www.enel.com/media/explore/search-press-releases/press/2017/01/enel-group-launches-its-first-green-bond-totalling-1250-million-euros-on-european-market-> accessed 12 August 2025.

22 Enel, 'Enel Group Launches Its First Green Bond Totalling 1,250 Million Euros on European Market' (Enel.com 9 January 2017) <https://www.enel.com/media/explore/search-press-releases/press/2017/01/enel-group-launches-its-first-green-bond-totalling-1250-million-euros-on-european-market-> accessed 12 August 2025.

23 TwentyFour Blog, 'Small Miss for Enel, Big Step for the Sector' (*Small Miss for Enel, Big Step for the Sector | TwentyFour AM*, 24 April 2024) <https://www.twentyfouram.com/insights/small-miss-for-enel-big-step-for-the-sector> accessed 12 August 2025.

24 Enel, 'Enel's Strategic Plan 2024–2026: Executive Summary' (Enel.com 2024) <https://www.enel.com/investors/strategy/strategic-plan-2024-2026> accessed 13 August 2025.

25 Reuters, 'Enel Teams up with Intesa Sanpaolo for Italy Payments Firm Mooney' *Yahoo Finance* (23 December 2021) <https://ca.finance.yahoo.com/news/enel-teams-intesa-sanpaolo-italy-210945325.html> accessed 13 August 2025.

26 EuropaWire PR Editor, 'Enel Enters Joint Venture with Macquarie Asset Management, Sells 50% Stake in Greek Subsidiary for 345 Million Euros' *EuropaWire* (23 July 2023) <https://news.europawire.eu/enel-enters-joint-venture-with-macquarie-asset-management-sells-50-stake-in-greek-subsidiary-for-345-million-euros/eu-press-release/2023/07/27/12/23/35/119534/>> accessed 13 August 2025.

27 Enel, 'Enel: Sustainability-Linked Revolving Credit Facility Increased to 13.5 Billion Euros' (Enel.com 11 May 2022) <https://www.enel.com/media/explore/search-press-releases/press/2022/05/enel-sustainability-linked-revolving-credit-facility-increased-to-135-billion-euros> accessed 13 August 2025.

28 Network for Greening the Financial System, *Network for Greening the Financial System Information Note* (Central Banks and Supervisors Network for Greening the Financial System 2024) <https://www.ngfs.net/system/files/import/ngfs/medias/documents/ngfs_information_note_on_improving_ghg_emission_data.pdf> accessed 15 August 2025.

29 Network for Greening the Financial System, *Network for Greening the Financial System Information Note* (Central Banks and Supervisors Network for Greening the Financial System 2024) <https://www.ngfs.net/system/files/import/ngfs/medias/documents/ngfs_information_note_on_improving_ghg_emission_data.pdf> accessed 15 August 2025.

30 Equifax, 'Measuring the Invisible: How Banks Calculate Financed Emissions' (Equifax.co.uk 5 March 2025) <https://www.equifax.co.uk/about-equifax/press-releases/-/intlpress/measuring-the-invisible-how-banks-calculate-financed-emissions/> accessed 16 August 2025; F Mirenzi, *Challenges and Strategies for Banks in Reducing Financed Emissions* (OMFIF 15 August 2025) <https://www.omfif.org/2025/08/challenges-and-strategies-for-banks-in-reducing-financed-emissions/> accessed 16 August 2025.

31 Asuene, *GFANZ: Finance's Role in the Net-Zero Transition | Blog | ASUENE | the Enterprise Climate Cloud Platform | Carbon Calculation Decarbonizated SaaS* (ASUENE 19 March 2025) <https://asuene.com/us/blog/gfanz-finances-role-in-the-net-zero-transition> accessed 16 July 2025.

32 M Segal, 'Bloomberg, Carney-Led Climate Finance Group Restructures after String of High-Profile Departures from Net Zero Coalitions' *ESG Today* (6 January 2025) <https://www.esgtoday.com/bloomberg-carney-led-climate-finance-group-restructures-after-string-of-high-profile-departures-from-net-zero-coalitions/> accessed 16 August 2025.

33 Industrial and Commercial Bank of China Limited, *Annual Report 2020* (ICBC 2021) <https://www.icbc-ltd.com/en/page/721858136553324554.html> accessed 17 August 2025; Industrial and Commercial Bank of China Limited, *Annual Report 2021* (ICBC 2022) <https://www.icbc-ltd.com/en/page/721852240511139844.html> accessed 17 August 2025; Industrial and Commercial Bank of China Limited, *Annual Report 2022* (ICBC 2023) <https://www.icbc-ltd.com/en/page/824694856168763392.html> accessed 17 August 2025; Industrial and Commercial Bank of China Limited, *Annual Report 2023* (ICBC 2024) <https://www.icbc-ltd.com/en/page/957353942088728576.html> accessed 17 August 2025; Industrial and Commercial Bank of China Limited, *Consolidated Annual Report 2024* (ICBC 2024) <https://v.icbc.com.cn/userfiles/Resources/ICBCLTD/download/2025/Announcement20250425_1.pdf> accessed 17 August 2025.

34 BloombergNEF, 'Global Investment in the Energy Transition Exceeded $2 Trillion for the First Time in 2024, according to BloombergNEF Report' *BloombergNEF* (30 January 2025) <https://about.bnef.com/insights/finance/global-investment-in-the-energy-transition-exceeded-2-trillion-for-the-first-time-in-2024-according-to-bloombergnef-report/> accessed 17 August 2025.

35 Industrial and Commercial Bank of China Limited, *2024 Sustainability Report* (March 2025) <https://v.icbc.com.cn/userfiles/resources/icbcltd/download/2025/esg2024en.pdf> accessed 20 August 2025.

36 Industrial and Commercial Bank of China Limited, *2024 Sustainability Report* (March 2025) <https://v.icbc.com.cn/userfiles/resources/icbcltd/download/2025/esg2024en.pdf> accessed 20 August 2025.

37 PBOC, 'PBOC, MEE, NFRA and CSRC Issue Opinions on Leveraging Green Finance to Support the Beautiful China Initiative' (Pbc.gov.cn 12 October 2024) <http://www.pbc.gov.cn/en/3688006/3995557/5480627/index.html> accessed 19 March 2025.

38 ICBC, 'ICBC (Europe) S.A. Launches the Pioneering Overseas ESG & Sustainable Finance Risk Management System' (Icbc.com.cn 2025) <https://europe.icbc.com.cn/en/page/1047463878289698816.html> accessed 19 August 2025.

39 Industrial and Commercial Bank of China Limited (n 35).

40 ICBC, 'ICBC Again Wins "Best Bank for Sustainable Finance, China" of the Asset' (Icbc-ltd.com 8 April 2024) <https://www.icbc-ltd.com/en/page/950788501396504576.html> accessed 19 August 2025.

41 蔺璐璐, 邓玉洁 and 林晓丽, '广州日报-工商银行广州分行：探寻创新之路　谱写绿色金融新篇章' (Gzdaily.cn 15 November 2024) <https://epaper.gzdaily.cn/news/html/2024/11/15/content_630_872970.htm> accessed 20 August 2025.

42 ICBC, 'ICBC Wins the Achievement in Climate Risk Management Award from the Asian Banker' (Icbc-ltd.com 17 November 2022) <https://www.icbc-ltd.com/en/page/766236023104475136.html> accessed 21 August 2025.

43 MSCI, 'ESG Ratings | MSCI' (Msci.com 2025) <https://www.msci.com/data-and-analytics/sustainability-solutions/esg-ratings> accessed 21 August 2025.

44 This is to comply with GHG Protocol Scope 3, Category 15 (Investments) as per the Global GHG Accounting and Reporting Standard for the Financial Industry developed by the Partnership for Carbon Accounting Financials.

45 LS Dong, C Tortajada, and A Biswas, *Key Green Finance Policies to Build China's Trillion-Yuan Water-Savings Industry* (CWR 22 May 2025) <https://cwrrr.org/opinions/key-green-

finance-policies-to-build-chinas-trillion-yuan-water-savings-industry/?utm_source=China+Water+Risk&utm_campaign=4d5e55db31-China_Water_Risk_Jan_2018_Newslette07_15_2017_COPY&utm_medium=email&utm_term=0_caee821f95-4d5e55db31-1205191764> accessed 21 August 2025.

46 IEA, *World Energy Outlook Special Report Energy and AI* (International Energy Agency 2025) <https://iea.blob.core.windows.net/assets/601eaec9-ba91-4623-819b-4ded331ec9e8/EnergyandAI.pdf> accessed 4 August 2025.

47 Latest company financial filings from Alphabet, Amazon.com, Apple, and Microsoft for the quarter ended 30 June 2025 found on the Investor Relations company website page of each company, accessed 5 August 2025.

48 Z Abdullah, 'Google's Latest Data Centre Raises Its Investment in Singapore to $6.7 Billion' *The Straits Times* (3 June 2024) <https://www.straitstimes.com/tech/tech-news/google-s-latest-data-centre-raises-its-investment-in-singapore-to-676-billion> accessed 14 August 2025.

49 Reuters Staff, 'Google to Invest $1 Billion in Thai Data Centre, Cloud Infrastructure' *Reuters* (30 September 2024) <https://www.reuters.com/technology/google-invest-1-billion-thai-data-centre-cloud-infrastructure-2024-09-30/> accessed 14 August 2025; Thai Embassy Washington, *Google Chief Says Firm Will Build Cloud Data Center in Thailand* (Royal Thai Embassy 10 February 2025) <https://washingtondc.thaiembassy.org/en/content/202502102> accessed 14 August 2025.

50 C Clifford, 'How Google Plans to Use 100% Carbon-Free Energy in Its Data Centers by 2030' *CNBC* (13 April 2022) <https://www.cnbc.com/2022/04/13/google-data-center-goal-100percent-green-energy-by-2030.html> accessed 5 August 2025.

51 G Fortunato, 'New Paths for Clean Energy in Asia-Pacific' (*Google*, 21 October 2024) <https://blog.google/around-the-globe/google-asia/new-paths-for-clean-energy-in-asia-pacific/> accessed 14 August 2025; M Silva, 'Advancing Renewable Energy in Australia through Collaboration' (*Google*, 19 December 2023) <https://blog.google/intl/en-au/company-news/outreach-initiatives/advancing-renewable-energy-in-australia-through-collaboration/> accessed 14 August 2025; Mercom, 'Google Partners with CleanMax, Adani for Renewable Energy Supply' (Mercomindia.com 3 October 2024) <https://www.mercomindia.com/google-partners-with-cleanmax-adani-for-renewable-energy-supply> accessed 14 August 2025; S Okuyama, 'New Agreements Bring Solar Energy to Japan's Electricity Grid' (*Google Cloud Blog*, 24 May 2024) <https://cloud.google.com/blog/topics/sustainability/new-agreements-bring-solar-energy-to-japans-electricity-grid> accessed 14 August 2025; PacificLight Power, 'PacificLight | Electricity Retailer in Singapore' (Pacificlight.com.sg 29 July 2024) <https://www.pacificlight.com.sg/media-centre/newsroom-article/advancing-green-data-centers-in-singapore> accessed 14 August 2025; AP Corio, 'Our Investment to Accelerate Clean Energy in Asia Pacific' (*Google*, 1 July 2024) <https://blog.google/outreach-initiatives/sustainability/google-clean-energy-asia-pacific/> accessed 14 August 2025; M Hanna, 'Let the Sunshine In: Opening the Market for More Renewable Energy in Asia' (*Google*, 22 January 2019) <https://blog.google/outreach-initiatives/sustainability/let-sunshine-opening-market-more-renewable-energy-asia/> accessed 14 August 2025; Hsiao I-Chun, 'We're Adding to Our Carbon-Free Energy Portfolio in Taiwan, with Our First Offshore Wind Deal in Asia Pacific' (*Google*, 22 April 2025) <https://blog.google/feed/google-offshore-wind-power-purchase-agreement-taiwan/> accessed 14 August 2025; M Chang, 'Our First Geothermal Energy Deal in Asia' (*Google*, 15 April 2025) <https://blog.google/around-the-globe/google-asia/geothermal-taiwan/> accessed 14 August 2025.

52 R Koningstein, 'We Now Do More Computing Where There's Cleaner Energy' (*Google*, 18 May 2021) <https://blog.google/outreach-initiatives/sustainability/carbon-aware-computing-location/> accessed 5 August 2025.

53 Alphabet Inc, *Annual Report 2020* (Alphabet 2021) <https://abc.xyz/investor/> accessed 6 August 2025; Alphabet Inc, *Annual Report 2021* (Alphabet 2022) <https://abc.xyz/investor/> accessed 6 August 2025; Alphabet Inc, *Annual Report 2022* (Alphabet 2023) <https://abc.xyz/investor/> accessed 6 August 2025; Alphabet Inc, *Annual Report 2023* (Alphabet 2024) <https://abc.xyz/investor/> accessed 6 August 2025; Alphabet Inc, *Annual Report 2024* (Alphabet 2025) <https://abc.xyz/investor/> accessed 6 August 2025.

54 Alphabet Inc, *Prospectus for 2.05% Sustainability Notes due 15 August 2050* (Alphabet 2020) <https://ciusb.com.uy/wp-content/uploads/2022/07/216_BONO-ALPHABET-INC-2.05pcnt-VTO.-15-08-2050-US02079KAF49.pdf> accessed 6 August 2025.

55 Google, *Sustainable & Efficient Operations – Google Sustainability* (Sustainability.Google 2024) <https://sustainability.google/operations/> accessed 7 August 2025.

56 E Wesoff, 'Google Signs Deal to Use Small Nuclear Reactors to Power Data Centers' *Canary Media* (14 October 2024) <https://www.canarymedia.com/articles/nuclear/google-agrees-to-multi-reactor-power-deal-with-nuclear-startup-kairos> accessed 7 August 2025.

57 E Howland, 'Google, Intersect Power to Develop Co-Located Energy Parks with $20B of Renewables, Storage' *Utility Dive* (11 December 2024) <https://www.utilitydive.com/news/google-intersect-power-co-located-energy-park-data-center-ferc/735198/> accessed 7 August 2025.

58 Commonwealth Fusion Systems, 'Google and Commonwealth Fusion Systems Sign Strategic Partnership' (Cfs.energy 25 June 2025) <https://cfs.energy/news-and-media/google-and-commonwealth-fusion-systems-sign-strategic-partnership> accessed 7 August 2025.

59 L Lukiyanova, *Energy Dome Inks a Strategic Commercial Agreement with Google* (Energy Dome 25 June 2025) <https://energydome.com/energy-dome-inks-a-strategic-commercial-agreement-with-google/> accessed 7 August 2025.

60 TPG, 'The Rise Funds | TPG' (Tpg.com2025) <https://www.tpg.com/platforms/impact/the-rise-funds> accessed 7 August 2025.

Conclusion

Looking ahead

The path forward: balancing risk and reward

Not a 'shift', not a 'transition', it's an 'overhaul'

The world is well on its way on the path to global carbon neutrality. The transition is not merely some future possibility, it is an unstoppable reality. The adoption of low- to zero-carbon technologies and solutions is not just a shift or just a transition. It is now a major progressive overhaul of huge portions of our economy.

The defence, energy, healthcare, ICT, transport, and infrastructure sectors each require annual investments in excess of a trillion dollars over the next ten years or longer. A major share of their capital expenditure goes towards sector-specific climate-friendly technologies and solutions. The resulting products are retooling these sectors as well as the whole global economy.

Defence. To enhance security at military bases and other defence and security facilities, governments are investing in energy self-sufficiency by sourcing electricity from on-site clean energy generation and storage facilities, and technologies and solutions catering for physical climate risk.

Healthcare. Governments and private investors have been adopting clean energy technologies and energy efficiency solutions to ensure reliability, especially for climate resilience, while cutting emissions and operational costs at hospitals, clinics, and other health facilities.

ICT. Transition investments overlap with the expansion in data centres, which require secure and reliable energy sources at a stable price, and they are also being adopted across the energy value chain to enable smarter, more efficient services, beyond renewables' integration.

Transport and Infrastructure. Capital is being invested in electrification and decarbonising logistics. For urbanisation, governments and developers are increasingly promoting energy-efficient and low-carbon buildings as well as rendering cities sustainable and the infrastructure climate resilient.

Climate-related spending on these sectors is only the tip of the iceberg. They are just some of the many examples where the transition to net zero is not isolated but deeply embedded within broader economic trends.

Grappling with complexity: the demands of transformation

The overhaul to net zero is a new paradigm. It requires new thinking and new approaches. Globally, many sectors of the economy are yet to fully grasp this new thinking and new

DOI: 10.4324/9781003666509-19

approach. All areas are lagging, from government to finance to business. The lack of understanding creates and nurtures misperceptions, such as 'solar PV is bad because it doesn't work at night', which have directly slowed the expected expansion in investments in clean energy generation and related solutions. Misunderstandings, aggravated by fossil fuels advocates and others, are the primary cause of the slowdown in all sorts of processes, as highlighted. The urgent first priority is improving capacity building, communications, education, and training. Thinking about the overhaul to net zero is something new; it is like learning a new language.

Powering the Unstoppable Green Shift is a compass to navigate the misunderstandings and misperceptions through the examination of the three actors – government, finance, and business – with a symbiotic relationship vital to a net-zero economic future.

The energy transition is the primary structural change of the 21st century. It is a generational economic transformation and a shift that the world has not witnessed in nearly 200 years. The convergence of the low cost of clean energy and related solutions, a broadly supportive policy framework, and corporate economic necessity mean that the shift is absolutely unstoppable. This presents an immense number of business and economic opportunities for those positioned to capitalise on it.

Transition strategies for success

The energy transition is an intricately complex subject from several perspectives. Being able to successfully identify its fundamental components will allow participants, particularly the finance and corporate sectors, to surmount the complexities. Often the first set of hurdles revolves around policy and regulation, which are driven by governments. Policy and regulation evolve over time, but their key role lies in sending a consistent signal to the markets. The government, at a minimum, must have endorsed that the transition is critical. The signal, even a weak one, must be consistent. It is the critical element before the finance and corporate sectors are able to move to identify business and investment opportunities.

A further essential factor for business and finance is access to transition projects that are financially viable and economically sustainable. Low to zero-carbon projects must be bankable, and no environmentally sustainable business can have any kind of longevity if it is not also economically sustainable. That is not to say that it is all about financial viability and that the environment is not a priority. The environment is a critical issue and there are many ways to undertake ecologically critical initiatives which may not be financially viable on a stand-alone basis.

One approach could be a financial mechanism such as government-backed carbon credits tied to the maintenance, operations, and expansion of a forest or a mangrove wetland. This would deliver biodiversity preservation, climate adaptation, support to local communities, and more. Another approach is blended finance. This is a vehicle for making such projects financially sustainable over the long term.

Governments, together with the finance and business sectors, must adopt a multidisciplinary approach to navigate the interwoven complexities of the long-term transition to carbon neutrality. There are a large number of disciplines that practitioners must grasp, which range from accounting to economics to engineering. This does not mean that a lawyer must also be an accounting, economics, or engineering expert. But it is crucial for practitioners to understand the basics, particularly with regard to how climate-related issues interact with these disciplines.

Those working in government must take a multidisciplinary approach so that they may develop the knowledge base to make better decisions. Those involved in the financial markets must take this approach so that they can service their clients or more easily identify investment opportunities. Those in business must have a broad understanding of the different disciplines so as to successfully address business operations and planning during the transition.

Investing in change: opportunities abound

At the core of the transition to net zero, the major growth engine for the sector is electrification, which itself is a cornerstone of decarbonisation. It allows us to consume fewer fossil fuels. Higher levels of electrification in the transport, building, or industrial sectors are invaluable drivers to carbon neutrality.

The fundamental direct elements of the energy sector are demand and supply, unit-cost and end-user price, market mechanisms, and technologies. These direct components, together with other indirect ones, offer enormous business and investment opportunities.

The first area of opportunity lies with the demand and supply of energy. Long-term electricity demand should rise at a compounded annual growth rate of at least 2 per cent in the next two to three decades. The average growth could be from acceleration in electrification and from digital services, especially AI. New supply will need to be ready to meet the growth in demand. In some regions, particularly in Asia Pacific, the increase will be much greater as emerging economies gradually become more mature. Possible economic, geopolitical, or extreme climate events may temporarily slow growth; however, electrification presents a significant upside factor.

On the cost side, mainstream clean generation per unit of energy produced is today highly competitive with thermal coal or natural gas in a great many jurisdictions around the world, including most of the EU and China. In the United States, energy from renewables is the most cost-competitive form of electric power generation on an unsubsidised price-per-kWh basis, according to the highly respected Lazard Levelised Cost of Energy+ report 2025.[1]

Cost competitiveness and stable input costs mean affordable and steady energy prices for consumers. These cost and consumer price stability are not yet globally understood. However, it is certainly much better understood than five or ten years ago when the unit price of mainstream clean energy was still quite high. For instance, the payback period for rooftop solar systems in Australia has decreased from approximately eight years in 2015 to four and a half years in 2024. Apart from the shorter payback period, the owner benefits from a stable and predictable electricity price from the rooftop solar facility, something which is not the case if one uses electricity from coal or natural gas generation plants whose price is neither stable nor predictable over the long term.

Market mechanisms are tricky to address for market participants. Almost no electricity market structure in the world is designed to accommodate clean energy today. As with everything else evolving in the transition world, so is the capability of grids to integrate clean energy into the energy markets. Grid modernisation will move at different speeds depending on the market. A broad view is that once the penetration rate of clean energy in the local energy pie becomes significant – which could mean 20 per cent for some countries or more for others – then the buildup of infrastructure to cater for clean energy will accelerate. The acceleration of power grid investments in China in recent years is an example.

Technological developments have been imperative for the transition since its beginnings. Yet since the early 2020s, beyond cost reductions, digital and other technologies and solutions have become a fully integrated component of the transition. All forms of technologies, directly or indirectly related to the energy transition, have been growing and evolving at great speed. Businesses and financial investors alike have recognised their transformative role. The efficiency and performance of mainstream renewable energy technologies, such as solar and wind power, continue to improve. Other technologies are progressively scaling up. Some, such as battery storage energy systems, are growing at a very fast pace. Others, such as green hydrogen, may need a few more years before they can significantly scale up and reach a competitive unit price. Beyond climate tech, there is the digital technologies dimension which by itself has many catalytic roles. Importantly, they can better assess demand while optimising supply. Digital solutions can reduce energy costs for consumers in numerous ways and are a critical component of energy market mechanisms undergoing transformation.

It bears repeating that these opportunities for growth and investment are conditional upon, and fostered by, the clear signal by government about its commitment to the energy overhaul.

Facing and beating transition barriers

Positive factors sharply outweigh negative factors in the transition to carbon neutrality. Tangible evidence lies in the absolute growth of clean energy generation and solutions as well as climate tech investments in recent years. The growth has not been linear but exponential, nonetheless. The many hurdles which existed, say five years ago, have mostly been surmounted while at the same time new challenges have appeared. While the current list of challenges is extensive, many may be addressed within the next five years. Thereafter, new challenges will certainly appear. Many of the hot issues in 2025 revolve around China, the United States, China–US relations, and infrastructure and bureaucratic barriers.

China Paradox. The nation faces major climate transition challenges: slower economic growth threatens investment in clean energy and grid upgrades; coal generation is difficult to phase out over the coming decades; local governments often prioritise economic targets over emissions reduction, misaligning with national policies; and the evolving carbon market lacks transparency, restricting its impact on emissions cuts

US Backward Step, Policy Risks. Since January 2025, the Trump 2.0 Administration has rolled back clean energy incentives, halted major projects, and increased regulatory uncertainty, leading to billions of dollars in cancelled investments and job losses. The new Trump import tariffs risk increasing inflation and potentially causing stagflation. This political and economic volatility is diverting energy transition capital to other jurisdictions.

China–US Geopolitical Risks. The tensions have increased geopolitical risk, especially for clean energy supply chains. Uncertainty over rare earth elements, essential for these technologies, is a significant mid-term concern. Limited cooperation between the two largest economies and GHG emitters is undermining global progress on carbon neutrality.

Infrastructure and Bureaucratic Fences to Growth. Grids in many countries require upgrades to integrate clean energy, yet grid bottlenecks often lead to curtailments and wasted output. Lengthy approval processes slow clean energy growth and deter investors. Furthermore, public-private financing for energy transition remains sluggish due to bureaucratic delays common across multiple jurisdictions.

These are just four issues slowing the growth of energy transition-related projects and solutions. Yet, while these issues have slowed the process, they did not kill it. Just a few years ago, some of the primary issues were high technology costs, limited financing options, perceived high risk and low bankability, weak policy support, and impossibility for grid integration. These challenges have today largely been overcome. There is strong tangible evidence to believe that today's challenges will also be overcome in future years.

Catching the net-zero wave

A central factor critical to the path to carbon neutrality is that the great majority of challenges have been identified and have been reasonably well understood by governments and that many jurisdictions are already taking actions which allow the world to continue on its path to net zero.

In the public sector, there are several types of actions which can be executed. First and foremost is the reduction of the amount of time that it takes to get a project approved. Red tape is seldom solely a problem for clean energy related projects. For example, in many European countries, residential housing shortages are often caused by the slow approval process. This involves taking too many steps and interacting with numerous departments. As far as energy transition-related projects go, a single central interdepartmental energy transition agency could be one solution. This would not replace the authority of other entities but would have the authority to coordinate and move the approval processes forward.

Policymakers must also simplify and accelerate Public–Private Partnerships. A private entity partnering with government will find it easier to seek financing for a project or secure a partner. The investment world is all about risk and returns; a public entity participating in the project reduces the risk and as such the reward required, or premium, may fall.

As larger companies transition, they force smaller companies in the supply chains to transition as well. Public entities must also do a better job in helping small companies. One of the major drivers to the transition to net zero is small to medium enterprises. As they are small, they have limited capital and need more support. For example, if a small enterprise wants to raise energy efficiency at its office or factory, it will need capital upfront. But a small company may not have the financial capacity for undertaking such a project. Among many actions, government could offer, for example, a low-interest loan for the capital expenditure for the whole of the project.

The finance sector plays a central role. There are a great number of things that it can do so as to accelerate the transition. It must work with all parties to innovate and to grow new climate finance instruments. There are already many fixed-income and carbon finance instruments, for instance. For these instruments to grow, the green capital markets may need to be significantly broader and deeper. This is an action that can be driven by financial institutions when they have the right financial or regulatory, or both, incentives.

The harmonisation of benchmarks and democratisation of information are other major areas where the finance sector can work with government. Currently, there are multiple climate rules related standards. For example, almost every large financial services provider has its own ESG-rating benchmarking system. The problem is that all of these benchmarks are slightly different and could be confusing. Importantly, some users may find the subscription unaffordable. The annual subscription to these benchmarks-related services costs tens of thousands, if not hundreds of thousands, of dollars. If a corporation or an asset management firm cannot afford the cost of subscribing to this information, then only a limited number of corporations will have access.

Financial institutions, given their reach and know-how, also play an essential role in capacity building, education, and training. This is something which is already taking place. Financial institutions typically organise meetings or seminars for their clients, so that these customers may better understand the various climate finance products the institution has available as well as for the financial institution to identify information pertinent to its own internal climate risk assessments, for example. This is another area where the finance sector can work closely with government to create a united approach. An example would be governments mandating companies to incorporate carbon price accounting in their operational and financial management, as well as providing training. This involves a company-assigned carbon cost to guide its investments, strategy, and emission reduction plans.

Final note: progress through a multidisciplinary approach

Across many Western democracies and other parts of the world, public opinion has become increasingly polarised on key policy issues. People are divided. Those who recognise the risks of climate change and support the journey to net zero often struggle to engage with voices that deny its existence or champion fossil fuels, and the reverse is just as true. The divide fuels 'confirmation bias' or 'selective perception' towards the green shift.

This polarisation is not limited to public opinion. It is also with governments, financial institutions, and companies in many jurisdictions, especially the United States. The reality is that for economic, political, energy security, and other reasons, a middle way must be identified. Picking on two extreme views, clean energy advocates must acknowledge that solar panels are unlikely to replace all energy sources worldwide. Fossil fuels advocates must understand that the carbon footprint full life cycle of an EV (from raw materials extraction to disposal) is sharply lower than that of an internal combustion engine vehicle. But what can be done for a more middle-of-the-way perspective? Should the world wait for the self-correcting pendulum to swing back to reality? Should the world wait for an extreme crisis?

One may not have noticed but the 'self-correcting pendulum' is already adjusting. One small piece of evidence is 'greenhushing'. Some corporations which have undertaken transition plans have been publicly attacked for having climate change bias. Many of these companies have kept the plans but gone into stealth mode.

An excellent article by *The Economist* notes companies that had previously announced bold climate transition strategies have begun to stay quiet about their progress. It noted that despite some high-profile backsliding, most firms continue to pursue their decarbonisation goals discreetly. It emphasises that corporate mentions of climate change have fallen significantly, reflecting reluctance to publicise efforts amid political and economic uncertainty.[2] The article quotes a report which found over two-thirds of companies with climate targets to be on track, with many improving target rigours by including supply chain emissions. The persistence of quiet action suggests corporations recognise the financial benefits of decarbonisation despite the lack of fanfare, as examined in detail in Section IV.

For the overhaul to accelerate worldwide, governments need to remain clear and consistent with their signals to the markets, similar to what China has done. This might imply that an acceleration towards the transition may only be successful in a control economy with a centralised administration. Yet regions like the EU can easily achieve this as well, for as long as the motivation and associated policies remain clear and consistent.

The way forward can only be better communication, capacity building, education, and training. The basis for this will be a multidisciplinary approach. The transition train has left the station, with government as the signal operator, and will accelerate as the finance sector works with business, and business works with the finance sector.

Notes

1 Lazard, *Lazard Releases 2025 Levelized Cost of Energy+ Report* (Lazard 2025) <https://www.lazard.com/media/0sopmth5/lazard-releases-2025-levelized-cost-of-energyplus-report.pdf> accessed 3 September 2025.

2 The Economist, 'The Remarkable Rise of "Greenhushing"' *The Economist* (29 July 2025) <https://www.economist.com/business/2025/07/29/the-remarkable-rise-of-greenhushing> accessed 9 August 2025.

Abbreviations and foreign exchange rates

CBAM	Carbon Border Adjustment Mechanism
CBI	Climate Bonds Initiative
CCS	Carbon Capture and Storage
CCUS	Carbon Capture, Utilisation and Storage
CDM	Clean Development Mechanism
CDP	Carbon Disclosure Project
CH4	Methane
CNG	Compressed Natural Gas
CO2	Carbon Dioxide
CO_2e	Carbon Dioxide Equivalent
COP	Conference of the Parties
CPI	Climate Policy Initiative
CSP	Concentrated Solar Power
CSR	Corporate Social Responsibility
CSRD	Corporate Sustainability Reporting Directive
DAC	Direct Air Capture
DER	Distributed Energy Resources
DOE	Department of Energy (US)
EIB	European Investment Bank
EPA	Environmental Protection Agency (US)
EPC	Engineering, Procurement, and Construction
ESCO	Energy Service Company
ESG	Environmental, Social, and Governance
ETS	Emissions Trading System
EU ETS	European Union Emissions Trading System
EV	Electric Vehicle
FIT	Feed-In Tariff
GDP	Gross Domestic Product
GFANZ	Glasgow Financial Alliance for Net Zero
GHG	Greenhouse Gas
GHGP	Greenhouse Gas Protocol
GRI	Global Reporting Initiative
HVDC	High-Voltage Direct Current
ICE	Internal Combustion Engine

IEA	International Energy Agency
IEEFA	Institute for Energy Economics and Financial Analysis
IMF	International Monetary Fund
IPCC	Intergovernmental Panel on Climate Change
IRA	Inflation Reduction Act of 2022 (Public Law 117-169) – the United States
IRENA	International Renewable Energy Agency
ISO	Independent System Operator
ISSB	International Sustainability Standards Board
JCM	Joint Crediting Mechanism
JRC	Joint Research Centre (EU)
Kyoto Protocol	Kyoto Protocol to the United Nations Framework Convention on Climate Change
LCOE	Levelized Cost of Energy
LEED	Leadership in Energy and Environmental Design
LNG	Liquefied Natural Gas
LULUCF	Land Use, Land-Use Change, and Forestry
MDBs	Multilateral Development Banks
MRV	Monitoring, Reporting, and Verification
NDC	Nationally Determined Contribution
NETs	Negative Emissions Technologies
NGFS	Network for Greening the Financial System
NZE	Net-Zero Emissions
OPEX	Operational Expenditure
Paris Agreement	Paris Agreement under the United Nations Framework Convention on Climate Change
PCAF	Partnership for Carbon Accounting Financials
PJM	Pennsylvania-New Jersey-Maryland Interconnection
PPA	Power Purchase Agreement
PPAs	Power Purchase Agreements
PRI	Principles for Responsible Investment
PV	Photovoltaic
RE	Renewable Energy
RE100	Renewable Energy 100% Initiative
REN21	Renewable Energy Policy Network for the 21st Century
RES	Renewable Energy Sources
RFS	Renewable Fuel Standard
RTO	Regional Transmission Organization
SAF	Sustainable Aviation Fuel
SBTi	Science Based Targets initiative
SDG	Sustainable Development Goals
SDR	Special Drawing Rights (IMF)
SE4ALL	Sustainable Energy for All
SFDR	Sustainable Finance Disclosure Regulation
T&D	Transmission and Distribution
TCFD	Task Force on Climate-related Financial Disclosures

TNFD	Taskforce on Nature-related Financial Disclosures
UN	United Nations
UNFCCC	United Nations Framework Convention on Climate Change
UNEP	United Nations Environment Programme
UNDP	United Nations Development Programme
VCM	Voluntary Carbon Market
VRE	Variable Renewable Energy
WRI	World Resources Institute
ZEV	Zero-Emission Vehicle

Currency	One USD buys	Currency	One USD buys
Australian Dollar (AUD)	1.53	Hong Kong Dollar (HKD)	7.80
British Pound (GBP)	0.74	Indian Rupees (INR)	88.14
Canadian Dollar (CAD	1.38	Japanese Yen (JPY)	148
Chinese Yuan (CNY)	7.13	Singapore Dollar (SGD)	1.28
Euros (EUR)	0.85	Norvegian Krone (NOK)	10.03

Figure 15.1 Notes on exchange rates: For the purposes of consistency, all currencies are translated to US dollars. Exchange rate as of 7 September 2025.

Source: XE.com Inc.

About the author

Joseph Jacobelli serves as Managing Partner at Bourne Impact Capital (B.I.C.). A leading expert in climate business and finance, he has spent decades driving research and investment in the field. Growing up across Europe and Australia, he developed a multicultural perspective that shapes his multidisciplinary approach to the energy transition.

At B.I.C., Joseph oversees a single-family office that invests in public capital markets and real estate. He has built a well-diversified portfolio that includes investment-grade Asian and European fixed-income instruments, blue-chip equities, and strategically selected real estate assets. His long-term asset allocation strategy prioritises stable and consistent absolute returns. He is also the founder of Asia Clean Tech Energy Investment, which provides ad hoc advice and research to corporations and institutions on clean energy investments and sustainability in Asia.

For three decades, Joseph worked as a financial analyst at leading global investment banks, including Bear Stearns, HSBC, ING Barings, Merrill Lynch, and Nomura. He led regional analyst teams, contributed to multiple initial public offerings, and earned top rankings in institutional investor surveys. At Bloomberg Intelligence (BI), he led regional research content and played a key role in expanding BI's Asia operations by leveraging his expertise and market relationships. Throughout his career, he evaluated dozens of listed clean energy and other companies across Asia.

Joseph gained hands-on experience in the energy transition as a senior executive at two energy corporations. As Group Director at CLP Holdings, a major regional electric utility, he executed alternative power projects, carbon transactions, and clean tech investments. As Asia Head of Cenfura, a green electricity-focused start-up, he spearheaded project development and financing in the region.

Passionate about driving climate awareness in business and finance, he regularly speaks at industry conferences and contributes to media platforms. He published *Asia's Energy Revolution* (2021) and *Powering the Unstoppable Green Shift* (2026). He is a regular contributor to *The Energy Industry Times* and hosts the Asia Climate Finance Podcast.

He holds a master's in international law from the National Taiwan University and a bachelor of arts from the University of Queensland. He is fluent in English, French, Italian, and Mandarin and has basic proficiency in Cantonese, Japanese, and Portuguese. His volunteer work includes mentoring entrepreneurs and supporting future business leaders.

For more details, visit: asiacleantechenergy.com

Index

Author's Note: This index reflects the multidisciplinary character of the energy transition. Cross-referencing technical developments (Electrotech) with regulatory frameworks (Strategy), digital capabilities (Digital Solutions), and capital mobilisation (Finance) will support fuller navigation of the material.